The Art of Advocacy

Editorial Advisors

ASPEN COURSEBOOK SERIES

The Art of Advocacy

Briefs, Motions, and Writing Strategies of America's Best Lawyers

NOAH A. MESSING

Lecturer in the Practice of Law and Legal Writing
Yale Law School

 Wolters Kluwer

Law & Business

Published by Wolters Kluwer Law & Business in New York.

Wolters Kluwer Law & Business serves customers worldwide with CCH, Aspen Publishers, and Kluwer Law International products. (www.wolterskluwerlb.com)

To contact Customer Service, e-mail customer.service@wolterskluwer.com, call 1-800-234-1660, fax 1-800-901-9075, or mail correspondence to:

Wolters Kluwer Law & Business
Attn: Order Department
PO Box 990
Frederick, MD 21705

Design and book composition by Keithley & Associates, Inc.

Printed in the United States of America.

5 6 7 8 9 0

ISBN 978-1-4548-1838-0

Library of Congress Cataloging-in-Publication Data

Messing, Noah A.
    The art of advocacy : briefs, motions, and writing strategies of America's best lawyers / Noah A. Messing.
        pages cm. — (Aspen coursebook series)
    Includes bibliographical references and index.
    ISBN 978-1-4548-1838-0 (alk. paper)
    1. Legal briefs—United States. 2. Legal composition. 3. Motions (Law)—United States. 4. Trial practice—United States. 5. Legal research. I. Title.
    KF250.M49 2013
    349.73—dc23
                                                                                        2013015119

About Wolters Kluwer Law & Business

Wolters Kluwer Law & Business is a leading global provider of intelligent information and digital solutions for legal and business professionals in key specialty areas, and respected educational resources for professors and law students. Wolters Kluwer Law & Business connects legal and business professionals as well as those in the education market with timely, specialized authoritative content and information-enabled solutions to support success through productivity, accuracy and mobility.

Serving customers worldwide, Wolters Kluwer Law & Business products include those under the Aspen Publishers, CCH, Kluwer Law International, Loislaw, ftwilliam.com and MediRegs family of products.

CCH products have been a trusted resource since 1913, and are highly regarded resources for legal, securities, antitrust and trade regulation, government contracting, banking, pension, payroll, employment and labor, and healthcare reimbursement and compliance professionals.

Aspen Publishers products provide essential information to attorneys, business professionals and law students. Written by preeminent authorities, the product line offers analytical and practical information in a range of specialty practice areas from securities law and intellectual property to mergers and acquisitions and pension/benefits. Aspen's trusted legal education resources provide professors and students with high-quality, up-to-date and effective resources for successful instruction and study in all areas of the law.

Kluwer Law International products provide the global business community with reliable international legal information in English. Legal practitioners, corporate counsel and business executives around the world rely on Kluwer Law journals, looseleafs, books, and electronic products for comprehensive information in many areas of international legal practice.

Loislaw is a comprehensive online legal research product providing legal content to law firm practitioners of various specializations. Loislaw provides attorneys with the ability to quickly and efficiently find the necessary legal information they need, when and where they need it, by facilitating access to primary law as well as state-specific law, records, forms and treatises.

ftwilliam.com offers employee benefits professionals the highest quality plan documents (retirement, welfare and non-qualified) and government forms (5500/PBGC, 1099 and IRS) software at highly competitive prices.

MediRegs products provide integrated health care compliance content and software solutions for professionals in healthcare, higher education and life sciences, including professionals in accounting, law and consulting.

Wolters Kluwer Law & Business, a division of Wolters Kluwer, is headquartered in New York. Wolters Kluwer is a market-leading global information services company focused on professionals.

To my wife, Lori Bruce

You deserve far more than this book, which,

like its author,

is dedicated to you.

About the Author

Noah Messing is Yale Law School's Lecturer in the Practice of Law and Legal Writing. He teaches appellate advocacy, advanced legal writing, drafting, and arbitration, and he will help to run Yale's Supreme Court Advocacy clinic during the 2013-2014 academic year. Noah has trained more than 1,000 judges and attorneys to write more effectively. During law school, Noah served as a Coker Fellow and as an editor of *The Yale Law Journal*. For his work in the Morris Tyler Moot Court of Appeals program, he received both the Benjamin Cardozo Prize for the year's best brief and the Potter Stewart Prize for winning the Spring semester moot court competition. Following graduation, Noah worked as a trial and appellate litigator in Washington D.C., as Counsel to Senator Hillary Clinton, and as Associate Counsel to the Hillary Clinton for President campaign. In 2013, he chaired the Legal Writing, Reasoning, and Research section's panel at the annual conference of the Association of American Law Schools, speaking about the "Past, Present, and Future of Appellate Briefs." His work on commercial speech has appeared in *The New England Journal of Medicine*, and he is an arbitrator with the American Arbitration Association.

Summary of Contents

Contents

Acknowledgments

The idea for this book arose in 2011 when Carol Rose recognized the value of a project that I had already started, but for which I had no grand designs. Without her vision, the examples of written advocacy that I had begun to gather for my students would have lingered in my private collection.

Doug Kysar shared with me his great secret, Carol McGeehan, so he is the reason that I wound up working with Aspen Publishers on this project. And that may have been the best decision that I made during the process: Carol makes publishing fun and, in a perfect world, everyone (and certainly every law professor) would know the joy of getting to work with her. She, Michael Ford, Julie Gaston, Rick Mixter, Deanna Proto, and Lisa Werhle at Aspen have the passion of artists and the precision of engineers: they kept me on the rails. Aspen's Christine Hannan and Dana Wilson demonstrated amazing insight and saintly patience. The formatting prowess of Keithley and Associates — including Meri and John Keithley and Nancy Danahy — was remarkable, as every page in this book demonstrates.

Roy Englert catalyzed the project. He fed me briefs, contacts, and enthusiasm. He is one of the best lawyers in the country, yet his character and generosity somehow dwarf his talent.

Then the cavalry arrived: I was plied with valuable materials and useful suggestions by Scott Ballinger, Elizabeth Bangs, Linda Berger, Eric Biber, Timothy Blevins, Ralph Brill, John Bronsteen, Charles Calleros, Rob Cary, Dave Chao, Kirsten Clement, Paul Clement, Walter Dellinger, Kate Desormeau, Neil Eggleston, Kathryn Fehrman, Judy Fisher, Sandy Glover, Doug Godfrey, Dick Goehler, Mel Greenlee, Rick Hess, Steve Hirsch, Steve Jamar, Lucille Jewel, Daniel Knudsen, Hon. Mark Kravitz, Mark Lemley, David Leopold, Sue Liemer, Bob Long, George Mader, Rich Marmaro, David Massengill, Patricia Millett, Seema Misra, Elliot Morrison, Anne Mullins, Michael Murray, Glen Nager, Kevin Newsom, Ben Opipari, Myra Orlen, Jonathan Pitt, Sara Rankin, Ana Reyes, Charles Rothfeld, Virginia Seitz, Kannon Shanmugam, Bob Silver, Lou Sirico, Micah Smith, Neil Sobol, Phil Spector, Sri Srinivasan, Tina Stark, Gail Stephenson, Hon. Richard Taranto, Gabriel Teninbaum, Joe Terry, Kristen Tiscione, Daniel Walfish, Hon. John Walker, Mal Wheeler, Pamela Ann Wilkins, Brian Willen, and others. Thank you.

My research assistants at Yale Law School provided enormous amounts of zeal, sweat, and firepower, so I extend deep thanks to Matt Andrews, Lewis Bollard, Christine Buzzard, Kathryn Cherry, Estella Cisneros, Kevin Jonke, Jeff Kane, Charanya Krishnaswami, Nic Marais, Iya Megre, Ester Murdukhayeva, Danielle Rosenthal, Jessi Samuels, Steve Seigel, Ray Treadwell, Caroline Van Zile, Emily Weigel, Rachel Weiner, Paige Wilson, Eileen Zelek, and Joanna Zhang. Lauren Hartz and Zach Keller went far beyond what I could have ever expected from research assistants, producing massive amounts of great work. Pat Florio was a pleasure to work with: her attention to detail and cheerful willingness to enter countless edits freed me to focus on the fun parts of this project. Robert Post and Brent Dickman of Yale Law School supported me at every step. I am grateful for their faith. Dean Post also shared me with Karl Llewellyn's unpublished advice about advocacy; it appears in print, for the first time, thanks to his keen eye — and thanks to the generosity of Professor Llewellyn's nieces, Sandy Mentschikoff Levedahl and Jeanne Mentschikoff, who authorized me to use that document, which appears in Appendix A. I am grateful to them for letting me share this spectacularly insightful document and for allowing me, in some tiny way, to link myself to one of law's titans.

Almost twenty anonymous reviewers sent detailed and helpful comments on various parts of the book. Thanks, to whomever you are, for both the encouragement and the valuable suggestions. Richard Neumann also reviewed a sample chapter when the project began; he provided priceless insights and more encouragement than he realizes.

Almost two hundred friends helped me to crowd-source the title of this book. Thanks to all of you.

Many colleagues at Yale and two luminaries at the University of Chicago helped in hundreds of selfless, kind ways, so I thank Emily Bazelon, Bill Eskridge, Gene Fidell, Larry Fox, Heather Gerken, Abbe Gluck, Linda Greenhouse, David Grewal, Yair Listokin, Daniel Markovits, Jeff Meyer, John Nann, David Odo, Nick Parrillo, Claire Priest, Judith Resnik, Lior Strahilevitz, Michael VanderHeijden, John Witt, and Judith Wright. My partnership with Dan Kahan during the course that we co-taught ripened my thinking about this subject. Dave Lat provided wise counsel about the project in its earliest stages. Ross Guberman shared great advice and gave a spectacular pep talk at a pivotal time. And Shay Dvoretzky is a champion: it's easy to prepare a book about advocacy when one of the most talented appellate lawyers in the country is willing to answer any question about any subject at any hour.

Then there's Rob Harrison. Rob pulled me into teaching, taught me most of what I know about this field, and then guided me through the shoals during this project. This book would never have happened without him.

Mom and Dad helped me in countless tangible and intangible ways — but most important to this project, they infused me with a love of good writing. My journey into most of the great books that I ever read began with Mom saying, "I think you'd like this." And Dad wrote the first brief that I ever read. He tried to save a man's life. I was eight years old and his writing was so clear that I understood most of what the brief argued. So I was blessed with two great, loving teachers from an early age. Mom, Dad — I love and thank both of you.

Owen Laszlo Messing generously shared me with this project during the first twenty months of his life, yet he still cheered me on every single day. And finally, to my wife, Lori Bruce: You are wonderful, brilliant, and beautiful, and I'm grateful for your love, support, patience, and stellar advice.

Introduction

John Roberts is widely regarded as one of the great legal writers in the country. His "crisp writing," "painstaking research," and "rigorous logic" — along with his twenty-five victories at the Supreme Court — led Roberts's peers to view him with "palpable awe" and to call him a "brilliant writer," "the best of the bar," and "perhaps the best advocate of the generation." In the first case that he argued at the Court, Roberts earned a unanimous victory, but the Court overruled the case (unanimously again) several years later; commentators suggested that the Justices had been "lured further than they wanted to go" by Roberts's advocacy. And, since joining the Supreme Court as Chief Justice, he has been called "the best writer on the Court" and a "dazzling judicial talent."

So what advice does he give to lawyers who want to write better briefs and motions? He offers a single tip: *The only good way to learn about writing is to read good writing.*

Roberts is hardly alone. Other judges tell lawyers to "read any type of good writing to become a better writer" and emphasize that "if you read well-written work, then writing well becomes second nature." A top Supreme Court litigator observes that "the only way" to turn young attorneys into "effective legal writers is to immerse them in as much outstanding legal writing as possible." And Associate Justice Anthony Kennedy admits that he has chastised his law clerks, telling them "you can't write anything good because you've never read anything good."

Many writers in many fields recognize the relationship between reading and writing. Among them are writing expert William Zinsser ("Bach and Picasso didn't spring full-blown as Bach and Picasso; they needed models. This is especially true of writing."); Stephen King ("If you don't have time to read, you don't have the time (or the tools) to write."); J.K. Rowling (telling aspiring novelists to "read as much as you possibly can . . . *nothing* will help you as much as reading"); and even President Obama (noting that reading taught him "how to write, but also how to be and how to think"). Countless other great judges, lawyers, professors, writers, and journalists offer the same advice. If you Google the phrase "reading is the *only* way to learn how to write," you'll retrieve almost half a million results. And if you Google "reading is the best way to learn to write," you'll get even more hits. We write what we read.

So here's the premise of this book: the best way to become a great advocate is to read and absorb great advocacy. You can certainly read genres other than law. In fact, you should. But consuming great written advocacy will help you to produce great written advocacy.

This book therefore pulls together examples of stellar legal writing. These examples are great. But not perfect. Some will seem too aggressive to you. Fine. Some will seem too meek. Fine. Others will seem too wordy, or too formal, or too playful, or too bogged down by citations, or too dependent on policy, or too laced with rhetoric. Fine, fine, fine. I even point out some shortcomings myself. But the examples reflect excellent (and often astounding) advocacy about a variety of subjects demonstrating a variety of styles and techniques. And I include so many examples precisely so that you can draw on an array of options to cultivate a style that suits *you*. That said, good advocacy tends to reside within certain boundaries, so I warn you when an example approaches the limits of how lawyers should write. Many of the best lawyers in the country are represented, and these examples collectively show you the best of what American lawyers produce on behalf of their clients. The sum is even greater than the parts.

The book seeks to act as an antidote to all of the dreadful things you've been reading since you began law school — whether that entails days or decades. As one judge observes, law schools "teach students to write like lawyers by asking them to read old cases by dead judges who learned to write by copying older, deader judges." And few practicing lawyers are exposed consistently to good legal writing, causing legal pundits like Fred Rodell to quip that "there are two things wrong with almost all legal writing. One is its style. The other is its content." Bad writing wages a steady, clandestine war on your ability to write well. "Writing style is not consciously learned," explains one linguistics expert, "but is largely absorbed, or subconsciously learned, from reading." Chief Justice Roberts echoes this view, observing that reading good prose improves one's writing because you "kind of absorb it."

More precisely, reading good and absorbing writing will *eventually* make you a better writer. But advice helps the medicine act faster. This book therefore annotates the examples that it reprints and offers countless tips to help you extract more value from each motion and brief.

Enough people have asked how I selected examples that I should explain my approach. I began by asking many of the best lawyers I know for their favorite motions and briefs. Then I asked these lawyers to nominate lawyers whom they admire and asked those nominees for the filings that made them proudest. Next, I reviewed legal blogs for exciting cases, watched the dockets of prominent courts, and tracked down the filings of lawyers who received acclaim in legal periodicals. Then I contacted numerous judges, legal writing professors, legal historians, and law clerks for suggestions. I also spent many, many hours looking at random motions and briefs on Westlaw based on key words that seemed promising. I wound up with approximately 12,000 motions and briefs, almost all of which I discarded summarily — too dry, too complicated, too average, or too old. The survivors (roughly 1,000 contenders) were impressive, and my team of research assistants and I discussed and trimmed them. We eventually rendered a manageable number of short examples, which are long enough to let you get into the flow of the document but short enough to prevent narcolepsy. They come from interesting, important, or notorious cases. And they also serve as vehicles to discuss a variety of points about advocacy.

To quote one of my favorite writing experts again, William Zinsser urges his readers to "find the best writers in the fields that interest you. . . . Don't worry that by imitating them you'll lose your own voice and your own identity. Soon enough you'll shed those skins and become who you are supposed to become."

So study this book's examples, but also just soak in them. Soon enough you'll become the advocate that you're supposed to become. And, through that process, you will write with greater skill, joy, and authenticity. Advocacy will no longer be a grind or a mystery. It will be your art.

How to Get the Most from This Book

Helping you to get the most value from this book requires a few additional comments. Each chapter begins with a short overview. Then I provide several examples of strong writing and advocacy. Each of those examples is accompanied by a short introduction and by several annotations that remark on both the chapter's core point *and* on a handful of other noteworthy details. I realize that my approach may jar some readers — this book, by design, is less focused than many writing books on teaching a single lesson at a time; my view is that great lawyers need to be able, in the same instant, to notice issues ranging from a problem with a comma to an opportunity to reimagine an entire field of law. Even so, on the inside cover, this book lists both the takeaway points that appear before the book's examples and the writing tips in Chapter 16.

I recommend that you read each example all the way through *without* looking at the annotations. Form your own ideas about the example. Pay attention to how the facts or argument build and flow. Assess what persuades or influences you (and what doesn't). *Then* look at my annotations, which are just a sideshow; the examples are the main event.

Ten other points warrant your attention.

1. I include a disproportionate number of appellate briefs because they're where I found the strongest writing. Appellate briefs give lawyers a chance to refine the arguments that they raised at trial. And at the Supreme Court, the writing grows even finer, partly because many of the lawyers are gifted, but also because the briefs are a *third* draft: each issue was raised at trial and then sharpened during the first appeal. Moreover, the trial judge and the appellate panel (and usually a dissenting judge, another court of appeals, or both) have further crystallized each side's best arguments. In short, appellate courts (and especially the Supreme Court) are fertile ground for good briefs to grow. But I devote Chapter 14 to trial motions to focus on some of the key differences between successful motions and successful appellate briefs.

2. My citation practice in this book is designed to be intuitive and useable, not to comport fully with *The Bluebook* or *The ALWD Citation Manual*. Some of the lawyers' formatting choices have been altered to prevent the book from looking chaotic or inconsistent.

3. This book's goal is to expose you to great advocacy, analysis, and writing, *not* to compile a mound of sentences that comport with some Platonic ideal of good prose. I'm far more worried about the flow and power of an argument than about any individual sentence. If you want to find a handful of bad apples in the roughly 3,500 sentences that I have reprinted, you will succeed. Moreover, if any sentences ruin your enjoyment of a passage, realize that judges will have the same experience: let the handful of lousy lines remind you to hone your own prose.

4. My annotations occasionally question choices that the lawyers made. I point out these choices (often with the word "WARNING!") not to damn the writing, but to cause you to think about whether you would have made the point differently. Each example has much to recommend it, even when it's slightly imperfect, and the skilled lawyers who wrote these passages may well have had valid reasons for their choices.

5. It's hard to find passages that can be dropped into a book without much explanation. I discarded many stellar motions and briefs simply because using them would have required too much background. I have provided some information about each excerpt that I use (except for the Introductions in Chapter 13), but that background is designed to tee up the examples, not to capture perfectly the nuances in each case. I have tried to make it possible to read chapters in whatever order you want, but I recommend reading it from start to finish (unless you want to begin with Chapter 16 to get a primer on style). If you want just the basics, read Chapters 1, 4, 5, 11, 13, and 16.

6. I have placed in boldface one annotation for each example. If you're pressed for time, the annotations in bold are the ones that most directly illustrate the "Takeaway Point" of each example.

7. This book presents a huge number of strategies. If you use them all, in every case, your writing will be cluttered and chaotic. So learn all of these techniques, but save most of them for some future brief. This compilation is like a playbook in football: your team won't execute every play in every game.

8. I added line numbers next to the examples. Those numbers make it easier to refer readers to a specific line.

9. Each chapter provides an overview. Some of those overviews track the chapter's Takeaway Points, but others synthesize or supplement the points made within the chapter.

10. And finally, the book excerpts motions and briefs that won as well as motions and briefs that lost. I sometimes mention the outcome, but generally I do not because I've been careful to select compelling arguments — even when those arguments compelled too few judges. Outcomes matter, of course, but some of your cases will be sickly and flawed; seeing how skilled lawyers make a good fight out of a weak case is just as important as learning to play a dominant hand. In fact, one of the most impressive passages in the book (Example 8.3) comes from an argument that the Supreme Court rejected *unanimously*. Once you see what the argument is built on, you'll be amazed that the lawyers created a facially plausible argument.

Feel free to email me with any questions or comments — my email address is noah.messing@yale.edu — or to send me any great motions or briefs.

Noah A. Messing
June 2013

The Art of Advocacy

PART I

FACTS

In this part of the book, we examine how lawyers use facts to advocate for their clients. Chapter 1 describes the basics: how to tell the court about a dispute in a way that favors your client while preserving your credibility. Chapter 2 explores a vital technique that inexperienced lawyers often overlook: using the procedural history of a case (i.e., what happened *during* the lawsuit) to help your client. And Chapter 3 presents a variety of advanced techniques that great lawyers use in their factual statements.

But do facts really matter? Absolutely — and demonstrably. In a recent study, a federal magistrate judge tested the effect of facts on decision making. He gave a group of approximately 300 judges (1) a criminal statute that prohibited undocumented immigration and (2) a short description of the defendant who was charged with violating this statute by entering the United States illegally. Everything was identical except for one detail. Some of the judges were told that the defendant had violated the law to earn money for his daughter's liver operation; other judges were told that the defendant had come to the United States to find someone for a drug cartel. Both hypothetical defendants raised the same legal argument. Even though each group of judges received an identical statute, the "good" defendant had a 43 percent better chance of avoiding prison than the "bad" defendant.[1] Thus, while an effective Statement of Facts won't win every case, framing facts effectively will greatly increase the chance of achieving favorable outcomes for your clients.

And a judge who thinks your client deserves to win can also influence the outcome of a case in many other ways, such as giving a plaintiff multiple chances to amend a complaint, allowing ample or narrow discovery, letting a case that relies on strained inferences to survive summary judgment, ruling favorably on objections, providing helpful instructions to a jury, awarding damages or making sentencing decisions, and so on. You do *not* want a court to view your client as the bad guy. And your facts, of course, introduce your client to the judge and thus shape the judge's view of the parties and the dispute.

Remember, however, that you need to keep your argument in mind as you write your facts; your client has a fool for a lawyer if you tell your client's story without assessing first whether, in light of the applicable law, those facts can support the outcome you want. To win lawsuits, you must tether facts to the law.

Let's review some examples to see how top lawyers achieve the various goals described above. If all goes well, you will tell tight, compelling stories that live up to the following insight from one of the nation's great jurists: "The mark of a master is that facts which before lay scattered in an inorganic mass, when he shoots through them the magnetic current of his thought, leap into an organic order, and live and bear fruit."[2] The next few chapters demonstrate how to achieve this goal.

---

1. Conversation with U.S. Magistrate Judge Andrew Wistrich (Feb. 9, 2011).
2. Oliver Wendell Holmes, *The Use of Law Schools,* in *Collected Legal Papers* 35, 37 (The Lawbook Exchange 1952) (1920).

Chapter 1

Facts: The Basics (Victims and Villains)

In this chapter, we review various examples of how to tell the court about the facts that led to your client's dispute.

Lawsuits are bigger than ever. Thanks to our ability to mail, store, and recover files electronically, modern cases often involve millions of documents and dizzying amounts of data. A case's record may also include scores of depositions, stacks of declarations, a slew of motions, and scads of letters. Lawyers therefore grind away countless hours trying to *summarize* what happened in the case. Instead, however, they should *frame* what happened in the case. This distinction is the central point of this chapter.

Effective storytelling involves two or three critical goals for the plaintiff: creating empathy toward your client or generating enmity toward the defendant (or both) as well as satisfying the relevant legal standard. For the defendant, the basic goals of a story are more varied, but usually involve one or more of the following: reducing the vitriol created by the plaintiff's story; explaining the reasons for the defendant's actions; showing the gaps, errors, and legal inadequacy of the plaintiff's story; and counterpunching (by exposing the plaintiff's own wrongdoing). Each side tries to tell a compelling story, not to prepare a mere summary of what happened.

CHAPTER OVERVIEW

1. Make the court *want* your side to win.
2. Present facts sufficient to support the legal outcome that you want or to undermine your adversary's legal theory.
3. Cause the court to focus on—and remember—a handful of facts that most help your client.
4. Let the court know what happened in your dispute (i.e., who did what to whom and when).
5. When your clients look like villains, use neutral language and tone to quell hostility toward them.
6. Build credibility with your reader.
7. Prune facts ruthlessly to keep the reader interested in your case.
8. Declaw and reframe bad facts before the other side raises them.

Example 1.1	**Takeaway point 1.1:** Judges want to feel just; making your client the "good guy" or the victim will let your client benefit from that inclination.

Your Statement of Facts should do more than summarize what sparked a lawsuit. It should make readers want your client to win. We see below a common way to advance this goal: depict your client as a likeable victim. In the following case, a city in Connecticut wanted to "take" a number of homes through the power of eminent domain, but nine homeowners opposed the city's efforts. They argued that the government's plan — to transfer the land to a drug manufacturer — did not qualify as a "public use" (as required by the U.S. Constitution's Takings Clause) because the property would be conveyed to another private party. Here, we meet the homeowners.

Source: Homeowners' brief in *Kelo v. City of New London,* 545 U.S. 469 (2005) (citations removed).

1　　Petitioner Wilhelmina Dery was born in her house in the Fort Trumbull
2　neighborhood of New London, Connecticut in 1918. Her family, the Ciavaglias,
3　first moved to Fort Trumbull from Italy in the early 1880s. Mrs. Dery still lives in her
4　home on Walbach Street, which was purchased by her family in 1901, as she
5　has for her entire life. Her husband, Charles, lives there as well, and moved into
6　the house when the couple married fifty-nine years ago.
7　　The Derys' son, Matthew, was born in Fort Trumbull and grew up there. He,
8　his wife, and his son currently live right next door to Mr. and Mrs. Dery at 28
9　East Street in a home he received from his grandmother as a wedding present.
10　The home has been in his family since 1903. Petitioner Susette Kelo, a registered
11　nurse, lives down the block from the Derys at 8 East Street. She purchased the
12　Victorian-era house in 1997 and since that time has made extensive improvements
13　to it. She loves the water view from her home, the people in the area, and the
14　fact that she can get in a boat and be out in the Long Island Sound in less
15　than ten minutes.

A

B

C

D

E

F

G

A This is a marvelous first sentence. We learn that New London is trying to seize the birth home of an octogenarian, making readers sympathetic to her.

B This sentence reinforces the subjective value of Mrs. Dery's home: her family has maintained ties to this neighborhood since it first arrived in the country. Both the majority and dissenting opinions discussed the family's enduring connection to the neighborhood.

C **If the lawyers had not mentioned Mr. Dery, readers might worry about Mrs. Dery more: this sentence thus reflects the difficult narrative choices that lawyers must make. It taps into one powerful meme ("the lovely elderly couple") rather than an even stronger one ("an old lady with nowhere else to go and no one to help her"). Tapping into these preconceptions and preferences (without being obvious) is an important part of how lawyers win cases.**

D This sentence shows that the home is unique not only because of the Derys' lengthy connection to it, but also because the Derys wouldn't live next door to their son and grandson if they moved.

E Kelo's name appears in the case's caption — *Kelo v. City of New London* — but this is the first time we hear about her. The lawyers wisely decide to lead the brief's Statement with the Derys, concluding (correctly) that their story is more compelling.

F This date (1997) may seem irrelevant. Not so. Adding it prevents the other side from attacking the lawyers' credibility. New London authorized its redevelopment project in January 1998 — just months after Kelo bought her home. Disclosing the date prevents the government from making Kelo's lawyers look dishonest by pointing out that Kelo bought her home *after* the city had announced that this neighborhood's homes might be seized. The homeowners' lawyers camouflage this bad fact, in the middle of a sentence, without any self-consciousness or defensiveness.

G WARNING! The brief lists details that are designed to convey that Kelo has a special connection to her property, but the list is not especially compelling. A stronger pre-trial declaration from Kelo would have helped years later at the nation's highest court.

Example **1.2**	**Takeaway point 1.2:** A Statement of Facts should make the court want your adversary to lose. Use facts — not adjectives or rhetoric — to achieve that goal.

We see below two ubiquitous strategies: creating enmity toward an adversary and organizing your Statement around the elements that you need to establish in order to prevail. Viacom sued YouTube, alleging that YouTube had infringed its intellectual property rights by allowing users to post copyrighted music, TV programming, and movie clips. The district court granted summary judgment for YouTube, holding that the relevant federal law (the Digital Millennium Copyright Act) contained a statutory "safe harbor" that shielded YouTube from liability: merely knowing that infringement was occurring was insufficient to establish liability. On appeal, Viacom argued that YouTube could not invoke the safe harbor because YouTube's infringement was willful and profitable. This excerpt from Viacom's Statement is organized around the elements of that argument and portrays YouTube as a greedy company willing to violate copyright law to achieve quick growth and easy profits.

Source: Viacom's brief in *Viacom International, Inc. v. YouTube, Inc.,* 676 F.3d 19 (2d Cir. 2012) (some citations removed).

B. YouTube Builds A Business Based On Infringement   A

In 2005, three former employees of the Internet payments company PayPal founded YouTube with hopes of replicating the financial success of PayPal, which eBay purchased in 2002 for $1.3 billion. YouTube was to be a "consumer media company" operating over a website (www.youtube.com). The content for YouTube would be provided primarily by its users, who would be invited to upload videos onto the website so long as they granted YouTube an unrestricted "worldwide...license to use, reproduce, distribute, prepare derivative works of, display, and perform the [video]...in any media formats and through any media channels." JAI-96, 336; *see also Viacom Int'l Inc. et al v. YouTube, Inc. et al,* No. 1:07-cv-02103-LLS, Docket (S.D.N.Y.) (hereinafter ("DCt.R.")), Dkt.No.210, Ex. 118. Once a video was uploaded, YouTube made it available to the entire YouTube audience, which could watch the video on YouTube's website, along with advertisements YouTube ran alongside the video. The goal, as one of the founders observed, was to make YouTube "just like TV," with users "who keep coming back," and advertisers who pay for access to that audience. YouTube   B accordingly assumed complete editorial control over the site, including by reserving and exercising the right to terminate user accounts or remove "content at [its] sole discretion for any reason whatsoever" and by requiring that uploaders provide a license to YouTube to sublicense uploaded material.

YouTube's three founders aimed to quickly establish—and cash in on—   C YouTube's popularity. JAII-191 ("our dirty little secret...is that we actually just want to sell out quickly"). To do that, however, YouTube needed to build its   D audience faster than its competitors. To this end, YouTube's founders applied a no-holds-barred approach, with one exhorting his colleagues to "concentrate all of our efforts in building up our numbers as aggressively as we can through whatever tactics, however evil."

From the outset, YouTube's founders knew that vast quantities of infringing   E videos were attracting traffic to the site. As early as June of 2005, YouTube's Internet service provider complained that YouTube was violating its user agreement by, YouTube founder Steve Chen believed, "hosting copyrighted content."

32   But Chen resolved that YouTube was "not about to take down content be-
33   cause our ISP is giving us shit." *Id.* And, in emails with the other founders, he
34   later remarked "we need to attract traffic. . . . [T]he only reason why our traffic
35   surged was due to a video of this type"—i.e., copyrighted and unauthorized.
36   Maryrose Dunton, YouTube's lead product manager, was even more explicit,
37   acknowledging that "probably 75–80% of our views come from copyrighted
38   material." Chen agreed that even removal of only the "obviously copyright in-
39   fringing stuff" would reduce views "from 100,000 views a day down to about
40   20,000 views or maybe even lower."

Ⓕ

41   The availability of unauthorized copyrighted material was a significant part
42   of the reason YouTube trounced its competitor Google Video in the race to build
43   an audience. As the Google Video team explained, "[a] large part of [YouTube's]
44   traffic is from pirated content. . . . [W]e are comparing our 'legal traffic' to their
45   mix of traffic from legal and illegal conduct."

46   In the wake of the Supreme Court's decision in *Metro-Goldwyn-Mayer Studios*
47   *Inc. v. Grokster, Ltd.*, 545 U.S. 913 (2005), condemning intentional facilita-
48   tion of infringement over the Internet, YouTube founder Chad Hurley emailed
49   the others: "[W]e need views, [but] I'm a little concerned with the recent

Ⓖ

50   [S]upreme [C]ourt ruling on copyrighted material." Chen also recognized that
51   the company would have "a tough time defending the fact that we're not liable
52   for the copyrighted material on the site because we didn't put it up when one of
53   the co-founders is blatantly stealing content from another site and trying to get
54   everyone to see it." Hurley ultimately advised his colleagues to "save your meal
55   money for some lawsuits!"

Ⓐ Here, an argumentative heading tells readers exactly what they should expect to take away from this section. Headings need not be neutral.

Ⓑ This excerpt analogizes YouTube to television just in case judges haven't used YouTube. Moreover, it seems obvious that a TV network would be liable if it broadcast another network's shows. By implying that YouTube is just like a TV station, Viacom taps into this intuition, to suggest that YouTube has infringed when it "broadcast" Viacom's shows.

Ⓒ **Viacom builds its facts around the elements of its claims. For example, Viacom needs to prove that YouTube had control over its viewers' videos; this paragraph thus emphasizes the sweeping license terms that YouTube imposed on users, the editorial control it exercised, and its power to terminate users. The next paragraph establishes YouTube's intent to profit. And the one after that establishes that YouTube executives knew about the infringement on the company's website. These facts track what Viacom needs to show to win and make YouTube sound venal.**

Ⓓ This parenthetical shows how to use the fruits of discovery. Viacom skewers YouTube with a document that YouTube produced during the litigation. This quote also enables Viacom to characterize all of YouTube based on a single e-mail from an unidentified author. This is a classic technique deployed by skilled lawyers: trying to paint multiple people (or an entire company) with the words of a single person. But use this technique judiciously: opposing counsel may point out your ruse, which can undermine your credibility.

Ⓔ This quote might not even discuss copyrighted content, but Viacom nevertheless uses it, showing YouTube's willingness to rely on "evil" tactics. Remember that litigation has no sense of humor: this line was a joke — Google's motto is "Don't be evil" — but on the naked page, it seems sinister and damning.

Ⓕ Notice how powerful it is to use an adversary's admissions. Coming from YouTube's own executive, these quotations seem like irrefutable evidence of massive, perpetual infringement.

Ⓖ The lawyers sneak some legal argument into their statement. Chapter 3 elaborates this technique.

Example **1.3**	**Takeaway point 1.3:** Emphasize your best facts, even if you need to repeat them. Better yet, use variations of these facts so that your statement doesn't seem repetitive.

Judges dislike it when lawyers repeat themselves. But for the key facts in your case, do it anyway. Repetition emphasizes the point, ensures that readers won't miss it, and helps readers to realize that a fact is important. The next passage arose after a jury in West Virginia awarded $50 million to plaintiffs in a lawsuit against a coal company. The coal company's CEO, Don Blankenship, then contributed significantly to the campaign of a state supreme court justice. That candidate, Brent Benjamin, won the seat and then joined the court's majority in a 3-2 decision that overturned the $50 million verdict. The jilted plaintiffs asked the U.S. Supreme Court to force Benjamin to recuse himself, arguing that the Due Process Clause of the Fourteenth Amendment so required (given Benjamin's indebtedness to Blankenship). Here, the brief chronicles Blankenship's donations to Benjamin's campaign, painting an image of a conflict of interest that the Supreme Court ultimately labeled "extreme."

The brief demanding that Justice Benjamin recuse himself, from , 556 U.S. 868 (2009) (some citations omitted).

1　　Mr. Blankenship played a significant—and very public—role in that elec-
2　tion, spending $3 million of his own money to support Justice Benjamin's
3　campaign and actively soliciting additional financial support from other do-　**A**
4　nors. Mr. Blankenship's extraordinary level of support for the Benjamin cam-
5　paign was unparalleled and virtually unprecedented. Indeed, the $3 million that
6　he expended in support of Justice Benjamin was more than the total amount
7　spent by all other Benjamin supporters combined, three times the amount spent
8　by Justice Benjamin's own campaign committee, and likely more than any
9　other individual spent on a judicial election that year.
10　　Most of Mr. Blankenship's campaign expenditures were made through And
11　For The Sake Of The Kids, a so-called "527 organization" that, according to
12　Mr. Blankenship, was formed after the verdict in this case for the purpose
13　of "beat[ing] Warren McGraw," the incumbent justice against whom Brent
14　Benjamin was running, and that was "named for its belief that McGraw's poli-
15　cies [were] bad for children and their future." Tom Diana, *W. Va. Coal Executive*
16　*Works to Oust McGraw*, Wheeling News-Register, Oct. 25, 2004; Brad McElhinny,
17　*Big-Bucks Backer Felt He Had to Try*, Charleston Daily Mail, Oct. 25, 2004, at 1A.
18　By the time of the election, Mr. Blankenship had donated $2,460,500 to And For
19　The Sake Of The Kids—more than two-thirds of the total funds raised by the
20　organization.[1]
21　　And For The Sake Of The Kids used most of these funds to finance hundreds
22　of campaign advertisements in the weeks preceding the election, including a
23　series of television ads that accused Justice McGraw of voting to release an
24　incarcerated child molester and to permit him to work in a high school. *See*
25　Deborah Goldberg et al., *The New Politics of Judicial Elections* 4–5 (2004) (de-
26　scribing one of these ads, which stated, "Letting a child rapist go free? To work
27　in our schools? That's radical Supreme Court Justice Warren McGraw. Warren
28　McGraw—too soft on crime. Too dangerous for our kids.").　**B**
29　　In addition to the nearly $2.5 million that Mr. Blankenship donated to And
30　For The Sake Of The Kids, he spent another $517,707 of his personal funds on
31　independent expenditures directly supporting the Benjamin campaign, mostly

32 | through payments to media outlets for television and newspaper advertise-
34 | ments....
35 | Mr. Blankenship also worked to solicit funds on behalf of Justice Benjamin's
36 | campaign. Most notably, he widely distributed letters exhorting doctors to
37 | donate to the campaign because electing Justice Benjamin would purportedly
38 | help to lower their malpractice premiums.
39 | Mr. Blankenship's significant efforts on behalf of the Benjamin campaign
40 | did not go unnoticed. *See, e.g.*, Adam Liptak, *Judicial Races in Several States*
41 | *Become Partisan Battlegrounds*, N.Y. Times, Oct. 24, 2004, at A1; Toby Cole-
42 | man, *Coal Companies Provide Big Campaign Bucks*, Charleston Gazette, Oct.
43 | 15, 2004, at 1A. Indeed, a number of observers openly questioned the motives
44 | behind Mr. Blankenship's extraordinary campaign expenditures at a time when
45 | Massey was preparing to appeal a $50 million verdict to the state supreme court.
46 | *See, e.g.*, William Kistner, *Justice for Sale*, American RadioWorks (2005), *at*
47 | http://americanradioworks.publicradio.org/features/judges/ ("One of [Justice
48 | Benjamin's] major backers was the CEO of Massey Energy Company, the largest
49 | coal producer in the region. The company happened to be fighting off a major
50 | lawsuit headed to the West Virginia Supreme Court. That prompted many in
51 | these parts to say that Massey was out to buy itself a judge."); Edward Peeks,
52 | Editorial, *How Does Political Cash Help Uninsured?*, Charleston Gazette, Nov. 9,
53 | 2004, at 2D ("[T]hese voices raise the question of vote buying to a new high
54 | in politics.").

---

55 | 1. Nationally, only four political groups directly involved in state elections in 2004
56 | outraised And For The Sake Of The Kids: the Republican Governors Association,the
57 | Democratic Governors Association, the Republican State Leadership Committee, and
58 | the Democratic Legislative Campaign Committee. Disqual. Mtn. Ex. 17.

A Within one sentence, the brief has caused readers to raise their eyebrows. Why would Blankenship spend so much of his own money unless he was getting a good return on his investment? In this Example, Caperton's lawyers mention the $3 million figure (and variations of it) four times. They ensure that readers spot this fact.

B The brief undermines Blankenship's credibility by quoting nasty political ads that seem disconnected from his presumptive concerns.

C The brief details Blankenship's fundraising tactics — which once again seem unrelated to his presumptive concerns — to insinuate a broader scheme to plant a friendly vote on the West Virginia court. Implying bad facts about an adversary (and letting readers reach their own conclusions) is often more effective than stating your allegation explicitly. Just be sure that readers won't miss the point.

D The case turns not just on the existence of a conflict of interest, but also on the appearance of one.

Rather than assert "this smells fishy," the brief lets the *New York Times* and National Public Radio make this point. Attacks on an opponent's motives or credibility are most effective when you quote either your opponent or a neutral party.

E We see again that third parties can say helpful things that litigants cannot. A court would gasp if the lawyers themselves alleged that Massey Coal "was out to buy itself a judge" and that this case involved "vote buying." But the lawyers impugn the other side through a third party's words.

F Use footnotes sparingly but powerfully, as with footnote 1 in Caperton's brief. Instead of stating that Blankenship's donation was wildly out of proportion to normal state election contributions, the footnote simply lists the four political juggernauts that gave more money that year, thus allowing readers to conclude for themselves that the size of Blankenship's expenditures was suspicious.

Example 1.4

Takeaway point 1.4: Provide readers with basic information about the dispute — who did what to whom and when, and why it matters. This tip is especially important for nondispositive trial motions (because judges will often be unable to tell how tangential issues fit into the overall case).

This example shows that legal writing need not be stiff and formal. While you might never write this playfully, develop your own style and don't feel that you need to write dry prose. This brief also manages to advance a morality tale between a hero and some villains. In addition to advancing your argument, framing the story in a way that glorifies your clients improves the chances that they will hire you again; by contrast, a defense built on a client's stupidity or ignorance can lead to client-relations difficulties.

In this case, several plaintiffs sued Facebook, and they settled their claims in exchange for Facebook stock. Then, however, they sought to cancel the settlement agreement, alleging that Facebook tricked them into settling by overstating the value of its stock. Below, Facebook's colorful brief introduces the parties and the dispute: the *who*, *what*, *where*, *when*, *how*, and *why* of the controversy.

Source: Facebook's brief in *Facebook, Inc. v. Pacific Northwest Software, Inc.*, 640 F.3d 1034 (9th Cir. 2011).

---

1 The plotline of this controversy is all too familiar: Wunderkind entrepreneur
2 conceives of a transformative business and propels it to a meteoric success, but
3 failed rivals insist they thought up the idea first and demand all the profits.
   A

4 The wunderkind in this case is Mark Zuckerberg. He is Chair and CEO of
5 Facebook, which runs the most popular social-networking website ever created.
6 Zuckerberg founded Facebook in 2004 when he was a Harvard undergrad.
   B
7 ER 152. Over the ensuing six years, through innovation, determination, and
   C
8 marketing genius, Zuckerberg steered Facebook to become an enterprise that
   D
9 now serves over 400 million users worldwide, and is probably the hottest start-
10 up in the world.

11 The rivals were fellow Harvard students: brothers Cameron and Tyler Win-
   E
12 klevoss and Divya Narendra. ER 150. After Zuckerberg launched Facebook, the
   F
13 rivals founded a competitor now named ConnectU. ER 152, 719. In October
14 2004, they filed a federal lawsuit in Massachusetts asserting that Facebook
15 was their idea. ER 148-61. They claimed that while they were at Harvard, they
   G
16 hatched the concept of a website, called Harvard Connection, with the much
17 more mundane mission of helping Harvard students find dates with each other
18 and land jobs with Harvard alumni. ER 150. They imagined eventually launch-
19 ing dating and networking sites on other campuses. *Id*. They alleged that they
20 enlisted Zuckerberg to help design their website. *Id*. They had never struck a
21 formal deal with Zuckerberg. Their whole case was premised on what the
   H
22 district judge in Massachusetts dismissed as "dorm room chitchat." SER 117.
   I
23 They asserted that Zuckerberg stalled and eventually co-opted their idea to
24 launch Facebook. ER 151-52. Among their causes of action were fraud and mis-
25 appropriation. ER 153-59.

26 From there, the plot took an unusual twist. Facebook discovered that its
27 accusers were themselves perpetrating a massive heist—from Facebook. The
28 discovery precipitated the filing of this lawsuit, which Facebook brought against

29 ConnectU and its Founders in San Jose, California, in 2005. In the California
30 action, Facebook alleged that the CU Founders scrapped their original Harvard
31 Connection concept and reconceived ConnectU as a new website with a two-
32 word business model: "copy [F]acebook." SER 127. Worse yet, in 2004 and
33 2005, the CU Founders hired programmers to illegally hack into the Facebook
34 system and use automated software to "scrape" and download millions of Face-
35 book users' email addresses and other personal information. SER 126-32, 623-
36 25. With this bounty, ConnectU spammed millions of Facebook users in hopes of
37 luring them to ConnectU's competing website. SER 109-12.

A In a single sentence, the authors frame their client as the good guy (a genius who built a "transformative business"), while the rivals are failures seeking to pilfer profits that they don't deserve. The line also feels brisk and engaging, resembling a Hollywood movie pitch. And that's not an accident: the word "plotline" alludes to the then-forthcoming movie *The Social Network*, which discusses this lawsuit extensively.

B **This sentence gives us some of the *who, what, and when* of the lawsuit. The rest of the Example supplements this information.**

C Earlier, we saw briefs that cited a joint appendix (JA), which is familiar to most attorneys; the Ninth Circuit, however, requires appellants to file an Excerpts of Record. The "ER" refers to the materials that the appellant prepares for the court; the "SER" refers to Supplemental Excerpts of Record, which the appellee prepares and which comprises materials that the appellee wants to use but that the appellant omitted from the ER. The difference between JAs and ERs shows that court rules can vary from one jurisdiction to another. You *must* check your local court rules.

D A good verb can bring a sentence to life. The verb "steered," which alludes to unspecified hazards that Zuckerberg had to dodge, is more powerful than possible substitutes. *See* Appendix C (listing short verbs). Likewise, the verb "imagined" (which appears later in this Example) swipes at the other side's failure to take concrete steps to build their company.

E Within three words we know what this paragraph will be about: the bad guys. Try to help readers identify instantly what a paragraph will discuss, whether a party, a stage in the dispute, or facts that relate to some legal issue.

F The word "after" plays an important role: it informs readers that the wunderkind started his business *before* the rivals, making it seem like, if any theft occurred, the rivals stole his idea.

G Using the word "they" to begin four consecutive sentences (a form of repetition known in rhetoric as "anaphora") would be more effective if hammering home related points; it is less so here when the four sentences relate to different topics. On the other hand, using the same subject in each sentence of a paragraph helps readers to absorb prose easily. Balance stylistic goals against the need to make your text absorbable. For those interested in an excellent primer about rhetoric, consult chapter 6 in Bryan Garner's *The Elements of Legal Style*.

H WARNING! Ideally, there should be a citation here; if the lawyers had an admission from the other side, they might quote the material or clarify who conceded this point. Alternatively, they should cite their own side's unrebutted testimony on this point. Evidence — even if it is uncontested — needs to be introduced into the trial court record to help on appeal. Facebook got lucky; it managed to sneak this in. Also, be wary of using absolutes like "always" or "never."

I Notice that this verb is ambiguous: did the court formally dismiss their claims or, more colloquially, find their claim undeserving of attention? Watch out for ambiguity — unless it helps you.

J This quote is brilliant. Substantively, it shows that the plaintiffs tried to rip off Facebook's idea (which is the very thing that they allege that Facebook's founder did to them). And stylistically, placing the words after a colon forces readers to focus on the quote.

K "Worse yet" is an excellent "signpost"; this beginning of the sentence tells readers what is coming and grabs their attention.

L We see again how effective short and engaging words can be: "scrapped," "bounty," "hack," "spammed," and "luring."

Example **1.5**	**Takeaway point 1.5:** When you represent the "bad guy," blame someone else, show that your client acted reasonably, and rebuild your client's credibility.

The examples we looked at so far involved an elderly homeowner, an alleged victim of copyright theft, a party alleging that a judge was crooked, and a wunderkind inventor. But what do you do when your client is the presumptive bad guy? Some lawyers counterpunch, and others tell their client's story in a neutral way to stanch the flames that the plaintiff has stoked. The following Example reflects both a "neutral" beginning and a novelistic writing style. The passage comes from a brief that reduced the client's liability by $2 billion.

In 1989, the oil tanker *Exxon Valdez* ran aground off the coast of Alaska, spilling oil into the Prince William Sound. Victims of the spill sued Exxon and won a jury award of $5 billion — 90 percent of which reflected punitive damages. Appellate courts eventually halved the award, and this brief convinced the Supreme Court to slash the punitive damages award again, by another 80 percent. Exxon argued that the punitive damages were excessive under both admiralty law and the Due Process Clause. In the following passage, Exxon sets up those substantive arguments by trying to show readers that the company was not grossly negligent, and the brief's tone tries to sound measured and credible as it seeks to make a historic disaster sound like a puzzling mishap that isn't attributable to Exxon.

Source: Exxon's brief in *Exxon Shipping Co. v. Baker,* 554 U.S. 471 (2008).

---

1   On March 24, 1989, the Exxon Valdez, a state-of-the-art, well-equipped tanker,
2   ran aground on Bligh Reef in Prince William Sound. The immediate cause was
3   the failure of Third Mate Cousins to steer the vessel away from the reef. The ves-
4   sel's master, Captain Hazelwood, instructed Cousins when and where to make
5   the turn, but then left the bridge—a violation of Exxon's explicit policy requir-
6   ing two officers to be present. For reasons that remain unknown, Cousins failed   **A**
7   to make the turn as instructed, and the ship went aground, spilling 258,000
8   barrels of oil. Pet. App. 61a-64a....   **B**
9   The vessel departed Valdez at 9:12 p.m. on March 23, 1989, and was guided
10   through the Valdez Narrows by a state-licensed pilot. JA271-72. Hazelwood
11   joined the pilot on the bridge, and at about 11:20 took active command of the
12   navigation of the vessel. The ship's radar showed ice in the inbound and out-
13   bound shipping lanes through Prince William Sound. Ships customarily steered
14   out of the defined lanes to avoid ice, JA1014; the two previous outbound tankers
15   had both done so. JA1021-25; DX 1735A. Hazelwood accordingly radioed the
16   Coast Guard that he was going to do likewise. JA76sa.
17   Cousins helped the pilot transfer to the pilot boat. When Cousins returned,
18   Hazelwood gave orders for returning to the shipping lanes after safely passing
19   the ice. JA350-53, 813, 838. He instructed Cousins to turn right when the ship
20   came abeam Busby Island light, an easily identifiable landmark. JA352, 834-35.
21   There was nothing dangerous or unusual about the turn Hazelwood planned.
22   The Commandant of the Coast Guard testified that these were *not* treacherous
23   waters. JA989-90. The ship was not traveling at an unusual speed. JA1011, 1016.
24   Visibility was good. The sea was calm. JA827-28, 264. Cousins reviewed the
25   planned maneuver with Hazelwood. JA834-37. The district court acknowledged   **C**
26   that Hazelwood's instructions were "specific" and "correct." Pet. App. 269a.   **D**

27 Having given his instructions, Hazelwood left the bridge and went to his
28 cabin, a few steps away, telling Cousins he needed to do some paperwork relat-
29 ed to avoiding a storm expected in the Gulf of Alaska. JA352-53, 813. His depar-
30 ture from the bridge violated Exxon's Bridge Manual, a statement of company
31 policy regarding the operation and navigation of its vessels, which was placed
32 on the bridge of every vessel, and which every watch officer was required to
33 read and sign. DX 3450, §§ 2.1.5, 8.5; JA945-46, 346-34. Because the Valdez was
34 leaving port, the Bridge Manual required both that the Master be on the bridge
35 and that two officers be on the bridge. By leaving Cousins as the only officer on
36 the bridge, Hazelwood violated both provisions. JA559. Exxon later discharged
37 Hazelwood for violating its rules. JA351-53.

38 When Hazelwood went below, the position abeam Busby Island light was
39 about two minutes away. JA342, 813-14. There was ample room for the Valdez
40 to pass between Bligh Reef and the ice. JA349-51, 826-27. At 11:55, Cousins de-
41 termined that the ship had come abeam the light. He noted his fix on the ship's
42 chart, ordered the helmsman to turn the rudder 10° right, and called Hazelwood
43 to tell him that the turn had begun. JA817-21, 353-54. The turn, however, had
44 not begun. The ship's course recorder indicates that the rudder did not go over
45 to 10° right until 12:02, seven minutes *after* the ship reached the turning point
46 on which Hazelwood and Cousins had agreed. JA1016-17. The rudder was then
47 held steady at 10° right for five minutes. This steered the Valdez back toward
48 the shipping lanes, but not soon enough to avoid the reef, where the Valdez
49 ran aground at 12:07 a.m. JA1017-18. Hazelwood immediately returned to the
50 bridge and took command. The objective evidence shows plainly that the turn
51 was not made in accordance with Hazelwood's instructions.

52 If the Valdez had begun turning abeam Busby Island light, as Hazelwood
53 had instructed, it would have missed Bligh Reef by a wide margin. Even a 5°
54 right rudder turn would have been enough. JA1018-20.

E

F

A Notice that Exxon frontloads its main theory: its policies were violated, and two rogue employees botched their jobs. Thus, the brief suggests that Exxon itself wasn't grossly negligent. A common strategy for a defendant is to blame someone else.

B The brief introduces quickly the worst fact in the case — to get it over with: lots of oil spilled. Exxon measures the spill in barrels rather than in gallons: "more than 10 million gallons" would sound worse and be more comprehensible, which would hurt Exxon. Use measurements that favor your client.

C The brief used these facts to undermine the argument that Exxon was grossly negligent. The short sentences would make Ernest Hemingway proud. They force readers to absorb Exxon's points, which suggest that Exxon's ship was not captained recklessly.

D The district court is cited for advantageous facts even though it pummeled Exxon: legal judo.

E The paragraph advances the view that Hazelwood was a rogue actor who, rather than acting *for* Exxon, violated its rules. Exxon presents itself as the victim (of a mischievous captain): like defendant Facebook in Example 1.4, Exxon tries to avoid being the villain.

F Lawyers rarely want to explore counterfactual situations, which tend to be abstract or unprovable. But here, Exxon doesn't stop at showing that the captain failed to follow Exxon's rules; it adds that the disaster would have been averted if the captain's orders had been followed. Why does this matter? Hazelwood was a lapsed alcoholic and Exxon knew it. This fact is the strongest piece of evidence supporting punitive damages against Exxon (and Justice Breyer mentioned this fact in his dissent). But if Hazelwood's orders would have steered the Valdez safely to port, then his addiction — and Exxon's decision to hire him — didn't cause the oil spill. Exxon's brief thus seeks to calm the furor against it, which is a critical goal for an unpopular defendant.

| Example 1.6 | **Takeaway point 1.6:** A formal tone gains credibility. |

Adapt your story's tone based on your client and the type of dispute. A trendy company like Facebook might benefit from a playful-sounding brief, while a client such as Exxon would not. Government briefs use perhaps the most formal and neutral tone of all, because of both custom and the government's role in the legal system. Public defenders often adopt the same formal tone (to build their clients' credibility). The brief that follows is quite formal but manages to avoid boring readers, which is the risk that accompanies a businesslike style.

In the following dispute, the government sought to reinstate the conviction of an al Qaeda operative, Ahmed Ressam, who was caught smuggling bomb components into the United States. He had planned to use the materials to kill travelers at Los Angeles International Airport. The legal issue related to a single word — "during" — in a federal criminal statute that criminalized "carr[ying] an explosive *during* the commission of any felony." The Ninth Circuit vacated Ressam's conviction, holding that "during" required the government to show that the explosives were related to Ressam's underlying felony, which was lying to a customs official when he tried to enter the United States. This brief convinced the Supreme Court to reverse.

Source: The U.S. government's brief in *United States v. Ressam*, 553 U.S. 272 (2008).

---

1   Respondent is an Algerian citizen. Pet. App. 3a. In 1998, he was recruited by
2   an al Qaeda operative while living in Canada. *Ibid*. After using a forged baptis-
3   mal certificate to obtain a Canadian passport in the name Benni Antoine Noris,
4   respondent traveled to Afghanistan, where he received advanced training in the
5   manufacture and use of explosives. *Id*. at 3a-4a. During that period, respondent
6   and others conceived a plot to target a United States airport to coincide with the
7   millennium. *Id*. at 4a.

8   On November 17, 1999, respondent and another al Qaeda operative trav-
9   eled to Vancouver, British Columbia, where they rented a Chrysler 300M and
10   checked into a motel. Pet. App. 4a. On December 14, 1999, the pair drove to
11   Tsawwassen, British Columbia, where they took a car ferry to Victoria on Van-
12   couver Island. *Ibid*.; J.A. 20, 41-42. Hidden in the Chrysler's spare tire well were
13   the components of a bomb, including explosives, timing devices, detonators,
14   fertilizer, and aluminum sulfate. Pet. App. 4a. Following their arrival in Victo-
15   ria, respondent's accomplice returned to Vancouver via public transportation,
16   and respondent boarded the day's only car ferry from Victoria to Port Angeles,
17   Washington. *Ibid*.; J.A. 27.

18   When the ferry arrived at Port Angeles, respondent's vehicle was the last to
19   off-load, and respondent became agitated when questioned by a United States
20   customs inspector. Pet. App. 5a; J.A. 29-30. The customs inspector instruct-
21   ed respondent to complete a customs declaration form, on which respondent
22   claimed to be a Canadian citizen and signed his name as Benni Noris. Pet. App.
23   5a; J.A. 30-31. The customs inspector then directed respondent to turn off his
24   car, open the trunk, and get out of the vehicle so that a secondary inspection
25   could be performed. J.A. 32-33. The car was searched, and the explosives and
26   other items were discovered. Pet. App. 5a; J.A. 36-39. An expert later deter-

A
B
C
D
E
F
G
H

27
28
29

> mined that a bomb made from the components found in respondent's vehicle could have killed or injured hundreds of people if detonated during the holiday travel rush at LAX. Pet. App. 5a.

A This sentence shows both that the respondent had a history of crossing borders with falsified documents — which is the underlying felony with which he was charged — and of violent terrorist training, which is the danger that (the brief hints) should lead the Court to lock up Ressam for a long time. Within several sentences, the brief has made it hard for readers to feel sympathy for Ressam.

B WARNING! The brief has listed two consecutive dates. On the one hand, these details are precise. Courts might use this information in an opinion. But listing consecutive dates taxes readers by forcing them to absorb numbers without necessarily grasping why that information is relevant. *Relative* dates, such as "four weeks later" or "the next month", are easier for readers to absorb. But there's more. The dates *do* matter here. The first date (November 17) shows that Ressam lurked in a sleepy town for a month; this plotting makes him seem more sinister — a professional terrorist. And the second date (December 14) shows that he entered the country with plenty of time to get to Los Angeles and scout the airport that he planned to target during the holidays.

C The details about where the bomb components were hidden ("in the Chrysler's spare tire") and what Ressam hid enables readers to visualize what is occurring. These details make it sound like Ressam was capable of detonating a major bomb, making readers *want* to lock him up.

D Avoid jargon. The word "by" would have been a better choice here than "via."

E This detail might seem irrelevant, but it suggests, without saying so, that Ressam tried to slip into the United States through a sleepy, vulnerable border town.

F **The respondent's agitation demonstrates why the customs inspector became suspicious. This detail is probably designed to preempt and quiet, subtly, any potential concerns that the customs official lacked a valid basis to search Ressam or that Ressam was searched because of racial profiling. The brief conveys this subtle point in an official and balanced tone.**

G The lawyers describe how the respondent's false statement was immediately followed by the inspector's discovery of the explosives, thereby highlighting the temporal element needed to trigger § 844(h)(2) — he was carrying explosives "during" the time that he made his illegal false statements to the customs official. Again, we see that good lawyers link the facts to their legal position.

H Notice how lawyers use passive verbs in this sentence to emphasize the nouns that matter most — the car, the explosives — rather than *who* conducted the search, which is irrelevant here. Avoid using passive constructions unless a passive verb will help you.

I The lawyers include this sentence to demonstrate the potential attack's severity and timing (during Christmas). The brief mentions earlier that Ressam was targeting Los Angeles's airport (and introduced the abbreviation "LAX") so this sentence reminds readers that Ressam planned to target a major airport.

Example 1.7

Takeaway point 1.7: Keep your Statement of Facts engaging to ensure that readers stay focused.

Formal writing need not be rigid or dry. The following example, for instance, reads like a thriller, even though it also came from a brief filed by the federal government. A federal jury convicted John Bell of attempting to murder a federal officer, rejecting Bell's argument that he fired his gun in self-defense when FBI agents raided the gas station where he worked. (The gas station was the hub of an illegal gambling ring.) Here, the government's brief describes the raid and summarizes the evidence that convicted Bell. The main actor, Detective Murray, is part of a team of police officers who raided the gas station. The excerpt begins midway through Detective Murray's attempt to arrest Bell.

Source: Brief of the U.S. government in *United States v. Bell*, 584 F.3d 478 (2d Cir. 2009).

1	Detective Murray instructed the defendant, "get your hand out of your
2	pocket." JA 188, 246. Although the defendant was within four feet of Detective
3	Murray and looking directly at him, the defendant did not comply with Detec-
4	tive Murray's commands. JA 188-189, 245. Initially, Detective Murray continued
5	to move toward the defendant, again stating "police," in an effort to prevent
6	the defendant from escaping, retrieving a weapon or destroying evidence. JA
7	189, 249. The defendant, however, continued to ignore Detective Murray's com-
8	mands. JA 249. Accordingly, Detective Murray determined that it was not safe
9	to move any closer to the defendant....
10	As Detective Murray stopped, he saw that the defendant had his sweatshirt
11	or coat wrapped around his right hand near his right hip. JA 189-191. Detective
12	Murray yelled to the defendant, "show me your hand." At that point, and for the
13	first time, Detective Murray raised his gun and pointed it at the defendant. JA
14	190-191. The defendant then pulled his right hand out from under his clothing.
15	JA 191. As he did, Detective Murray saw that the defendant had a silver revolver
16	in his hand, which the defendant raised and pointed at Detective Murray; the
17	defendant's finger was on the trigger. JA 191, 235, 678. Detective Murray yelled
18	"gun" to alert his fellow officers that the defendant had a weapon. JA 191, 259-
19	260, 292, 353, 366-368, 545, 596, 631-632, 646. Detective Murray then dove to
20	the left and fired his gun at least once, but possibly twice. JA 191-92, 632-35,
21	658. The defendant also fired his gun twice at Detective Murray. JA 192, 235-
22	236, 244, 635.
23	Both of the defendant's bullets went through the window directly behind
24	where Detective Murray had been standing before he dove for cover. JA 27,
25	190. One of the defendant's bullets exited the window at 68½ inches above the
26	ground. JA 488. The defendant's second shot exited the window several inches
27	below the first. JA 27, 485-487. Detective Murray stands approximately five feet
28	nine inches tall. JA 210. Accordingly, the defendant's shots were precisely at the
29	height of Detective Murray's head and chest. JA 211.

A B C D E F G H I J

A Some lawyers would use the more precise term "appellee" to refer to Bell — but that term is confusing and abstract, and "defendant" reminds readers that Bell was charged with a crime. Consider, too, the brief's use of "Detective Murray"; since most courts view the police favorably, this is a sensible choice. (That said, the word "Detective" appears in this short passage seventeen times. Try to make your semantic choices invisible.)

B The government begins the description of Bell's attempted murder with Murray's mundane request — not with guns blazing. This detail emphasizes Murray's compliance with procedure and his desire to avoid violence.

C The brief stretches out a three-second event into three paragraphs of riveting narrative. Keep in mind that subtle details can jeopardize credibility. The prior sentence says that Murray was within four feet of Bell. How much could he have "continued to move toward the defendant"? You are bound by the trial record, however; those facts become inviolable on appeal — and you need to do the best you can with hazy or puzzling facts. Consult your clients, comb trial materials, and hunt down answers to inconsistencies in the factual record.

D The brief puts readers in the protagonist's shoes. The brief tells the story from Detective Murray's vantage, leading us to sympathize with him. Bell's brief, of course, told the story from Bell's perspective. When you could tell your case's story from multiple perspectives or begin at various points, take special care to figure out how to start and tell the story.

E The lawyers resisted the urge to guess which type of clothing Bell was holding. Once again, we see great discipline — and sound ethics — by the lawyers who wrote this brief. As an attorney, you are bound to comport with your duty to the courts, as these lawyers do admirably (by sticking to the unclear record).

F **This part of the brief exemplifies the adage that good writers "show rather than tell." The lawyers recount concrete details that lead readers to conclude that Bell did not fire in self-defense: we are shown that Bell's hand was on the trigger of his silver revolver, that Murray was scared, and that Bell was about to shoot. Stories are vastly more effective and engaging when the facts speak for themselves and when the readers reach conclusions on their own.**

G This issue is one of the critical disputes in the trial: was Bell acting in self-defense? If Murray had shot at Bell without provocation, he wouldn't have yelled "gun." Thus, the *nine* citations that support this point are designed to convince readers that Bell pulled out his gun to shoot Murray. A number of the briefs in this chapter use an onslaught of citations to win credibility battles.

H Lawyers want, of course, to write with certitude. But here, the lawyers arguably increase their credibility about other issues by acknowledging once again the limits of their knowledge on this specific issue (i.e., how many times Murray fired his gun). But avoid uncertainty whenever possible because it raises questions; here, for example, readers might wonder why it isn't possible simply to check Murray's gun to see how many rounds had been fired. The answer becomes clear in a subse-quent part of the Statement of Facts when readers learn that Murray fired his gun again later in the shootout.

I By using the word "also" — and by mentioning the defendant's gunshots so prominently — the brief obscures the damaging facts that Murray shot *first* and that the defendant shot back in response, which sounds like self-defense. Replicate this technique to downplay bad facts.

J Yet again we see that *show* is better than *tell*. After showing the exact heights of the bullet holes and of Murray, the brief lets readers figure out for themselves that these shots were intended to kill Murray.

Example 1.8

Takeaway point 1.8: Anticipate and confront especially damaging facts and figure out how to defang them.

It's easy to tug heartstrings when your client is an elderly homeowner or to have your concerns taken seriously when you're prosecuting criminals. But what can you say about a client who is a war criminal to make him seem like a victim? Keep reading.

The following passage discusses Daniel Negusie, who sought asylum in the United States. He had previously been a prison guard during a war between Eritrea and Ethiopia, and he was denied asylum because of his role during that conflict. He argued that the federal immigration laws, which bar persecutors from obtaining asylum in the United States, do not apply to asylum applicants who were coerced into being persecutors. To give a sense of what the government alleged, here is an excerpt from the other side's brief, making Negusie look like a typical prison guard:

> [Negusie] carried a gun and was responsible for keeping control over prisoners and preventing their escape. His duties also included "punish[ing] the prisoners . . . by exposing them to the extreme sun heat" and denying them water, forbidding them to take showers, and keeping them from ventilation and fresh air. Petitioner routinely stood guard over prisoners who were kept in the sun as a form of punishment or execution. Petitioner was aware that prisoners died when ex- posed to the sun "for more than a couple of hours," and he knew that at least one person he guarded died as a result of sun exposure. Petitioner acknowledged his integral role in the torture and execution of prisoners . . . .

And yet Negusie won at the Supreme Court largely by showing that he was a *victim* not a war criminal. The following passage reveals how he accomplished this goal.

Source: Negusie's brief in *Negusie v. Holder*, 555 U.S. 511 (2009) (citations omitted).

1　　*2. Petitioner's Persecution in Eritrea.*[4]　Petitioner Daniel Girmai Negusie was
2　a citizen and resident of Eritrea during the Ethiopian-Eritrean war. One day in
3　1994 when petitioner was 18 years old, he went to his town's theater to see a
4　movie. Soldiers surrounded the theatre; when the audience left the theatre at
5　the movie's conclusion, everyone was "apprehended and hand-tied by rope."
6　The soldiers shot at anyone who attempted to escape. His captors subsequently ⟶ A
7　forced petitioner to perform "hard labor" in a salt mine. Anyone who attempted
8　to escape and was caught was "kept in the sun for three days without food
9　and water."

10　　After a month in the salt mines, petitioner was forced to undergo military
11　training for six months. Following his training, he was pressed into service as
12　a gunner on a naval vessel patrolling the Red Sea. He testified that during this
13　service, he never fired the gun at any person or vessel.

14　　Following his conscription in the Eritrean navy, petitioner was discharged
15　and took a job as a painter aboard a ship. In 1998, however, the conflict with ⟶ B
16　Ethiopia re-erupted, and petitioner was conscripted once again. Petitioner
17　refused to fight because he considered Ethiopians his "brothers." As a result
18　of his refusal to fight and because he is half-Ethiopian, petitioner was taken to

---

19　　4. The Board of Immigration Appeals upheld the Immigration Judge's finding
20　that petitioner was credible. The court of appeals did not address that determination,
21　because it found petitioner's claim of duress irrelevant as a matter of law. ⟶ C

22   prison, where he was placed in solitary confinement for six months. Petitioner
23   remained imprisoned under harsh conditions, forced to perform hard labor, for
24   an additional one and a half years after his solitary confinement.

D

25   During his imprisonment, petitioner converted to Protestant Christianity, for
26   which he was subjected to additional persecution. At one point, he was forced
27   to roll on the ground in the hot sun while being beaten with a stick every day
28   for two weeks for talking with fellow Christians in the prison.

E

29   Once petitioner was released from prison in 2001, the prison camp's com-
30   manding officer directed him to assume "duties as a prison guard and also in
31   the surveillance...of the base." Petitioner was never permitted to leave the
32   military base and would have been executed had he tried to flee. In fact, peti-
33   tioner testified that at least two of his friends were killed in the course of trying
34   to escape from their forced service as guards.

F

35   While forced to serve as a prison guard, petitioner was told to "bring out the
36   prisoners from their cells and punish[] them." Petitioner, however, "objected
37   [and] declined taking such an action of punishing the prisoners" because it of-
38   fended his beliefs as a Christian. Instead, in the face of threatened execution,
39   when ordered to punish and torture the prisoners, petitioner "did the [opposite]
40   of what they ordered me [to do]." Rather than denying the prisoners showers,
41   for instance, he permitted them to take showers in secret at night. He also gave
42   the prisoners food, water, and cigarettes in secret, and let them out into the
43   fresh air at night. Although he witnessed torture take place, he never himself
44   beat or killed anyone during his forced service.

45   After almost four years of coerced service at the military base and prison,
46   petitioner resolved to risk death in escape rather than continue coerced service
47   for his captors. He fled in the dark of night to a friend's house. Each night for the
48   next five nights, he and another escapee swam out to a container ship anchored
49   in the Red Sea. On the fifth night, they finally opened a ventilation shaft and
50   sneaked into a container, bringing food and water with them. Over one month
51   later, petitioner arrived in the United States and filed for asylum.

A Notice how the word "subsequently" obfuscates (intentionally) how much time passed.

B This fact — that Negusie painted ships — is designed to show that Negusie left the prison system during peacetime, suggesting that he worked as a guard only because he was forced to do so.

C The lawyers cleverly use this footnote to prevent the Court from questioning the truthfulness of Negusie's account of his prison service. Appellate courts will rarely revisit a trial court's (or agency's) factual findings — and you should remind reviewing courts when facts cannot be second-guessed.

D The lawyers demonstrate that Negusie was coerced; he was punished when he disobeyed orders.

E The implicit message of this passage is that Negusie was persecuted for being Christian. Those facts are designed both to increase empathy toward him and to improve his chance of getting asylum, which is available to individuals who reasonably fear religious persecution. Eritrea, however, is at least 48 percent Christian — hardly a helpless minority. Only 1 percent of citizens, however, are Protestants. Rather than delving into Eritrean demographics or the risk of persecution to Protestants in Eritrea, the brief just states Negusie's religion and lets readers draw their own conclusions, which likely help Negusie.

F Earlier, we learned that Negusie would be punished harshly if he refused to work as a prison guard. This fact anticipates another question on readers' minds: why didn't he try to escape? Top lawyers anticipate readers' concerns and address bad facts — without saying that they are doing so.

FREQUENTLY ASKED QUESTIONS ABOUT THE BASICS OF USING FACTS

Q. How much can I characterize facts?

A. Judges expect some "spin." But if you materially distort facts, omit important facts, or manufacture facts, your credibility will be shot. A test: if the judge caught you, would you be embarrassed? If so, don't do it.

Q. Do I need to recount *all* of the facts that I use in my Argument?

A. Usually, yes. But rather than, for instance, listing fifty provisions of a contract in your Statement of Facts, you might just tell readers that additional provisions are quoted later, in the Argument. Alternatively, if your case involves multiple parties or legal issues that rest on entirely distinct facts, you can provide a short Statement that applies to the entire case, and then add additional facts just before you discuss each party or issue. As Example 6.6 shows, very complicated cases sometimes benefit from saving facts for your Argument.

Q. Should I organize my facts chronologically?

A. Sort of. You should not bounce forward and backward in time. But you should tell a compelling, coherent story rather than begin with whatever fact happens to have occurred first in time. Consider using creative "flashback" techniques to avoid beginning with bad facts; for instance, you can wait until you describe what the trial court found before listing bad facts that would otherwise appear early in your Statement if you adhered to strict chronological order.

Q. When you say that lawyers should disclose bad facts, does that principle apply to every bad fact in the case?

A. No, that rule applies only to the ones that the court will need to consider or that the other side will use to bludgeon you if you fail to disclose them.

Chapter 2

Facts: Using a Case's Procedural History to Help Your Client

When top lawyers discuss the procedural history of their case, they use that discussion to advance their clients' interests. Novices, by contrast, usually ignore a case's posture or treat it cursorily — or neutrally. This chapter shows how to frame the posture of your case in a way that helps readers learn what happened in the lawsuit while *also* helping your client.

The discussion of the case's posture typically appears toward the end of a Statement of Facts — once you've explained how the dispute arose. It can therefore usually be placed in its own subsection within your facts. In some instances, the posture can be very short; in other instances, a detailed sketch proves helpful. A procedural section is a fixture of appellate briefs. Trial motions also frequently use a dispute's procedural background to persuade a court to award the relief that the motions are requesting. Indeed, the procedural details sometimes reflect the nub of the dispute in a trial court, such as in a motion for sanctions, a motion to compel production of documents, or a motion to dismiss for failure to exhaust administrative remedies. Posture matters.

This book devotes a whole chapter to this skill — using a case's posture effectively — because posture is so important to effective advocacy and is almost certainly the most overlooked aspect of preparing a stellar Statement.

CHAPTER OVERVIEW
1. Explain how the case reached its current state (e.g., on appeal from a summary judgment order, on remand from an appellate court).
2. Tell the court which relevant decisions and orders were issued earlier in the case.
3. Emphasize a lower court's helpful factual findings and legal reasoning.
4. Deemphasize or subtly undermine adverse findings and reasoning.
5. Use the posture to smuggle in helpful atmospheric details from the earlier stages of the case.
6. Show that your client preserved (or that the other side waived) objections and arguments.
7. Steer readers to the location of important record materials.
8. On appeal, emphasize helpful dissenting or concurring opinions from earlier in the case that support your client.
9. When you want to reverse or vacate a lower court's order or opinion, help the reviewing court to see exactly what orders or opinions it would need to reverse or vacate.

Example **2.1**	**Takeaway point 2.1:** Explain the key procedural developments in your case in a way that helps your client while also helping the court to see what happened. Treat procedural history, in other words, just like the rest of your Statement of Facts. The resolution of some cases depends on the posture. In those cases, the procedural history serves not merely an informative function, but goes to the heart of the dispute. Lawyers need to explain what the lower court did and what relevant decisions the lower court issued. To see this technique, we return to the case in which Don Blankenship, the CEO of a coal company, spent millions of dollars to elect a justice in West Virginia. The plaintiffs (i.e., petitioners) argue that the Due Process Clause requires that Justice Benjamin recuse himself from the case. *Source:* The brief challenging Justice Benjamin's failure to recuse himself, from *Caperton v. A.T. Massey Coal Co.,* 556 U.S. 868 (2009).

1   **5.** The West Virginia Supreme Court of Appeals thereafter granted Massey's

2 petition for review. In a 3-2 decision, the court reversed the $50 million verdict

3 against Massey and dismissed the case with prejudice—while "mak[ing] per-

4 fectly clear that the facts of this case demonstrate that Massey's conduct war-

5 ranted the type of judgment rendered" against it. J.A. 357a. Justice Benjamin

6 joined the majority's opinion reversing the verdict against Massey.

7   Creating nearly a dozen new points of West Virginia law, the majority held

8 that petitioners' suit against Massey was barred by a forum-selection clause

9 in the coal supply agreement that Sovereign Coal Sales, Inc., and Harman

10 Mining Corporation had entered into with Wellmore, which provided that

11 "[a]ll actions brought in connection with this Agreement shall be filed in and

12 decided by the Circuit Court of Buchanan County, Virginia." J.A. 358a. The

13 majority reached this conclusion even though it acknowledged that neither

14 Massey itself nor two of the petitioners—Harman Development Corporation

15 and Mr. Hugh Caperton—were parties to the agreement and that the causes

16 of action on which petitioners prevailed sounded in tort, rather than contract.

17 *Id.* at 377a, 386a-87a....

18   Justices Albright and Starcher filed vigorous dissents. Both expressed alarm

19 at the "result-driven effort" of the majority to relieve Massey of liability. J.A.

20 423a; see also id. at 420a. According to Justice Albright, the majority "went out

21 of its way to make findings that fit its intended result" and did so "by twisting

22 logic, misapplying the law and introducing sweeping 'new law' into our juris-

23 prudence." *Id.* at 429a, 430a-31a (emphasis omitted).

24   6. Petitioners timely petitioned for rehearing. While that petition was pend-

25 ing, photographs were made public showing Chief Justice Maynard, who had

26 joined the majority's opinion in favor of Massey, vacationing with Mr. Blanken-

27 ship on the French Riviera during the pendency of Massey's appeal.

Ⓐ This brief numbers the various subsections of the Statement of Facts. This "numbering" approach is common at the Supreme Court. In most courts, however, lawyers use subheadings to signal that a new phase of the case is about to be discussed. The first three parts of the brief provided background about Justice Benjamin's indebtedness to Blankenship. The fourth part described petitioners' initial motion to recuse Justice Benjamin, which was denied.

Ⓑ Notice the beautiful subtlety here: litigants have the right to an *appeal*, but a "petition for review" means that the appellate court gets to decide whether to hear a case. Thus, the very fact that the West Virginia court agreed to hear this case could hint that Massey received favorable treatment from the court. This point is not a critical one, but it shows that great lawyers are trying to advance their cause — even at the margins — at all moments.

Ⓒ By including the vote count, the brief shows that Justice Benjamin's vote dictated the outcome.

Ⓓ Once again, the lawyers' mastery of the procedural details advances the clients' cause. The appellate court "dismissed the case with prejudice," thus preventing the case from being retried on remand. The resolution of the case hints that the West Virginia court was trying to end the case.

Ⓔ The brief quotes the West Virginia court itself to suggest that its opinion clashed with the evidence. Again, the subtle implication is that bias produced that result. Each of the subtle procedural details merely nudges readers; the brief does not overstate the relevance of any single detail.

Ⓕ The brief specifies that Benjamin cast one of the three votes that reversed the verdict. Less skilled lawyers would stop here. But these lawyers know that they bolster their case if they can show that the West Virginia court's opinion was dubious, which the brief demonstrates in the following paragraph.

Ⓖ The brief makes the court's opinion seem radical by stating that it created many new points of law. The implication, once again, is that impartial judges wouldn't have reached this result. Some readers will think that this phrase overreaches and that this sentence is too long. But I applaud it: it renders the balance of the sentence (which summarizes unfavorable facts) irrelevant and forgettable. And the helpful fact sticks — that the West Virginia court created new law to favor Massey.

Ⓗ **The majority's reasoning *sounds* preposterous. Characterizing the lower court's reasoning this way makes readers skeptical of both the court's integrity *and* its reasoning. And that ultimately caused the Supreme Court to scrutinize what the state court did and to require Justice Benjamin to recuse himself. The lawyers decided not to describe exactly who these parties (Sovereign, Harman, and Wellmore) were; readers might be curious, but the lawyers elected not to enter a detailed battle about whether the West Virginia court's reasoning was valid. They chose brevity.**

Ⓘ A strong dissenting opinion is a great ally on appeal. This brief exemplifies how dissents and concurrences can provide succor to your client.

Ⓙ Before petitioning the Supreme Court to hear a case, litigants must exhaust their other options. Thus, they often need either to ask federal appellate courts to hear cases en banc or to petition state supreme courts to rehear the case. This topic sentence signals a new stage in the case and also assuages the Justices' concern that the litigants might have failed to take all of the steps necessary to launch a challenge at the Supreme Court.

Ⓚ Here, the brief uses the old guilt-by-association trick. Two justices voted with Justice Benjamin, and the brief gives us no reason to doubt *their* integrity. Readers might thus suspect that Massey's arguments have merit. The colorful facts in this paragraph seem irrelevant to the legal issue because the case is about Justice Benjamin's failure to recuse himself, *not* about Chief Justice Maynard. But in a single sentence, the brief makes the Supreme Court of Appeals of West Virginia appear like a den of corruption — and makes readers want to do something about it.

Example 2.2

Takeaway point 2.2 Emphasize the helpful rulings, findings, and evidence that appeared earlier in your case even if you lost.

Good lawyers weaponize the procedural history of their cases, even when the dispute does not revolve around the procedural posture. The next brief does exactly that in describing the lower court proceedings.

In this case, police stopped a motorist named Albert Florence and found an outstanding bench warrant for his arrest. The warrant reflected a recordkeeping error; Florence had paid the ticket several years earlier. He was nevertheless arrested. As a result, he was processed through two prison facilities and was subjected at each prison to searches that included undressing, delousing, and a strip search. Florence filed a lawsuit for monetary damages against the state police, alleging that the searches were unconstitutional and unreasonable. The district court granted summary judgment for him, holding that unless there is reasonable suspicion, "strip-searching" someone who is not indictable violates the Fourth Amendment. On appeal, the Third Circuit reversed — a win for the prison. Here, the prison's lawyers tell the Supreme Court what the district court did. As you will see, the description of these procedural facts is hardly meek or neutral.

Source: Brief for the prison system in *Florence v. Board of Chosen Freeholders*, 132 S. Ct. 1510 (2012).

COUNTERSTATEMENT OF THE CASE

The court granted summary judgment for petitioner and the class.... The court brushed aside respondents' penological interests justifying their policies. It rejected respondents' showing that the searches uncover gang activity and potential health problems because, in its view, such searches are not the least intrusive means for achieving these goals. Pet. App. 85a-86a.

It was equally dismissive of respondents' demonstration that the policies were justified by significant security interests in deterring contraband. Pet. App. 85a-86a. The court noted (at 85a) that Essex submitted an expert report by George M. Camp, whose studies this Court credited in *Turner v. Safley*, 482 U.S. 78, 92-93 (1987). Dr. Camp opined that conducting strip searches — including the type of visual body-cavity searches at issue in *Wolfish*, see J.A. 381a-82a, 386a — for all new arrivals is "an essential function in protecting the security and institutional integrity of jail," *id.* at 385a. In fact, non-indictable detainees "can be more dangerous and ... more likely to bring in contraband." *Id.* at 380a. He also explained that "interaction and mingling between misdemeanants and felons" make it imperative that all inmates are searched, *id.* at 381a, and that if arrestees know that certain categories of offenders will not be searched, "[t]hese weak links [will be] discovered by the inmate population and exploited to the detriment of both prisoners and staff," *id.* at 382a. Despite this and other evidence — including concessions by the lone expert designated by petitioner, whom petitioner attempted to withdraw once he discovered that the expert's opinions supported respondents' policies — the district court faulted respondents for not submitting "supporting affidavits that detail evidence of a smuggling problem specific to their respective facilities." Pet. App. 87a. It did so despite acknowledging that *Wolfish* stated "that evidence of a smuggling problem is 'of little import' to the analysis." *Id.*

Ⓐ A "counterstatement" is the appellee's (or non-movant's or respondent's) stand-alone version of facts, which should retell the dispute in a way that favors that litigant. Throughout this passage, the lawyers restrict their attacks to the trial court's *reasoning*, not to the court itself. Judges work in the same building, see each other at conferences, and swap stories about lawyers who irritate them. Attacking one judge tends to make other judges feel attacked or disrespected. Comment on judicial *actions* with which you disagree in an intellectually critical but respectful manner. But, in general, don't attack the judge. (Example 2.1 is a very rare exception to this rule.)

Ⓑ That this case was decided against the prison on summary judgment means that the prison's facts must be accepted as true (because that legal standard governs the disposition of a summary judgment motion). When the standard of review favors your client, emphasize it.

Ⓒ This sentence seems like it is describing the posture. Hardly. It is using a procedural fact to suggest that the prison should be allowed to "uncover gang activity and potential health problems," without judicial babysitting, as it deems appropriate. The procedural history advances the first of several policy arguments.

Ⓓ **The "posture" walks through each of the prison's arguments — thus, for all practical purposes, the posture is an argument. But the discussion sticks to facts by stating *that* it argued something rather than by simply repeating the argument.**

Ⓔ The Supreme Court itself previously credited the expert's work, which helps to establish the expert's credibility. Moreover, the brief concisely repeats the expert's arguments, converting this "factual" discussion into a powerful piece of advocacy that raises another policy argument.

Ⓕ This detail is *very* helpful to the prison (because it explains why arrestees like Florence need to be searched). But burying this helpful detail in a long paragraph reduces the chances that readers will focus on this quotation. Try to keep paragraphs no longer than about 200 words.

Ⓖ As we'll see again in the next chapter, sophisticated lawyers smuggle case law into their facts. How? By making it a fact! This quote rests on the word "acknowledging": that word allows the prison to include favorable case law (because the district court mentioned it). As Comment D above mentions, stating that the court or some other party said something qualifies as a fact, even if that statement happens to contain an argument. There's a second benefit from including this case citation: showing that the trial judge disregarded the Supreme Court's opinion paints the lower court as reckless, undermining its reasoning and making appellate judges more willing to second-guess its conclusions.

Example	**Takeaway point 2.3:** Atmospheric details about the procedural history can advance your client's main argument.
2.3	

Let's look at another example in which a brief undermines lower courts' reasoning. Here we revisit Exxon's attempt to convince the Supreme Court to reduce a $2.5 billion punitive damages award after Exxon's tanker spilled oil in waters near Alaska. This passage also exemplifies how to use atmospheric facts from the case's history to advance your client's substantive arguments. Exxon explained earlier in the brief that the trial court hammered Exxon with a $5 billion punitive damages award. We learn below what the appellate courts did. Two details may help to illuminate this discussion. First, the *State Farm* case (discussed below) capped punitive damages; the more reprehensible a defendant's conduct, the higher the acceptable ratio between the punitive damages and the actual damages. Second, in most courts, a ship's owner is not liable for the torts committed by the ship's captain.

Source: Exxon's brief in *Exxon Shipping Co. v. Baker*, 554 U.S. 471 (2008) (record citations omitted).

C. Appellate Proceedings

1. The Ninth Circuit issued its first opinion in November 2001. The court rejected Exxon's arguments that no punitive damages were authorized, but added a number of significant caveats. Addressing whether judge-made maritime punitive damages remedies could expand the penalties already provided in the CWA [Clean Water Act], the court acknowledged that the question was "serious," "not without doubt," and "close." On the propriety of the jury instructions authorizing vicarious punitive damages liability, the court pronounced itself bound by its decision in *Protectus Alpha Nav. Co. v. North Pac. Grain Growers*, 767 F.2d 1379 (9th Cir. 1985), but acknowledged that *Protectus* conflicted with the historic maritime-law rule as well as with modern maritime decisions of other circuits. And while the court did not accept Exxon's argument that maritime law and due process bar punitive damages when prior sanctions and liabilities have satisfied any public interest in punishment and deterrence, it acknowledged that the argument had "force as logic and policy."

The Ninth Circuit[, however, nevertheless held] that a $5 billion award could not stand. Applying the due process guideposts of *BMW of North America v. Gore*, 517 U.S. 559 (1996), the court held that Exxon's conduct was not sufficiently reprehensible to justify so high an award because (1) the spill was not intentional; (2) punishment was for economic injuries only; (3) "fuel for the United States at moderate expense has great social value"; and (4) Exxon had spent billions to mitigate harm in the aftermath of the accident. The court further held that pretrial claims payments and settlements generally should not be included in the "harm" used to analyze the ratio between punitive and compensatory damages, and that a high ratio was unnecessary for deterrence because the $3.4 billion that Exxon had already paid constituted a "massive deterrent" independent of any punitive damages.

2. The Ninth Circuit remanded the case for determination of the appropriate remittitur. The district court reduced the award to $4 billion, but asserted that it saw no "principled" basis for any reduction at all. Exxon again appealed, but the Ninth Circuit *sua sponte* remanded the case for reconsideration in light of *State Farm Mut. Auto. Ins. Co. v. Campbell*, 538 U.S. 408 (2003). This time

33 the district court increased the award to $4.5 billion, asserting that *State Farm*
34 presumptively validated punitive damages of up to nine times the total harm
35 (which the district court calculated to be $500 million). Exxon appealed for the
36 third time.
37   3. The Ninth Circuit issued its second opinion in December 2006. The court
38 again reviewed the award under the *Gore* guideposts, but this time rational-
39 izing a multibillion dollar award. On reprehensibility, for example, the court
40 emphasized that the spill had physically endangered the crew and rescuers of
41 the vessel, even though no one was injured and none of the crew or rescuers
42 was a plaintiff in the lawsuit. On ratio, the court repudiated its earlier statement
43 that pretrial payments and settlements should not be included in the harm,
44 stating incorrectly that *State Farm* mandated this change of view. Accepting the
45 district court's calculation of $500 million in total losses, the court held that due
46 process would permit a 5:1 ratio because the tort fell within the "mid range" of
47 reprehensibility. By this reasoning, the court upheld an unprecedented punitive
48 award of $2.5 billion, 200 times the next largest award affirmed by a federal ap-
49 pellate court for unintentional conduct. *See Mason v. Texaco, Inc.*, 948 F.2d 1546
50 (10th Cir. 1991). Judge Browning would have affirmed $5 billion.
51   4. Exxon filed a timely petition for panel rehearing and rehearing en banc.
52 The court denied it on May 23, 2007, amending its decision to remove its incor-
53 rect statement about *State Farm*, but not otherwise changing its result or at-
54 tempting to justify the repudiation of its prior decision. Two judges filed dissents
55 from the denial of en banc review. Judge Kozinski argued that the court had
56 unjustifiably departed from 200 years of maritime precedent prohibiting vicari-
57 ous punitive damages, in conflict with every other circuit that had considered
58 the issue. Judge Bea agreed with Judge Kozinski, and also dissented because a
59 $2.5 billion award was excessive under *State Farm*.

E

F

G

(A) Lawyers can (and often do) use a separate sub-heading for each stage of the procedural history.

(B) Rather than simply saying "Exxon lost," the lawyers mine the appellate opinion for dicta and factual conclusions that help Exxon.

(C) This is subtle, brilliant advocacy: the plaintiffs-petitioners alleged "Exxon Irretrievably Waived Its [Clean Water Act] Argument." By mentioning the CWA right away in its procedural section, Exxon plants the idea that the CWA issue has been fiercely litigated throughout the lawsuit.

(D) The court's conclusions give Exxon a chance to parade helpful facts as procedural history. Good lawyers revel in the chance to let judges tell their client's story and advance their client's arguments.

(E) Notice again that, just as in Example 2.2, the lawyers try to make the court in which they lost look feckless, fickle, and biased, but they assiduously refrain

from insulting the court or the individual judges. They let the facts register their complaints about how the Ninth Circuit handled the case. They also smuggle in helpful facts yet again.

(F) **Rather than celebrating that "the court therefore cut the award in half," Exxon *complains* here, presenting a decision that reduced its liability by $2 billion as a defeat. Exxon then sneaks in a citation to show that the punitive damages award was massive and historic, even after it was reduced. Each court picked a different amount to punish Exxon: $5 billion, $4 billion, $4.5 billion, and $2.5 billion. This variability makes the award seem arbitrary, which is a valuable atmospheric fact for Exxon.**

(G) Exxon highlights the lower court's misreading of a case and its self-repudiation to undermine that court's credibility. This "atmospheric" fact has little to do with the current dispute but makes Exxon look reliable about the law.

Example 2.4	**Takeaway point 2.4:** Procedural history dictates the outcome of many trial motions, so find compelling ways to address procedural facts that harm your client.

In trial court motions, the procedural history often lies at the heart of a dispute — especially when a motion seeks a procedural remedy, such as to compel production of documents or force a witness to testify. The following example shows how to use procedural history in a motion.

An independent prosecutor was trying to force President Bill Clinton to testify in front of a grand jury about his alleged sexual relationship with his former intern, Monica Lewinsky. The president had denied throughout early 1998 that he and Lewinsky had been sexually intimate; his litigation goal appeared to be to avoid testifying as long as possible (and at least until after the November 1998 midterm elections). Below, we see Clinton's attempt to quash a subpoena ordering him to testify: the motion revolved primarily around his lawyers' skirmishes with the independent prosecutor, a form of procedural history.

Source: President Clinton's motion from *In re Motion To Continue*, Misc. No. 98-267 (D.D.C. July 28, 1998).

---

1   For the first time, a sitting President has been subpoenaed to testify before a
2   grand jury. On Friday evening, July 17, 1998, the Office of Independent Counsel
3   ("OIC") delivered a subpoena to counsel attempting to compel President
4   William J. Clinton to testify before the grand jury today, Tuesday, July 28, 1998.
5   In response, President Clinton, through counsel, has indicated a willingness to
6   provide voluntary testimony for the grand jury. Despite this response, the OIC
7   has refused to continue or withdraw the subpoena returnable today, necessitat-
8   ing this request to the Court. This refusal creates the prospect of a constitutional
9   confrontation that, with a short continuance, may well be avoided. Accordingly,
10   President Clinton moves this Court for a two-week continuance of the return
11   date of the subpoena, to August 11, 1998, to permit the parties to seek such
12   a resolution or adequately to prepare appropriate legal papers if a resolution
13   cannot be reached.

14   I. Background

15   Six times after January 21, 1998, the OIC invited President Clinton to testify
16   before the grand jury investigating the Monica Lewinsky matter. *See* Exhibit 1
17   (correspondence between Mr. Kendall [the Presdent's lawyer] and the OIC regard-
18   ing the President's testimony). In response, counsel for President Clinton outlined
19   serious concerns to be addressed before any such testimony would be considered,
20   including issues that had arisen over the origin and conduct of the OIC's Lewinsky
21   investigation. The OIC's most recent mention of the possibility of such tes-
22   timony was almost four months ago, on April 3, 1998, with a response by
23   Mr. Kendall on April 17, 1998. *See* Exhibit 1. The OIC did not respond to the
24   April 17 letter and did not raise the issue with counsel for the President in any
25   way in the almost four months since its last letter.
26   After this long period of silence, on Friday, July 17, 1998, without warning,
27   the OIC delivered a subpoena to counsel for the President purporting to require
28   President Clinton to testify before the grand jury today, July 28. Exhibit 2 (sub-
29   poena and accompanying letter). At the time, President Clinton was traveling
30   outside of Washington, D.C., and he did not return until early Tuesday, July
31   21, 1998. In light of the need to consider properly the serious issues presented

A
B
C
D
E
F

32 by the subpoena, counsel for President Clinton telephoned Mr. Bittman (of the
33 OIC) on July 22, 1998, and requested that the OIC provide another week,
34 until August 4, for counsel to respond to the July 17 delivery. On July 23, 1998,
35 the OIC offered three more days, if the President would agree not to seek any
36 additional time from the OIC or the Court. Exhibit 3 (July 23, 1998 Letter of
37 Mr. Bittman).

38 On July 24, 1998, counsel for President Clinton informed the OIC that the
39 President "is willing to provide testimony for the grand jury, although there are
40 a number of questions relating to the precise terms and timing of the testimony
41 which must be worked out." Exhibit 4 (July 24, 1998 Letter of Mr. Kendall).
42 Counsel for the President also requested that the subpoena be withdrawn
43 while these issues were resolved. The OIC declined to withdraw the subpoena.
44 Exhibit 5 (July 24, 1998 Letter of Mr. Bittman). Subsequently, by letter yester-
45 day, Mr. Kendall wrote to the OIC with a detailed and specific proposal regard-
46 ing both the format and timing of potential testimony by the President. Exhibit
47 6 (July 27, 1998 Letter of Mr. Kendall). Despite this responsive and good faith
48 offer, and the prospect of immediate continuing negotiations, the OIC refused to
49 withdraw or even continue the return date of the subpoena beyond 1:30 p.m.
50 today unless "the President commits in writing to testify on a date certain on
51 or before August 7, 1998." *See* Exhibit 7 (July 27, 1998 Letter of Mr. Bittman).

G

H

I

A This is a great first sentence. It states the stakes, captures readers' attention, and frames the other side's acts as outlandish and unprecedented.

B This sentence is designed to make Clinton seem reasonable. The phrase "indicated a willingness" is much less direct than "agreed" and reflects the successful hunt for a weak verb that lawyers conduct when they *want* to avoid committing to a position.

C Clinton seeks a clear and modest remedy — a short extension — reflecting the general rule that motions need to specify what relief they seek. Notice, too, that the motion does *not* commit to having the president appear in two weeks; it merely seeks an extension "to permit the parties to seek" a resolution or for the president to prepare for a legal battle. The long sentence obscures that Clinton is not agreeing to testify voluntarily.

D WARNING! Why begin with such a bad fact, namely that the other side tried repeatedly to get the president to appear before a grand jury? On the one hand, President Clinton's lawyers know that this detail is the Achilles heel of their argument, so they raise it immediately and then try to neutralize it by showing the lengthy delay between the penultimate and final request. Even so, stating up front that the president evaded *six* requests to testify is unfavorable enough that this detail probably should have been de-emphasized. Indeed, the trial judge harped on this fact during a hearing on this motion, leading the president to testify lest she order him to honor the subpoena.

E This vague sentence aspires not to convince or win the case, but merely to make readers think that Clinton had *some* valid basis for refusing the multiple requests to appear before the grand jury. A strong basis to stay the subpoena would have helped.

F This effective beginning to the paragraph suggests that there's no urgency to forcing the president to testify.

G Notice how the posture of the dispute *becomes the relevant factual background for the motion. And as a result, the same principles that govern facts apply here. For instance, you want your client to sound reasonable and you want your adversary to seem aggressive and insincere.*

H Lawyers can characterize facts favorably as in the motion's comment (a "good faith offer"). Don't overdo this approach, however: when every fact is accompanied by commentary — a trait that appellate lawyer Peter Keisler calls "sportscasting" — judges may roll their eyes.

I This sentence tees up the president's argument — that the August 7 deadline is, as the motion says elsewhere, "particularly arbitrary here because there are no impending deadlines, no statutes of limitations are about to run, and no trials are imminent."

| Example 2.5 | **Takeaway point 2.5:** Emphasize how your client was wronged — both procedurally and substantively — during administrative proceedings. |

Lawyers can target *procedures,* too — not just the substantive issues such as orders, opinions, and reasoning. Indeed, the flawed process by which, for example, an agency reached its decision might form the core of your client's lawsuit. The following example shows how to use procedural facts to make an agency look like it acted arbitrarily.

The Federal Communications Commission (FCC) decided not to repeal or modify a long-standing regulation that imposed a cap on how many broadcast television stations any single company could own. Federal law required the FCC to reassess that cap every two years to decide whether it remained necessary. Here, several TV networks that opposed the cap use the procedural record to show that the FCC failed to take its duty seriously. And that storytelling supports the TV networks' legal argument: the agency acted "arbitrarily and capriciously" (which is the legal standard under the statute that lets parties challenge agency actions).

Source: Fox's (and other TV networks') brief in *Fox Television Stations, Inc. v. FCC,* 280 F.3d 1027 (D.C. Cir. 2002), modified on reh'g, 293 F.3d 537 (D.C. Cir. 2002).

---

1 With its 1998 review complete, the FCC summarily dispatched its 2000 biennial **A**
2 review of the cap less than eight months later. Buried in an Appendix to a 209-
3 page Staff Report referenced in the FCC's Report, it consists of a conclusory rec-
4 ommendation that the existing ownership limits remain unchanged. See 2000 **B**
5 Biennial Regulatory Review, Updated Staff Report, Appendix IV at 176 (Jan. 17,
6 2001) (S.A. 119). There is no assessment of the effects of "changes made to the
7 local television station ownership rule" on competition and diversity, as the FCC
8 had promised in its 1998 review. See 1998 Report ¶¶ 25-26 (J.A. 708-709). The **C**
9 Staff Report merely echoes in one paragraph the statements made in the FCC's
10 1998 review, see Staff Report at 176 (S.A. 119), and the FCC accepted those
11 "staff recommendations" without discussion. **D**

A The crux of Fox's argument is that the FCC lacks a rational basis for maintaining the cap. Thus, rather than stating that the FCC "issued" the contested biennial review, petitioners rebuke the FCC for "summarily dispatch[ing]" its duty, and for doing so hastily — in eight months rather than after two full years.

B This extraordinary sentence contains *five* strategic moves. First, its use of the vivid verb "buried" hints that the FCC sought to hide either its recommendation or the feebleness of its efforts. Second, the fact that the FCC included the crucial recommendation in an appendix, which was mentioned only briefly in the main report, suggests that the agency failed to wrestle seriously with the numerous objections that Fox raised about the ownership cap. Third, that the appendix was prepared by staff — not by the Commission itself — shows both that the FCC did not reassess the cap and that the D.C. Circuit should be less deferential to the agency's conclusion because it came from agency minions. Fourth, even the FCC's staffers were so disengaged from this issue that they failed to spend a single sentence in their

209-page report evaluating whether the cap should survive; only the report's appendix touched this issue. And *fifth,* the word "conclusory" tells readers that the FCC failed to analyze whether the cap reflected good public policy; rather, the FCC stated a conclusion without explaining its reasoning.

C Fox points out that the FCC backed away from its own promise to study the cap seriously. Moreover, the FCC's past conclusion that the cap *deserved* to be scrutinized implies that the rule is flawed.

D The brief manages to stay on the attack even as it quietly admits two bad facts. First, the Staff Report *did* explain the agency's reasoning. But by using the brilliant verb "echoes," the brief implies that the agency just cut and pasted its past analysis without thinking seriously about whether to preserve the cap. Second, the FCC ratified the recommendation of its staff. Thus, the agency — rather than mere staffers — did decide this issue. Nevertheless, the scare quotes around "staff recommendations" quietly mock the FCC's procedures. Bad facts are airbrushed until they *seem* benign.

FREQUENTLY ASKED QUESTIONS ABOUT USING PROCEDURAL HISTORY

Q. **How do I use exactly the right verb to describe what courts did?**

A. If you are in doubt about how to use verbs that describe particular judicial acts, consult an authority like *Black's Law Dictionary* or look to see how courts have used that term in similar cases.

Q. **Do I need a procedural history section in trial court motions?**

A. The answer depends on the motion—and on what will help your client. For instance, in a motion to dismiss a third amended complaint, it might be helpful for a defendant to chip away at a plaintiff's credibility by showing the flaws in the prior complaints. Or, in a discovery dispute, you may want to show that your client already bent over backwards to accommodate the other side.

Q. **Should I discuss favorable procedural history if I won at the earlier stage or stages of the case?**

A. Absolutely. This chapter presented examples of how to deal with adverse decisions, because that skill is trickier—the art of attacking a court's reasoning without attacking the court itself. But wise lawyers emphasize why a judge agreed with them and what helpful facts that judge found.

Q. **Do I need to discuss every stage of the case?**

A. No. You need only to discuss every *relevant* stage. Thus, on appeal, you need not mention that the trial court denied your motion to dismiss or your motion to exclude an expert's report—unless those details are relevant to your appeal or create important atmospheric benefits.

Chapter 3

Facts: Advanced Techniques

We're not done with facts. While the first two chapters, if mastered, will make you more dangerous than most lawyers, we haven't yet explored some of the advanced storytelling techniques that elite lawyers deploy to win their cases.

CHAPTER OVERVIEW
1. Call into question your opponent's credibility.
2. Rebuild your client's credibility (if your client's intentions or honesty are attacked).
3. Explain the relevant law (yes, in your Statement of Facts).
4. Use legislative history in your Statement.
5. Import facts extrinsic to your lawsuit to contextualize your dispute.
6. Explain unfamiliar terms and concepts.
7. Adopt a unique tone or style to gel with your theme.

Example 3.1

Takeaway point 3.1: Use facts to undermine the opposing party's credibility.

Credibility battles are common in briefs. Conventional wisdom says that lawyers should not target opposing counsel. That advice is sound, to a point: judges often report that they dislike these tactics and that gratuitous or nasty attacks hurt both parties. But careful, targeted attacks on your adversary's credibility might nevertheless work, just as negative advertising in political campaigns both irks *and* influences voters.

There are two primary ways of attacking an adversary's credibility: proactively (as an *ad hominem* attack) or reactively (when an adversary overreaches). You should not lightly decide to target your adversary or its lawyers. But if the other side has behaved in some improper way, you should at least consider whether to emphasize that misconduct.

Source: AT&T Mobility's brief from *Selby v. AT&T Mobility LLC* (Cal. App. 4th Dist. May 9, 2012).

---

1   A. Serial Plaintiff Susanne Ball Initiates This Lawsuit.   **A**

2   Susanne Ball, the original plaintiff in this action, filed suit on May 27, 2004,
3   seeking attorneys' fees for her counsel and an injunction against the enforce-
4   ment of seven purported provisions in the standard wireless service agreement
5   of [AT&T Mobility] predecessor Cingular Wireless LLC ("Cingular")....
6   Ball was not and had never been a Cingular customer, and none of the chal-   **B**
7   lenged provisions had been enforced against her. As she had done in many
8   other lawsuits, however, Ball allowed plaintiffs' counsel to sue in her name   **C**
9   as a self-anointed private attorney general under the Unfair Competition Law
10   ("UCL").[1] After Proposition 64 was enacted to prevent precisely this kind of
11   lawyer-driven litigation, the superior court (Hon. Gregory L. Lewis) concluded
12   that Ball lacked standing. . . .

---

13   1. Ball was a frequent plaintiff in UCL cases before Proposition 64 removed
14   her ability to sue over practices to which she bore no connection. *See, e.g., Ball v.*
15   *T-Mobile USA, Inc.*, No. G043210; *Ball v. Fleetboston Fin. Corp.*, No. G038894; *Ball v.*
16   *Citibank*, No. [redacted]; *Ball v. Blue Cross of Am.*, No.G033976.

A The attack on the plaintiff (and, implicitly, on the lawyers who use her as their pawn) begins immediately — in the first two words of the brief's Statement of Facts. Even though Ball is no longer the named plaintiff in this case, targeting her undermines the lawsuit itself and weakens the credibility of the lawyers who filed it. Footnote 1 shows that Ball is a "serial plaintiff."

B The first swipe at Ball is a mild one that relates to an actual legal issue: whether she has standing to sue.

C The next swipe has little to do with substantive issues. It is not hateful or vitriolic, but it is sharp, and it seeks to discredit Ball because of her past conduct rather than because of the merits of her position. This technique (an example of an *ad hominem* attack) can also be used in Arguments. I strongly discourage you from exceeding the level of vitriol reflected in this passage.

The Art of Comparing

One other advanced technique that lawyers often use in their Statements (or in their Arguments or Introductions) is to compare something unfamiliar to something familiar. You've experienced the power of this phenomenon whenever someone tells you that a band sounds "like U2 with a reggae vibe" or that a cuisine is "like Thai, but spicier." Without a reference point, the new object or idea can be hard to grasp. Explanatory comparisons—often metaphors—appear throughout the examples in this book.

Comparisons help us to process new information, but the best ones also stick, becoming a permanent part of how we perceive the new object. Some examples of effective comparisons include: *beyond a shadow of a doubt*; a *penumbra* of constitutional provisions; commerce is a *stream*; church and state are separated by a *wall*; states are the *laboratory* of democracy; there is a *revolving door* between regulators and regulated industries; money is *speech*; corporate *veils* are pierced; and the threat of punishment creates a *chilling effect*. The most subtle comparisons, or as Professor Linda Berger calls them, "the unnoticed ones that make the results seem natural," are often the most potent.

Thus, the comparisons that irrevocably shape how we see complicated objects and ideas are often the most useful, as in these examples:

- During the late-2008 financial crisis, the bewildering financial instrument known as a "credit default swap" was described as "buying fire insurance on your neighbor's house."
- Famed investor Warren Buffett described corporate junk bonds (which yield high dividends but are very risky) as "weeds priced as flowers."
- On the question of whether a tweak in a regulation was meant to overhaul a regulatory system, Justice Scalia observed that Congress does not "hide elephants in mouseholes."
- Dissenting in a case that allowed the U.S. military to intern American citizens during emergencies, Justice Jackson observed that the Court's principle "lies about like a loaded weapon."

To maximize the punch of your comparisons, keep them short and sharp. The longer they run, the greater the likelihood that they will sputter.[1] Politicians are great at snappy comparisons:

- President Franklin Delano Roosevelt urged Congress in 1941 to let him sell, lease, or lend weapons to allies in Europe by observing that if a neighbor's home is on fire and he asks to borrow your garden house, "you lend the garden hose to your neighbor and he puts out the fire."
- One political candidate referred to Governor Mitt Romney in 2012 as "a perfectly lubricated weather vane."
- Another candidate referred to the "narcotic" of government spending.
- When running to become president, Ronald Reagan argued that the Republican Party needed to nominate a candidate of bold colors, not "pale pastels."
- Before becoming president, Abraham Lincoln said about the growing rift between the North and the South, "a house divided against itself cannot stand."

Metaphors can be either persuasive or explanatory or, best of all, both. Supreme Court nominee John Roberts achieved this double-barreled success when he commended judicial restraint during his Senate confirmation hearing; he observed that "judges are like umpires" whose job it is to "call balls and strikes and not to pitch or bat." Use short, sharp similes, metaphors, and analogies to convey your points and explain key facts. Avoid prolonged allegories.

---

1. One 2007 motion addressing a real estate dispute, for example, used the following convoluted analogy in a California court: "The relationship between KWR and Szuch is best described by a baseball metaphor, the famous double play combination of the Chicago Cubs, 'From Tinker to Evers to Chance.' RAFEH is Evers, the guy in the middle. That is, KWR exerted control of RAFEH, and as discussed factually and legally below, Szuch was RAFEH's agent/employee."

Example 3.2

Takeaway point 3.2: Use facts to undermine opposing counsel's credibility

When the other side fires an ad hominem attack you, rebut it, but don't dwell on it. Credibility battles, especially for a plaintiff, can derail the process of getting the court to focus on the reasons your client should win. Simply counter the attack and move on. But when the other side has systematically stretched the truth, delve into one or two examples to make the court doubt *everything* that your adversary has written. The following example uses this technique, attacking opposing *counsel* (as opposed to the opposing party).

The passage below comes from a filing prepared by YouTube, which was being sued for copyright infringement by foreign copyright holders. Here, YouTube responds to a motion in which the plaintiffs misquoted a document purportedly showing that executives at YouTube admitted that they knew that their website contained loads of unlicensed copyrighted material. This example shows that opposing lawyers will both (i) try to spin your client's statements unfavorably and (ii) pummel you for any mistakes or overreaches. You'll immediately notice that the style is acerbic, approaching the limit of how venomous a motion should be.

Source: YouTube's opposition to plaintiffs' motions for partial summary judgment in *Football Ass'n Premier League Ltd v. YouTube, Inc.*, 633 F. Supp. 2d 159 (S.D.N.Y. 2009), *aff'd in part and vacated in part*, 676 F.3d 19 (2d Cir. 2012).

Plaintiffs further manipulate the evidence to fit their story (A) when they cite a September 7, 2005 email from [YouTube's co-founder, Steve] Chen. Chen was responding to an inquiry from board-member Roelof Botha about "racy" videos. Botha asked: "Should we create a 'mature' section for this content? Or should we put in the equivalent of a 'safe search' function (just like Google has) so we don't alienate the moms that are uploading videos on the site?" Viacom mangles Chen's response:

How Viacom quotes the document (B)	What the document actually says
"That way, the perception is that we are concerned about this type of material and we're actively monitoring it. [But the] actual removal of this content will be in varying degrees. That way... you can find truckloads of... copyrighted content... [if] you [are] actively searching for it." (C)	I think it's an accepted [sic] that in an environment such as YouTube, relying on user-generated content, copyrighted and inappropriate content will find its way onto the site. On the dev environment, we've implemented a flagging system so you can flag videos as being inappropriate or copyrighted. That way, the perception is (D) that we are concerned about this type of material and we're actively monitoring it. The actual removal of this content will be in varying degrees. We may want to keep some of the borderline content on the site but just remove it from the browse/search pages. That way, you

25	can't find the content easily. Again, similar to Flickr, if you search for the right tags on Flickr, you can find truckloads of adult and copyrighted content. It's just that you can't stumble upon it, you have to be actively searching for it.
26	
27	
28	
29	
30	

E

31   Viacom claims that this document shows that YouTube's founders "deliberately and intentionally chose to leave up other infringing clips when they
32   thought the additional site traffic was worth the legal risk." Viacom Br. 6-7. To
33   manufacture that charge, Viacom turns Chen's reference to "borderline" content
34   into "infringing" content. It turns a thought ("we may want to keep") into
35   an implemented plan. Chen Opp. Decl. at 2 (explaining that YouTube never
36   adopted Chen's idea). And it turns Chen's statement about "truckloads" of
37   content available on Flickr (a photo-sharing site owned by Yahoo!) into a
38   description of what was on YouTube. Viacom also suggests something sinister
39   about Chen's reference to "perception"—but there is nothing wrong with being
40   concerned about how a site is perceived by the "moms" who may want to use
41   it. *See* Schapiro Opp. Ex. 222 (141:4-23).
42

F

G

A Some books suggest understatement here, such as "Viacom appears to have misquoted a critical YouTube document and to have thereby altered that document's meaning." But that subtler approach is less effective at ensuring that judges *remember* that the other side distorted the document. These choices — *how* to point out an opponent's deceitfulness — are difficult decisions without a clear answer, and they likely depend on the judge, how he or she seems to think the other side has behaved throughout the case, and the culture within your office. Targeting the other side increases the risk that you'll have a hostile relationship with opposing counsel, which can make your job awfully unpleasant. Think carefully and breathe deeply before attacking.

B Presenting information in a visually appealing and absorbable way is important. It helps readers grasp your point, and it entices them to spend time on your argument. Don't be shy about using tables, photographs, or other visual tools. *See* Example 6.6.

C Keeping quotes short and snappy is a good goal, and you can certainly use ellipses or brackets. Viacom's version of the quote, however, contains three bracketed phrases and three sets of ellipses. Performing aggressive rhinoplasty on a quotation exposes you to a heightened risk that the other side will point out mischaracterizations.

D Viacom's use of the word "perception" implies that YouTube is trying to *feign* a commitment to policing its content; in YouTube's version, YouTube is actually committed to policing this content and wants to ensure that users perceive its position accurately. Opposing counsel will often distort what your clients have said. Clarify — concisely, but decisively — what your clients actually said (thus deterring opponents from chicanery).

E YouTube's lawyers undermine Viacom's credibility by exposing how selectively Viacom has quoted the email. That said, judges may resent the implicit suggestion that YouTube expects them to read and compare two block quotes.

F Rather than trust judges to juxtapose the two quotations, YouTube summarizes how Viacom mischaracterized its document. This is a textbook move in a credibility battle. YouTube manages to show not only that Viacom mischaracterized the document but also that it drew an overbroad inference based on this inaccurate quote. YouTube helps its cause by making its points in short, sharp sentences.

G You will seem defensive if you deny every allegation, including valid ones. Thus, if you or your client get "accused" of something innocuous, legal, reasonable, or justified, point out that the allegation, even if true, is toothless. YouTube demonstrates this tactic here.

Example

3.3

Takeaway point 3.3: Repair your clients' credibility when their intentions or honesty are attacked.

When you or your clients are attacked, you need to counter the other side's allegation, as YouTube did in Example 3.2. But for some issues, a counterattack won't prove helpful; instead, you need to help readers see the issue from your client's perspective to alter the perception that your client is venal, greedy, guilty, or otherwise contemptible.

Rhetoricians have known for thousands of years that ethos — the advocate's character and believability — is a critical part of persuasion. If a listener (or reader) greets your arguments with skepticism because you are perceived as untrustworthy, you need to reestablish your credibility before your substantive arguments will be given a fair hearing. The following Example illustrates this principle, as it manages to recast a litigant's controversial actions.

Exxon challenged a $2.5 billion punitive-damages award after its vessel spilled oil in Alaskan waters. The plaintiffs blasted Exxon on numerous grounds, including that it had knowingly hired a lapsed alcoholic, Joseph Hazelwood, to captain the ship. They alleged that Hazelwood's recklessness and drunkenness caused the crash. Exxon's decision to retain him was one of the cornerstones of the massive punitive damages award. But in the following excerpt, Exxon's lawyers try to rebuild the company's credibility, and they nearly achieve the unthinkable: making a multinational oil company seem more humane than the plaintiffs whose livelihoods were harmed by the spill.

Source: Exxon's brief in *Exxon Shipping Co. v. Baker,* 554 U.S. 471 (2008).

---

1 **Exxon's Alcohol Policy.** Plaintiffs argued that Hazelwood was impaired by
2 alcohol,[3] and that but for his impairment he would not have left the bridge to
3 work in his cabin. Plaintiffs further asserted that Hazelwood was an alcoholic,
4 that Exxon knew it, and that Exxon was therefore *independently* reckless for
5 allowing Hazelwood to serve as master and for not supervising him sufficiently.   A
6 Exxon's evidence showed that its alcohol policy conformed to industry stan-
7 dards, guaranteed that employees seeking treatment would not lose their jobs,
8 and rested on the premise that without job security those needing treatment
9 would hide their affliction—disserving safety, not enhancing it. PX 158; JA684-   B
10 85, 1082-83, 1088. As this Court has held, it is perfectly consistent with public
11 policy for an employer's substance-abuse policy to provide for reinstatement of
12 relapsed employees, even to safety-sensitive positions. *Eastern Associated Coal*   C
13 *Corp. v. United Mine Workers,* 531 U.S. 57 (2000). The Ninth Circuit acknowl-
14 edged that the jury "could have decided that Exxon followed a reasonable policy
15 of fostering reporting and treatment by alcohol abusers, knew that Hazelwood

---

16   3. This was hotly disputed. All 20 witnesses who observed Hazelwood on the
17 night of the grounding, Exxon employees and unrelated parties alike, testified that
18 his actions were normal and professional, and that he was not impaired in any way.
19 *E.g.,* JA999, 273-74, 1003-08, 942-45, 934-39, 981-84, 1013-14, 497-98, 380-83, 833. A   D
20 state court jury *acquitted* him of operating a vessel under the influence. JA1495-97.
21 And even the district court held as a matter of law that Hazelwood's actions before
22 the pilot left the ship (47 minutes before the grounding) gave no basis to believe he
23 was impaired. JA1577, 1580-82.   E

24 had obtained treatment, did not know that he was an alcoholic, and did not
25 know that he was taking command of his ship drunk." Pet. App. 88a-89a; see
26 OCCP 16-25. As will be seen, the district court instructed the jury that it did not
27 need to reach or resolve these issues.

F

A In general, avoid restating your adversaries' allegations. Why spend your limited word count summarizing their position? But when their attack goes to the central issue in the case and targets your client's intentions, restating the allegation adds to your credibility and makes you sound reasonable.

B This point masterfully reframes the discussion. By focusing on the implications of its general employment policy, rather than on the specific decision to retain Hazelwood, Exxon sneaks a policy argument into its Statement of Facts (i.e., that Exxon's policy *promotes* safety). This passage makes Exxon's policy seem reasonable and defends the company's credibility against allegations that it was reckless, greedy, and indifferent to the risk of harm to the wilderness. At the same time, Exxon resists the temptation to wax on about how much it cares for its employees; that might seem insincere, thus damaging its ethos rather than restoring it.

C Exxon uses a variety of techniques in this passage, such as incorporating the procedural history as a source of advocacy (*see* Chapter 2) and using legal authorities in a Statement of Facts (*see* Examples 3.4 and 3.5).

D The plaintiffs who were harmed by the oil spill challenged Exxon's story, reflecting that the party that wins the trial needs to defend aggressively the trial court's findings when the other side attempts to retry the case on appeal. Here is how the plaintiffs responded to this brief:

> Exxon's suggestion that Hazelwood was not drunk illustrates just how brazenly its Statement of the Case ignores the detailed decisions below and how severely Exxon slants the record. The jury heard testimony about Hazelwood's drinking on March 23 from crew members who drank with him, bartenders, another customer, and Hazelwood himself. JA21921, 239-55, 334-35; Tr. 2729, 2766-67. The state-employed pilot testified that he smelled alcohol on Hazelwood's breath before the

grounding, JA267-71, as did Coast Guard officers who boarded the ship after the grounding. JA489-92, 1015-16. Coast Guard blood alcohol tests confirmed that Hazelwood had been extremely drunk. Pet. App. 108a, 256a-257a. Even Exxon's Chairman conceded shortly after the spill that Hazelwood was "drunk," PX2 at 7:05 (Resps' DVD); SJA207sa, and Exxon fired him for that reason. SJA198sa.

Did Exxon overreach? No. It presented information truthfully: just as Exxon claimed, the plaintiffs "argued" and "asserted" the above information and "Exxon's evidence showed" otherwise. And, as its brief also notes, the district court told the jury not to address these specific issues. Exxon is litigating aggressively *and* truthfully. A longer excerpt of the plaintiff's counterstatement appears in Example 15.1.

E The example yet again blends the techniques discussed in this chapter and Chapter 2, citing both the district court's helpful conclusions and a separate criminal case involving Hazelwood. While these techniques have independent value, Exxon is deploying them for the goal described in this section: to win a credibility battle by convincing readers that hiring Hazelwood was neither reckless nor the actual cause of the oil spill.

F Exxon now tries to win a credibility battle about whether Hazelwood was actually drunk when the crash occurred. Exxon does not need to prevail on this point to win the lawsuit, which is why this detail was demoted to a footnote. Even so, Exxon accurately concludes that it would look less culpable if Hazelwood was sober, so it introduces the evidence to support that conclusion. The reference to "unrelated parties alike" reflects another subtle attempt to build credibility: third parties corroborated that Hazelwood seemed sober on the night of the accident.

Example **3.4**	**Takeaway point 3.4:** Your Statement of Facts may explain — in nonargumentative language — your case's key statutory or regulatory issue.

Facts can contain law. This will strike some lawyers as counterintuitive, but when a case involves a complicated statutory or regulatory scheme (or some other unfamiliar law), you *help* judges when you explain the relevant law right away rather than forcing them to wait ten, twenty, or even thirty pages until the Argument. And there's an additional payoff: your Argument can begin with an actual argument rather than a dry explanation of how the law works. Make your discussion of the law seem even-handed, but frame the law in a way that favors your client. Be wary, however, of using this technique when your case revolves around a well-known legal issue, as your explanation of the law is unlikely to seem helpful to judges.

Here, Michigan enacted statutes that required Michigan-based subsidiaries of national banks to register in Michigan, to pay fees to Michigan, and to submit periodic financial statements to Michigan. A national bank, Wachovia, challenged the Michigan statutes, arguing that the National Bank Act and federal banking regulations preempted (i.e., voided because of a conflict) the state legislation. As you read the following excerpt, notice how masterfully Wachovia frames its case within a larger historical framework. The seemingly neutral summary of the banking law not only informs readers but also advances Wachovia's theory of this case — that letting states burden out-of-state banks is dangerous.

Source: Wachovia's brief in *Watters v. Wachovia Bank, N.A.,* 550 U.S. 1 (2007).

---

1   The National Bank Act grants enumerated and "incidental" powers to
2   national banks to engage in the business of banking. *See* 12 U.S.C. § 24. It has
3   long been established that, "in the context of national bank legislation, . . . grants
4   of both enumerated and incidental 'powers' to national banks" are "not nor-
5   mally limited by, but rather ordinarily pre-empt, contrary state law." *Barnett*
6   *Bank of Marion County, N.A. v. Nelson,* 517 U.S. 25, 32 (1996).   **A**

7   The National Bank Act also provides that "[n]o national bank shall be sub-
8   ject to any visitorial powers except as authorized by Federal law, vested in the
9   courts of justice or . . . exercised or directed by Congress." 12 U.S.C. § 484(a).
10   "[V]isitorial powers" include examination of the bank's "manner of conducting
11   business" and enforcement of applicable laws and regulations. *Guthrie v. Hark-*
12   *ness,* 199 U.S. 148, 158 (1905). The limitation on visitorial powers in Section   **B**
13   484 was among the provisions enacted by Congress in 1864 to protect national
14   banks against potentially hostile state actions. Congress was aware of the earlier
15   history of state hostility to the First and Second Banks of the United States, and
16   it was foreseeable that new frictions would arise from the new national bank
17   system.[1]

---

18   1. *See, e.g.,* Cong. Globe, 38th Cong., 1st Sess. 1893 (Apr. 27, 1864) (statement
18   of Sen. Sumner) (comparing the potentially hostile use of state laws against national
20   banks to the Maryland tax invalidated by the Court in *McCulloch*).   **C**

(A) **This is an effective case citation — and it appears in the Statement of Facts. The language is directly on point with Wachovia's position, and though it serves an argumentative function, it belongs in the Statement of Facts because it helps to explicate the development of national bank regulations. Wachovia has successfully laundered an argument into its facts while also helping readers understand how the disputed statute operates.**

(B) Wachovia explains the unfamiliar term "visitorial powers"; once again, readers are likely to be grateful for the explanation. Yet the definition also introduces the term in a way that suggests (without saying so) that laws which regulate how a bank conducts business — such as Michigan's — are preempted by the National Bank Act. The brief plants in readers' minds a definition of this critical term — *visitorial powers* — that favors Wachovia. The brief even gilds the lily by adding an old Supreme Court opinion that hints that tradition is on Wachovia's side, implying that history has shown the perils of letting states regulate national banks.

(C) Wachovia masterfully chooses examples from famous and critical moments in U.S. history to show the perils of letting states regulate banks. Michigan's laws seem banal — are filing reports really as fearsome as undercutting Union banks during the Civil War? But Wachovia has subtly tapped into the menace that state regulation can pose so that readers will think of the worst-case scenario: an open war by states on out-of-state banks. Separately, Wachovia uses the term "hostile" three times in three sentences, priming readers to think that state banking regulations are anathema to good national banking policy. The brief alludes to the famous holding of *McCulloch v. Maryland,* 17 U. S. 316 (1819), which struck down a tax that Maryland levied on out-of-state banks. The "theory" of this case is that Michigan's statutes are a modern-day analogue of the Maryland state tax in *McCulloch* (and should, similarly, be struck down). Raising the specter of this famous case (and the risks that the *McCulloch* Court saw in letting states burden out-of-state banks) once again makes a strong subliminal argument. This excerpt is an expert act of weaving law, history, and policy together into a passage that seems fairly neutral.

Example 3.5

Takeaway point 3.5: Slip helpful case law into your Statement of Facts by making those authorities factually relevant to your client's story.

In addition to explaining statutes, Statements of Facts can discuss cases. Just as the procedural history of a dispute can help judges to understand the controversy, a terse discussion of relevant cases helps judges — and your client. Make the case relevant to *your* client's dispute. We see an example of this trick below.

In the following case, several TV networks sued the Federal Communications Commission (FCC) for deciding not to repeal or modify a long-standing regulation that imposed a cap on networks' ownership of broadcast television stations.

Source: The final paragraph of Fox's (and other TV networks') Statement of Facts in *Fox Television Stations, Inc. v. FCC*, 280 F.3d 1027 (D.C. Cir. 2002), *modified on reh'g*, 293 F.3d 537 (D.C. Cir. 2002).

---

1   **F. This Court's Decision In Time Warner II**   Ⓐ

2   One further development demands attention. On March 2, 2001, this Court
3   struck down the FCC's analogous rule imposing a horizontal cap on national
4   cable television ownership. *See Time Warner Entm't Co. v. FCC*, No. 94-1035,   Ⓑ
5   2001 WL 201978 at *4-11 (D.C. Cir. Mar. 2, 2001) ("*Time Warner II*"). In particu-
6   lar, the Court found that the FCC's stated concern about the "risk of anti-com-
7   petitive behavior" by cable operators if they were permitted to exceed the cap
8   was entirely "conjectural." *Id.* (citation omitted). The Court also struck down   Ⓒ
9   the FCC's vertical limit on cable television ownership because the FCC had
10   made no "rational connection between the facts found and the choice made,"
11   *id.*, and seemed to "ignore its own conclusions about cable companies' incen-   Ⓓ
12   tives and constraints," *id.* at *13. The same considerations apply equally to the
13   national television station ownership rule.   Ⓔ

Ⓐ This final section of the brief's Statement implies that if the FCC's rule on letting *cable operators* own TV stations was "arbitrary and capricious," the agency's rule on letting networks own stations was equally cavalier.

Ⓑ Know your audience. Some judges may have no idea what a "horizontal cap on national cable television ownership" is. But the D.C. Circuit had just decided the *Time Warner II* case, and the court routinely hears antitrust cases, so the lawyers concluded that they didn't need to explain the term. The test of good writing is how it serves your decision maker, not a randomly selected reader. That said, the law clerks who worked on the case probably didn't know this area of the law very well. So perhaps a hint (about what this term means) would have helped.

Ⓒ This sentence is brilliant. Fox smuggles into its Statement of Facts a quote from a judicial decision (about a related issue) to show that the same government agency suffered "conjectural" delusions of "anti-competitive behavior." The implication: the FCC imagined risks in the other case, so the risks in this case are also phantasmal.

Ⓓ The quote supports Fox's legal burden: it needs to show that the FCC's rule is "arbitrary and capricious." Showing that the agency failed to link its decision to the facts (or to its own conclusions) undermines the decision maker's credibility.

Ⓔ WARNING! This final sentence crosses the line into Argument. There is no penalty for doing so, but the choice might irritate some judges or clerks.

Example 3.6

Takeaway point 3.6: Use legislative history in your Statement of Facts to make the legislature's motives, statements, or process part of your client's story.

Legislative history can appear in your Statement to help readers grasp a statute's purpose. And that purpose should, of course, favor your client's position.

In 1996, the Massachusetts legislature passed a statute that effectively withheld lucrative government contracts from most companies that conducted any business with Burma/Myanmar, a country with a poor human rights record. During the lawsuit, Massachusetts maintained that the law was intended to "dissociate" Massachusetts from Myanmar; it disputed that the law was intended to pressure Myanmar in any meaningful way. A business group (NFTC) challenged the law and sought to show that the law both infringed on the exclusive power of the federal government to regulate foreign affairs and tried to influence foreign policy, which the Supreme Court had previously restricted states from doing.

Source: Statement of Facts from the brief challenging Massachusetts's law, from *Crosby v. National Foreign Trade Council*, 530 U.S. 363 (2000).

1	Massachusetts' avowed purpose in enacting the Law was...to condemn
2	Myanmar and to affect the domestic policies of that nation. The Law's legisla-
3	tive history, wholly ignored by Massachusetts' brief, is revealing. Its sponsor
4	called the Law a "foreign policy" initiative whose "identifiable goal" was "free
5	democratic elections in Burma." Pet. App. 9a; J.A. 39-40. Other Massachusetts
6	legislators described the Law as Massachusetts "engag[ing] in their own little
7	version of foreign policy" (J.A. 35), "set[ting] up some foreign policy business
8	guidelines" (J.A. 46), "dabbl[ing] in foreign affairs" (J.A. 50), and "promot[ing]
9	and stand[ing] for civil and human rights" in Burma. J.A. 53. The Law's
10	proponents lauded it as a vehicle for pressing the federal government to alter
11	its foreign policy toward Myanmar. J.A. 47, 102. The Governor's signing state-
12	ment said the Law "ma[de] a stand for the cause of freedom and democracy
13	around the world"; he expressed hope that "Congress will follow our example."
14	J.A. 57. Neither the sponsor of the bill, nor the legislators who debated it,
15	nor the Governor who signed it into law mentioned any economic benefit to
16	Massachusetts, its agencies, or its citizens. *See* Pet. App. 10a. The purpose, as
17	Massachusetts conceded below (Pet. App. 9a), was " 'to apply indirect economic
18	pressure against the Burma regime for reform.' "

A This phrase suggests that Massachusetts either (1) failed to research the case diligently or (2) misrepresented its intentions. Either conclusion hurts Massachusetts.

B Notice that the source of these statements might not be legislative debates: these quotes might have come from speeches on the campaign trail or a quote in a newspaper. Nevertheless, this brief weaponizes these great quotes to show that Massachusetts legislators all but make the NFTC's case: they envision the law as their own version of foreign policy.

C Not only is the legislative history substantively helpful, but it also furnishes colorful language that makes the point more effectively than the NFTC could have otherwise done. For instance, the word "dabbling" implies a lack of seriousness, an encroachment into unfamiliar territory, or both.

D The double "nor" serves as a lovely rhetorical flourish. Moreover, this sentence shows that silence in the legislative record can suggest that certain issues did *not* motivate the legislature. One of Massachusetts's alternative arguments was that it was acting as a "market participant"; this sentence anticipates that argument, and suggests that Massachusetts's concerns about participating effectively (or ethically) in the market are an after-the-fact rationalization by the Commonwealth.

Example 3.7	**Takeaway point 3.7:** A Statement of Facts can include multiple types of legal authority.

As we wrap up our discussion about the art of using authorities in a Statement of Facts, it is worth emphasizing that you don't need to choose whether to discuss statutes, cases, or legislative history in a Statement. You can use all of these tools, as one of the country's most respected advocates does in the following passage.

A record company sued a student for copyright infringement after he illegally downloaded thirty songs from peer-to-peer downloading networks. The company won, and the court ordered the student to pay $67,500. He challenged the decision, alleging that the copyright law — by imposing massive "statutory damages" for civil offenses that caused little economic harm — violated his due process rights. Here, the record company uses its Statement to oppose his legal theory.

Source: Sony's Opposition to a Petition for a Writ of Certiorari, seeking to uphold *Tenenbaum v. Sony BMG Music Entertainment*, 660 F.3d 487 (1st Cir. 2011).

1 Rather than impose upon a copyright owner the often difficult or impos-
2 sible burden of establishing the value of the copyright and the amount of harm
3 caused by the infringement, Congress has long provided that a copyright owner
4 may choose between actual damages or statutory damages as recovery for
5 infringement. *See, e.g.,* Act of May 31, 1790, ch. 15, §§ 2, 6, 1 Stat. 124, 125   **A**
6 (authorizing recovery of "fifty cents for every sheet which shall be found in
7 [the infringer's] possession"). The availability of statutory damages not only
8 obviates the need for difficult or impossible proof, but also deters infringement
9 and ensures appropriate incentives for the creation of copyrighted works. *See*
10 *F.W. Woolworth Co. v. Contemporary Arts, Inc.*, 344 U.S. 228, 232-33 (1952).   **B**
11 In its current form, the Copyright Act provides that, for any act of infringe-
12 ment, the owner of the copyright may recover either the actual damages
13 suffered plus any additional profits of the infringer, 17 U.S.C. § 504(b), or in
14 the alternative "may elect, at any time before final judgment is rendered, to
15 recover...an award of statutory damages," *id.* § 504(c)(1). The choice belongs
16 exclusively to the copyright owner. A copyright owner is entitled to statutory   **C**
17 damages for each work infringed of "not less than $750 or more than $30,000 as
18 the court considers just." *Id.* That baseline range for garden-variety non-willful
19 infringement is subject to two exceptions: If the copyright owner proves that
20 the infringement was willful, the statutory range increases to "not more than
21 $150,000" per infringed work. *Id.* § 504(c)(2). By contrast, if, subject to certain
22 exceptions, *see, e.g., id.* § 402(d), the infringer proves that he or she "was not
23 aware and had no reason to believe that his or her acts constituted an infringe-
24 ment of copyright," the award may be reduced to "not less than $200" per work.
25 *Id.* § 504(c)(2).
26 The damages provision of the Copyright Act has existed in the same basic
27 form since 1976, subject only to amendments to increase both the minimum
28 and maximum amount of statutory damages available. *See* Copyright Act of   **D**
29 1976, Pub. L. No. 94-553, 9 Stat. 2541, 2585 (authorizing minimum damages of
30 $250, maximum damages of $10,000, and maximum for willful infringement of
31 $50,000); Berne Convention Implementation Act of 1988, Pub. L. No. 100-568,
32 § 10, 102 Stat. 2853, 2860 (increasing minimum to $500, maximum to $20,000,
33 and maximum for willful infringement to $100,000); Digital Theft Deterrence

34   and Copyright Damages Improvement Act of 1999, Pub. L. No. 106-160, § 2,
35   113 Stat. 1774, 1774 (increasing minimum to $750, maximum to $30,000, and
36   maximum for willful infringement to $150,000).

37   Because the Copyright Act's statutory damages provisions refer to the
38   "court," statutory damages were typically awarded by the judge, rather than
39   the jury. In *Feltner v. Columbia Pictures Television, Inc.*, 526 U.S. 340 (1998),
40   however, this Court held that the Seventh Amendment provides a right to a jury
41   trial on the amount of statutory damages. Although the Court "discern[ed] no
42   statutory right to a jury trial" in the language of section 504(c), it concluded
43   that a statutory damages action is an action at law in which juries have histori-
44   cally had the authority to determine what amount of damages to award. *Id.* at
45   347, 351-52. Accordingly, the Court held that "the Seventh Amendment provides
46   a right to a jury trial on all issues pertinent to an award of statutory damages
47   under § 504(c) of the Copyright Act, including the amount itself." *Id.* at 355.   E

48   Since *Feltner*, Congress has amended section 504(c) but has not altered the
49   statutory damages scheme under which the jury, not the judge, has authority
50   to decide the amount of statutory damages to award within the ranges that
51   Congress has specified. Indeed, in the wake of *Feltner*, Congress' only relevant
52   action has been to increase the amount of statutory damages available, thus
53   substantially increasing the jury's discretion. *See* Digital Theft Act, *supra*
54   (increasing minimum to $750, maximum to $30,000, and maximum for willful
55   infringement to $150,000). The legislative history explains that these amend-
56   ments were designed to provide greater deterrence of copyright infringement in
57   light of new technologies that substantially increase the ease and scale of copy-
58   ing. *See* H.R. Rep. No. 106-216, at 6 (1999).   F

A The brief subtly adds a historical argument to its facts by using a 221-year-old statute to point out that federal law has allowed statutory damages for copyright violations since the nation's founding.

B Next, the brief uses a case to smuggle a policy argument into the facts.

C The brief uses a third type of legal authority here: the current statute, which the brief cites to explain to readers how liability works in the U.S. copyright system.

D Next, the brief looks at statutory history — the precursors to the current statute — to show that statutory damages have existed in their current form for decades and to tee up the next helpful legal fact, which is that Congress has increased damages in recent years, suggesting that the legislature wants to punish copyright violations harshly.

E The Statement then discusses a case (to squelch a potentially harmful legal argument — a Supreme Court opinion that could be read to limit the availability of statutory damages). The brief defangs the case by framing it as merely requiring the *jury* (rather than a judge) to decide whether statutory damages should be awarded.

F Having already discussed legal history, the current copyright statute, two cases, and the current law's statutory history, the Statement now discusses legislative history to introduce the helpful point that Congress wanted to deter copyright infringement by increasing the statutory damages. Thus, the brief — in its facts — has used five different types of authorities to advance its position as well as a number of thinly veiled policy arguments. Your adversaries may use these techniques; you should, too.

| Example 3.8 | **Takeaway point 3.8:** Use extrinsic facts to show the scope of your client's problem and to make subtle policy arguments. |

Providing insightful or favorable facts that shine light on your dispute — even though they might not have arisen during your case — can help your client's cause in various ways. For instance, if you were seeking punitive damages in a race discrimination lawsuit, wouldn't you want the judge to know that the same defendant had been found liable seventeen previous times for racial discrimination? Extrinsic facts can show that your client's injury is part of a recurring pattern or that ruling against your client might have drastic implications. Below, we see an example of how to use extrinsic facts to help a client.

We consult again a case in which a former Eritrean prison guard, Negusie, sought asylum in the United States. His claim was denied; an immigration court found that Negusie has persecuted prisoners. He countered that he was coerced into guarding those prisoners. Here, his lawyers — perhaps recognizing that "I was forced to be a war criminal" sounds implausible — use extrinsic facts to show that young people in war zones are routinely coerced into military service. The passage also implies that many deserters deserve asylum because they will be endangered if they return to their home countries.

Source: Negusie's brief in *Negusie v. Holder,* 555 U.S. 511 (2009).

---

1 Violent conflicts around the world today frequently involve civil wars that
2 have as a hallmark coerced participation in armed conflict. Thus, the United
3 Nations recognizes over thirty ongoing conflicts around the world in which
4 more than a quarter million young people have been coerced into violent armed
5 conflict. The Secretary-General, *Report of the Special Representative of the*   A
6 *Secretary-General for Children and Armed Conflict,* ¶ 11, U.N. Doc. A/61/275
7 (Aug. 17, 2006). As one former child soldier has testified,

8 [T]here are thousands of children from ages 8 to 17 in Burma, Sri Lanka,
9 Congo, Uganda, Ivory Coast, Colombia, just to name a few places, that
10 are being forced to fight and lose their childhoods and their families.
11 They are maimed and they lose their humanity, and these are the fortu-
12 nate ones. Those who are less fortunate are killed in the senseless wars
13 of adults.   B

14 *Casualties of War: Child Soldiers and the Law: Hearing before the U.S. Sen.*
15 *Comm. on the Judiciary, Subcom. on Human Rights and the Law,* 110th Cong.
16 (2007) (testimony of Ishmael Beah, former child soldier from Sierra Leone); *see*
17 *also Hearing on the "Material Support" Bar Before the Subcomm. on Human*
18 *Rights and the Law of the S. Comm. on the Judiciary,* 110th Cong. (2007) (testi-
19 mony of Anwen Hughes, Senior Counsel, Refugee Protection Program, Human
20 Rights First) (hundreds of thousands of child soldiers from African countries are
21 forced to serve in state and opposition armies); Matthew Happold, *Excluding*
22 *Children from Refugee Status: Child Soldiers and Article 1F of the Refugee Con-*
23 *vention,* 17 Am. U. Int'l L. Rev. 1131, 1131 (2002) ("[T]he majority of refugees
24 in the world today are . . . fleeing civil conflicts in which the distinction between
25 oppressor and oppressed is often unclear." (citing United Nations High Commis-   C
26 sioner for Refugees, *Refugees by Numbers* 8 (2000))).

27   Examples of countries in which combatants force innocent victims to take
28   part in their persecutory acts include:

29   • Burma (see *Burma Country Report, available at*
30   http://www.state.gov/g/drl/rls/hrrpt/2006/78768.htm);

31   • Columbia (see *Columbia Country Report, available at*
32   http://www.state.gov/g/drl/rls/hrrpt/2006/78885.htm);

33   • El Salvador (see *Doe v. Gonzales*, 484 F.3d 445, 447-48 (7th Cir. 2007));

34   • Guatemala (see *Hernandez v. Reno*, 258 F.3d 806 (8th Cir. 2001);

35   • Iraq (see *Iraq Country Report, available at*
36   http://www.state.gov/g/drl/rls/hrrpt/2006/78853.htm (citing
37   occurrences of compelled child participation in violent activities
38   of opposition groups);

39   • Peru, *Miranda Alvarado v. Gonzales*, 441 F.3d 750 (9th Cir. 2006),
40   modified on reh'g, 449 F.3d 915 (9th Cir. 2006); *Castaneda-Castillo v.*
41   *Gonzales*, 488 F.3d 17 (1st Cir. 2007);

42   • Somalia (see *Somalia Country Report, available at*
43   http://www.state.gov/g/drl/rls/hrrpt/2006/78757.htm) (citing reports
44   from previous year that militia groups forced minority groups into
45   forced labor);

46   • Sudan (see *Sudan Country Report, available at*
47   http://www.state.gov/g/drl/rls/hrrpt/2006/78759.htm) (noting forced
48   military conscription of underage men and numerous abuses carried
49   out by security forces).

D

A This sentence establishes that many people in many countries have been coerced in a similar way as Negusie. The lawyers bundle together various types of forced service to make the number of people involved as large as possible.

B When possible, avoid block quotes: readers often skip them.

C WARNING! These citations have language in them that is extremely helpful to Negusie, but the dense look of the paragraph makes it less likely that readers will absorb each point. Document design is an important feature of good advocacy. One recent book, Matthew Butterick's *Typography for Lawyers*, offers heaps of valuable advice about fonts, layout, and other features of making your documents visually appealing to readers. *See also,* Ruth Anne Robbins, *Painting with Print: Incorporating Concepts of Typographic*

and Layout Design into the Text of Legal Writing Documents, 2 J. A.L.W.D. 108 (Fall 2004). As you'll see, these lawyers use a common typographical trick (bullets) in the next paragraph, to make the information easier to scan.

D During another part of the Statement, the brief showed that the problem of child-soldiers described on these two pages is also a problem in Eritrea. *See* Negusie Br. 12-13 ("The Eritrean government routinely 'round[ed] [up]' young men and women for national service,' and 'incarcerat[ed] and tortur[ed] family members of national service evaders.'") (quoting a State Department report). When your client is likely to be perceived as unsavory or unusual or not credible, beginning with extrinsic facts deflects attention from your client and focuses instead on the broader problem. Negusie was not mentioned *until thirteen pages into the brief.*

Example 3.9

Takeaway point 3.9: Explain unfamiliar terms and concepts to (i) avoid confusing readers and (ii) frame those new ideas in a way that favors your client.

Facts sometimes need to introduce the reader to unfamiliar information, such as a doctrine, a device, or some other complicated object or idea. This principle is especially important when a case involves obscure or complicated issues such as patents, technology, or financial instruments. And even when readers think that they know what a term means, they might not know important details about it. While lawyers err when they heap endless details on readers, they also miss an opportunity when they fail to explain an unfamiliar term or to reveal subtleties about terms that readers *think* they know. The following example demonstrates how to describe technology that readers think they know in a way that advances a client's interests.

The passage arose from a case in which the government, without a valid warrant, used a GPS device to track all movements of a suspected drug dealer's Jeep for almost a month, resulting in the suspect's conviction.

Source: Brief of Jones, whose car was monitored by GPS, from *United States v. Jones*, 132 S. Ct. 945 (2012).

---

1 In 1978, the U.S. Department of Defense launched the Navigational Satellite
2 Timing and Ranging Global Positioning System, or GPS, for the U.S. military's
3 use. *See* Renée M. Hutchins, *Tied Up in* Knotts? *GPS Technology and the Fourth*
4 *Amendment*, 55 UCLA L. Rev. 409, 414 (2007) (citing Def. Sci. Bd. Task Force,
5 Dep't of Def., The Future of the Global Position System 4, 25-26 (2005)) (here-
6 inafter Hutchins). The system operates through 25 government-owned satellites
7 orbiting the earth, each of which "continuously transmits the position and orbit-
8 al velocity of every satellite in the system." *Id.* at 415. A GPS device " 'listens' to
9 the transmissions of the four closest satellites," and, through a process known
10 as trilateration, "determines its precise location on earth." *Id.* at 415-17.

11 GPS devices produce an accurate, continuous, and three-dimensional digital
12 record of their position and velocity over any period of time—as well as that
13 of any person or object carrying them. See Muhammad U. Iqbal & Samsung
14 Lim, *Privacy Implications of Automated GPS Tracking and Profiling*, IEEE Tech.
15 & Soc'y Magazine (2010), *available at* http://www.gmat.unsw.edu.au/snap/
16 publications/usman&lim2007c.pdf. These data can be communicated to a
17 remote computer through a cellphone connection and translated onto an
18 interactive map. *Id.* Even without the application of additional software, a GPS
19 device is "accurate within 50 to 100 feet." Pet. Br. 3-4. With additional software,
20 the FBI can identify the most likely exact longitude, latitude, and address "on
21 the mapping system," JA 80-81, with accurate "positioning to within a few cen-
22 timeters" or even "millimeter[s]," *see* "GPS Accuracy," http://www.gps.gov/
23 systems/gps/performance/accuracy (last visited Sept. 25, 2011). And the tech-
24 nology is rapidly improving. *See* Hutchins, *supra*, at 421.

A

B

C

D

Ⓐ Good lawyers use citations to support not only the point that precedes the citation but also their larger message. Does this brief succeed with this strategy? Beautifully. The brief is arguing that the government must obtain a warrant before tracking suspects with GPS devices. And Hutchins's article concludes that "the unfettered use of such surveillance [GPS] is inimical to fundamental Fourth Amendment principles. The most defensible treatment of GPS tracking under the existing analytical framework is that it is a search and, as such, must be preauthorized by a warrant issued only upon probable cause." 55 UCLA L. Rev. at 409. The citation supports the overall argument as well as the specific point that precedes it.

Ⓑ This passage makes great use of quotations to explain a technical concept. It doesn't explain the term "trilateration," but readers don't need to know that phrase; therefore, using the term hints that the lawyers have become experts in this area. If readers need to understand a term, however, you must explain it to them.

Ⓒ Once again, this citation serves multiple roles. It supports the preceding proposition. The title primes readers to think about how GPS devices can undermine personal privacy. And the article favors Jones's position, noting that GPS monitoring "enables various privacy abuses." Think carefully about what you cite; here, if the lawyers were citing this piece for its legal conclusions, the article would be inapposite because the authors are Australian. But the authors' citizenship is irrelevant given that the piece is being cited for a fact and, to a lesser extent, for its conclusions about the policy implications (rather than the legal validity) of using GPS devices to monitor suspects.

Ⓓ **These factual points hint at an Orwellian monitoring of citizens: of the government knowing, within millimeters, where people are. The brief later argued that the policy implications of warrantless GPS tracking are Big Brotherish, and the final sentence in the reprinted passage tees up that argument with the ominous prediction that the technology (which is already eerily accurate) could improve further.**

Example

3.10

Takeaway point 3.10: On rare occasions, adopt a distinctive tone to track the theme of your motion or brief.

Few lawyers have the moxie to intentionally sound different from most other lawyers. But in some cases, an unconventional style can advance your client's goals, provide respite for brief-weary judges, and increase your job satisfaction. Just be certain that the style advances your client's themes and goals and won't irk your boss or client. The following Example comports beautifully with these guidelines.

This case reflects a fitting way to end our discussion of facts, as it demonstrates that facts (and the way they are presented) can alter the outcome of a dispute. In 2005, two similar cases reached the Supreme Court at the same time. Both challenged the constitutional right of state governments to display the Ten Commandments outside of government buildings. Texas won by a 5-4 vote; Kentucky lost by the same margin. Why did the similar cases produce opposite outcomes? Because of the facts. In Kentucky, the display of the Ten Commandments provoked challenges almost immediately after the monuments were installed outside a number of Kentucky courthouses. The Supreme Court's opinion noted the "short (and stormy) history" of those courthouse displays (which were removed, slightly altered and reinstalled, and challenged again). Writing for the majority, Justice Breyer emphasized the divisive effect of Kentucky's monuments.

By contrast, the Court observed that Texas's six-foot-tall monument had stood unchallenged for forty years, was donated by a nongovernmental secular organization, and was designed to showcase "the historical 'ideals' of Texans." Additionally, the Ten Commandments appeared in a nonreligious context, like a religious artifact in a secular *museum*. Notice how the brief's prose reflects this theme.

Source: Texas's brief in *Perry v. Van Orden*, 545 U.S. 677 (2005).

---

1   The Capitol and its Grounds are listed on the National Registry of Historic
2 Places and designated as a protected National Historic Landmark. J.A., at 93,   **A**
3 103. The State Preservation Board is charged with preserving, maintaining, and
4 promoting the cultural resources of the Capitol and its Grounds. Meeting the
5 federal statutory definition of a "museum," 20 U.S.C. § 9172, the Capitol and its   **B**
6 Grounds are cared for by a professional curator, who is given the duties of cata-
7 loguing and preserving their historical materials. Tex. Gov't Code § 443.006. . . .
8   Those wishing to tour the Grounds have access to brochures, laying out a
9 self-guided tour, that the State Preservation Board makes available to Capitol
10 visitors. [J.A.], at 35, 112, 204. The self-guided tour begins in the southeast   **C**
11 portion of the Grounds, where the first monument encountered is a memorial
12 to John B. Hood's Texas Brigade. *Id.*, at 115, 125. The tallest monument on the   **D**
13 Capitol Grounds (at over forty-four feet in height), it is inscribed with quotes
14 from Jefferson Davis and Robert E. Lee, and is topped by the bronze figure of a
15 Confederate soldier. *Id.*, at 205. Moving north, the tour continues to the Texas   **E**
16 Peace Officers memorial and the Disabled Veterans monument. *Id.*, at 117, 128-
17 29.
18   The tour then crosses over to the Capitol's northwest quadrant, which
19 contains seven of the Grounds' seventeen monuments. This area is the larg-   **F**
20 est grouping of monuments on the Capitol Grounds. Three monuments honor
21 veterans—a tribute to veterans of the Korean War (the largest monument in
22 the northwest quadrant), a tribute to veterans of World War I, bearing the in-

23 scription "God–Country–Peace," and a monument to Texans who died at Pearl **G**
24 Harbor. *Id.*, at 131-33. And four concern children—a replica of the Statue of
25 Liberty in honor of the Boy Scouts of America (at nearly sixteen feet, the tallest
26 monument in the northwest quadrant), *id.*, at 134; a tribute to the Texas Pioneer
27 Woman, depicting a pioneer mother cradling a baby in one arm, *id.*, at 135; a
28 tribute to Texas Children, portraying six children on a visit to the Capitol, one
29 of whom wears a necklace bearing a small cross, *id.*, at 54, 136; and the Ten
30 Commandments monument at issue in this litigation, donated by the Fraternal
31 Order of Eagles and dedicated in 1961 "to the Youth and People of Texas," *id.*, **H**
32 at 87, 137.
33   Continuing south, the tour passes monuments commemorating veterans of
34 the Texas National Guard and the Spanish-American War, *id.*, at 139-40, and a
35 Texas Cowboy statue paying tribute to the "rough and romantic riders of the
36 range," *id.*, at 142, 206. . . .
37   The self-guided tour ends at the "Great Walk," which connects the Capitol's
38 main, south entrance with Congress Avenue and downtown Austin. *Id.*, at
39 37, 118-19, 145. Here visitors will find the four oldest monuments on the
40 Grounds. . . .

A The brief emphasizes the vintage of Texas's monument: it is "historic."

B The grounds are *literally* a museum, and the Board's mission — to preserve Texas's culture — reflects a secular mission (i.e., to advance Texas's culture, rather than any religious agenda).

C This adjective seems innocuous. Not so. It signals that no state official accompanies visitors, discusses the Ten Commandments, or forces visitors to look at them. That detail is designed to protect the monument against the Court's various Establishment Clause tests, which assess whether a state is promoting or endorsing religion.

D This adjective also plays a role: it signals that a secular monument is bigger than the monument of the Ten Commandments. Elsewhere, the brief mentions that the statue of the Ten Commandments is one of the smallest displays at the statehouse. Notice, too, that the tour's sequence matters: secular content comes first, again making the Ten Commandments seem like a small afterthought in this display. The next two monuments are also secular.

E This phrase *sounds* like the words of a tour guide. The style reflects the theme.

F Notice that the sheer number of monuments — seventeen — suggests that including the Ten Commandments was not designed to achieve a religious goal. Taking readers on a virtual tour of the grounds helps to demonstrate that the Ten Commandments do not dominate the site.

G This fact is a two-edged sword. On the one hand, it shows that there is a second religious monument, which is harmful: the site is more religious than it would otherwise be. But this detail also raises implicitly the helpful point that all sorts of references to God (such as on U.S. currency) might become unlawful if mere religious words, without government endorsement, created a constitutional problem. This disclosure avoids hiding a bad fact (which would jeopardize the lawyers' credibility) and — even more importantly — hints at the difficulty that the Court would face in drawing lines between acceptable and unacceptable religious content. The next paragraph (in a deliberately long sentence) mentions that another statue depicts a girl wearing a cross around her neck. The same principles apply to that disclosure.

H By mentioning the Ten Commandments in a long sentence, surrounded (both physically and in words) by numerous secular monuments, the brief downplays the religiosity of the display.

FREQUENTLY ASKED QUESTIONS ABOUT ADVANCED TECHNIQUES WITH FACTS

Q. If I catch my opponent making an error, should I always point it out to the judge?

A. Adapt your response to the situation, to the importance of the error, and to the relationship that you have (or want) with opposing counsel. For isolated, minor errors, I recommend ignoring them; highlighting an adversary's irrelevant gaffes can make you seem petty. At most, point out those errors gently, and in a footnote. When your adversary makes major mistakes, however, or a large number of smaller ones, point out the errors if doing so will undermine your adversary's credibility.

Q. What if the other side attacks me or my client?

A. Karl Llewellyn's advice was to "shrug it" when an adversary attacks you. *See* Appendix A. Likewise, Bryan Garner's *The Winning Brief* sensibly encourages litigators to remain calm and thereby make your adversary look like a hothead. *See, e.g., Polar Tankers, Inc. v. City of Valdez*, 2009 WL 788634 (Appellate Brief) (U.S. Mar. 23, 2009), Reply Brief for the Petitioner (No. 08-310) ("We respectfully suggest that this harsh characterization of our argument is a tad over-caffeinated. It also is just plain wrong. . . ."). Be sure, however, that your credibility remains sound.

Q. What if I accidentally misquote a document or a case and get caught by my adversary?

A. Don't mess up: proof your documents repeatedly and check all of your citations carefully. But if an error slips past you, assess whether there's a way to explain why it doesn't matter. Some law offices will own up to the error, emphasize that it was accidental, express embarrassment, and assure the court that the error was atypical. Their goal is to minimize the harm to a specific client. But other top lawyers will worry about bad publicity and will deny that the error actually occurred, endure the criticism (without responding), or engage in tit-for-tat counterpunching by hunting down similar errors made by their adversary. Don't err. But learn to forgive yourself if you do.

Q. If I include law or legislative history in my Statement of Facts, how do I know when it crosses into the sort of outright advocacy that belongs in an Argument?

A. There's no bright line. Top lawyers increasingly sprinkle legal authorities into their Statements. I recommend this test: will the legal authority provide (1) insight into the meaning, mechanics, or purpose of a law in a (2) noncontroversial way that (3) judges will actually benefit from?

Q. I included law and extrinsic facts in my Statement, but now my Statement is long — approximately thirty pages. Is that too lengthy?

A. A thirty-page Statement of Facts is likely to cause judges to lose focus and become impatient when they do not immediately see the relevance of what they are reading. The tips in this chapter are not intended to encourage you to submit behemoth Statements. One trick: if your case implicates multiple legal issues, you can provide a short overview of the facts and then have a series of mini-briefs in which each piece of your Argument is preceded by a short Statement. In other words, you break your facts into pieces and place each piece next to the relevant part of your Argument. Judge John Walker (Second Circuit) has endorsed this approach, which he reports seeing in briefs filed by various assistant U.S. attorneys. Alternatively, cut some details to limit the size of your Statement. Also, an Introduction (see Chapter 13) helps judges to grasp why facts that might not seem relevant immediately are important to the case.

Q. **Should I look for evidence that my adversary (or opposing counsel) made inconsistent arguments either earlier in the case or in past cases?**

A. Yes, you can and should hunt down evidence that your adversary or opposing counsel took positions previously that conflict with their current positions — either in the same lawsuit or in previous cases. Highlighting hypocrisy and self-contradiction is a great way to undermine an adversary's argument and its credibility, but don't overdo it. Focus on major "shifts" related to key points. You can mention these inconsistencies in either your Statement or your Argument.

PART II

ARGUMENTS

As we saw in the first three chapters, facts persuade. And they often come close to arguing. But legal arguments — which appear in the Argument section of a brief or motion — more openly and comprehensively advance a client's legal position. This part of the book explores a variety of strategies for building winning arguments.

The chapters in this part reflect my view that lawyers often fail to appreciate the array of authorities that they can marshal. While a single argument can win *some* cases, lawyers maximize their chances of winning when they deploy all available tools that are likely to convince a judge.

The following chapters therefore cover nearly all of the types of arguments that appear in a typical brief or motion. While lawyers need not (and typically *should* not) use every type of argument in every case, they should hunt for more varied authorities than they usually cite. For instance, if your brief discusses five strong cases, elaborating on the sixth- through tenth-best cases will rarely help your client. By contrast, discussing five helpful cases *and* pertinent regulations *and* an airtight textual argument *and* powerful policy arguments *and* a lengthy national history of the disputed practice will, in most cases, improve a client's prospects. The following chapters encourage you to use a wide range of tools to persuade judges.

The skills discussed in the following chapters can also help you avoid the most common blunder of novice legal writers: being overly defensive. For instance, new lawyers regularly cite a helpful case or two and then shift into rebuttal mode. They have nothing else to say in support of their position, but they have lots of reasons that the other side's position is flawed. So they parry the other side's actual or anticipated arguments rather than build a robust affirmative argument. Worse yet, some lawyers begin their rebuttal even sooner, offering a point-by-point refutation of the other side's arguments without advancing *any* affirmative case. The great Karl Llewellyn (as shown in Appendix A) pilloried this approach, warning that "an answering case" is a losing case.

Successful lawyers advance their affirmative points, exploring a variety of arguments that favor their client on a particular issue — usually from strongest to weakest (but ending with a decent finale) — *before* countering the other side's arguments. As you get more comfortable with building robust, multifaceted affirmative arguments, you can and should adapt this default rule. But as a starting point, tell readers why you win *before* you explain why you don't lose.

This book's exploration of arguments begins in familiar territory. Chapter 4 discusses how to build arguments with authorities such as cases and statutes. Chapter 5 then discusses how to dismantle these same arguments when your adversary makes them.

The subsequent chapters each discuss a discrete type of argument:

- Fact-based arguments (Chapter 6)
- Textual arguments (Chapter 7)
- Arguments built on legislative history and statutory history (Chapter 8)
- Policy arguments (Chapter 9)
- Historical arguments (Chapter 10).

A subsequent segment of the book (Chapter 11) looks at how to organize your arguments. But let's take one argument at a time for now. The first step in that process is to remember how to organize individual arguments — the basic technique by which lawyers persuade courts. This technique goes by many names: CRAC, CREAC, TREAT, TREAC, TRAC, and so on. The approaches aren't very different from one another when you use them correctly.

CRAC remains the most popular mnemonic among legal writing professors, so this book uses it.[1] CRAC stands for *Conclusion, Rule, Application,* and *Conclusion.*[2] Whatever you call it, use it — at least most of the time. But don't cling to it too tightly, either.[3]

Here's how CRAC, which is basically a way of telling readers what you're going to prove and then proving it, works:

Conclusion	Write a topic sentence that tells the court what proposition you're going to establish.
Rule	Describe the authorities and principle that governs this proposition. In many instances, the Rule also explains how the legal principle works, provides details about the case that established that principle, or both.
Application	Explore how the legal authorities and principle relate to the facts in your case.
Conclusion	Remind readers what you just proved, but state it differently from the opening conclusion.

Here is a paradigmatic CRAC paragraph (from a hypothetical case in Maryland). But remember that the Rule and the Application often contain multiple sentences (or, even, multiple paragraphs):

> *[Conclusion]* The statute of limitations on Wilson's claim has expired, so his claims must be dismissed. *[Rule]* Under Maryland law, contract claims must be filed within three years of the date on which they arise. Md. Cts. & Jud. Proc. Code Ann. § 5-101. *[Application]* Wilson's complaint acknowledged that King's alleged breach occurred on March 1, 2006 — far more than three years

---

1. For *memos,* the mnemonic IRAC is used. The *I* stands for *Issue*—and intends to signal that the typical topic sentence in a memo is more objective and less argumentative than a typical topic sentence in a brief. For instance, a typical paragraph in a memo might begin, "The Court will first need to assess whether the statute of limitations has expired on Wilson's copyright infringement claim." In a brief, this sentence would instead state its position more directly, beginning with something like "The statute of limitations on Wilson's copyright claim expired eight months ago" or "Wilson's copyright claim remains timely." Modern memos, however, often follow CRAC rather than IRAC.

2. Cf. Handout, "IRAC/CRAC," *available* at http://www.law.berkeley.edu/files/IRAC_handout.doc (last visited Feb. 15, 2013) (describing the A in CRAC as *Analysis* rather than *Application*).

3. I largely agree with the view of Boston College's Jane Kent Gionfriddo, who observed, "The bottom line is that our profession should not use formulaic concepts like 'IRAC' that do not adequately teach the very real complexity of legal analysis and its communication." *See* Jane Kent Gionfriddo, *Dangerous! Our Focus Should Be Analysis, Not Formulas Like IRAC,* 10 *Second Draft* 2, 3 (Nov. 1995), *available* at http://www.lwionline.org/publications/seconddraft/nov95.pdf. But these tools make a good starting point; the training wheels come off eventually.

ago. Compl. ¶ 22. Maryland law thus required Wilson to file his complaint by February 28, 2009. He did not. In fact, he waited another *four* years (until March 4, 2013) to file. *[Conclusion]* Thus, Wilson missed the filing deadline, and Maryland law bars his lawsuit.

CRAC also helps lawyers to organize counterarguments. For instance:

> *[Conclusion]* Wilson's attempt to salvage his lawsuit — by arguing that the statute of limitations was tolled while he arbitrated a related contractual claim — is meritless. *[Rule]* Maryland's highest court rejected this *exact* argument last year, holding that the statute of limitations may "not be tolled by the pursuit of arbitration." *Kumar v. Dhanda*, 426 Md. 185, 204, 43 A.2d 1029, 1040 (2012).[4] *[Application]* Wilson's complaint admits facts that doom his case: "this lawsuit could have been filed earlier, but Wilson sought to resolve as many of his disputes as possible through arbitration before filing this case." Compl. ¶ 22. *[Conclusion]* Maryland law precludes this approach and bars Wilson's lawsuit.

Most textbooks fail to specify whether CRAC should be used to organize single paragraphs or entire sections of arguments. The answer: either. CRAC helps to organize discussions or individual paragraphs. When discussing a fact-intensive issue, you might need just one line of Rule but five pages of Application, such as in a case about whether an employer's objectionable conduct suffices to support an employee's sex discrimination claim. Conversely, your Rule might require multiple pages, but the Application might be straightforward. And you might raise four distinct points in support of an argument, and each of those points could follow CRAC. Thus, the components of CRAC expand or contract to meet the demands of an argument.

To go even further, lawyers can manipulate the C, the R, the A, and the C, cutting one or more of these components, flipping their order, combining them, and otherwise sculpting them. For instance, top lawyers often combine two of the letters of CRAC into a single sentence, as in this example: "*[Rule]* The Supreme Court held X, *[Application]* which is exactly what happened in this case: [add details.]" Lawyers also sometimes introduce and apply multiple Rules quickly. Or they lop off one of the Conclusions in a short paragraph lest the passage sound too repetitive. They even invert the Rule and Application, especially when the facts are short but when the Rule requires a prolonged explanation: for instance, "*[Application]* Marshall defrauded and bankrupted hundreds of senior citizens, *[Rule]* which is the exact type of conduct that led this court to 'permit punitive damages for egregious fraud.'" Thus, very few paragraphs or sections in superb briefs resemble paradigmatic uses of CRAC — good writing is more flexible than that — but CRAC nevertheless is a stellar *default* organizational strategy, especially for new attorneys.

Here's one warning about CRAC: avoid listing multiple Rules at once. Readers are better at absorbing facts (Application) than abstract principles (Rules).[5] Thus, if you list multiple Rules, readers will drown. Think of Rules as *water* and Application as *air*; if you force a typical reader to endure more than an uninterrupted minute of Rules, she will be desperate for a breath. Facts provide that air. The solution is to keep your discussion of Rules brisk and engaging. Admittedly, different customs govern within different courts; when construing a dense statutory provision at the Supreme Court, your Rule might need

---

4. If this counterargument was a major issue, lawyers would probably want to elaborate on the facts of *Kumar* to show that *Kumar* resembled the hypothetical lawsuit brought by Wilson.

5. *See generally* Daniel Kahneman, *Thinking, Fast and Slow* 20-24 (2011).

to grind on for pages. But if your child custody motion discusses the statute for seven consecutive pages without mentioning the orphan whom you represent, you should consider revising your draft.

Remember, too, that readers yearn for variety, but some legal standards are built to bore. For instance, the *Georgia-Pacific* patent infringement test has *fifteen* factors, and many briefs and motions march through each of the elements in monotonous CRAC-compliant paragraphs. Try to spare your readers from this approach — somehow. Good lawyers find ways to avoid stultifying judges; if judges are bored, your points won't stick. Thus, figure out a way to engage judges lest you lull them to sleep by the sixth element of a twenty-element test.

Let's continue our exploration by looking at a familiar type of argument: those based on legal authorities such as cases, statutes, and regulations.

Chapter 4

How to Build Arguments Based on Authorities

The effective use of authorities requires three primary skills. First, lawyers must build affirmative arguments with *favorable sources:* lawyers must find the best possible authorities, describe those authorities clearly, and show the court why those authorities require or favor the outcome that the lawyers' clients want. Second, when important authorities can be read to support either side's position, lawyers must show that the law supports their client. This chapter focuses on these two skills and on a variety of related ways of building arguments based on authorities. (The third critical skill involves protecting a client from the slings and arrows of the other side's favorable authorities: the art of countering arguments. Chapter 5 will explore this skill.)

The term "authorities" is broad. This chapter focuses on statutes, cases, and regulations. Nonbinding authorities such as treatises can also be very influential in some cases, and this chapter points out several instances where lawyers used secondary sources effectively.

CHAPTER OVERVIEW

1. When your position is supported by one or more *controlling* authorities, ensure that the court sees those sources early and clearly. Emphasize that your authorities compel an outcome, but also make readers *want* to follow those authorities.

2. When no controlling authorities support your argument, present relevant, helpful *persuasive* authorities. Omit any meek, self-conscious admissions that these sources are merely advisory.

3. When a critical authority can be read to support either party, make sure that the court sees it your way.

4. Quoting authorities concisely is helpful, but avoid block quotes. Many readers skip them altogether.

5. Supplement quotations by synthesizing and explaining doctrines so that the court sees *why* the authorities reached their conclusions. Quotations seek to restrict a court based on mere words, like a person who justifies a command by stating "Because I said so!" Showing the *reasons* for a command makes the point more persuasive. Quotes bark orders; reasoning makes readers want to follow them.

6. When a point is critical *and* disputed, you may wish to provide readers with a string cite — a list of multiple authorities — to show that your position has been accepted broadly. But do not add a string cite to substantiate an obvious or uncontested point.

7. When you cannot find satisfactory authorities to support a key proposition, show that the law has favored your position in analogous situations.

8. In addition to cases, search for other helpful authorities (statutes, regulations, treatises, and so on) that support your position. Too often, lawyers hunt only for cases.

9. Attune yourself to the relative value of various authorities and to how their value differs from case to case. For instance, Restatements are sometimes authoritative on unresolved issues of state law, but they exert far less sway on federal statutory issues.

Example 4.1

Takeaway point 4.1: Emphasize controlling authority, but remember to make a court *want* your client to win.

In those wonderful instances when controlling authorities support your position, make sure that the court sees those authorities early and clearly. An example of how to play this sort of dominant hand appears below.

The excerpt comes from a federal district court's review of an administrative agency's decision involving Laura Liston, who was a citizen and national of Mexico. In 2004, Liston's father, a U.S. citizen, applied for her Certificate of Citizenship under a federal law called the Child Citizenship Act. That statute offers an easy path to citizenship for foreign children of U.S. citizens — but only until children turn eighteen years old. The federal agency that handles immigration (USCIS) scheduled an interview with Liston, who was approaching her eighteenth birthday. She missed her mandatory interview, and USCIS denied her application when she reached her eighteenth birthday. She brought this lawsuit, claiming that she is entitled to citizenship, and that she never received notice of her interview. As you will see below, the government had an airtight case. In clear and capable prose, it presented an ironclad statutory argument, a helpful regulation, and a controlling case, but its motion was denied. What went wrong? The denial of this motion illustrates one of the most important lessons in persuasion: telling readers that they *need* to do something rarely works as well as making them *want* to do it.

Source: Government's motion to dismiss in *Liston v. Chertoff*, No. CV-06-265-LRS, 2007 WL 681178 (E.D. Wash. Jan. 11, 2007).

1	The adjudication of Plaintiff's application for citizenship is not left to the
2	open-ended discretion of the Attorney General and USCIS. On the contrary,
3	under the relevant section of the Immigration and Nationality Act ("INA"), sev-
4	eral procedures and conditions must be met before USCIS may approve such an
5	application:
6	a) A parent who is a citizen of the United States . . . may apply
7	for naturalization on behalf of a child born outside the United States
8	who has not acquired citizenship automatically under section 320. The
9	Attorney General shall issue such a certificate of citizenship upon proof
10	to the satisfaction of the Attorney General that the following conditions
11	have been fulfilled: . . . .
12	(3) The child is under the age of 18 years and in the legal cus-
13	tody of the citizen parent. . . . .
14	8 U.S.C. § 1433 (2006); INA § 322 (2006). Federal regulations further address the
15	conditions of eligibility, including the requirement that the child be under the
16	age of 18 years at the time the certificate of citizenship is issued: "A child will
17	be eligible for citizenship under section 322 of the Act, if the following condi-
18	tions have been fulfilled . . . (3) the child *currently* is under 18 years of age." 8
19	C.F.R § 322.2(a)(3) (2000) (emphasis added). The plain language of the statute
20	and regulation make clear that USCIS is simply not allowed under this statute to
21	issue a certificate of citizenship to an applicant who is 18 years of age or older,
22	even if the application was filed when the applicant was a minor. Thus, much
23	to the contrary of Plaintiff's assertion that USCIS' denial of her application was
24	arbitrary and capricious, USCIS had no choice but to deny Plaintiff's application.

A

B

C

25	While the law may admittedly operate harshly on some applicants, USCIS	
26	is simply not empowered to substitute more lenient requirements for those	
27	imposed by Congress. In a case dealing with a similar provision of the Child	
28	Citizenship Act ("CCA"), the Ninth Circuit has recognized that despite seem-	
29	ingly harsh results, the Act has firm and explicit age requirements that must be	
30	followed. *Hughes v. Ashcroft,* 255 F3d 752, 760 (9th Cir. 2001). In *Hughes,* the	D
31	Court held that the CCA granted automatic citizenship only to those children	
32	who were under the age of 18, and who met the other criteria, as of the effec-	
33	tive date of the CCA. *Id.* The Court recognized that throughout the text of the	
34	entire CCA, the emphasis was on children only. *Id.* The Court further found that	
35	this emphasis was not irrational, stating that "Congress could have decided, for	E
36	example, that a person who already is an adult has an independent opportunity	
37	to apply for citizenship. On the other hand, children are in need of greater help	
38	and protection." *Id. See also Langhorne v. Ashcroft,* 377 F.3d 175, 181 (2d Cir.	
39	2004) ("Thus the overarching statutory scheme that was in place when Lang-	
40	horne claims he was covered by Section 321(a) was clearly keyed to the age of	
41	eighteen."). In short, case law confirms that Congress meant what it said when	
42	it limited the Child Citizenship Act to children, and USCIS is therefore not free	
43	to grant citizenship to adult applicants under this Act.	F

A Avoid nouns or verbs that obscure who is acting (e.g., "adjudication"). *See* Chapter 16, Tip 6.

B The motion reprinted all five statutory requirements, but I reprinted only the disputed one. Although many readers skip block quotes (or perhaps suspect that they represent shortcuts to the hard work of creating original persuasive language), the key language of a statute, regulation, or contractual provision is important enough to quote verbatim. Even so, make readers *want* to read the quote, for example, by preceding it with a sentence explaining *why* it matters or by using a teaser (such as by prefacing a block quote with the sentence, "The defendant's CEO then made a stunning admission: . . ."). Likewise, italicize key parts of a block quote so that readers can instantly spot the most important bits.

C Having quoted the statute, the motion does *not* begin to rebut the other side's argument. Rather, it continues to build its affirmative argument — just as it should do. Here, the government invokes a regulation to support its statutory argument.

D This passage exemplifies the risks of telling a court that a law "must be followed" rather than making the court want to do so. The motion twice admits that the consequences of denying Liston's citizenship application would be "harsh." When possible, avoid such concessions and focus instead on why an outcome is fair or unjust — such as by emphasizing the variety of alternative paths to citizenship for Liston. While concessions sometimes protect your credibility, they usually backfire.

E Notice how defensive the motion becomes here; it argues that its position is "not irrational" — hardly a compelling argument. Instead, frame your position positively, like this: "Clear rules are vital to the orderly administration of an immigration system that processes millions of applications every year. If the Court grants to Liston an exemption from an unambiguous statute, countless other applicants will seek exemptions from ironclad laws."

F This stellar example of the second Conclusion in CRAC ensures that readers will grasp the lawyers' point.

Example
4.2

Takeaway point 4.2: Cite and quote key cases, but also explain and emphasize the salient facts and relevant principles from those cases.

Resist the urge to cite your key supporting cases without any discussion or to dump quotes from them into your brief. Instead, drill into the cases' facts and reasoning to show readers *how* they mirror the issues in your case.

We look next at football and cheating. In 2007, a young assistant for the New England Patriots was caught videotaping a rival's defensive coaches during a football game. Videotaping allows one team to "steal" the other team's plans and thus gives it an advantage. The NFL traced the orders to videotape the game to the Patriots' head coach, Bill Belichick, who eventually admitted that he had taped NFL games since 2000. The NFL punished Belichick and his team for violating the league's rules. A New York Jets fan (and season ticket holder) sued Belichick, the Patriots, and the NFL, claiming that because the quality of the Patriots-Jets game was compromised by cheating, all of the Jets' season ticket holders had been wronged in various ways that warranted damages. After prevailing on a motion to dismiss, the NFL here tries to convince the Third Circuit to affirm the dismissal.

Source: NFL's brief from *Mayer v. Belichick*, 605 F.3d 223 (3d Cir. 2010) (some case citations omitted).

1	Plaintiff-Appellant has offered no legal theory under which a spectator may
2	assert a claim based on his subjective view of the quality of a sporting event.
3	Indeed, as discussed above, the district court rightly observed that the great
4	weight of the case law holds that any such claim is not actionable.
5	*Castillo v. Tyson,* 701 N.Y.S.2d 423 (App. Div. 2000), a purported class
6	action in which the court rejected essentially the same claims as those here, is
7	instructive. The plaintiffs in *Castillo* were fans who paid to view a boxing match
8	between Mike Tyson and Evander Holyfield. When Tyson was disqualified for
9	biting Holyfield's ear, the plaintiffs brought suit against Tyson, fight promoters,
10	and fight telecasters seeking a refund because they allegedly were denied the
11	right "to view a legitimate heavyweight title fight fought in accordance with
12	the applicable rules and regulations of the governing boxing commission." The
13	plaintiffs advanced a litany of legal theories in support of their claims, includ-
14	ing many of those found in the Complaint here, such as breach of contract,
15	unjust enrichment, fraud, and tortious interference with contractual relations. The
16	appellate court affirmed the lower court's dismissal of the plaintiffs' complaint
17	for failure to state a cause of action, holding that the plaintiffs were not in con-
18	tractual privity with any of the defendants, *id.*, and that the plaintiffs received
19	exactly what they paid for, "namely, *the right to view whatever event transpired.*"
20	Here, in an assertion almost identical to that made by the boxing fans in
21	*Castillo,* Mr. Mayer complains that he was denied the right to observe an honest
22	game played "in compliance with all laws, regulations and NFL rules." And as
23	in *Castillo,* Mr. Mayer's claims for unmet expectations fail as a matter of law.
24	Spectators have no express or implied right to see a sporting event free of penal-
25	ties or free from any one particular type of penalty. Thus, fans who purchased
26	tickets to a game between the Patriots and the Jets have no cause of action for
27	disappointment in its quality.

A

B

C

D

E

F

G

Ⓐ This topic sentence foretells the argument that will follow. For more advice on topic sentences, *see* Chapter 16, Tip 4, and Appendix B. The topic sentence in the next paragraph substantiates the claims in this paragraph. The lawyers split this CRAC discussion into several paragraphs to make the passage readable.

Ⓑ The brief hints that it will cite multiple cases. And it did — six others. This exemplar, however, focuses only on the case that the brief discussed most extensively.

Ⓒ **This New York State case is not controlling on the Third Circuit. So what? The brief emphasizes the prior case's similar facts and sensible reasoning to make readers *want* to follow that case. This approach reflects what Chief Judge Richard Posner (7th Cir.) meant when he advised lawyers to use case law "not** as a club with which to beat your opponent to death, but as a source of policies to guide decision."

Ⓓ The discussion emphasizes the ways in which the prior case mirrors the lawsuit against Coach Belichick and the other football defendants.

Ⓔ The discussion ends with a snappy quote that sticks with readers and that captures the defendants' theme. Themes are discussed more extensively in Chapter 13.

Ⓕ The brief alerts readers that it is about to apply the *Castillo* case to the pending lawsuit. Or, in the language of CRAC, the brief is moving from Rule to Application.

Ⓖ The brief tells readers what it just proved: the final "C" or Conclusion in CRAC.

Example 4.3	**Takeaway point 4.3:** You can cite numerous cases, but you should *discuss* only some — not all — cases that help your client. You will sometimes cite multiple cases. The next example omits the contents of the paragraphs and focuses instead on how to flow from one case to the next. The passage excerpts the brief filed by the struggling city of New London, Connecticut, which wanted to seize some private homes to build a business park for a pharmaceutical company. Several homeowners who sought to retain their homes filed a lawsuit asserting that New London would violate the U.S. Constitution by taking land from one private party and then "retransferring" it to another private party. New London leaned on precedent to support its plan. New London won 5-4, and the majority based its decision on the weight of these prior cases. New London also emphasized in its brief the poverty and blight that it was combating; it thus motivated the Court to follow the precedents that are discussed below. *Source:* City's brief in *Kelo v. City of New London*, 545 U.S. 469 (2005) (some citations omitted).

1　　On five occasions in the past half-century, this Court has upheld the re-
2　transfer of private property to another private party against Takings Clause chal-
3　lenges because of the public benefits created by the re-transfer. This clear line of　**A**
4　precedent — which receives scant attention in the petitioners' brief — should be
5　controlling on the general question of whether economic development is permit-
6　ted under the Takings Clause.
7　　The seminal case in this Court's modern Takings Clause jurisprudence is
8　*Berman v. Parker.* In *Berman* . . . .　**B**
9　　This Court reached a similar conclusion in *Hawaii Housing Authority v.*　**C**
10　*Midkiff,* in which the Court unanimously upheld the constitutionality of Hawaii's　**D**
11　Land Reform Act. . . .
12　　This Court issued yet another clear statement regarding the constitutionality
13　of re-transfer to a private party in *National Railroad Passenger Corp. v. Boston &*
14　*Maine Corp., supra.* . . .
15　　. . . *See also Brown,* 538 U.S. at 232 (taking of interest on clients' funds
16　to fund legal services for indigent litigants valid public use); *Ruckelshaus v.*
17　*Monsanto Co.,* 467 U.S. 986, 1014-16 (1984) (public disclosure of pesticide data
18　pursuant to FIFRA, which made data available to other manufacturers and
19　effected taking, valid public use).　**E**
20　　At the end of the day, the petitioners advance no cogent reason for this Court
21　to reverse this long line of decisions upholding the re-transfer of condemned
22　property to a private party, so long as the re-transfer will result in a substantial
23　public benefit.　**F**

A This is *almost* a stellar sentence, but it goes on a bit too long. Even so, the point comes across: five Supreme Court opinions support New London. Readers also know that a discussion of these cases will follow.

B Notice that the paragraph's first sentence tees up *Berman*, explaining that this opinion is important before discussing it. You should generally tell readers what principle you will establish in a paragraph *before* you discuss the case that establishes that principle. Thus, notwithstanding Example 4.1 (line 5), few paragraphs should begin "In *X v. Y,* . . . ."

C These words signal that the brief is moving to the next case — and is still making its affirmative argument. Other phrases ("by contrast," "only one case," or "this Court has rejected the argument that") signal that lawyers are about to deal with negative arguments, those that support the other side's case. These types of "signposts" immediately let readers know what point the rest of the sentence will make.

D A unanimous decision has no special legal effect, but unanimity hints that a prior court found an issue uncontroversial (or obvious).

E **You do not need to discuss in detail every case that favors your client. After telling the Court that the brief will present five favorable cases, the lawyers discuss all five of them, but two of the "discussions" are mere parenthetical summaries of the holdings. Notice that the two cases that received little attention involved money and information — not real property. The lawyers, in other words, deprioritized the two least analogous cases and thereby shortened their argument. You should usually do the same. Force readers to focus on the strongest and most analogous cases.**

F This sentence acts as the Conclusion of this part of the argument (i.e., the final "C" in CRAC).

Example **4.4**	**Takeaway point 4.4:** Synthesize doctrines to help judges see what a line of cases is really about.

Quoting an authority is more effective when you also crystallize what that authority sought to do. The following exemple shows how to extrapolate sensible, unspoken principles from cases: the passage synthesizes a century of case law.

This case involves a telecommunications company. When a phone call is placed from or to a landline telephone, the call passes through a local phone network. The local network's owner could refuse to connect the calls of other companies' customers, thereby monopolizing that calling area. Congress decided to prevent this potential conduct by requiring phone companies to lease access to their networks so that competitors could offer landline service. Verizon thus leased access to its network to AT&T, but a class of AT&T customers in New York City sued Verizon, alleging that it deliberately provided poor service to AT&T customers. The class claimed that this behavior violated § 2 of the Sherman Act — an antitrust law that prohibits acquiring or maintaining monopolies through anticompetitive conduct. The class sought to force Verizon to sell some of its network to competitors. While the Second Circuit agreed with the plaintiffs, the following brief persuaded the Supreme Court to reverse.

Source: Brief for Petitioner-Verizon from *Verizon Communications Inc. v. Law Offices of Curtis V. Trinko, LLP*, 540 U.S. 398 (2004).

---

1   Respondent's claim confronts fundamental limits on Section 2. Most basi-
2   cally, acquiring or continuing a monopoly is not unlawful; Section 2 condemns   **A**
3   only limited types of unilateral conduct for doing so.[10] A firm that has lawfully
4   obtained monopoly power thus need not dismantle its monopoly by subjecting
5   itself to a process of creeping divestiture, shedding its customers one at a time
6   by meeting every would-be rival's demand to buy its facilities or services at
7   wholesale rates. *See Cavalier,* at *11 ("if a company such as Verizon, which was
8   a longstanding legal monopoly, were asked to share its office space and to rent its
9   telephone lines and other facilities to a competitor when it was not already in the
10 business of renting office space, lines, or facilities, it could have legally refused
11 the request to expand into such a business without violating § 2").
12   The "'central message of the Sherman Act'" is, instead, that all firms, includ-
13 ing new entrants, "'must find new customers and higher profits through internal
14 expansion — that is, by competing successfully rather than by arranging trea-
15 ties with its competitors.'"[11] The Sherman Act promotes independent, unilateral
16 rivalry; it treats cooperation among competitors with suspicion.[12] For a century,   **B**

---

17   10. *United States v. United States Steel Corp.,* 251 U.S. 417, 451 (1920) (Section 2
18 "does not compel competition"); *Kodak,* 504 U.S. at 480 (power plus conduct); *Aspen,*
19 472 U.S. at 596 n.19; *see United States v. Microsoft Corp.,* 253 F.3d 34, 51, 58 (D.C. Cir.
20 2001) (en banc) ("merely possessing monopoly power is not itself an antitrust viola-
21 tion"; "having a monopoly does not by itself violate § 2"; "'the successful competitor,
22 having been urged to compete, must not be turned on when he wins,'" quoting *United*
23 *States v. Aluminum Co. of America,* 148 F.2d 416, 430 (2d Cir. 1945) (per L. Hand, J.)).   **C**
24   11. *Aspen,* 472 U.S. at 600. . . .
25   12. *Copperweld Corp. v. Independence Tube Corp.,* 467 U.S. 752, 767-69 (1984). . . .

26 the Act has overwhelmingly focused on *negative* duties (to avoid acts that hinder
27 rivals' independent efforts to attract customers) and not *affirmative* ones.[13]
28   The distinction between acts negatively interfering with others, on one hand,
29 and a failure to lend affirmative assistance, on the other, is fundamental else-
30 where in the law. *See DeShaney v. Winnebago County Dep't of Social Servs.*, 489
31 U.S. 189 (1989) (relying on same line to hold that failure to provide assistance is
32 not "deprivation" under Due Process Clause).

—————————— D

33   13. *See Illinois ex rel. Burris v. Panhandle Eastern Pipe Line Co.*, 935 F.2d 1469,
34 1484 (7th Cir. 1991) (negative/affirmative line); *Olympia Equip.*, 797 F.2d at 375-76
35 ("'There is a difference between positive and negative duties, and the antitrust laws,
36 like other legal doctrines sounding in tort, have generally been understood to impose
37 only the latter.'"); S. Breyer, *Regulation and Its Reform* 157 (1982) (antitrust laws "act
38 negatively, through a few highly general provisions *prohibiting* certain forms of pri-
39 vate conduct. They do not affirmatively order firms to behave in specified ways; for
40 the most part, they tell private firms what not to do.").

A   This passage does an exemplary job of explaining the principles embedded in a line of cases. Rather than simply quoting cases or holdings, it synthesizes a century's worth of jurisprudence into a few paragraphs.

B   This is a common tactic: when you have old cases, you want to present them as part of a glorious and consistent tradition. When old cases disfavor your client, you want to diminish their value by dismissing them as outdated.

C   Notice how the footnotes use short, effective parentheticals both to explain the law *and* to support Verizon's legal position. Many lawyers strive to avoid footnotes. However, when you footnote multiple authorities in a string cite, it keeps your textual passages uncluttered. Some writing specialists recommend placing most citations in footnotes. I strongly disfavor this approach because many readers like and expect citations in their text so that they can weigh the quality of a brief's authorities without plunging to the bottom of the page. But no answer is objectively right. Follow the custom that prevails in your office and in your court. If there is no custom, try to avoid footnotes.

D   This paragraph shows one way to flow into a new point. As you see in footnote 13, several intermediate federal courts (and Justice Breyer) had concluded that antitrust law distinguishes between affirmative and negative duties. But the Supreme Court had not done so yet. Thus, the lawyers looked to *analogous* cases and situations to show that the affirmative-negative distinction has (i) been used by the Supreme Court previously and (ii) provided a useful (and, indeed, "fundamental") way of interpreting laws. Reasoning by analogy is a critical part of effective advocacy: when you want a court to accept a novel proposition, show that it is not actually novel — by illustrating that the proposition has been embraced in other, similar contexts.

Example 4.5	**Takeaway point 4.5:** When a critical authority can be read to help either side, emphasize the ways in which the case supports your client's position.

Let's now discuss a common, challenging, and critical scenario that will eventually confront you: how to use cases effectively when they either (1) do not need to be followed or (2) do not address the exact issue implicated by your dispute. The following example demonstrates that when a court is not required by any authority to resolve a case in a particular way, you should make your authorities *seem* compelling. This process involves writing with confidence, synthesizing the rationales that led to the prior decisions, emphasizing the similarities between your case and the relevant authorities, and downplaying the differences.

To illustrate this point, we return to the YouTube dispute in which numerous intellectual property owners sued YouTube, claiming that the site infringed their copyrights. Here, YouTube discusses the dominant case, *MGM Studios, Inc. v. Grokster Ltd.*, 545 U.S. 913 (2005), which the Supreme Court had issued several years earlier. This passage shows how to claim ambiguous precedent for your client while undermining key points in your opponent's argument.

Source: YouTube's opposition to plaintiffs' motion for summary judgment from *Football Premier Ass'n League Ltd. v. YouTube, Inc.*, 718 F. Supp. 2d 514 (S.D.N.Y. 2010), *vacated in part*, 676 F.3d 19 (2d Cir. 2012).

---

1 **V. VIACOM'S INDUCEMENT CLAIM FAILS AS A MATTER OF LAW.**   **A**

2 The Supreme Court in *Grokster* announced a clear — and strict — standard
3 for inducement: "We hold that one who distributes a device with the object
4 *of promoting its use to infringe copyright,* as shown by clear expression or other
5 *affirmative steps taken to foster infringement,* is liable for the resulting acts of   **B**
6 infringement by third parties." *Grokster,* 545 U.S. at 919 (emphases added).
7 *Grokster* requires that the defendant act with the specific purpose of promoting
8 infringing uses and that it take affirmative steps to foster infringement. Plaintiffs
9 cannot make that showing. Perhaps for that reason, Viacom rests its inducement
10 motion on (1) an unsupportable effort to dilute the *Grokster* standard; and (2) a
11 series of factual misrepresentations.

12 **A. Viacom's Effort To Rewrite The Grokster Standard For Promoting Infringe-**   **C**
13 **ment Is Unsustainable.**

14 Viacom ignores *Grokster's* actual holding. Instead, it tries to shift the legal
15 playing field, disavowing the term "inducement" and contending that liability
16 "rests on the existence of the unlawful purpose itself." Viacom Br. 23. Viacom   **D**
17 suggests that businesses "are liable for infringement when they operate a website
18 with the unlawful intention, purpose, or objective that it will be used, *at least in*
19 *part* for infringing activity." *Id.* at 25 (emphasis added). The murky standard that
20 Viacom proposes diverges from *Grokster* in two critical respects.   **E**

21 First, Viacom glosses over the point, repeatedly emphasized by the Supreme
22 Court, that inducement liability is not based on some amorphous bad purpose,
23 but instead requires that the defendant have the specific objective of "promot-
24 ing" the use of its service "to infringe copyright." *Grokster,* 545 U.S. at 936-37.
25 Second, Viacom ignores the Supreme Court's admonitions that the inducer must
26 not simply possess that unlawful objective, but must actively seek to further it   **F**
27 "by clear expression *or other affirmative steps* taken to foster infringement." *Id.*

28 (emphasis added). To establish inducement, therefore, there must be a "showing
29 that *active steps* were taken with the purpose of bringing about infringing acts."
30 *Id.* at 938 (emphasis added). Viacom tries to read these elements out of *Grokster*
31 to create a new species of "passive" inducement that has no basis in the law.

G

32   Viacom's effort must be rejected not just because it conflicts with what *Grokster*
33 says, but because it threatens to undermine the careful balance that the Supreme
34 Court struck in delineating the contours of the inducement rule. The Court was

H

35 "mindful of the need to keep from trenching on regular commerce or discouraging
36 the development of technologies with lawful and unlawful potential."

A The short, sharp heading reminds us that we're at the summary judgment stage, which means that the district court needed to assess whether Viacom's claims could succeed as a matter of law. The heading directly addresses the legal burden that confronted YouTube at this stage of the lawsuit.

B If you emphasize too many words in a sentence, readers will tire of this technique. But some emphasis is very helpful.

C Inexperienced advocates often include two consecutive headings with nothing in between them — bone on bone. By contrast, the prior paragraph in YouTube's filing exemplifies how to provide an overview of a section, which also provides a bit of cartilage between your headings.

D YouTube explained these concepts earlier in its opposition brief. But the lawyers sense that readers need a hint, so they provide one in the next two sentences. Whisper helpful hints and reminders to your readers.

E The paragraph ends by foreshadowing what will come in the next two paragraphs: the two "critical respects" in which Viacom's arguments have diverged from the law. This approach exemplifies how good lawyers telegraph their moves, letting readers know what is coming next.

F Notice how aggressively YouTube characterizes the law: the Court did *not* use the word "must." The next annotation elaborates on this point.

G Reading YouTube's brief, you might assume that *Grokster* restricted copyright infringement lawsuits. And yet the Supreme Court in *Grokster* held 9-0 that a website that allowed users to share music files *could* be sued for copyright infringement. This whole example reflects my point from the opening of this chapter that great advocates make turf wars about cases look like the law supports their position. Here, to achieve that goal, YouTube focuses on the doctrinal rule rather than the outcome and injects a *requirement* into *Grokster* — by using the word "must" — that did not actually appear in the opinion. YouTube stretches the law slightly, but not extravagantly. Your discussions of doctrine, similarly, should emphasize whichever parts of leading cases help your client.

H YouTube camouflages a policy argument as a doctrinal point. (Chapter 9 explores policy arguments more closely.) One nit: when briefs promise that they will make a specific number of points, each ensuing paragraph should ordinarily begin with ordinal numbers: thus, this paragraph should probably have begun "Second, ..."

Example
4.6

Takeaway point 4.6: Use a string cite to establish nonobvious points and to signal to readers that disagreeing with your client's preferred outcome would be unwise, unusual, or reversible.

Some disputes swing on a single fact or a single authority. But in others, lawyers find it useful to show how many cases have supported their client's position. Thus, when a point is important *and* disputed, you may wish to provide a string cite to show that your position has been accepted broadly. For instance, when Chief Justice Roberts was a litigator, he wrote that the Sixth Circuit had rejected an "approach adopted . . . by every federal court of appeals," and then he added a footnote listing twelve circuit court opinions — including a prior opinion by a different Sixth Circuit panel. Even without knowing what that case was about, the sheer volume of authority suggests that the Sixth Circuit erred; after all, even the same court had previously reached the opposite conclusion. Used properly, string cites either survey the law or show that a controversial, vital, or nonobvious proposition has been widely accepted, which exerts subtle peer pressure on readers. Avoid string cites in most other instances. Used incorrectly, they will clog your prose with a heap of needless authorities. Let's look at a passage that uses a string cite effectively.

Here, a man in Oregon sought damages after he was injured while riding a three-wheeled "all-terrain vehicle" manufactured by Honda. A jury ordered Honda to pay $5 million in punitive damages. Under Oregon law, appellate courts in Oregon could not review punitive damages awards. Honda nevertheless appealed, arguing that Oregon's ban on letting appellate courts reduce punitive damages awards violated the U.S. Constitution's Due Process Clause. Basically, Honda said that it is unconstitutional to prevent parties from appealing excessive jury awards. The Supreme Court agreed, holding that punitive damages awards must be reviewable. The following passage shows how Honda used authorities — a boatload of authorities — to establish its legal claim, demonstrating that a string cite can serve multiple roles at the same time.

Source: Honda's brief from *Honda Motor Co. v. Oberg*, 512 U.S. 415 (1994).

---

1   Common sense thus suggests that jurors will make errors in setting dam-
2   ages awards. But we need not rely on logic to establish that proposition: em-
3   pirical data demonstrate that trial and appellate judges frequently find it neces-
4   sary to reduce or remit damages awarded by juries. These actions are significant
5   because every case in which a judge finds an award excessive is, by definition, a
6   case in which the jury's award, if uncorrected, would have worked an erroneous
7   deprivation of property.
8   We have reviewed all reported cases, state and federal, in which punitive
9   damages awards were contested as excessive during 1992 and 1993. In 90 of the
10 271 cases in our sample, the awards were set aside altogether. (These cases are
11 listed in Appendix C, *infra*.) And most important for present purposes, of the
12 remaining 181 cases, 51 — or more than 28% — saw reductions in the punitive
13 damages award. (Cases in which awards were reduced or remitted are listed in
14 Appendix A, *infra;* cases in which excessiveness arguments were rejected are
15 listed in Appendix B, *infra*.) These findings are consistent with the conclusions
16 of all of the published empirical studies on the subject. . . .

17   APPENDIX A
18   In the following fifty-one cases reported on Westlaw as decided in 1992 and
19 1993, remittiturs were granted or affirmed based on the excessiveness of the jury
20 verdict. *Dunn v. Hovic*, 1 F.3d 1371 (CA 3) (en banc) (reducing punitive damages

21 award of $2 million, which had been reduced by trial court from $25 million,
22 to $1 million), *modified in part,* 13 F.3d 58 (CA 3), *cert. denied,* 114 S. Ct. 650
23 (1993); *King v. Macri,* 993 F.2d 294 (CA 2 1993) (remitting punitive damages
24 award of $250,000 to $150,000); *Keenan v. City of Philadelphia,* 983 F.2d 459
25 (CA 3 1992) (affirming remittiturs with respect to three of four defendants); *Ross*
26 *v. Black & Decker, Inc.,* 977 F.2d 1178 (CA 7 1992) (remitting $10 million punitive
27 damages award to $5 million), *cert. denied,* 113 S. Ct. (1993); *Vasbinder v. Scott,*
28 976 F.2d 118 (CA 2 1992) (reducing $150,000 awards against each defendant
29 to $30,000 and $20,000); *Phelan v. Local 305 of United Ass'n of Journeymen &*
30 *Apprentices of Plumbing and Pipefitting Indus.,* 973 F.2d 1050 (CA 2 1992) (af-
31 firming remittitur but remanding because of magistrate's failure to offer plaintiff
32 option of a new trial), *cert. denied,* 113 S. Ct. 1415 (1993); *Brown v. Soldier of*
33 *Fortune Magazine, Inc.,* 968 F.2d 1110 (CA 11 1992) (trial court remitted $10 mil-
34 lion jury award to $2 million; remittitur not challenged on appeal), *cert. denied,*
35 113 S. Ct. 2992 (1993); *Hill v. Marshall,* 962 F.2d 1209 (CA 6 1992) (reversing
36 remittitur of entire punitive damages award, but remanding with directions to
37 approve an amount of punitive damages reasonably supported by the evidence);
38 *Ash v. Georgia-Pacific Corp.,* 957 F.2d 432 (CA 7 1992) (affirming reduction of
39 $2.5 million to $500,000); . . . [omitting *38* citations].

A "Common sense," of course, is *not* an authority; the lawyers refer to it only because they also have a heap of authorities.

B Most lawyers would have cited a case or two. Honda goes much, much further citing 271 cases in three appendices. Pay attention to how exhaustively top lawyers hunt for authorities that help their clients. But as we see later, Honda probably used a clever shortcut to find these cases.

C Honda uses a technical verb: as used here, *remit* means to send a case back to a lower court to revise the damages award.

D Some readers may find the word "sample" confusing: the word could mean that Honda looked at only some of the available cases (i.e., it sampled the cases). But the prior sentence clarifies that Honda looked at "all reported cases"; thus the word "sample" is meant to sound scientific and serious.

E This "most important" phrase exemplifies how to write empathically: it provides a useful hint to readers at the exact moment that they might otherwise become confused.

F Appendix A provides parentheticals for each of the 51 cases that reduced or remitted an award

of damages. Notice, too, the clever mathematical game played by the lawyers: they cut 90 of the cases from the sample size. Thus, their preferred outcome occurred in 28 percent of cases rather than just 51 cases from the total pool of 271 cases, or 19 percent. We see once again that lawyers frame cases — and numbers — in a way that aids their clients.

G Appendices B and C are even longer.

H This massive string cite (which has been shortened here) orders its cases using *The Bluebook's* Rule 1.4: federal circuit court opinions appear before district court opinions, which appear before state court opinions (starting with state supreme court opinions).

I This citation format (which does not comport with *The Bluebook*) suggests that the authors may have cut and pasted these citations from some other source, such as a treatise, an article, or an ALR report. (ALR reports compile authorities in various areas of the law.) Tapping into resources like these can speed your research and save your client money. Just make sure the authorities support your proposition, have not been reversed or overruled, and do not contain comments that undermine other arguments that you are making.

Example
4.7

Takeaway point 4.7: Remember to hunt for statutes and regulations that help your client; citing only cases weakens your client's prospects.

Most of the examples in this chapter rely on cases, but don't forget to search for additional authorities (such as statutes, regulations, rules, and treatises) that support your client's position. Law school focuses on cases, so much so that some students graduate without even reading a statute or regulation. But the words of statutes and regulations can be priceless because they are rigid — and thus harder for your adversary to counter than dicta or an amorphous holding. Great advocacy requires you to weave together a variety of helpful authorities.

In the next excerpt, a record company sued a student for copyright infringement after he illegally downloaded thirty songs. The company won, and the trial court ordered the student to pay $67,500. He challenged the decision, alleging that the copyright law's massive penalties violated his due process rights. Here, the record company contests the student's claim and focuses on the relevant statute, 17 U.S.C. § 504. The excerpt below demonstrates a number of techniques discussed thus far in this chapter, and it also shows how to use statutes to persuade judges.

Source: Respondent's Opposition to a Petition for a Writ of Certiorari to challenge *Tenenbaum v. Sony BMG Music Entertainment*, 660 F.3d 487 (1st Cir. 2011).

---

1   Petitioner's strained efforts to recharacterize his conduct as noncommercial
2 and uninjurious are for naught, as the plain text of the statute forecloses his
3 attempt to remove such infringement from its purview. Section 504 draws no
4 distinction between "commercial" and "noncommercial" infringers, but instead
5 broadly renders any "infringer of copyright" liable for actual or statutory damages.
6 17 U.S.C. § 504(a). Section 504(c), in turn, does not require a copyright owner
7 seeking statutory damages to prove actual damages, but instead allows a plaintiff
8 to elect statutory damages *"instead of* actual damages and profits." *Id.* § 504(c)
9 (emphasis added); *see also L.A. Westermann,* 249 U.S. at 106 ("[t]he fact that
10 these damages are to be 'in lieu of actual damages' shows that something other
11 than actual damages is intended"). Indeed, statutory damages were adopted in
12 large part to relieve copyright owners of the "'difficult or impossible'" burden
13 of proving actual damages or lost profits, which is precisely why this Court has
14 concluded that Congress intended statutory damages to be available "[e]ven for
15 uninjurious and unprofitable invasions of copyright." *F.W. Woolworth,* 344 U.S.
16 at 231, 233 (quoting *Douglas,* 294 U.S. at 209). It would turn Congress' intent on
17 its head to accept Petitioner's contention that they are unavailable absent proof
18 of commercial purpose and/or actual damages.

A

B

C

D

E

F

A In every court, lawyers need to decide whether to use a party's actual name, some modified version of its name (to achieve a semantic goal), or its procedural name. Names like "plaintiff," "movant," "indemnitor," "petitioner," "appellee," and "defendant–cross-claimant" are harder for readers to keep straight. Even so, at the Supreme Court, a sad convention has emerged of using "Petitioner" and "Respondent," so this brief wisely follows the standard approach.

B The language in this sentence is formal: "for naught," "forecloses," "purview." This sort of style is fine in some courts (including the Supreme Court, where this brief was filed). But in general, keep your language simpler.

C **Rather than beginning with a case — as a student might — the lawyers bludgeon their adversary with statutory commands. The doctrine comes later and is used to confirm that the statute means what the lawyers claim it means.**

D This separate subsection of the statute — 504(c) rather than 504(a) — addresses the second of the student's arguments (i.e., that his conduct was "uninjurious").

E Notice that the *words* of a statute matter rather than the *principles*. Thus, while lawyers can (and are often wise to) quote a case or to explain the legislative goals of a statute, they need to quote statutes to compel a court. Paraphrasing a case can be helpful; less so with a statute.

F This phrase ("turn on its head") is overused — one of law's many tired tropes. Avoid clichés and hunt for fresh phrases. But these phrases are handy, if imperfect, crutches when you are writing under a tight deadline.

Example
4.8

Takeaway point 4.8: When you have few favorable authorities, invoke helpful principles that arose in analogous situations.

Good lawyers are creative — especially when little law addresses (or supports) the exact issues raised by their client's case. These situations require a search for *analogous* authorities. For instance, imagine that a car company auctions off one of its car dealerships. A woman submits the highest bid but still loses. She then sues for sex discrimination. As her lawyer, your search turns up no sex discrimination cases involving standard auctions. Now what?

You need to look for something analogous. For instance, you might cite cases involving *race* discrimination in auctions. Or you might look for other instances in which a woman offered more money than a man but lost out on the opportunity, such as a case in which a property management company was found liable for renting an apartment to a man, even though a woman offered to pay higher rent. Or you might hunt down a case in which a business was found liable for sex discrimination after it hired a male contractor to plow snow, even though a female plow driver offered to do the same job for less money — a different type of auction. And, of course, all of these cases probably would provide valuable *supplemental* support, even if you found a perfectly germane case (i.e., a favorable case involving sex discrimination during a standard auction).

Reasoning by analogy is a critical part of advocacy, and it can take many forms. Think creatively about the analogous principles and situations that support your client's position. To illustrate this advice, we return to the *Jones* case in which the government placed a GPS tracker on a man's car without obtaining a warrant. The applicable test for whether an unlawful search occurred was whether the car's owner had an "expectation of privacy" that was violated when the government used a GPS device to monitor his movements. This passage argues that Jones reasonably expected that no one was monitoring his movements constantly because state law made that same activity illegal for *private* parties.

Source: Car owner's brief from *United States v. Jones*, 132 S. Ct. 945 (2012).

---

1   The reasonableness of Jones's privacy expectations is confirmed by the fact
2   that no private individual could lawfully engage in similar conduct. A private   A
3   individual's surreptitious installation of a GPS tracker onto the property of
4   another to monitor the owner's movements is not only a trespass to chattels, *see*   B
5   Restatement (Second) of Torts § 217(b) & cmt. e (1965), but can form the basis   C
6   for criminal liability under the laws of various states.[3] And the police would cer-
7   tainly not expect that anyone could permissibly affix GPS devices onto city patrol
8   cars to secretly track police movement. For these reasons, the government can-   D
9   not plausibly argue that by installing the GPS device onto Jones's vehicle, it was
10   merely doing what any member of the public could do to any other. No one has
11   the right to affix a GPS device onto another person's vehicle without her consent.

12   3. *See, e.g., People v. Sullivan*, 53 P.3d 1181 (Colo. Ct. App. 2002) (husband using
13   GPS against wife found guilty of harassment by stalking); *L.A.V.H. v. R.J.V.H.*, 2011
14   WL 3477016, at *4 (N.J. Super. Ct. Aug. 10, 2011) (ex-husband's use of GPS to follow
15   and monitor ex-wife constitutes stalking); *M.M. v. J.B.*, 2010 WL 1200329 (Del. Family
16   Ct. Jan. 12, 2010) (father convicted of felony offense of stalking for placing GPS de-
17   vice on mother's vehicle); *Heil v. State*, 888 N.E.2d 875 (Ind. Ct. App. June 12, 2008)
18   (husband convicted of first degree stalking for using GPS device to track his wife).   E

19	And Jones reasonably expected that no one — not private individuals and cer-
20	tainly not the government acting without a warrant — would usurp his property
21	in order to generate and record GPS data about his movements and locations.
22	*See* William J. Stuntz, *The Distribution of Fourth Amendment Privacy,* 67 Geo.
23	Wash. L. Rev. 1265, 1268 (1999) (because the government "can easily condition
24	the citizenry to expect little or no privacy," "Fourth Amendment privacy protec-
25	tion must be tied to something other than what people expect from the police,"
26	and "[t]he law's solution is to tie its protection to what people expect from one
27	another.").

A This excerpt draws an analogy between the government's installation and use of a GPS tracking device on Jones's vehicle and a private individual's performance of the same action.

B Does analogical reasoning matter? Here's how a concurring opinion summarized the majority's decision (which held in Jones's favor): "By attaching a small GPS device to the underside of the vehicle that respondent drove, the law enforcement officers in this case engaged in conduct that might have provided grounds in 1791 for a suit for trespass to chattels. And for this reason, the Court concludes, the installation and use of the GPS device constituted a search." 132 S. Ct. at 957-58 (Alito, J., concurring). Thus, extending an old common law principle to a new technology carried the day in this case.

C The brief shows that private individuals have been prosecuted for engaging in the same conduct that the government contends is constitutional.

D The absurdity of this idea — letting private individuals track patrol cars twenty-four hours a day — demonstrates how to use simple hypothetical situations to advance your argument. That said, the government can routinely do things that private citizens cannot; the lawyers here are careful not to overstate the strength of this analogy, using the term "certainly not expect" rather than something more definitive like "would be illegal."

E The brief could have gone even further — by listing *every* state in which attaching a GPS device to a car would be unlawful. And the lawyers probably considered this approach. Most statutes, however, do not specify whether using GPS qualifies as stalking. Courts would need to decide that issue. Thus, the lawyers stuck with reported cases rather than guessing whether an antistalking statute would cover this activity. They showed admirable restraint.

Notice, too, that the brief does *not* mention whether tracking someone with a GPS would be illegal in the District of Columbia (which is where Jones lived) or in Maryland (which is where the government actually attached the GPS to Jones's car). Why not? Because discussing these jurisdictions' laws would lead to an easy counterpoint and would *undermine* the authorities that Jones cites: the two jurisdictions banned stalking only when it was done to intimidate the victim, so attaching GPS devices secretly could not violate the stalking laws in Washington D.C. or Maryland. Thus, Jones's lawyers, yet again, showed impressive judgment and restraint by omitting Washington D.C.'s and Maryland's unhelpful stalking statutes.

FREQUENTLY ASKED QUESTIONS ABOUT BUILDING AFFIRMATIVE, AUTHORITY-BASED ARGUMENTS

Q. **How many cases should I cite to support each section of a brief or motion?**

A. The real issue is how many cases you should discuss, not how many you should cite. In general, it's worth discussing only a handful of cases in each section — the ones that exert the greatest gravitational tug on your dispute. Beyond that number, it usually makes sense to cite supplemental cases merely to confirm specific, narrower points or to corroborate the premise of your dominant cases. Lawyers often use parenthetical descriptions to discuss nonessential cases quickly (as shown in Examples 4.3, 4.4, and 4.6, among others).

Q. **How much detail should I provide about the cases that are essential to the resolution of my dispute?**

A. You should provide enough information to ensure that the judge knows what happened in the case, how the case came out, why the case came out that way, and why it supports your side. These facets of a good discussion can devour multiple pages or nibble up only a few lines, depending on both the complexity and importance of the case. Unless a case is enormously influential on your dispute, you can probably discuss it sufficiently in a single paragraph (or less).

Q. **Within a given part of my Argument, in what order should I discuss my authorities?**

A. Discuss your most powerful point first, then your second most powerful point, and so on. The word "powerful" refers to the composite strength of a point including (1) how intuitively compelling the point is, (2) how analogous and helpful the authorities are that support that point, and (3) how much sway those authorities exert on your judge. If you are litigating in a federal district court and have a controlling circuit court opinion and a merely persuasive Supreme Court opinion, you will usually begin with the controlling authority (unless some other reason — such as maintaining flow or explaining the evolution of a doctrine — convinces you to put the more-prominent but less-relevant case first). The text of a statute should usually appear before the cases that construe that text.

Q. **May I list my authorities in footnotes?**

A. As noted in Example 4.4 (comment C), I don't recommend it. Try to minimize the number of footnotes in a brief or motion. Also, remember that many jurisdictions will treat a point as being "waived" — not capable of being raised on appeal — if an argument is mentioned only in a footnote, so be wary about relegating a substantive point to a footnote. Footnotes are fine, however, for string cites.

Q. **Should I cite precedent from other jurisdictions?**

A. Yes, but when authorities do not compel an outcome, don't overplay their importance. Instead, focus on the *principles* that compelled those courts, not on *which* courts acted. For instance, this sentence comes from a case in which a plaintiff who failed to opt out of a settlement with a bank later objected to the settlement: "Circuit and District Courts across the country agree that the opt-out right completely protects against any impairment of an absent class member's interests." That sentence emphasizes *who* acted: courts in other jurisdictions. The topic sentence, instead, should have emphasized the *principle,* as in the following revision: "A class member's right to opt out of a settlement completely protects his legal interests. For example, ..." The revision emphasizes the key point rather than the identity of who made that point (i.e., noncontrolling courts). You can signal, however, that your position has been adopted broadly, such as by writing, "Nearly every court to assess this issue has concluded that . . . ." Avoid buzz words such as "control," "must follow," and "requires this Court to" that imply that your judge *needs* to follow these non-controlling authorities.

Q. Should I ever cite authorities such as treatises and law reviews?

A. Yes, but be selective about how you cite them. Emphasize the reasoning and evidence offered in these authorities. Merely telling a court that a professor recommended something will ordinarily gain you little ground unless the treatise or scholar is especially influential within a field (such as Nimmer's treatise on copyright or Areeda's treatise on antitrust). Showing that your adversary's expert wrote an article supporting your position is also helpful — and fun.

One good example of how to use secondary sources comes from a case in which a party challenged a patent. Its brief offered this information from journalists and scholars to suggest that the Patent & Trademark Office rubberstamps nearly all patent applications, but that a closer look at these patents ("reexamination") proves nearly all of them to be invalid:

> Generally, when reexamination occurs, . . . nearly 74% of the time the PTO finds the patent invalid or restricts its claims. Anne Marie Squeo, *BlackBerry Gambles Patent Office Will Be on Its Side in Court*, Wall St. J., Jan. 17, 2006, at B1. This rate is unsurprising given that the overworked PTO can spend a mere 18 hours on average to review a patent application before initial issuance. . . . Cecil D. Quillen, Jr., *Continuing Patent Applications and Performance of the U.S. Patent and Trademark Off.*, 11 Fed. Cir. B.J. 1, 3 (2001) (estimating rate of patent approvals by the PTO to be 97%).

Q. I have a current case that cites an old case for the proposition that I want to establish. Should I cite the new case, the old case, or both?

A. In general, cite newer cases to show judges that the proposition that you want to establish is still followed; older cases may cause judges to wonder whether the law has evolved since your case was decided. You can cite the new authority and then add a parenthetical noting that it cited or quoted an older case. In some instances, however, you'll want to show that a proposition is timeless: cite the old case (or both cases). Citing just an old case and a new case, however, can cause a court to infer that the proposition was not followed during the interval. Thus, if you cite both, consider indicating that the principle is well established or widely followed, such as by using a "see, e.g.," signal (to convey that you are listing only a subset of the available cases) or by adding a parenthetical that states something to indicate that the authority is robust, such as "(citing twenty-six cases that followed this rule)."

Q. How can I best use a case that contains a helpful legal principle but in which the facts are completely different from those in my client's case?

A. Neither emphasize that the case was distinguishable — that's your adversary's job — nor claim that the cases are identical. If the principle from the other case applies to your case, you can usually proceed safely. If the quote sounds good but is from a totally distinct context, be aware that the other side will point out that the quote arose in a different situation and then assess whether you'd be embarrassed if the judge asked you about the other case. Protect your credibility and make preemptive concessions if necessary.

Q. **If a case is helpful on one issue but contains language that supports my adversary's position on a separate issue, should I omit it?**

A. Tread carefully. Lawyers usually scour the authorities cited by their adversaries — as we will see in the next chapter. Once you cite a case, it becomes "yours"; thus, you need to assess whether the benefits of citing the case justify the pain that you'll experience when the other side finds that the very case you cited supports an essential part of its argument. Try to find equally helpful but nontoxic cases. If the tainted case is the only viable option you have, weigh carefully whether it is worth the risk. Similarly, consider whether to milk the venom from the case before the other side can use it.

Chapter 5

Countering Your Adversary's Arguments

We just considered how to build arguments with authorities. We now explore how to dismantle these arguments.

CHAPTER OVERVIEW

1. Build your affirmative argument before you confront the other side's arguments.
2. When your brief or motion raises multiple issues, build your first affirmative argument (as described in Chapter 4) and then counter the other side's points on that issue. Repeat this sequence for each of the other issues.
3. Rebut every nontrivial point that the other side makes. Otherwise, you should brace yourself for opposing lawyers to trumpet your "implicit admission" or "tacit acknowledgment" that their unrebutted points are correct. Learn to counter minor points quickly and decisively.
4. Find some way to show that adverse authorities do not dictate your dispute. Point out, for instance, that an adverse case involved a different law, a different jurisdiction, different facts, different legislative history, different procedural posture, and so on. You must distinguish controlling authorities to avoid dooming your case, but you should also distinguish important persuasive authorities lest those cases beguile your judge.
5. In addition to distinguishing an adverse persuasive authority, *diminish* it, such as by undermining the court's reasoning, by showing that many courts have criticized that opinion, or by revealing the woeful policy implications that the opinion, if followed, would produce.
6. Attack your opponent's research, such as by pointing out flaws in its discussions of authorities and by calling attention to the absence of support for any of its arguments.
7. When your opponent is a repeat offender, bring up his or her past sins. For example, discredit a lawyer who files the same lawsuit repeatedly or a litigant who has raised the same claims (or violated the same law) repeatedly.
8. Search for evidence that the opposing party (or its counsel) has previously agreed with your position.
9. If you are appealing a case, do *not* attack the judge; instead, undermine his or her reasoning firmly but respectfully.
10. Avoid asking courts to overrule a case. Do so only when necessary, and distinguish the adverse precedent, too — or else you are essentially admitting that the precedent bars your argument.

Example 5.1	**Takeaway point 5.1:** Explain what happened in your adversary's best cases and then provide clear, trenchant reasons that these cases should not apply to your dispute.

We begin our exploration of how to counter the other side's arguments by looking at how to distinguish adverse authorities. *Distinguishing* is different from *diminishing*. The former seeks to show that a precedent is inapplicable; the latter seeks to show that a precedent *should* not be applied. The former is like dodging a boxer's punch; the latter involves shrugging it off. Lawyers use both techniques to undermine adverse authorities, but distinguishing is more common, especially when seeking to escape the influence of a harmful controlling authority.

We return to the Facebook dispute. Facebook sought to preserve a settlement that its opponents (the "CU Founders") wanted to void. The CU Founders argued that the settlement was not binding because it specified that Facebook would finalize the agreement later. Facebook countered that the settlement agreement was final and binding, even though the parties still needed to resolve some details (because those details were minor and because the agreement gave Facebook the power to resolve those details). As you will see in the first paragraph below, the description of the adverse case's facts is a bit hard to follow, but Facebook then does a great job distinguishing the case in the second paragraph.

Source: Facebook's brief in *Facebook, Inc. v. Pacific Northwest Software, Inc.*, 640 F.3d 1034 (9th Cir. 2011).

---

1   The one case the CU Founders discuss in support of their position — *Terry*
2   *v. Conlan*, 33 Cal. Rptr. 3d 603 (Ct. App. 2005) — falls into a completely dif-
3   ferent category than *Sheng, Core-Vent*, and this case. In the course of a judi-
4   cially supervised settlement discussion, the parties there assented to some terms
5   expressed orally on the record. Two terms in particular were central to the court's
6   conclusion that "[t]he facts clearly show there was no meeting of the minds on
7   material terms." *Id.* at 613. First, the parties appeared to agree to two irreconcil-
8   able propositions for how a disputed parcel of property would be managed: One
9   term specified that an "*independent trustee* or . . . a manager" would manage the
10 property, while another specified that the "trustee" of the property would be one
11 of the parties to the case, who was obviously not independent. *Id.* at 610 (em-
12 phasis added). Second, the parties agreed that "everyone is going to cooperate to
13 obtain the most favorable tax benefits that everybody can under the framework
14 of the settlement," *id.* at 606 (internal quotation marks omitted), but the parties
15 immediately disagreed on whether they were actually under any obligation to
16 achieve the "favorable tax benefits," and whether the trust must be qualified as
17 a particular form of trust that was mentioned on the record. *Id.* at 613. As to both
18 terms, the trial court imposed on the parties its own Solomonic arrangement that
19 no one had agreed to. *Id.* at 611, 613.
20   *Terry* is distinguishable for several reasons. First, unlike *Terry*, the parties here
21 explicitly addressed the question of what structure the transaction would take,
22 and agreed to vest one party with the discretion to determine that structure. ER 483.
23 Second, in *Terry*, unlike here, the parties indicated that the tax treatment and the
24 management were material to them by referring to them in . . . the agreement;
25 it was just impossible to know *what* they agreed as to those terms. Third, the

A
B

C
D

E

26 agreement in Terry was so ambiguous that it left the trial court "with no other
27 option than to fill in the gaps of the agreement to enforce settlement," 33 Cal.
28 Rptr. 3d at 614, whereas here the Settlement Agreement was so clear that the
29 district court was able to enforce it without crafting any additional terms . . . . —F
30   In the end, this case boils down to a fundamental question about the viabil-
31 ity of mediation in settling a high-stakes dispute. This Court would deal a mortal —G
32 blow to mediation if it were to accept the CU Founders' position that a com-
33 plex litigation can never be settled without resolving a laundry list of ancillary
34 terms that are "'typically' addressed 'in formal acquisition documents,'" OB 69
35 (quoting expert at ER 760), and that settlements are vulnerable unless lawyers
36 show up at mediations with a "laptop . . . [and] a draft of a possible settlement
37 agreement," OB 54. That is not how mediation works. The best mediators, from
38 JAMS to judges, follow the practice that Mr. Piazza [who mediated the Facebook —H
39 dispute] displayed: the art of "getting to yes" on the terms the parties consider
40 material, and securing a binding agreement on those terms.

A This technique — pointing out that the other side lacks abundant authorities — is common. While it is better to have one great case than fifty marginal ones, the number of authorities can signal to a court whether a legal argument is novel or well established.

B These are cases that Facebook had discussed earlier: it *first* showed why its position is correct. *Then* it dealt with the other side's argument. Follow this approach, which this book refers to as the "affirmative to negative" principle, meaning that you should generally advance your argument before you respond to (or anticipate) the other side's objections.

C The brief omits a critical detail: why the appellate court reversed. The discussion would be more helpful to readers if it explained the appellate court's reasoning. But the lawyers also want to avoid giving too much air time to the other side's best case.

D We learn immediately what this paragraph will establish. This sort of clear topic sentence is exemplary, but many lawyers like to be subtler when they are distinguishing cases, preferring to distinguish without using the word "distinguish." The brief distinguishes *Terry* based on the factual difference between the two cases.

E Earlier in the brief, Facebook explained that the settlement said that Facebook could finalize the deal in whatever form it wanted.

F **This point is Facebook's best one — and is the main reason that this book reprints part of Facebook's brief. As shown here, a single detail can undermine the other side's main authorities; the best way to distinguish a case is usually by making one or two sharp strikes rather than by pointing out a heap of ticky-tack differences.**

G This paragraph basically makes a policy argument (*see* Chapter 9, which shows more examples of policy arguments). But it does so to further the discussion about why *Terry* should not govern this case: namely, parties need to be able to end their lawsuits without hammering out every conceivable detail in the settlement agreement. Having distinguished *Terry*, Facebook now diminishes its allure.

H This phrase reflects a catchy use of alliteration. The authors presume that readers are familiar with JAMS, which is one of the nation's preeminent organizations of mediators.

| Example 5.2 | **Takeaway point 5.2:** Take special pains to distinguish the other side's best case, even if you need to dive into that case's record or into academic commentary about that case. |

We just looked at a brief that distinguished an adverse authority quickly and incisively. But distinguishing adverse cases sometimes requires you to drill deeper into the adverse authority — especially when a single adverse authority looms over your dispute. Just remember that spending multiple pages on an adverse authority signals to judges that the case is important and harmful, or else you would not spend so much time addressing it.

In the following example, a woman in California grew marijuana for herself. She claimed that she was using it as medicine (which is legal under California law). But in 2002, federal Drug Enforcement Administration (DEA) agents came to her home and destroyed her cannabis plants, even though she was not selling the drug to other people. She filed a lawsuit against the U.S. Attorney General and the head of the DEA, seeking relief against the officers' actions. The district court rejected her suit, but the Ninth Circuit reversed, holding that the Controlled Substances Act (CSA) exceeded the federal government's Commerce Clause authority when applied to personal, local, noncommercial cultivation of marijuana. But the Supreme Court reversed again, holding that the CSA's ban on growing marijuana for oneself is within Congress's powers. In spite of the outcome, the following discussion reflects a great attempt to counter an adverse case — *Wickard v. Filburn*, 317 U.S. 111 (1942) — that allowed Congress to regulate the amount of wheat that a farmer could grow.

Source: Amicus brief for several states from *Gonzales v. Raich*, 545 U.S. 1 (2005).

---

1   Despite superficial similarities, this case is not a *Wickard* redux. The Gov-
2   ernment's description of *Wickard* as a case about a lone farmer's "home-grown
3   production of wheat" (U.S. Br. 37) for his own "personal use" (U.S. Br. 16)
4   is, with respect, an oversimplification. It is just not true that it is "impossible
5   to distinguish the relevant conduct surrounding the cultivation and use of the
6   marijuana crop at issue in this case from the cultivation and use of the wheat
7   crop that affected interstate commerce in" *Wickard*. U.S. Br. 8 (quoting Pet. App.
8   26a). Understanding why not — and, correlatively, why the Government's argu-
9   ment would carry the Court well beyond *Wickard* and into uncharted Commerce-
10 Clause waters — requires a fuller understanding of the economic and agricultural
11 facts underlying *Wickard* than the Government's brief provides.

12   As noted, the aggregation principle, as announced in *Wickard* and as
13 reiterated in subsequent cases, permits a reviewing court to consider the effect
14 on interstate commerce of an individual litigant's conduct "taken together with
15 that of many others similarly situated." *Wickard*, 317 U.S. at 127-28. Accord-
16 ingly, the first order of business in understanding aggregation is discerning what,
17 exactly, Roscoe Filburn was doing on his farm such that his conduct, when
18 "taken together with that of many others similarly situated" to him, would
19 substantially affect interstate commerce.

20   He was *not* just baking bread. There is a persistent myth — to which the
21 Government's brief seems to subscribe — that *Wickard* stands for the proposi-
22 tion that "wheat a farmer bakes into bread and eats at home is part of 'interstate
23 commerce'" subject to congressional regulation. *Village of Oconomowoc Lake*
24 *v. Dayton Hudson Corp.* 24 F.3d 962, 965 (7th Cir. 1994). The myth is just that:

A

B

25	a myth — an urban (or rural, as the case may be) legend. As one scholar has
26	noted, "Farmer Filburn was not an organic home baker who had decided to raise
27	wheat for a few loaves of bread"; rather, he "raised wheat commercially and
28	regularly sold a portion" of his crop on the open market. Deborah Jones Merritt,
29	*Commerce!*, 94 Mich. L. Rev. 674, 748-49 (1995). Indeed, the math shows that
30	"[t]o consume the 239 excess bushels at issue in the July 1941 wheat harvest,
31	the Filburns would have had to consume nearly forty-four one-pound loaves of
32	bread each day for the following year." Jim Chen, *Filburn's Legacy*, 52 Emory
33	L.J. 1719, 1759 (2003).
34	Far from organic home baker, Roscoe Filburn owned and operated a large
35	and multifaceted farming operation. As to scope, this Court's opinion reflects
36	that Filburn's annual "wheat acreage allotment" under the Agricultural Adjust-
37	ment Act ("AAA") was 11.1 acres, at a normal yield of 20.1 bushels of wheat per
38	acre, for a total of more than 223 bushels. 317 U.S. at 114. Filburn planted an
39	additional 11.9 acres and harvested an additional 239 bushels, bringing his total
40	harvest to 462 bushels (or 27,720 pounds) of wheat. *Id.* Notably, the marketing
41	quota at issue in *Wickard* applied only to large farms; it expressly exempted
42	"any farm on which the normal production of the acreage planted to wheat was
43	less than 200 bushels." *Id.* at 130 n.30. Plainly, then, Filburn was no small player.
44	Had he been the organic baker of legend, his case never would have arisen;
45	Congress had not even attempted to extend its regulatory reach to activities so
46	local in character.

A Avoid major concessions. This phrase, for example, merely acknowledges that the similarities are "superficial," making this sentence a safe concession.

B The tone of the brief is informal, almost conversational — a choice that offers both benefits and risks. Research, for example, suggests that some judges may disfavor this approach, but the style makes the brief enjoyable and engaging. Before including light touches in your filings, make sure that your judge isn't stodgy and that the stylistic touches represent a deliberate strategy.

C In general, avoid humor in briefs.

D Notice that the brief doesn't overplay the value of legal scholarship: it simply uses it to establish factual points. That said, by turning to scholars rather than *Wickard* itself, the brief tacitly signals that the opinion falls in line with the other side's reading. Watch out for the signals that you convey to judges about whether an authority supports your client.

E **This brief now drills into *Wickard*'s record to set up the argument that *Wickard* involved a greater effect on commerce than the personal use of marijuana in *Raich*. Notice how carefully the lawyers studied *Wickard* to figure out how to undermine it.**

F Why is this detail so helpful? It suggests that *Wickard*'s supposed holding — that Congress can regulate agricultural products grown for personal use — is in fact a dictum because Congress did not try to regulate personal use in such a case. Footnote 30 of *Wickard* provided a solid way for these lawyers to distinguish the other side's best case. Mimic their stellar and careful reading of adverse opinions. This excellent point, however, gets consumed by the detailed calculations that precede it. When you calculate figures, keep the paragraph as short as possible and don't place anything important later in the paragraph because readers may otherwise tune out by the time they get to your key point.

Example
5.3

Takeaway point 5.3: Don't just distinguish: *devalue* the other side's most important persuasive authorities.

The two previous examples showed you how to distinguish a case. Now let's look at how to *diminish* adverse authority. To do so, help readers see why the other side's key cases are badly reasoned, dangerous, contrary to the trend of judicial authority, or otherwise flawed. Both techniques — distinguishing and devaluing — are key strategies to counter the other side's arguments.

The following passage comes from a case involving three drug smugglers. One, Michael Adams, was convicted. The other two smugglers testified against Adams in exchange for lighter sentences. On appeal, Adams challenged his conviction, claiming that the government had violated a federal statute, 18 U.S.C. § 201, by offering the other two smugglers reduced sentences in exchange for favorable testimony. Section 201 prohibits "promis[ing] anything of value" to "influence . . . testimony under oath." Adams found two cases (*Lowery* and *Singleton*) that agreed with his reading of § 201, and his brief trumpeted those two authorities. Here, the government obliterates those two cases.

Source: Government's brief in *United States v. Adams*, 176 F.3d 493 (11th Cir. 1999).

1	Adams's entire argument with respect to section 201 rests on *United States v.*
2	*Lowery,* No. 97-368-Cr-ZIoch (S.D. Fla. 1998), which, in turn, relies for support
3	on *United States v. Singleton,* 144 F.3d 1343 (10th Cir. 1998), which the Tenth Cir-
4	cuit vacated and set for rehearing en banc within ten days of the panel's issuance
5	of its opinion. The *Singleton* opinion has since been criticized and disapproved
6	by nearly every court in the country that has considered it. [The brief cites seven
7	cases here.]
8	Second, the *Singleton* panel acknowledged that its ruling conflicted with the
9	law of the Eleventh Circuit. . . .
10	Third, Congress first enacted a version of section 201 as part of its revision
11	of the criminal code in 1948. Since enacting [section 201], Congress has estab-
12	lished a statutory and regulatory scheme that not only permits, but affirmatively
13	encourages, the United States to offer leniency and other benefits to cooper-
14	ating witnesses to obtain their testimony. Indeed, the Supreme Court recently
15	noted that two federal rules, Fed. R. Crim. P. 11 and Fed. R. Evid. 410, have the
16	"goal of encouraging plea bargaining." *United States v. Mezzanatto,* 513 U.S. 196,
17	207 (1995). As the Court recognized in *Mezzanatto,* plea bargaining frequently
18	requires the prosecutor to decide "whether to extend leniency or full immunity
19	to some suspects in order to procure testimony against other, more dangerous
20	suspects" because "prosecutors often need help from the small fish in a con-
21	spiracy in order to catch the big ones." 513 U.S. at 207, 208. Accordingly, Rule
22	11 allows prosecutors to seek dismissal of other charges, agree on sentencing
23	issues, and make other "promises" in a plea agreement that must be disclosed to
24	and accepted by the court. Fed. R. Crim. P. 11 (d, e, g). Rule 11 recognizes "the
25	propriety of plea discussions" and that "a plea agreement may also contribute to
26	the successful prosecution of other more serious offenders." *See* 1974 Advisory
27	Committee Notes.
28	Similarly, the Sentencing Reform Act of 1984, as amended, contains three
29	provisions authorizing sentencing reduction — upon government motion — for

A

B

C

30 cooperators who provide "substantial assistance in the investigation *or prosecu-*
31 *tion* of another" criminal (emphasis added). See 18 U.S.C. § 3553(e) (reduction
32 below minimum statutory sentence); 28 U.S.C. § 994(n) (requiring Sentencing
33 Commission to allow guideline reductions); Fed. R. Crim. P. 35(b) (reduction for
34 post-sentencing cooperation). . . .

35 Moreover, before and after enacting section 201(c)(2) and its predecessors,
36 Congress authorized prosecutors to confer immunity on witnesses in return for
37 testimony. *See Kastigar v. United States,* 406 U.S. 441, 445-47 (1972) (outlining
38 history of immunity statutes dating back to Eighteenth Century). The current
39 immunity statutes, 18 U.S.C. §§ 6001-6005, specifically allow federal prosecu-
40 tors to give immunity to witnesses to obtain testimony in any judicial pro-
41 ceeding. . . .

42 Likewise, the Witness Relocation and Protection Act authorizes the Attorney
43 General to give things of value — housing, payment of living expenses, and
44 other services — in return for a witness's agreement "to testify" and provide
45 cooperation. . . .

46 As the *Singleton* panel itself acknowledged, 144 F.3d at 1356-58, no court
47 has found that the government violates section 201(c)(2) by providing leniency
48 in return for truthful testimony. Instead, every federal court of appeals with
49 jurisdiction over criminal cases has allowed, and trusted juries to evaluate, testi-
50 mony of cooperating government witnesses testifying in return for sentencing or
51 financial considerations. For example, in *United States v. Valle-Ferrerr,* 739 F.2d
52 545, 546-547 (11th Cir. 1984), this Court sustained testimony from a witness
53 who was a paid government informant. *See also* [ten other cases]. . . .

54 [Finally, the] panel's conclusion plainly works absurd results. The United
55 States relies on witnesses who testify in return for leniency in literally thousands
56 of cases each year, including major cases such as the Oklahoma City bomb-
57 ing prosecutions. Without such testimony, the government could not success-
58 fully enforce the drug laws, could not prosecute organized crime figures under
59 RICO, and could not prosecute many other cases "of such a character that the
60 only persons capable of giving useful testimony are those implicated in the
61 crime." *Kastigar,* 406 U.S. at 446. . . . Consequently, Adams's argument that
62 the government violated section 201 by entering into plea agreements with his
63 co-defendants in which they agreed to provide truthful testimony must fail.

A The brief emphasizes that the Tenth Circuit itself gasped when *Singleton* was decided (by vacating the case and rehearing it en banc almost immediately).

B While I have omitted the string cite to save space, this spot in the brief is a perfect place to add a string cite to show that many courts have rejected *Singleton*.

C Remember where you are litigating. The government noticed that *Singleton* (Tenth Circuit) acknowledged that the Eleventh Circuit had reached a contrary conclusion. Thus, wisely, this brief emphasizes that fact to the Eleventh Circuit.

D This passage reflects a blunderbuss attack against *Singleton*: it raises doctrinal arguments, statutory arguments, rule-based arguments, and policy arguments. You do not need to challenge so aggressively every case that your adversary cites, but undermining its best case (as well as distinguishing it) usually proves valuable.

| Example 5.4 | **Takeaway point 5.4:** Point out the absence of authority for the other side's position and any meaningful errors in what it says about its authorities. |

Attack your opponent's research in two ways. First, call attention to the absence of support for its position. For instance, one litigant submitted a reply brief observing, "Plaintiff bases its entire conclusory claim on nothing more than an unreported decision from the District of Montana that has never been followed by any other case and has since been vacated . . . ." Second, undermine the authorities that the other side *does* cite — not just by undermining those cases (as in Example 5.3), but also by showing that those cases do not say what your adversary claims. The following example demonstrates both techniques, reflecting that good lawyers will (i) pummel you if you fail to cite authorities and (ii) dissect and demolish the authorities you *do* cite. Thus, ensure that the legal support for your position is ample, strong, and resilient.

This case arose when a city in Alaska started to tax some of the boats that docked in its ports. The tax law was written in a way that caused the tax to fall exclusively on large oil tankers. Polar Tankers, which owned large oil tankers, challenged the tax, alleging that it violated the U.S. Constitution's Tonnage Clause — a provision that prevents states from discriminating against specific ships or shipowners. (Even the creative spark to *think* of the obscure Tonnage Clause reflects stellar, innovative advocacy.) This brief persuaded the Supreme Court that the tax was an unconstitutional violation of the Clause.

Source: Shipowners' reply brief from *Polar Tankers, Inc. v. City of Valdez*, 557 U.S. 1 (2009).

---

1 The City is unable to identify a single decision — in this Court or elsewhere
2 — in which a discriminatory *ad valorem* tax on vessels has been upheld. And
3 it is able to construct its argument only by omitting from its quotations of this
4 Court's opinions unfavorable or limiting language. In fact, when the Court has
5 discussed the "settled" rule on the constitutionality of generally applicable prop-
6 erty taxes, it has explicitly noted that vessels were not treated less favorably
7 than other personal property. *See Moran v. New Orleans*, 112 U.S. 69, 74 (1884)
8 (vessels "valued as other property in the State"); *Transp. Co. v. Wheeling*, 99
9 U.S. 273, 284 (1879) (vessels "taxed in the same manner as the other property");
10 *The Passenger Cases*, 48 U.S. (7 How.) at 402 (vessels treated "the same as other
11 property"); *see also* Pet. Br. 17-18.
12 The same is true of the "leading early commentators on the Constitution"
13 invoked by the City. Three of the four treatises cited by Valdez refer to the non-
14 discrimination criterion in the very excerpts quoted by the City at Br. 19.[3] The
15 fourth quotation, which Valdez attributes to Justice Story's *Commentaries*, did
16 not, in fact, originate with Justice Story; it is an editor's note to the fifth edition of
17 the Story treatise, published more than 40 years after the Justice's death. *See* 1 J.
18 Story, *Commentaries on the Constitution of the United States*, at v (M.M. Bigelow,

---

19   3. Miller, *supra*, at 254 (a vessel "is liable to be taxed *like any other property* that
20 [the owner] may possess.") (emphasis added); T.M. Cooley, *A Treatise on the Con-*
21 *stitutional Limitations* 689-691 (7th ed. 1908) (vessels "may be taxed *like other prop-*
22 *erty*") (emphasis added); W.H. Burroughs, *A Treatise on the Law of Taxation* 91 (1877)
23 ("The prohibition only comes into play where they are not taxed *in the same manner*
24 *as other property* of citizens of the State. . . .") (emphasis added).

25	Bigelow, ed., 5th ed. 1891) (explaining the significance of lettered footnotes). That
26	editor deferred to Judge Hare for further discussion of the Tonnage Clause. *Id.*
27	§ 1016, at 738 n.(a). Judge Hare, in turn, unequivocally stated that, under the Ton-
28	nage Clause, "[s]hips cannot be singled out by a State for taxation." 1 J.I.C. Hare,
29	*American Constitutional Law* 253 (1889).

A The brief explains *ad valorem* taxes in an earlier section. *Ad valorem* is a tax based on the value of a piece of property.

B Define the terms of the debate in ways that favor your client — even if you have to narrow and qualify your claims. For example, the highlighted passage merely states that there has not been a (i) *discriminatory* tax of a (ii) *specific kind* (i.e., *ad valorem*) that (iii) applied to *vessels* (as opposed to other property), and (iv) that reached a final, favorable judicial judgment.

C This passage makes two very clever moves simultaneously: it criticizes the City for failing to cite authorities, and it uses the City's own quotations against it. This tactic is the result of good research; where another lawyer may have seen an ellipsis and assumed something irrelevant or uninteresting had been omitted, Polar Tankers found an argument. Be wary, however, about making allegations against the other side's integrity without providing evidence. Here, an example would have proved helpful. The lawyers presumably did not want to dwell on the other side's errors — such digressions can derail an argument's flow. One solution in extreme cases: lawyers could (if the court rules do not prevent this approach) attach a separate appendix showing each of the misleading quotes submitted by the other side. Few judges want to read so much detail, but that approach would let judges see the other side's mischief without fattening the brief. *See* Example 14.2, lines 44–45.

D Notice that the brief does not repeat the City's argument. Repeating an argument risks burning it into a reader's memory. Even so, attacking an argument without restating the argument increases the risk that readers won't understand your point. Thus, I recommend reminding readers what the other side argued when responding to its arguments, but frame the argument in your client's favor as if it were an affirmative argument.

E The brief molds these three quotations so that they are pithy, punchy, and pertinent. Keep quotes short, when possible — especially when you actually want readers to read them.

F In a reply brief, lawyers can steer a judge back to their opening brief. *See* Chapter 15.

G The prior paragraph of this brief attacks the City for its dearth of cases; this sentence launches a paragraph that shreds the authorities that the City *does* cite. In the real world, smart, aggressive lawyers will skewer you for your errors.

H Polar Tankers has landed a stinging blow: the Justice never wrote this quotation, which was issued long after his death. Out-research your adversaries or they will out-research you. That said — and this is critical — do not confuse a blow that stings the other side from one that knocks it out. Good research is helpful. But it is infinitely more vital to build an *affirmative* case: to present facts and arguments that compel a favorable outcome rather than to weaken the other side's case.

I Notice that the first two quotes are ambiguous: what does it mean to say that a boat may be taxed "like" other property? A town may choose to tax homes but not cars; by analogy, these treatises could be read to say "cities may tax boats however they want — just like they could do with other property." Rather than dwell on the ambiguity, however, Polar Tankers wisely construes the quotes in its favor and shunts them to a footnote so that readers are less likely to dwell on the ambiguity.

J Footnote 3 disposes three of the four quotations. Then the brief obliterates the fourth quotation in the highlighted text, showing that the relevant treatise helps Polar Tankers, not the City.

Example **5.5**	**Takeaway point 5.5:** An adversary's past misdeeds undermine its credibility and improve the likelihood that your client will get a favorable result.

No one likes a repeat offender. If your opponent is such a character, make sure the judge knows it. Pointing out the other side's repeated misconduct can win credibility battles and motivate a court to act in your client's favor. Example 3.1 showed you how to discredit a repeat offender in a Statement of Facts, but you can also use this technique in your Argument. Discovering that a plaintiff — or even an amicus — serially files lawsuits is easier than ever because online research databases now make it possible to search for a party's (or lawyer's) name in case filings. Even better, at least one legal database (Bloomberg) already has compiled party-specific docket sheets *by topic*; thus, with a few clicks of a mouse, you can find heaps of cases in which a given company was sued for a specific misdeed. The next two examples show how to target adversaries for a pattern of misbehavior.

In the following case, a jury in Louisiana convicted Juan Smith of murder. The prosecutors, however, failed to turn over information showing that their star witness, who identified the defendant from the witness stand, had previously told police that *he had not seen the murderer*. The Supreme Court's opinion in *Brady v. Maryland* requires prosecutors to disclose this sort of exculpatory information. Here, Smith's lawyers show the Supreme Court that this ethical lapse was not an accident.

Source: Juan Smith's brief in *Smith v. Cain*, 132 S. Ct. 627 (2012).

---

1 This Court is already familiar with the long and disturbing history of *Brady*
2 violations in Orleans Parish during the tenure of district attorney Harry Connick.
3 *See, e.g., Connick v. Thompson,* 131 S. Ct. 1350, 1356-1357 (2011); *id.* at 1382
4 (Ginsburg, J., dissenting) (describing the "culture of inattention to *Brady* in Or-
5 leans Parish"). In four cases in which defendants were sentenced to death dur-
6 ing Connick's tenure, appellate courts (including, on one occasion, this Court)
7 have found *Brady* violations and overturned the convictions. *See Kyles,* 514 U.S.
8 at 421-422; *State v. Bright,* 875 So. 2d 37, 44-45 (La. 2004); *State v. Cousin,* 710
9 So. 2d 1065, 1066 n.2 (La. 1998); *State v. Thompson,* 825 So. 2d 552, 557 (La. Ct.
10 App. 2002). In numerous other cases, moreover, appellate courts have vacated
11 non-capital convictions for *Brady* violations. *See, e.g., State v. Knapper,* 579 So.
12 2d 956, 961 (La. 1991); *State v. Rosiere,* 488 So. 2d 965, 969-971 (La. 1986); *State*
13 *v. Perkins,* 423 So. 2d 1103, 1107-1108 (La. 1982); *State v. Curtis,* 384 So. 2d 396,
14 398 (La. 1980); *State v. Falkins,* 356 So. 2d 415, 417 (La.), cert. denied, 439 U.S.
15 865 (1978); *State v. Carney,* 334 So. 2d 415, 418-419 (La. 1976); *State v. Lindsey,*
16 844 So. 2d 961, 969-970 (La. Ct. App. 2003).
17 In *Kyles* — decided shortly before petitioner's trial — this Court overturned
18 an Orleans Parish capital conviction based on the prosecution's failure to dis-
19 close multiple pieces of exculpatory evidence. *See* 514 U.S. at 421-422. In so
20 doing, the Court warned prosecutors to err on the side of disclosure in order to
21 avoid *Brady* violations. *See id.* at 439. That warning, however, appears to have
22 gone unheeded in Orleans Parish: when Connick was asked many years later
23 about the effects of *Kyles* on his office's practices, he responded that he "saw no
24 need, occasioned by *Kyles,* to make any changes." *Connick,* 131 S. Ct. at 1382
25 (Ginsburg, J., dissenting). Connick's successor as district attorney, Eddie Jordan,

A

B
C

26 confirmed that "[t]he previous administration had a policy of keeping away as
27 much information as possible from the defense attorney." Gwen Filosa, *Jordan*
28 *Targets Backlog of Cases; Volunteer Lawyers To Pitch In, DA Says*, New Orleans
29 Times-Picayune, Feb. 25, 2003, at A1.

30   In addition, the lead prosecutor in petitioner's case, Roger Jordan, was sanc-
31 tioned by the Louisiana Supreme Court for committing the underlying *Brady* vio-
32 lation in *Cousin*, one of the cases in which capital convictions were overturned
33 during Connick's tenure. *See In re Jordan*, 913 So. 2d 775, 782 (La. 2005). The
34 Louisiana Supreme Court noted that it had never previously disciplined a pros-
35 ecutor for a *Brady* violation. *Id.* at 781. The court observed, however, that the
36 evidence at issue — as in this case, a prior statement by the prosecution's only
37 eyewitness casting doubt on the veracity of that witness's identification — was
38 "clearly exculpatory." *Id.* at 782. The court accordingly suspended Jordan from
39 the practice of law for three months. *Id.* at 784. Notably, Jordan was assigned the
40 case for which he was sanctioned in the summer of 1995, *id.* at 778 — roughly
41 the same time he was assigned petitioner's case.

A This example starts with authority that the Court can't dispute — its own opinion from the prior Term. This opening also sets the theme: this case isn't just a stray *Brady* allegation, but the latest violation in a series.

B **We see here another benefit of a string cite (which we considered in Chapter 4). Citing so many cases might ordinarily be unnecessary, but here the bulk of violations underscores that a *pattern* of violations has occurred.**

C This detail about the timing of *Kyles* is doubly valuable. First, readers will infer that the prosecutors would be just as likely to violate their duty to disclose evidence in Smith's case as they were in *Kyles*. Second, the brief insinuates that this county's prosecutors brazenly committed *Brady* violations immediately after the Supreme Court ordered them to stop violating *Brady*. And this fact will irk the Court; judges seethe when parties ignore their orders.

D The brief draws on Connick's statements (as reported by Justice Ginsburg in a prior case) to discredit him. You should mine cases and news articles for *information* (and not just authorities) that can help your clients.

E Information should generally be organized from "general to specific," and this passage exemplifies that technique. The prior paragraphs looked at the pattern from all of Orleans Parish. Now, the brief narrows its attack to a single prosecutor.

F Innuendo is often more powerful than allegation. The brief could have written that "a reasonable onlooker would infer that if Jordan was violating *Brady* in one case, he was probably doing so in a concurrent case." But this brief sticks to facts, and lets readers form their own conclusions. Yet again, *showing* is more convincing than *telling*. Notice that the critical "hint" appears at the end of the paragraph to ensure that readers won't overlook it.

Example
5.6

Takeaway point 5.6: Showing that opposing counsel has filed the same case repeatedly and unsuccessfully damages his or her credibility.

Here is another example of an effective attack, this time targeting counsel. The next example arose after purchasers of an antibiotic drug (Cipro) sued the drug's manufacturer, Bayer. They alleged that Bayer had violated California's antitrust laws when it settled an earlier case to avoid competing against rivals: under that earlier settlement, Bayer allegedly paid a generic drug manufacturer several hundred million dollars not to manufacture a generic version of Cipro. Bayer then promptly raised the price of Cipro by 16 percent. In this brief, Bayer argues in favor of immunizing it from antitrust liability for its settlement agreement; more specifically, it counters arguments that a group of law professors, led by one of the nation's top intellectual property experts, raised in an amicus brief.

Source: Bayer's supplemental brief in *In re Cipro Cases I and II*, 200 Cal. App. 4th 442 (Ct. App. 2011) (record citations omitted).

1   Professor Mark A. Lemley ("Lemley") has authored an amicus brief on behalf
2 of a group of professors (collectively "Amici") supporting plaintiffs. . . .
3   Lemley has filed numerous briefs on behalf of various professors making the
4 same argument made here. Indeed, much of the current brief has been taken
5 verbatim from the prior briefs. But no court has ever agreed with (or even cited)
6 a Lemley brief, much less granted the relief requested. Here is the track record :

    A

Case	Party	Date	Relief Requested	Result
Tamoxifen 2d Circuit No. 03-7641	37 Professors	12/5/2005	Grant rehearing	Rehearing denied
Tamoxifen Supreme Ct. 2007 WL 527488	41 Professors	2/15/2007	Grant certiorari	Certiorari denied
Cipro-III Federal Circuit 2008 WL 644392	28 Professors	2/28/2008	Reverse *Cipro-II*	*Cipro-II* Affirmed
Cipro-III Supreme Ct.	54 Professors	4/24/2009	Grant centiorari	Centiorari denied
Cipro-IV 2d Circuit No. 05-2852	86 Professors	5/20/2010	Grant rehearing	Rehearing denied

7   B
10   C
16   D
20   E

22   . . . . [A]mici fail to address many of the dispositive issues in this case.
23 The brief ignores California law and does not cite a single California case.
24 Amici do not state what legal rule they propose this court should adopt. They
25 acknowledge that they "differ in their views on precisely what standard should be
26 applied to judge the legality of exclusionary settlements." Nonetheless, they ask
27 the court to impose liability on defendants without considering the substantial
28 issues of federal preemption and exclusive patent jurisdiction that such a holding
29 would implicate.

    F

30 Amici also ignore the key facts of this case, never citing the record. They
31 ignore that the Cipro patent at issue claimed the drug's active ingredient. Because
32 a generic drug must have the same active ingredient as the pioneer drug it copies,
33 all generic versions of Cipro infringed Bayer's patent, a fact to which the generic
34 challenger, Barr, stipulated. The settlement thus did not exceed the exclusionary
35 effect of the patent itself.

G

36 Amici further ignore that Bayer repeatedly defeated subsequent challenges to
37 the validity of its Cipro patent. After the settlement, Bayer submitted its patent for
38 reexamination before the Patent and Trademark Office ("PTO"), which reaffirmed
39 the claims relating to Cipro. Bayer then defeated three district court challenges by
40 other generics: two on motions for summary judgment, which were affirmed by
41 the Federal Circuit, and one after a bench trial, which the losing generic did not
42 appeal. The strength of Bayer's patent may explain why the plaintiffs here did not
43 allege that the patent was invalid or unenforceable in any way.

44 In sum, Amici mischaracterize the law, fail to address controlling legal issues,
45 and ignore the facts of record.

A The brief *begins* by trying to discredit the author — an *ad hominem* attack. In general, lawyers should avoid this technique — and judges consistently state that they dislike quarreling. But these attacks sometimes make sense. As one top judge admitted, he *"forgot all about the legal issues when he read a spat between lawyers."* And, for a defendant on trial or for a party that wants to get a summary affirmance on appeal, having the judge forget about the legal issues might prove helpful.

B Inexperienced lawyers generally avoid tables, pictures, graphs, and other multimedia tools that help readers to absorb information. That's a mistake. Your goal is to win — and if a table, picture, chart, or video helps you to do that, use it. Example 6.5 also demonstrates this technique.

C The column to the far right shows that, in each instance, the court did exactly the opposite of what Lemley requested.

D This line and the next two hint that the amici have been targeting Bayer because amici sought to meddle in the Cipro litigation, which involved Bayer.

E WARNING! As illustrated by the table, more and more professors had joined Lemley's amicus briefs. Bayer would probably counter "who cares?" Even so, the increasing support for Lemley's position might cause some judges to wonder whether his briefs raised valid points.

F This portion of the brief reflects a skill discussed earlier in the chapter — attacking absences and omissions of evidence — thus showing how legal-writing techniques can and should be used alongside one another.

G Having damaged amici's credibility, Bayer takes several additional jabs at the amicus brief.

Example 5.7	**Takeaway point 5.7:** Try to give the court a way to decide in your client's favor without overruling past cases — but, when absolutely necessary, ask the court to overrule itself.

Courts do not like overruling their prior opinions. They would greatly prefer to distinguish your case from the adverse case or to find some alternative ground on which to rule, such as a procedural defect (e.g., a lack of jurisdiction or of standing). But when necessary, ask a court to overrule a case.

We look again at the case in which the government placed a GPS device on a suspect's car without a warrant. Two prior opinions posed major problems for the car's owner, who wanted the Court to vacate his conviction and to exclude the evidence gathered by the GPS device. Those cases — *Knotts* and *Karo* — held that the government was able to place a "beeper" (a rudimentary tracking device that worked only when police remained in close proximity) in a container of chemicals and to use the beeper to track suspects along public highways. The *Jones* Court ultimately distinguished *Karo* from *Jones*. Even so, Jones's lawyers were rightly scared of these opinions, both because they upheld the government's attempt to track a suspect and because the opinions contained problematic dicta. Thus, Jones's lawyers both distinguished those cases and, to be safe, asked the Court to overrule those opinions.

Source: Car owner's brief from *United States v. Jones*, 132 S. Ct. 945 (2012).

---

1 **2. *Knotts* And *Karo* Did Not Involve The Features That**
2 **Make GPS Surveillance A Search**

3 To be sure, *Knotts* states that a "person traveling in an automobile on public
4 thoroughfares has no reasonable expectation of privacy in his movements from
5 one place to another." 460 U.S. at 281. But the Court "must read this and related
6 general language in [*Knotts* and *Karo*] as [it] often read[s] general language in
7 judicial opinions — as referring in context to circumstances similar to the circum-
8 stances then before the Court and not referring to quite different circumstances
9 that the Court was not then considering." *Lidster*, 540 U.S. at 424. *Knotts*'s general
10 language should be understood as applying to visual surveillance augmented by
11 technology that did not involve (i) a challenged, unauthorized physical intru-
12 sion onto and usurpation of another's property, (ii) the realistic threat of mass
13 and unending monitoring, or (iii) the acquisition of unique satellite-generated
14 digital data. But if the Court were to conclude, contrary to its customary manner
15 of reading prior decisions, that *Knotts* and *Karo* establish a more general prin-
16 ciple that governs this case, then they should be confined to their specific facts
17 and otherwise overruled. General language written thirty years ago — and at a
18 time when the seamless, perpetual surveillance that GPS makes possible was
19 merely "science fiction," *Cuevas-Perez*, 640 F.3d at 279 (Flaum, J., concurring in
20 the judgment) — should not be stretched beyond the facts on which they were
21 based.

A
B

C

D

E

A When terrible language conflicts with your position, confront it. Build your affirmative case before doing so — this passage, for instance, appeared near the end of Jones's brief, after Jones had built his own affirmative argument. But then acknowledge the adverse authority. When you hide from bad cases, your adversary will point out your furtive conduct, and the court will infer that you have no response to the problematic opinion.

B The quick counterpunch that words like "But" and "Yet" offer at the start of a sentence is particularly useful right after you concede a point. Alternatively, the prior sentence could have placed the bad information in a subordinate clause, such as "Although *Knotts* states X, ..." Used here, however, that technique would have created an unwieldy sentence, so the lawyers select a snappy way (i.e. the word "But") to begin addressing the harmful language in *Knotts* and *Karo*.

C This is a common move when dealing with terrible dictum that *looks* like a holding: point out,

gently, that the court used overly broad language and inadvertently opined on situations that it did not anticipate.

D Numbers are a useful way to signal that a case is being distinguished in multiple ways (without needing to say so explicitly). As noted in Example 5.1, lawyers usually avoid *saying* that they are distinguishing a case; they just do it. Here, the lawyers deploy expertly the technique of punching adverse cases quickly. They concisely raise three grounds for distinguishing the adverse cases, and then they move on.

E **Notice that the request that the Court overrule *Knotts* and *Karo* is both subtle and a backup argument. Some cases require more extensive explanation as to why a past opinion should be overruled. That approach is necessary when your case cannot meaningfully be distinguished from the adverse controlling case. Here, the brief's affirmative argument had already shown the problems that warrantless GPS searches pose to civil liberties.**

FREQUENTLY ASKED QUESTIONS ABOUT COUNTERING AN ADVERSARY'S ARGUMENTS

Q. This chapter shows several ways to distinguish cases: what are some other common approaches?

A. Here are some common grounds for distinguishing an adverse case: argue that your case involves (1) a different *procedural posture* (e.g., one case was resolved on a motion to dismiss, the other followed a full trial); (2) different *governing law* (e.g., Nevada law applies here, California law applied in the other case); (3) a different *standard of review or legal standard* (e.g., another statute was upheld under rational basis but this statute must be assessed under strict scrutiny); (4) different *facts* (e.g., different language appears in a contract); (5) a different *type of party* (e.g., a municipal police officer might have immunity that a private security guard lacks); (6) different *amounts of evidence* (e.g., your client has six witnesses whereas the previous party had just one); (7) different *language* in the applicable statutes or regulations; (8) a different *doctrinal or legislative history* (e.g., that trademark and copyright law are not coextensive, so authorities from one field do not presumptively apply to the other); and (9) different *policy implications* (e.g., the consequences of letting someone sell fireworks are less than those of letting someone sell grenades).

Q. How much time should I spend distinguishing an adverse opinion?

A. As little as possible — usually. For all but the most influential cases, the more quickly and decisively you can discard the other side's strong cases, the better. One to three sentences should usually suffice, and you can even bundle multiple authorities together and discard them by pointing out their common flaws. Indeed, when you spend lots of time on adverse authorities, you signal to the court that those cases are worth worrying about. But for key cases, be sure to provide enough detail to help the court understand that case and see why it should be disregarded. These battleground cases will sometimes require extensive discussion: a paragraph, a page, or even more.

Q. Why did you discourage me from beginning paragraphs with phrases like "the other side's cases are distinguishable"?

A. That approach makes your argument sound defensive. Some lawyers prefer to state openly that they are about to rebut an opponent's argument, which ensures that a reader realizes that he or she is about to read a counterargument. But that approach advertises the other side's position, giving it air time. A more elegant approach phrases even your rebuttals in language that asserts your client's affirmative point rather than merely countering the other side's point. (E.g., "Even the three cases relied on by the defendant support our position.") That approach tends to make a brief more persuasive and avoids calling attention to the other side's argument.

Q. Another lawyer did a great job distinguishing a case. Can I take material from her motion or brief?

A. Although lawyers often borrow heavily from other lawyers' motions and briefs, some judges blast this practice and call it unethical, even when lawyers recycle their own work. Some judges even steer these "cannibalization" matters to ethics boards. So, to protect yourself, change the wording and phrasing enough that the brief is transformed into your own work. This instruction is especially vital for any readers who are still in law school, as plagiarizing will subject student lawyers to academic penalties.

Q. **In addition to distinguishing adverse cases, should I always try to highlight the analytic flaws in adverse authorities?**

A. No. Minor cases are rarely worth discrediting. More generally, some of the "discrediting" will likely take place earlier in your brief as part of your affirmative argument (such as by invoking helpful authorities to show why a contrary result would be imprudent or reversible).

Q. **What do I do when a controlling authority is squarely against my client on an important point?**

A. The duty of candor to the tribunal requires you to bring the case to the court's attention, even when the other side does not do so. You can and should try to distinguish the case. Also, you can dig into that case's record to see whether the decision failed to consider any arguments that might help your client. And remember, cases are not controlling except on the issues that the prior court actually considered. You can also see whether an intervening act (such as a decision from an even higher court or from the legislature) abrogated the adverse authority. If these techniques all fail, try to transfer your case to another jurisdiction (in which the unhelpful authority isn't controlling) or preserve the issue for appeal. Or settle fast.

Q. **Do I really need to rebut *every* argument that the other side makes?**

A. You should rebut any argument that you don't want the court to accept as true. If you fail to rebut a point, the other side will claim that your silence is an admission that you have no response. Learn to bundle arguments and counter them quickly.

Q. **How sharply should I criticize other authorities (including a trial court)?**

A. Be firm but respectful. Avoid name calling. One court sanctioned a lawyer who (in addition to other misconduct) referred to the judge's findings as "half-baked." Instead, use procedural facts and sound reasoning to highlight the problems in the court's approach.

Chapter 6

Applying Facts in Arguments

This chapter focuses on the most important technique for proving that a rule applies or should apply (or that it doesn't apply): using facts. You will weaken your clients' prospects if you simply pile legal authorities on judges and then assume that they will figure out why those authorities are applicable. Instead, draw on facts to compel a court to invoke (or reject) a particular line of cases.

Some of the major ways of achieving this goal appear below.

CHAPTER OVERVIEW

1. Remind readers of the applicable legal rule, so that they remember what your client needs to prove to clear the relevant legal hurdle; this reminder is especially important when the legal rule is complicated.
2. Remind readers of the pertinent details from your client's dispute — the background facts (with citations to the record) — to show that your case resembles in meaningful ways the favorable cases that govern the court's decision (or to show that the cases are distinguishable). Do not assume that judges will recall every fact that they read earlier in the brief. By page 40, few judges will recall a detail that appeared on page 3. Try, however, to avoid being repetitive; this chapter offers some tips on how to revisit the same facts without repeating them.
3. Use procedural details to advance your argument. Top lawyers are astoundingly creative at using record materials to show that an adversary failed to plead adequate facts to state a claim, contradicted itself, waived an argument, failed to record an objection to an evidentiary ruling, or stipulated a fact. All sorts of strategic advantages await the party that has a superior command of the case's procedural history.
4. Look for opportunities to point out that the other side has failed to present evidence; the absence of facts can be extremely persuasive.
5. Search for extrinsic facts to support your position, such as government reports, articles, surveys, industry manuals, an adversary's public statements or filings, and so on. Just be sure that you either get those materials into the case's record or that your judge can take judicial notice of them.
6. Don't be afraid to use multimedia tools — photographs, charts and graphs, videos, and the like — to establish or clarify a critical point.

Example
6.1

Takeaway point 6.1: To prevail on a critical legal issue, provide a detailed fact-based explanation of why your client satisfies the applicable legal standard.

You must prove that your client satisfies the relevant legal rule. That proof requires you to restate the legal standard and to show that the facts meet that standard.

To observe this technique, we return to the judge in West Virginia who refused to recuse himself even though the chairman of one of the litigants spent $3 million on the judge's campaign. The excerpted passage presents facts designed to meet the applicable rule, which requires recusal if "the probability of actual bias on the part of the judge or decisionmaker is too high to be constitutionally tolerable."

Source: Brief arguing that Justice Benjamin was required to recuse himself, from *Caperton v. A.T. Massey Coal Co.*, 556 U.S. 868 (2009) (some citations omitted).

---

1   For at least five reasons, any reasonable observer would conclude that Mr.
2   Blankenship's support for Justice Benjamin's campaign generated a constitu-
3   tionally unacceptable probability that Justice Benjamin was biased in favor of
4   Massey in this case.

A

5   First, the sheer volume of Mr. Blankenship's financial support for Justice Ben-
6   jamin's campaign is truly staggering. West Virginia law imposes a $1,000 limit
7   on contributions to judicial campaigns. W. Va. Code § 3-8-12(f). Through his
8   donations to And For The Sake Of The Kids and direct expenditures on campaign
9   advertising, Mr. Blankenship spent *3,000 times* that amount supporting Justice
10 Benjamin. The $3 million that Mr. Blankenship spent is three times the amount

B

11 spent by Justice Benjamin's own campaign committee (J.A. 288a) and $1 mil-
12 lion more than the *total* amount spent by Justice Benjamin's committee and the
13 committee of his opponent, Justice Warren McGraw. *See* Goldberg, *supra*, at 16.
14 Indeed, the $2.5 million that Mr. Blankenship spent to fund And For The Sake Of
15 The Kids' campaign to elect Justice Benjamin is more than any other individual
16 or group contributed to a 527 organization involved in *any* 2004 judicial election
17 campaign. The next largest donor gave $600,000 less than Mr. Blankenship. *Id.*

18 Second, the appearance of bias generated by the size of Mr. Blankenship's
19 campaign expenditures is reinforced by the fact that his expenditures represent
20 60% of the *total* amount spent to support Justice Benjamin's campaign.[4] Thus,
21 this is not a case where the expenditures in question — even though large in
22 absolute terms — were matched by equally large donations from other parties
23 that could conceivably have diminished the probability of judicial bias in favor
24 of one specific donor.

25 Third, Mr. Blankenship did more than spend vast sums of money to support
26 Justice Benjamin's campaign. He also actively campaigned for Justice Benjamin
27 and solicited donations on his behalf. Most notably, he distributed letters urging
28 doctors to "send $1,000 to Brent Benjamin" because "[i]f Warren McGraw gets
29 re-elected to the West Virginia Supreme Court your insurance rates will almost
30 certainly be higher for the next twelve years than they will be if Brent Benjamin
31 gets elected." J.A. 181a. Mr. Blankenship's letters are directly responsible for a por-
32 tion of the more than $800,000 donated to Justice Benjamin's campaign committee.

C

---

33   4. A total of $4,986,711 was spent supporting Justice Benjamin's 2004 campaign:
34   $3,623,500 by And For The Sake Of The Kids (Disqual. Mtn. Ex. 17), $845,504 by the
35   Benjamin for Supreme Court Committee (J.A. 288a), and $517,707 by Mr. Blankenship
36   through direct expenditures (*id.* at 186a, 200a).

D

37 Fourth, the timing of Mr. Blankenship's campaign support strongly suggests
38 that it was intended to influence the outcome of this $50 million appeal. Mr.
39 Blankenship's campaign expenditures and fundraising efforts were made between
40 August 2004 and November 2004 (J.A. 119a, 199a), when Mr. Blankenship was
41 preparing to appeal this personally and professionally significant case to the court
42 on which Justice Benjamin was seeking a seat. Indeed, after the jury returned
43 its verdict against Massey in August 2002, Mr. Blankenship immediately made a
44 public vow to appeal the verdict to that court. *Id.* at 115a. Although the appeal
45 was delayed by Massey's post-trial motions, there was no doubt during the 2004
46 campaign that the case would ultimately be decided by the state supreme court
47 and that, if elected, Justice Benjamin would have the opportunity to cast a vote
48 in that appeal.

49 Fifth, Justice Benjamin's decision to participate in Massey's appeal was not
50 subject to review by the other members of his court. Where a judge's decision
51 not to recuse himself is endorsed by the court's other members, the likelihood
52 of judicial bias may be diminished because the allegations of bias have been ex-
53 amined — and rejected — by the judge's colleagues. In this case, not only were
54 the other justices of the West Virginia Supreme Court of Appeals precluded by
55 state law from considering petitioners' recusal motions, but three members of the
56 court (two justices and a circuit judge appointed to replace one of the recused
57 justices) expressed strong concerns about Justice Benjamin's participation in the
58 case. *See* J.A. 633a n.16 (Albright, J., joined by Cookman, J., dissenting); *id.* at
59 462a (Starcher, J., recusing). His colleagues' discomfort with Justice Benjamin's
60 refusal to recuse himself underscores the strong probability of bias generated by
61 Mr. Blankenship's support for Justice Benjamin's campaign.

E

F

A The topic sentence concisely restates the Rule and tells readers what will follow, namely, the evidence in the record that supports the relevant legal standard. Then it delivers on that promise. Mimic this approach.

B The term "3,000 times" sounds even more egregious than "$3 million." Relative numbers are often clearer and punchier than absolute numbers.

C To avoid repeating your Statement of Facts in your Argument, save a juicy quote for the Argument, as the lawyers do here. The Statement provided a more general description of Blankenship's letter: "[Blankenship] widely distributed letters exhorting doctors to donate to the campaign because electing Justice Benjamin would purportedly help to lower their malpractice premiums." The trick: even if you reiterate facts, rephrase or reframe them so that they don't *seem* repetitive.

D One sensible use for footnotes is to show your calculations: the text stays uncluttered, but readers can probe the footnotes to see how you reached your mathematical conclusions. Omitting this data could make readers doubt that the calculations are accurate.

E Lawyers need to exercise judgment about when to make obvious points, and this brief makes the right call: readers might intuit that Blankenship's huge contribution was intended to influence the $50 million appeal. But the brief makes this critical point explicitly lest readers miss it, and the phrase "strongly suggests" avoids overreaching..

F Example 1.3 showed how to repeat a strong point to emphasize it; here, the same brief expertly fuses two mediocre points to hide each one's frailty. Judges rarely review their colleagues' recusal decisions. Thus, it's no surprise that Justice Benjamin's colleagues were unable to force him to recuse himself and it's *legally* insignificant that his own colleagues thought he was biased. The points work better together than they would if made separately.

| Example 6.2 | **Takeaway point 6.2:** Master the record so that you can use facts and procedural details to advance a client's arguments. |

Lawyers use a variety of record facts and procedural facts to explain why their clients should win. To illustrate how lawyers pluck evidence from public reports, trial transcripts, the other side's filings, and expert reports, we look at a case in which a private citizen wanted crime scene photographs of a White House lawyer (Vincent Foster) who had committed suicide. The brief had just discussed a case (*Ray*) which observed that "unsubstantiated allegations of governmental misconduct" should not enable citizens to acquire sensitive government records.

Source: U.S. government's brief in *Office of Independent Counsel v. Favish*, 541 U.S. 157 (2004).

1   This case is precisely what *Ray* warned against. Respondent wants the pho-
2   tographs of Foster at the scene of his death to satisfy himself that Foster was not
3   murdered or to prove that he was. But six pathologists and numerous forensic
4   scientists, law enforcement investigators (not only from the Park Police and the
5   FBI, but also those retained by the Office of Independent Counsel), a commit-
6   tee of the United States Senate, Members of the House of Representatives, and
7   two Independent Counsels already have studied the matter at length and have
8   *unanimously* concluded that Foster committed suicide. And detailed reports of
9   those investigations, explaining their conclusions, already have been released to
10 the public.
11 Respondent's personal interest in the "blowback" and "backspatter" of blood
12 and other morbid matters (*see, e.g.*, Br. in Opp. 7-15) are all fully and com-
13 prehensively addressed in those prior investigations by persons who (unlike
14 respondent) are trained experts in pathology and the forensics of murder and sui-
15 cide. *See, e.g.*, J.A. 111 (retention of expert in bloodspatter). As the district court
16 noted, moreover, each subsequent investigation was undertaken for the express
17 purpose of addressing and resolving doubts that had been posited both about
18 Foster's death and the predecessor inquiries. 3/9/98 Tr. 10 ("[T]here were just lit-
19 erally scores of people out there trying to prove your points; namely, something
20 was amiss here, something was rotten, and none of them did."); *id.* at 6-7 ("[A]ll
21 [the different investigators] were driven to find a negative aspect of things, not
22 just Mr. Foster dispatching himself. And despite their demonstrated inclination,
23 they didn't come up with anything."). The pictures that respondent wants to see
24 to confirm or dispel his own doubts were fully examined by numerous investigators,
25 without a single individual determining that they evidenced a murder. . . . And all of
26 those investigations came *unequivocally* to the same conclusion: Vincent Foster
27 committed suicide.

A

B

C

(A) Here, the brief uses a common technique — intentionally lengthening a sentence that lists evidence — so that the evidence seems overwhelming.

(B) The lawyers *try* to disgust readers here. The issue in the case was whether the risk of embarrassment or suffering to the Foster family could overcome a citizen's general right under the Freedom of Information Act to obtain government records. If the lawyers can cause readers to recoil, they help their cause: readers will find compelling the premise that Foster's family would be upset if the photos of his corpse became public. Manipulating readers' emotions is dangerous, but top lawyers manage to do so. Subtly.

(C) **The brief uses procedural facts, namely the transcript from trial-court proceedings, to corroborate its claims.**

Example
6.3

Takeaway point 6.3: Use your adversaries' own words against them when writing your Argument.

The best facts to use in your Argument often come from your adversary, as we see below. The energy corporation Enron engaged in bogus accounting in the late 1990s to make itself seem very profitable. When the company's cooked books were discovered, Enron collapsed, costing investors more than $60 billion. One of Enron's outside bankers, Bayly, allegedly helped Enron to manipulate its earnings. The federal government indicted him. At trial, the district court admitted into evidence an email that tied Bayly to the fraud, but this email contained inadmissible hearsay. Bayly was nevertheless convicted. On appeal, Bayly argued that the email was inadmissible. But *harmless* evidentiary blunders cannot vacate a conviction, so he needed to rebut the government's claim that admitting the email was inconsequential. Here, Bayly's lawyers use the prosecutors' own words to show that admitting the email into evidence was a turning point in the trial.

Source: Reply brief for Bayly in *United States v. Brown*, 459 F.3d 509 (5th Cir. 2006).

---

1   **C. The Government Has Failed To Show Harmless Error**   A

2   Although the prosecutors repeatedly sought to move the Brown e-mail into

3   evidence (*see* Op. Br. 42) — and relied heavily on the e-mail once it finally *was*

4   admitted (*see id.* at 52-53) — the government now contends that the evidence

5   was "harmless beyond any shadow of doubt and under any standard of review."   B

6   (G.Br. 201.) This is the same evidence, it must be noted, that the government

7   hailed at trial as "powerfully probative evidence" concerning the very "nub" of

8   the case. (Tr. 2970.) This is the same evidence that the government described   C

9   before trial as being "at the heart of the issues in this case." (Dkt. 285 (6/25/05

10   Hearing Tr.) at 77.) And this is the same evidence that the government paraded,

11   at every turn, as critical evidence against Bayly.

12   The prosecutors who tried this case used exactly the right descriptions — the

13   Brown e-mail was indeed the "nub" of the case against Bayly and at the "heart"

14   of it. [T]he Brown e-mail was the *only* document cited by the government in its

15   pretrial memorandum supposedly tying Bayly to the alleged conspiracy. (*See* Dkt.

16   420, at 24.) The government used the Brown e-mail to suggest to defense witness

17   Katherine Zrike [a lawyer at Bayly's bank] that perhaps she should reconsider

18   her favorable testimony about Bayly's honesty and integrity. (Tr. 4285-87.) The

19   government argued in its opening summation that the Brown e-mail was "a criti-

20   cal document that you should focus on when you're back in the jury room delib-

21   erating." (*Id.* 6274.) The government invoked the e-mail against Bayly yet again

22   in its rebuttal summation. (*Id.* 6508-09.) In short, as the government expressly   D

23   told the district court at least three times at trial: The Brown e-mail is "powerfully

24   probative." (*Id.* 2970, 2973, 2979.)

Ⓐ The government bears the burden of showing that improperly admitted evidence was *harmless*; it is not the defendant's duty to show that the admission was harmful. Pay attention to whether you need to prove something or whether you need to show that the other side has failed to prove something.

Ⓑ The lawyers' repeated use of the phrase "this is the same evidence" creates momentum that pulls readers along with it.

Ⓒ **We see more legal judo: the government's prior arguments now help the defendant show that the email affected the trial's outcome.**

Ⓓ Bayly's lawyers introduce four separate helpful facts — in fewer than 100 words — and then end the paragraph with a memorable quotation. Presenting facts this concisely and clearly maximizes their persuasiveness.

Example
6.4

Takeaway point 6.4: When your adversaries fail to present evidence, point out to the court that the record does not corroborate their claims.

Just as an absence of authorities undermines an argument (*see* Example 5.4), an absence of facts can hobble your adversaries. The following example emphasizes the absence of facts in the other side's brief. In this dispute, a law school (Hastings) allowed any student group to apply to become a registered student organization (RSO). Only RSOs received school funds. One group, the Christian Legal Society (CLS), adopted bylaws requiring all members and officers to sign a "Statement of Faith" opposing homosexuality and premarital sex. The law school rejected CLS's application to become an RSO, concluding that the group's bylaws violated the law school's policy that all students can participate in all RSOs. CLS sued, claiming that Hastings' policy violated its First Amendment rights to speech, association, and religion.

Source: Brief of Hastings College of the Law in *Christian Legal Society v. Martinez*, 130 S. Ct. 2971 (2010).

1   In this Court, petitioner devotes almost its entire argument to attacking a pol-
2 icy that has never existed at Hastings — one that selectively "targets solely those
3 groups whose beliefs are based on 'religion' or that disapprove of a particular
4 kind of sexual behavior," and leaves other student groups free to choose mem-
5 bers based on their beliefs. Pet.Br.19; *see* Pet.Br.42. As its lead example petitioner
6 says that, under Hastings' policy, a "political . . . group can insist that its leaders
7 support its purposes and beliefs" whereas "a religious group cannot." Pet.Br.20.
8   The parties, however, jointly stipulated that Hastings' policy is that student
9 groups must open their membership to "any student . . . regardless of their status
10 or beliefs." JA-221 ¶ 18. Moreover, the parties specifically stipulated that a po-
11 litical student group like the Hastings Democratic Caucus is *not* free to close its
12 doors to students who have different beliefs. *Id.* Petitioner apparently just refuses
13 to accept the "joint" in "joint stipulation." Indeed, it says in one sentence that
14 "*[r]espondents* maintain" that Hastings has an open-membership policy, but in
15 the very next sentence admits that this policy is "described in *Joint* Stipulation
16 No. 18." Pet.Br.47 (emphases added). . . .   A
17   The government engages in viewpoint discrimination when it "targets not
18 subject matter, but particular views taken by speakers on a subject." *Rosenberger,*   B
19 515 U.S. at 829. An open-membership policy like Hastings', applicable to all
20 student organizations without regard to their mission or viewpoint, is quintes-
21 sentially viewpoint-neutral.
22   Petitioner eventually concedes at the tail-end of its brief that Hastings' open-
23 membership policy is "nominally" viewpoint-neutral. Pet.Br.51. It is no less
24 viewpoint-neutral in practice. Hastings' policy applies equally to every RSO. It
25 does not target any particular viewpoint or make any distinction between reli-
26 gious and non-religious speech. Pet.App.35a-36a. To be eligible for RSO status,   C
27 Hastings Outlaw [a student organization that supports gay and lesbian rights]
28 cannot exclude students who believe homosexuality is morally wrong any more
29 than CLS is permitted to exclude students who believe it is not.
30   The record in this case — which petitioners repeatedly ignore — reveals "no
31 evidence" of discriminatory motive or practice with respect to CLS or religious
32 viewpoints generally. Pet.App.35a. A number of organizations that, like CLS,   D

34 engage in worship, Christian fellowship, and Bible study have thrived at Hast-
35 ings as RSOs — both before and after CLS refused to comply with the policy —
36 including the Law Students' Christian Fellowship and Hastings Koinonia. And
37 CLS's own predecessor group, HCF, was an RSO for a decade before this litiga-
38 tion (when it allowed any interested Hastings student to be a member). In short,
39 the policy plainly does not exclude speech because of its "religious viewpoint."
40 *Good News Club*, 533 U.S. at 111. Nor any other viewpoint. . . .

41 Petitioner repeatedly suggests that the policy "requir[es] CLS to accept leaders
42 who do not follow its moral teachings." Pet.Br.32; *see also* Pet.Br.2, 27. Again, the
43 policy does not *force* CLS to do anything; it gives it a choice. Moreover, for those
44 groups that accept RSO status, the policy obligates them only to permit members
45 "to *seek* leadership positions." JA-221 ¶ 18 (emphasis added). The policy places no
46 restrictions at all on the selection process. . . . By ensuring that all students who
47 join RSOs are *eligible* for leadership positions, the policy simply ensures that stu-
48 dents are admitted as full-fledged members — not second-class ones.

49 Petitioner hypothesizes that if it chooses to honor the policy, it will be subject
50 to "sabotage," or even a "hijack[ing]." Pet.Br.28-29 & n.4. But Hastings' open-
51 membership policy is two decades old and there is not one shred of evidence
52 in the record before this Court that any of the scores of RSOs at Hastings has
53 ever been threatened with — much less subjected to — a takeover. [The Court
54 may not] invalidate the policy on the basis of a hypothetical theory that has no
55 support in the record and, indeed, virtually no support in the history of higher
56 education in America. *Cf. Crawford v. Marion County Election Bd.*, 128 S. Ct.
57 1610, 1623 (2008). . . .

58 Though petitioner's opening brief promised that amici would provide "nu-
59 merous examples" of sabotage and takeover (Pet.Br.29 n.4), petitioner's amici
60 have failed to identify a *single* actual "takeover" — anywhere.

A As reprinted, this paragraph omits authorities showing that litigants are bound by their stipulations. The reprinted text shows why this admission was so deadly to CLS.

B The brief discussed the applicable legal rule in greater detail earlier. Here, we see the importance of reminding readers of the law so that they know why the ensuing facts matter. And this standard shows why CLS's factual stipulation was so deadly: the entire legal standard turns on whether the government's policy is neutral or discriminatory. CLS had stipulated at trial that the policy did not discriminate against religious groups. If Hastings' lawyers had failed to inform the court of this procedural fact, they would have missed a huge strategic opportunity.

C Describing how a law or policy operates in practice is another sort of fact-based technique that lawyers use when building fact-centered arguments.

D Citing facts that are in the record — or noting the conspicuous absence of facts, as Hastings does here — is another way to build a fact-based argument.

E Past conduct and treatment of your adversary can also support your client's position.

F This sentence makes an overly broad claim: Hastings would almost certainly object if a student group prohibited gays and lesbians (or African Americans or women) from voting to select the leaders of a group. You need to balance persuasion and precision; here, the lawyers write too imprecisely.

G The lawyers use the absence of problems (at either Hastings or elsewhere) to advance their point. But the lawyers engage in dangerous writing here: although amici provided no examples, CLS itself (in the very footnote that Hastings cites) reported an incident in which College Republicans "at another university" hijacked the Young Democrats' election process.

Example 6.5	**Takeaway point 6.5:** Don't be afraid to use multimedia tools to help your client.

Including multimedia images such as photographs, charts, graphs, and video links in your Argument or Statement of Facts can help your clients in a wide array of cases. Explains Judge Richard Posner: "*Seeing* a case makes it come alive to judges." Suppose that your client was in a horrible car crash and received punitive damages. Including a photo of her — mangled and broken — after the accident might make an appellate court less likely to disturb the punitive damages award. Or suppose you allege that someone copied your client's logo. Including photos of the two logos will help to convince readers that the defendant infringed.

We see another situation below in which photos helped to build an argument. The passage comes from a Supreme Court case that addressed whether Texas could maintain a statue of the Ten Commandments outside its State Capitol. The brief reprinted below, which supported Texas, emphasized that the Ten Commandments appear on countless government buildings — including one that was especially important to this case.

Source: Amicus brief in *Van Orden v. Perry*, 545 U.S. 677 (2005) (formatting adjusted).

1   The Texas monument is neither unique nor isolated; to the contrary, the
2 Decalogue motif has been incorporated time and again by the artists and archi-   A
3 tects responsible for designing the halls of American government. For example,
4 in the Main Reading Room of the Library of Congress stands a large bronze
5 statue of Moses holding the Ten Commandments [image omitted]. This promi-
6 nent statue is on display for the one million people who visit the Library of
7 Congress each year.

8   Similarly, the recently completed Ronald Reagan International Trade Build-
9 ing features a very large statue with the Ten Commandments that is visible to
10 all who pass along Pennsylvania Avenue [image omitted]. And the millions of
11 visitors to the National Archives pass over a bronze plaque inscribed with the
12 Decalogue tablets [image omitted].   B

13   Indeed, Decalogue imagery graces the homes of all three Branches of our fed-
14 eral government. Moses and the Ten Commandments appear on both the south
15 frieze of the courtroom in which this Court sits [*see* fig. 1] and the pediment of
16 the Court's building [*see* fig. 2]. . . .

Figure 1 *God in the Temple of Government.*

Figure 2 *God in the Temple of Government.*

17   This established practice of integrating the Ten Commandments and other
18 religio-historical symbols into the fabric of our public institutions has been
19 repeated over and over again in the multitudinous town halls, public parks,
20 courthouses, educational institutions, and state capitals throughout this Nation.
21 In statues, paintings, sculptures, friezes, murals, and the like, religious iconogra-
22 phy has been part and parcel of American public architecture since the Found-
23 ing. It is fair to say that the inclusion of such iconography is the norm rather than
24 the exception.[3] . . .

25   Implementing the counter-historical regime that petitioner posits would
26 require this Court . . . to remove the Decalogue emblem from the doors of this
27 Court [*see* fig. 3].

C

Figure 3 *God in the Temple of Government.*

---

28   3. The images reproduced in this brief come from a photographic essay that vividly
29 captures the prominence and prevalence of religious symbols in and around public
30 buildings in the District of Columbia alone. *See* Carrie Devorah, *God in the Temples*
31 *of Government*, Human Events, Nov. 24, 2003, at 14, & Dec. 22, 2003, at 20. . . . An
32 illustrative, but by no means exhaustive, list of government properties outside of the
33 District of Columbia that contain Ten Commandments monuments can be found in
34 the appendix to the brief for the United States in the companion case.

A The brief does not explain this term. The lawyers reasoned that the Justices could infer from the context (and from the prefix "dec," meaning "ten") that "Deca-logue" refers to the Ten Commandments.

B Notice that the lawyers build up to the most com-pelling photos. This approach deviates from the gen-eral rule that your best point should come first. Bravo. These lawyers correctly sense that brief's brevity (eight pages) would prevent the Justices from tuning out. And the buildup to the final photos helps the brief end with a bang.

C This example uses photographs to strong effect. As noted above, other visual tools can also be helpful to your clients. For instance, in the investigation and litigation about BP's role in 2010's Deepwater Hori-zon oil spill, the litigants prepared elaborate videos for the trial judge to explain how the massive spill occurred. (Example 7.4 provides some background about that dispute.)

Example **6.6**	**Takeaway point 6.6:** Contrary to conventional wisdom, you do *not* need to include in your Statement every fact that appears in your Argument. And in complicated cases, you shouldn't. Somewhere in the shadows of the past, a custom evolved that a Statement must include every fact that the motion or brief discusses. That can be a dangerous rule. It weakens many briefs badly by making them boring and slow, and by heaping facts on judges before they know why those facts are relevant. Disregard this "rule" if doing so will help your client. Instead, indicate in your Statement that further details will be discussed in the Argument. This approach is reflected below. The Statement merely says "many professional content owners — including plaintiffs — routinely post their material on YouTube and authorize marketers and licensees to do the same. *Infra* 44-50." Then, all of this information (and more) is used to carpet bomb the other side in the Argument. (The same technique was used *five* other times in the Statement, shortening it significantly.) Here, YouTube uses facts to advance two arguments: (1) Viacom planted copyrighted material on YouTube (suggesting that Viacom is suing for injuries that it caused to itself), and (2) Viacom's difficulty in identifying its own copyrights demonstrates the infeasibility of Viacom's suggestion that the Second Circuit should require YouTube to monitor every video posted on its website. *Source:* YouTube's brief in *Viacom v. YouTube*, 676 F.3d 19 (2d Cir. 2012) (omitting dozens of citations to the record).

1　Like many other media companies, Viacom directly and through its marketing
2　agents posted to YouTube countless videos containing its copyrighted material.
3　Several aspects of Viacom's embrace of YouTube are particularly significant.
4　　*First*, Viacom's posting of content to YouTube was extensive. Viacom's own
5　documents reveal that it uploaded a "boatload of clips onto YouTube for distribu-
6　tion" and was "VERY aggressively providing clips on an ongoing basis"[13] Via-
7　com's uploading activity started early in YouTube's existence, and even Viacom's
8　decision to sue could not curb its desire to "continue to 'place' authorized clips
9　on YouTube." Indeed, Viacom kept uploading material to YouTube throughout
10　this litigation. *E.g.*, JA-V:306 (Paramount in March 2007: "We are still uploading
11　content to YouTube"); JA-V:308 (MTV lawyer in August 2007: "Actually we're OK
12　with uploading our own material on youtube for promotional purposes."); SJA-
13　VIII:2075 (August 2008 email from marketer to YouTube: "We work with MTV
14　(Viacom) on several of their shows and upload a lot of their content."); JA-IV:285
15　(MTV authorizing postings to YouTube in February 2008).[14]
16　　*Second*, Viacom and its agents posted a wide variety of videos on YouTube,
17　including long excerpts (or even full episodes) of television shows and clips taken

---

18　　13. *See also* JA-VI:682 (Viacom lawyer reporting that "there are A LOT of clips they
19　[VH1] have seeded to you tube"); JA-IV:317 ("We actually provide clips to YouTube
20　quite aggressively."); JA-VI:782 ("it would be a significant task to keep you updated
21　on each and every clip we post ongoing"). . . .
22　　14. Viacom has admitted that its employees uploaded "approximately" 600 clips
23　through May 2008, but that number (while significant) is wildly inaccurate. It omits
24　Viacom's extensive use of third-party marketing agents who uploaded thousands of
25　additional clips at Viacom's direction. It also ignores Viacom's acknowledged inability
26　to provide a full accounting of its postings on YouTube.

from its films with nothing indicating their origins. JA-VI:640(¶2); JA-VI:657-659; JA-VI:694; SJA-VII:1752-54 (Paramount explaining that "MI:3 scenes found on YouTube.com" were "brought online this week as pa[r]t of normal online publicity before the release of the film"). These videos were not obvious advertisements, and indeed many clips were calculated to look unauthorized. Viacom uploaded what its documents describe as footage from the "cutting room floor" and clips "rough[ed] up" to "add to the 'hijacked' effect" (JA-IV:234) — which Viacom now calls a "common" practice (JA-II:755(¶1.61)).

Third, while YouTube knew that Viacom was posting some clips, YouTube did not know, and could not have known, the full extent of Viacom's marketing activities. Viacom uploaded certain clips using its "official" YouTube accounts, but it did more of its posting using obscure accounts and agents. JA-VI:641-643(¶¶3-5); JA-IV:102(¶4); JA-IV:184(¶¶5-6); SJA-VI: 1301-03; SJA-IX:2163-66; SJA-VI:1234-38. The extent of Viacom's stealth-marketing emerged only in discovery, when YouTube uncovered no fewer than 50 Viacom-related accounts that collectively uploaded many thousands of clips to YouTube. JA-IV:212-216(¶5(a)-(f)); JA-VI:641-642(¶4). There is no way to tell from the names of these accounts — including "demansr," "gooddrugy," "thatsfunny," "ultrasloppyjoe," and "waytoblue" — that they were linked to Viacom or to distinguish them from other run-of-the-mill YouTube accounts.

Blurring its connection to the videos it authorized was an important part of Viacom's strategy. JA-IV:238. Examples abound: **B**

- MTV employee in 2006: "Spoke with Jeff [another MTV employee] and we are both going to submit clips to YouTube.com — him through his personal account so it seems like a user[] of the site and me through 'mtv2'";
- Paramount executive asking that clip be posted on YouTube "NOT WITH A PARAMOUNT LOGO OR ASSOCIATION";
- Paramount executive instructing marketer that clips were "to be uploaded from his personal acct and not associated with the film";
- Paramount executive advising that clips posted to YouTube "should definitely not be associated with the studio — should appear as if a fan created and posted it";
- MTV approving marketer's request to post clips on YouTube, "if u can do it the in cognito [sic] way";
- Paramount employee discussing uploading YouTube clip from Kinko's in order to mask its origin.

Such practices not only left YouTube users (and YouTube itself) at a loss to know who was posting the videos, they often made it difficult for Viacom itself to distinguish between authorized and unauthorized clips.

A The amount of evidence that YouTube produces in this section borders on overwhelming. It refers to multiple executives at multiple networks all uploading — and disguising — multiple videos. With such a volume of content, a judge might think that no one could possibly keep track of which videos violated copyrights. And that is exactly the effect that YouTube wanted.

B YouTube referred to these facts (and the other facts in this example) in its Statement, but signaled there that it would discuss them in greater detail in the Argument (to prevent the Statement from becoming too long).

FREQUENTLY ASKED QUESTIONS ABOUT APPLYING FACTS IN ARGUMENTS

Q. **I want to include the same basic facts in my Statement and Argument. How do I keep my motion or brief from being repetitive?**

A. Phrase the facts differently. Or provide more detail in one place than the other. Or provide a longer quote in your Statement and then quote just a few key words in your Argument so that your motion *reminds* judges of what a witness said or an exhibit showed. You can also quote a document in one place and then characterize or paraphrase it in another place. Repetition impairs the flow of your argument, so keep things fresh for readers. Also, as Example 6.6 demonstrates, if your case involves multiple litigants (or multiple distinct issues or very fact-intensive issues), you may simply tell readers in your Statement that your Argument will delve into the relevant facts of a given subject in more detail.

Q. **The chapter overview mentions using extrinsic facts (such as government reports) to support my position. If those extrinsic facts are not in the record, how do I place those facts in front of my judge?**

A. At the trial court, you can submit materials into the record; write a declaration authenticating those documents and then submit the document as an attachment to your or your witness's declaration, which accompanies your motion. On appeal, you can often discuss facts that aren't in the record if the court can take "judicial notice" of those facts — a term that usually refers to government documents. Lawyers try to stretch the limits of this exception.

   For example, Facebook used this technique effectively during a recent appeal. Its adversaries claimed that Facebook had duped them during settlement talks into accepting Facebook shares by falsely claiming that the shares were worth almost $36 apiece when in fact they were worth less than $9 per share. Facebook (on appeal) countered that California law required it "to report the values of stock options to the California Department of Corporations, which proceeds to post them on the Web for all to review." Facebook then added — even though this fact had not been raised to the trial court — that its adversaries could "easily have looked up" these valuations just "as this Court could even now." That public website showed that the shares were worth just $6.61. In other words, Facebook used a public website to show that it reported publicly that its shares were worth "far less than the $35.90/share value" that its adversaries "now say they had attributed to the stock." Facebook thus supplemented the record.

Q. **How do I include photographs, videos, instructional films, charts, or other visuals in my motion or brief?**

A. Lawyers rely on multimedia with increasing frequency. Photos are easy to deploy: just insert them into the body of your motion or brief (or into an appendix). *See* Example 6.5. This is a common technique; indeed, it is nearly ubiquitous in certain cases, such as trademark disputes. Likewise, you can include a URL in your motion or brief (so that judges can watch a video or see a report). Before including URLs, try to assess the tech-savviness of your judge. Also be mindful of how images will affect your page count.

Q. **During oral arguments, it's common for judges to ask hypothetical questions of lawyers to test the limits of the lawyer's position. Can I use this sort of hypothetical argument in my motion or brief?**

A. Do so sparingly and concisely (if at all). In general, leave elaborate hypotheticals for the judges. For lawyers, hypotheticals are most useful when they are short and concrete (e.g., "this case would be different if any witnesses had seen the accident") or when they present metaphors that help readers grasp a complicated concept by comparing it to something more accessible. Here is an example of using an elaborate hypothetical effectively, but I urge new lawyers not to indulge in such involved analogies, metaphors, or hypotheticals. The passage came from Oracle's appellate brief in its lawsuit against Google. The brief alleged that Google's Android operating system infringed on Oracle's copyrighted software. The brief analogizes Google to someone who plagiarizes:

> Ann Droid wants to publish a bestseller. So she sits down with an advance copy of *Harry Potter and the Order of the Phoenix* — the fifth book — and proceeds to transcribe. She verbatim copies all the chapter titles [and] copies verbatim the topic sentences of each paragraph. . . . She then paraphrases the rest of each paragraph. She rushes the competing version to press before the original under the title: *Ann Droid's Harry Potter 5.0.* The knockoff flies off the shelves. J.K. Rowling sues for copyright infringement. Ann's defenses: "But I wrote most of the words from scratch. Besides, this was fair use because I copied only the portions necessary to tap into the Harry Potter fan base." Obviously, the defenses would fail.

Q. **Can I make a fact-based argument based on what my judge previously said?**

A. Yes, and Example 14.7 provides a good example of how to point out respectfully that the court has already addressed an issue and reached a helpful conclusion. By contrast, playing "Gotcha!" (e.g., "it would be hypocritical of you, Your Honor, if . . . .") can be very dangerous, as judges may resent feeling cornered.

Chapter 7

Textual Arguments

The meaning of words is surprisingly elusive. Inexperienced lawyers assume at their immeasurable peril that they can skim statutes and contracts just as they might peruse a magazine article. Don't make that mistake. Study the relevant provisions of a statute or contract at a fraction of your normal reading speed. When reviewing a tricky statute, your reading speed can easily plunge to one-hundredth of your normal rate.

Why so slow? Because every word, every comma, every ambiguity, every hint of vagueness provides a potential opportunity — a "loophole." For instance, imagine that a statute requires a person to receive a minimum five-year criminal sentence if he or she embezzles "from his corporation." Simple enough, until you assess critically whether each word could help your client:

from — What if your client obtained the loan by falsifying a letter of approval from her company's board of directors to obtain a loan from *the company's bank*. She might be guilty of some other crime, but did she embezzle *from* her company?

his — Your client doesn't *own* the business, so you could argue that the corporation is not *hers*. Would owning some stock in the company negate this argument? Would a single share suffice? Or can you argue that "his corporation" means that the defendant needs to control the company — and that the statute seeks to ban not all embezzlement but merely misconduct by the company's owners?

corporation — Your client's business is a limited liability partnership, not a *corporation*. Would a court dismiss the indictment based on this fact? Moreover, the crime of embezzlement usually means money was taken from one's employer. Can you construe that the words "from his *corporation*" deliberately narrow the traditional crime of embezzlement?

(And in case you're wondering, legislative codes almost always define "he" or "his" to include women too, unless the context dictates otherwise.)

You need to train yourself to spot and take advantage of these sorts of subtleties. Spotting textual arguments requires patience, practice, and creativity. Then, discarding weak arguments requires judgment and discipline. And then you'll eventually need to convince a court that your interpretation of a statute or other textual passage is correct.

This chapter focuses on this final skill: convincing judges to follow your interpretation of a piece of binding text such as a statute. But a major, secondary goal is to get you to think like a lawyer by training you to spot statutory arguments. After all, if you don't notice a loophole, your client can't slip through it.

The following pages do not offer a comprehensive guide to statutory or contractual interpretation. But they show how a word or two — or even the absence of a word — can dictate the outcome of a case. For instance, we see below one case that hung on whether one can "file" a complaint *orally*. We see another case in which a group that tortured a U.S. citizen escaped liability because of a single word. And we see a case in which an oil company sought to escape billions of dollars of liability because a single word did *not* appear in a contract. Page 115 also introduces ten common textual canons of statutory interpretation.

CHAPTER OVERVIEW

1. Familiarize yourself with the various canons and doctrines that courts use to construe a word or phrase. Some common ones appear on the next page.
2. Hone your research skills so that you can find numerous types and pieces of evidence that will help readers to glean the meaning of the disputed text. Hunger for clues that support your reading of the text. Do not stop researching simply because you find one piece of support.
3. Think creatively about how a word or phrase is used. When making a textual argument, one of the hallmarks of great advocacy is to show how the disputed term is used in other contexts. Similarly, think of alternate words that could have been used in the statute — but that the legislature declined to use.
4. Do not simply grab the nearest dictionary to obtain a definition of a disputed word. Learn which dictionaries are favored by courts. Consult (and cite) multiple dictionaries and pay attention to which edition of a dictionary you use.
5. Emphasize the statute's overall purpose if that purpose is consistent with your reading of the specific provisions that the parties are disputing. That might require you to sneak into your textual argument either dicta or a few lines of legislative history (which is discussed in Chapter 8).
6. Refer the court to materials from the case's record or from prior cases in which your adversary (or the court) used the disputed term consistently with your interpretation.

INTRODUCTION TO INTERPRETIVE CANONS

To familiarize you with some common canons, and to demonstrate how two sides might present their respective canonical arguments, consider this hypothetical statute and scenario:

§ 1. Punishing any and all violence at schools

(a) *Committing an act of violence with a weapon, including a gun or knife, an explosive device, or a weapon of mass destruction at a school shall be punishable by imprisonment of not less than ten years.*

(b) *Committing an act of violence at a school without using a weapon, explosive device, weapon of mass destruction, or other device capable of inflicting harm shall be punishable by imprisonment of not more than one year.*

Wielding a baseball bat, Smith attacks Jones at a public high school. Prosecutors charge him with violating § 1(a) in the above statute and seek to imprison him for ten years. Smith seeks to dismiss the indictment. What canons can each side invoke? Notice that *both* sides invoke one major canon.

DEFENDANT'S ARGUMENTS	PROSECUTION'S ARGUMENTS
Ordinary meaning. A "weapon" is primarily used to inflict harm, unlike a baseball bat, which is used *primarily* to play a game. Thus, a bat is not a "weapon."	*Ordinary meaning.* A weapon is any instrument that can be used to attack another person, whether or not it has some other use. A baseball bat qualifies.
Noscitur a sociis. A word derives meaning from the company it keeps. Section 1(a) prohibits using "an explosive device" or "a weapon of mass destruction." These objects *primarily* exist to cause harm, and can cause *mass* harm, unlike a baseball bat. These neighboring items in § 1(a) suggest that a baseball bat is outside the statute's ambit.	*Ejusdem generis.* Examples of what a term means illuminate the term's meaning. Thus, the inclusion of a "knife" as an example of a weapon § 1(a)—a tool with a potential non-violent purpose that cannot easily cause mass harm—shows that dangerous tools like a baseball bat are fairly included in the meaning of "weapon."
Expressio unius est exclusio alterius. Expressing something in one place but excluding it elsewhere implies that the exclusion was intentional. Section 1(b) refers to using any *"other device capable of inflicting harm,"* which would apply to a baseball bat. But § 1(a) omits any mention of "other devices capable of inflicting harm." The *expressio unius* canon therefore suggests that the legislature did not intend § 1(a) to reach "other devices" such as Smith's baseball bat.	*Absurdity doctrine.* A bat isn't a "weapon" under Smith's reading, so Smith couldn't be charged under § 1(a). But § 1(b) only applies if someone *does not* use some other "device capable of inflicting harm." Thus, using a baseball bat means that Smith cannot be charged under § 1(b) either. Thus, hitting a schoolchild with a baseball bat would go unpunished under Smith's argument. Statutes must be read to avoid that sort of absurd result. Smith's approach would produce an absurd result.
Surplusage canon. Statutes should be read to ensure that every word has some meaning. If "weapon" included a baseball bat, there would be no need in § 1(b) to refer to "other device[s] capable of inflicting harm."	*Presumption of nonexclusive "include"*: The word "including" in § 1(a) shows that the statute is merely presenting examples, not a complete list of what qualifies as a "weapon."
Rule of Lenity. Ambiguities in criminal law should be resolved in a defendant's favor. If the court thinks the statute is ambiguous, that ambiguity should be resolved against incarcerating Smith.	*Title-and-headings canon.* Courts may look at headings for guidance about a law's meaning. Here, the heading shows that the legislature intended to punish "any and all" violence at schools, and Smith plainly cannot be punished under § 1(b). Thus, § 1(a) should be construed as applying to his assault on Jones.

| Example 7.1 | **Takeaway point 7.1:** Use dictionaries, usage, and commonsense examples to illustrate the "ordinary meaning" of a disputed term. |

When lawyers battle over the meaning of a disputed term, they use "canons" — interpretive rules for construing the meaning of a word or phrase. We look next at one of the primary canons: ordinary meaning. Courts usually conclude that a disputed term in a statute or contract means whatever that term typically means.

In the next example, an American who traveled to the Middle East was tortured and killed. His family sued the Palestinian Authority, which had allegedly overseen and approved the torture and murder. The lawsuit was based on the Torture Victim Protection Act (TVPA), which authorizes suit against any "individual" who violates the TVPA's provisions. The Palestinian Authority moved to dismiss, arguing that "individual" refers only to human beings, not organizations. The example shows how lawyers argued that the word "individual" barred the lawsuit.

Source: Brief of the Palestinian Authority from *Mohamad v. Palestinian Authority*, 132 S. Ct. 1702 (2011).

1   This Court has "stated time and again that courts must presume that a legis-
2 lature says in a statute what it means and means in a statute what it says there."
3 *Conn. Nat'l Bank v. Germain*, 503 U.S. 249, 253-254 (1992). This Court's analysis
4 "begins with 'the language of the statute,'" and "where the statutory language
5 provides a clear answer, it ends there as well." *Hughes Aircraft Co. v. Jacobson*,   A
6 525 U.S. 432, 438 (1999).
7   The TVPA imposes liability on an "individual." Where, as here, a statute uses
8 a term that it does not define, the term must be given its ordinary meaning. *See*
9 *FCC v. AT&T Inc.*, 131 S. Ct. 1177, 1182 (2011). As the court below unanimously
10 recognized, the ordinary meaning of "individual" is a natural person, not a legal
11 entity like a corporation. Pet. App. 6a-8a.   B
12   In ordinary usage, "individual" refers to "a single human being, as distin-
13 guished from a group." *Random House Dictionary of the English Language*
14 974 (2d ed. 1987); *see also Webster's Third New International Dictionary* 1152
15 (1986) ("a single human being as contrasted with a social group or institution").
16 Because "individual" does not have a different specialized legal meaning, legal
17 dictionaries define the term in a manner consistent with its ordinary usage: "As
18 a noun, [individual] denotes a single person as distinguished from a group or
19 class, and also, very commonly, a private or natural person as distinguished
20 from a partnership, corporation, or association." *Black's Law Dictionary* 773
21 (6th ed. 1990). "*[I]ndividual* is best confined to contexts in which the writer   C
22 intends to distinguish the single (noncorporate) person from the group or crowd."
23 B. Garner, *A Dictionary of Modern Legal Usage* 291 (1987).
24   We thus use "individual" in both common and legal parlance to make clear
25 that we are referring to a human being and not a group, corporation, or institu-
26 tion. We contrast an individual tax return with a corporate return, individual tax
27 rates with corporate rates, and individual campaign contributions with corporate
28 contributions. We contrast individual responsibility with corporate responsibil-
29 ity, individual defendants with corporate or governmental defendants, individ-
30 ual investors with institutional investors, and an individual mandate with one
31 imposed on businesses. . . .   D

32   This Court routinely uses "individual" to distinguish a human being from a
33   corporation or other artificial entity. In *Goodyear Dunlop Tires Operations, S.A*
34   *v. Brown*, 131 S. Ct. 2846 (2011), the Court stated that, "[f]or an individual, the
35   paradigm forum for the exercise of general jurisdiction is the individual's domi-
36   cile; for a corporation, it is an equivalent place, one in which the corporation is
37   fairly regarded as at home."[The brief cites eight more cases here.]
38   Precisely because its meaning is so obvious, "individual" is not frequently
39   defined in the U.S. Code. When provisions do define the term, they routinely
40   do so merely to confirm that the term includes only natural persons (or certain
41   categories of natural persons). *See* 5 U.S.C. §552a(a)(2) ("[T]he term 'individual'
42   means a citizen of the United States or an alien lawfully admitted for permanent
43   residence. . . ."); 20 U.S.C. §5602(3) ("[T]he term 'eligible individual' means
44   a citizen or national of the United States or a permanent resident alien of the
45   United States. . . ."); 29 U.S.C. §1301(a)(14)(C)(ii)(V) ("'[I]ndividual' means a
46   living human being. . . ."); 43 U.S.C. §390bb(4) ("The term 'individual' means
47   any natural person, including his or her spouse, and including other dependents
48   thereof. . . ."). Those statutes include legislation passed by the same Congress
49   that enacted the TVPA in 1992. *See* Pub. L. No. 102-229, §214, 105 Stat. 1701,
50   1719 (1991) (codified at 29 U.S.C. §1301(14)(C)(ii)(V)); *see also* 137 Cong. Rec.
51   2255 (1991) ("'The term "individual" means a human being.'").
52   The Code of Federal Regulations reflects the same consensus: "Individual
53   means a natural person." [The brief cites nineteen regulations here.] As one
54   regulation explains, "[i]ndividual means a citizen of the United States or an alien
55   lawfully admitted . . . but does not include proprietorships, businesses, or corpo-
56   rations." 10 C.F.R. §1008.2(f); *see also* 20 C.F.R. §401.25 ("Individual . . . means
57   a living person who is a citizen of the United States or an alien lawfully admitted
58   for permanent residence. It does not include persons such as sole proprietor-
59   ships, partnerships, or corporations.").
60   Federal law is hardly unique. *Every one* of the 50 States has at least one stat-
61   ute defining "individual" as a "natural person." [The brief cites the laws of fifty
62   states and the District of Columbia here.]

A Textual arguments often begin by emphasizing that text — not legislative history or policy — is the primary method of interpreting a statute or clause.

B The brief introduces its first canon: ordinary meaning. The next paragraph applies this canon to the word "individual." The brief also draws a clear line between its interpretation and the other side's interpretation.

C The brief cites four dictionaries that were published from 1986 to 1990. But there are more current editions of these dictionaries. Did the lawyers err? No. The TVPA was enacted in 1991, so the brief cites the dictionaries that reflect what the word "individual" meant when Congress acted. This choice reflects stellar attention to detail.

D These creative examples suggest that the meaning of "individual" is apparent from the word's ordinary use. Chief Justice Roberts used a similar passage in his opinion in *AT&T Inc.*, 131 S. Ct. at 1182 (cited above) ("We do not usually speak of personal characteristics, personal effects, personal correspondence, personal influence, or personal tragedy as referring to corporations or other artificial entities. This is not to say that corporations do not have correspondence, influence, or tragedies of their own, only that we do not use the word 'personal' to describe them.").

E The next few paragraphs reflect common techniques for construing a statute under the ordinary meaning canon, such as looking at how courts have used a term and at how other statutes and regulations define a term.

Example
7.2

Takeaway point 7.2: Familiarize yourself with and use interpretive canons but don't forget to use common sense.

The last example showed how lawyers use a term's ordinary meaning to construe a statute. When a statute is ambiguous (and even when it isn't), lawyers delve into various other canons to show that a statute means what their clients want it to mean.

There are dozens of canons — 57 according to the book *Reading Law* by Justice Scalia and Bryan Garner, and even more (almost 200!) according to the 2012 supplement to *Legislation* by Professors William Eskridge, Elizabeth Garrett, and James Brudney. Familiarize yourself with the canons, but also trust your instincts: if some piece of information clarifies the meaning of a disputed term, mention that information (even if you do not know the name of the applicable canon). Think of these canons as clues about a disputed term's meaning.

We look below at how lawyers use some of these clues. The case involves an employee who complained *orally* when his company violated the Fair Labor Standards Act of 1938 (FLSA) by underpaying him. Later, the company fired the employee, leading him to file an antiretaliation suit. He based his suit on a separate provision of the FLSA (29 U.S.C. § 215(a)(3)) that prevents any employer from firing employees because they *"filed* any complaint" about FLSA violations. The district court, however, granted summary judgment for the employer, holding that the antiretaliation provision applies only when an employee complains in writing — not orally. After losing again on appeal, the fired worker took his case to the Supreme Court; if "file" included oral complaints, he could revive his lawsuit and, potentially, reclaim his job.

Source: Terminated employee's brief in *Kasten v. Saint-Gobain Performance Plastics Corp.*, 131 S. Ct. 1325 (2011). (Some footnotes omitted.)

1   The Seventh Circuit's decision rests on a single mistaken premise: that [o]ne
2   cannot 'file' an oral complain . . . .
3   Had the framers of the FLSA wished to limit section 215(a)(3) to written com-
4   plaints, they would undoubtedly have said so in just those terms. Three other
5   provisions of the FLSA itself expressly require that something be "written" or "in
6   writing." Section 210(a) provides that judicial review of an order of the Secretary
7   under section 208 may be obtained "by *filing* . . . a *written* petition praying
8   that the order of the Secretary be modified or set aside in whole or in part." 29
9   U.S.C. § 210(a) (emphasis added). Section 214(c)(5)(A) states, regarding cer-
10 tain lawsuits, that "[n]o employee may be a party to any such action unless the
11 employee or the employee's parent or guardian gives consent *in writing* to
12 become such a party and such consent is *filed* with the Secretary." 29 U.S.C.
13 § 214(c)(5)(A) (emphasis added). Similarly, section 216(b) provides that "[n]o
14 employee shall be a party plaintiff to any such [civil] action . . . unless he gives
15 his consent *in writing* to become such a party and such consent is *filed* in the
16 court in which such action is brought." 29 U.S.C. § 216(b) (emphasis added).
17   Each of these provisions contains an express requirement of a written docu-
18 ment despite the fact that they also require that the matter be "filed," the piv-
19 otal disputed term in section 215(a)(3). If Congress had intended or understood
20 "filed" to mean "filed in writing," it would not have included the additional
21 requirement of a written document in sections 210(a), 214(c)(5)(A) and 216(b).
22 If "filed" invariably meant "in writing," it would be redundant to refer to the
23 filing of a written document. . . . As the Seventh Circuit dissent explained, "[I]t

A

B

is noteworthy that Congress in many other statues has specifically required written complaints. . . . These statutes suggest that when Congress means to require
that complaints take a written form, it sets forth that requirement expressly."[28]
(P. App. 7.) . . . .

It is not uncommon for an "employee" protected under the FLSA to communicate with supervisors orally when they interact on a day-to-day basis. (P. App.
59.) This is particularly true in the context of the blue-collar industry, factory,
and retail employees that the FLSA was primarily adopted to protect. Workers
who are illiterate also most often find hourly paid employment, and would be
most likely to communicate complaints verbally.[31]

---

28. *E.g.,* 2 U.S.C. § 437g(a)(1) ("complaint shall be in writing"); 5 U.S.C.
§ 3330a(a)(2)(B) (same); 7 U.S.C. § 193(a) ("complaint in writing"); 7 U.S.C. § 228b-2(a)
(same); 7 U.S.C. § 1599(a) (same); 15 U.S.C. § 80b-9(a) ("file with it a statement in
writing"); 19 U.S.C. § 2561(a) (stating a federal agency may not consider a complaint
unless the agency is informed "in writing"); 33 U.S.C. § 392 ("a statement of complaint, verified by oath in writing"); 38 U.S.C. § 4322(b) ("complaint shall be in writing"); 42 U.S.C. § 2000b(a) ("complaint in writing"); 42 U.S.C. § 2000c-6(a) (same);
42 U.S.C. § 3610(a)(1)(A)(ii) ("complaints shall be in writing"); 42 U.S.C. § 15512(a)
(2)(C) ("[C]omplaint filed . . . shall be in writing and notarized, and signed and sworn
by the person filing the complaint."); 47 U.S.C. § 554(g) ("A complaint by any such
person shall be in writing, and shall be signed and sworn to by that person."); 49
U.S.C. § 46101(a)(1) ("A person may file a complaint in writing . . . .").   `C`

31. The most recent data available to Congress when it enacted the FLSA was
from the 1930 Census[, which] reflected the following statistics: 73% of the American
workforce was employed in blue-collar labor professions; there were 63,489 individuals who were blind; there were 4,283,753 (4.3%) individuals who were illiterate; and
869,865 (7%) Caucasian individuals who were foreign-born could not read and write
in English. . . . Congress therefore would have likely been aware of the extremely large
population group that would be unlikely or unable to submit a written complaint in
1938.   `D`

A Notice that the three provisions are less probative than advertised; each merely shows that something that was written down was being filed — *not* that something can be filed orally. Nevertheless, this sort of clue is worth citing. In the next paragraph, the lawyers cite clues from statutes other than FLSA.

B The brief does not specify which canons it is rely-ing on. That's fine. What matters is that you find good clues of a statute's meaning, whether or not you iden-tify which canon makes that clue probatitive.

C These citations are strong, and the lawyers proba-bly wrestled with the choice of whether to move them

— or the strongest of them — to the text (rather than placing them all in a footnote). Replicate this dogged, creative research for your own clients.

D This point is a sophisticated attempt to make a fact-based and policy argument look like a canonical argument (about what Congress is pre-sumed to know about Census data). And it worked. The seven-Justice majority relied on this point, dem-onstrating that good advocacy sometimes depends less on rigid canons or doctrines than on common sense and policy.

Example 7.3

Takeaway point 7.3: Organize textual arguments like doctrinal arguments: build your affirmative case and then rebut the other side's position.

Once you explain the textual arguments that support your client, you need to rebut textual arguments that disfavor your client. Confront whichever canons pose a problem to your client's reading of the text just as you would counter adverse cases: dodge or diminish the other side's arguments.

We see below an example of how to respond to the other side's reliance on a canon. A number of hedge funds wanted to hide their coordinated attempt to seize control of a major railroad. Federal law, however, appeared to require the hedge funds to alert the target railroad that they were working with other groups to seize control of the company. The funds failed to do so. (Think of the hedge funds as wolves slipping as close to their prey as possible before springing their attack.) The railroad used the funds' failure to disclose their plan to try to block the wolf pack from voting its shares. The hedge funds' argument turns on the phrase "beneficial owner," which they argue renders the next section of the statute superfluous. But courts generally refuse to read statutes in a way that renders any term meaningless, which is called the canon against superfluity. The following passage attacks that canon.

Source: Brief for hedge funds from *CSX Corp. v. Children's Investment Fund Management (UK) LLP,* 292 Fed. App'x 133 (2d Cir. 2008).

---

1   Canons are helpful guideposts, not rigid or inflexible rules. *See, e.g.,* William
2   N. Eskridge, Jr. et al., Cases & Materials on Legislation: Statutes & The Creation
3   of Public Policy 849 (4th ed. 2007). . . . [T]he American legal profession is to a
4   large extent devoted to designing transactions to avoid legal or regulatory bur-
5   dens, and there is nothing inherently wrong with that. But lawmakers and regu-
6   lators often respond by taking a "belt and suspenders" approach in which words
7   and categories overlap. One need look no further than the venerable aiding and   **A**
8   abetting statute, 18 U.S.C. § 2, for an example: that statute makes anyone who
9   "aids, abets, counsels, commands, induces or procures" a federal crime punish-
10 able as a principal. Needless to say, it is hard to imagine "aiding" that is not also
11 "abetting," or "inducing" that is not also "procuring." But Congress obviously   **B**
12 chose to err on the side of caution to avoid the risk of leaving a legal loophole.
13 And that is hardly an unusual situation. *See, e.g., Gutierrez v. Ada,* 528 U.S. 250,
14 258 (2000)("There is no question that the statute would be read as we read it
15 even if the phrase were missing. But as one rule of construction among many,
16 albeit an important one, the rule against redundancy does not necessarily have
17 the strength to turn a tide of good cause to come out the other way."); *Bab-*   **C**
18 *bitt v. Sweet Home Chapter of Communities,* 515 U.S. 687, 703 (1995) ("Any
19 overlap . . . is unexceptional, . . . and simply reflects the broad purpose of the
20 Act."); *cf. M'Culloch v. Maryland,* 17 U.S. (4 Wheat.) 316, 420 (1819) ("If no
21 other motive for its insertion can be suggested, a sufficient one is found in the
22 desire to remove all doubts.") (Marshall, C.J.).

(A) This metaphor — based on the point that a belt renders suspenders superfluous — is a common term among lawyers who draft contracts.

(B) **The lawyers realize that, to win, they need to make superfluity seem normal and common: that will render their argument plausible. So they focus on well-known examples, even though the subject matter of the authorities that they cite is totally different. All judges will be familiar with aiding and abetting, and there's really no debate over whether the meanings of these terms overlap. This passage demonstrates how a well-known example can help to rebut your adversary's argument, even when the example has nothing to do with the case's subject matter.**

(C) While this language is dicta, the quotation is directly on point from the Supreme Court. Using it reflects stellar research and excellent instincts, as the lawyers realize that a good citation will add vital credibility to an argument that might otherwise seem implausible. The lawyers recruit to their cause both recent and time-tested cases. Case law supports their textual argument.

Example
7.4

Takeaway point 7.4: Construe disputed contract clauses by using both general and subject-specific canons.

The techniques that lawyers use to construe statutes often apply to contracts, too. The next example — from a multibillion-dollar dispute arising out of one of the decade's worst environmental disasters — demonstrates this point.

On April 20, 2010, the Deepwater Horizon drilling unit exploded in the Gulf of Mexico. Eleven workers died, the rig sank, and millions of gallons of oil spewed into the Gulf. More than 200,000 plaintiffs filed lawsuits against the companies involved in the botched drilling effort, which caused the disaster. Two of the primary defendants were BP, which supervised the drilling of the oil well, and Transocean, owner of the drilling unit (which is like a mobile oil platform). Transocean potentially faced billions of dollars in liability, but it argued in a pretrial motion that the parties' contract required BP to indemnify (i.e., reimburse) Transocean for all of its liability. Below, BP acknowledges that the contract requires it to indemnify Transocean if Transocean acted negligently. But BP denies that it had any obligation to indemnify Transocean for *gross negligence* or for *strict liability*. The outcome of this contractual skirmish would shift billions of dollars from one party to the other.

Source: BP's Cross-Motion for Partial Summary Judgment, *In re Deepwater Horizon*, 2:10-md-02179-CJB-SS Dock. 4827-1 (E.D. La. Dec. 7, 2011) (altering the name of a BP affiliate from "BPAP" to "BP").

---

1   **A. The Plain Terms of the Drilling Contract Provide No Indemnity for Losses**
2   **Resulting from Gross Negligence or Strict Liability.**

3   Paragraph 24.2 of the Drilling Contract defines BP's duty to indemnify Trans-
4   ocean for pollution losses, and by its terms does not extend to pollution caused
5   by Transocean's gross negligence or conduct for which Transocean is strictly
6   liable, such as violations of [the federal Oil Pollution Act] or the duty to provide
7   a seaworthy vessel. The paragraph states that BP will indemnify Transocean
8   "without regard for *negligence* of any party or parties and specifically without
9   regard for whether the pollution . . . is caused in whole or in part by the *negli-*
10 *gence or fault* of [Transocean]." Ex. 1, Drilling Contract ¶ 24.2 (emphases added).
11 By specifying that the indemnity covers "negligence" or "fault," the parties did
12 not extend it to cover the distinct concepts of strict liability or gross negligence.
13 Where the parties have specified particular causes of loss that are covered by an
14 indemnity, the indemnity cannot be expanded to cover *other* causes not within
15 the natural meaning of the terms the parties have chosen. *See, e.g., Babcock v.*
16 *Cont'l Oil Co.*, 792 F.2d 1346, 1350-51 (5th Cir. 1986); *Corbitt v. Diamond M.*
17 *Drilling Co.*, 654 F.2d 329, 332-33 (5th Cir. 1981); see also *Smith v. Tenneco Oil*
18 *Co.*, 803 F.2d 1386, 1388 (5th Cir. 1986) ("Indemnity agreements are to be strictly
19 construed.").
20 This is especially the case here, since other provisions of the Drilling Contract
21 show that the parties knew how to specify gross negligence and strict liability
22 when they intended to address them. For example, Paragraph 23.1 specifically
23 addresses obligations in the event of "gross negligence" or "willful misconduct"
24 resulting in loss of or damage to the hole. [The "hole" refers to the passage
25 drilled into the seabed from which oil is extracted]. Ex. 1 ¶ 23.1. Likewise, Para-
26 graph 25.1 expressly includes losses arising from "strict liability" and "unsea-
27 worthiness." *Id.* ¶ 25.1. As this Court has explained, in these varying indemnity
28 provisions, the parties "made specific, 'blow-by-blow' allocations of liabilities

29 between themselves." Dkt. 4588, Order and reasons at 38. The different terms

30 the parties chose to specify the causes of loss that would be covered by the differ-

31 ent indemnities must be given effect. *Matador Petroleum Corp. v. St. Paul Surplus*

32 *Lines Ins. Co.*, 174 F.3d 653, 656-57 (5th Cir. 1999). . . . Indeed, the importance

33 of the different terms used in each paragraph of the indemnity provisions is but-

34 tressed by the Court's determination that the *expressio unius* canon of construc-

35 tion applies to interpreting this contract. Dkt. 4588 at 38-39. Here, the *inclusion*

36 of "negligence or fault" in Paragraph 24.2 necessarily *excludes* from the indem-

37 nity losses resulting from other causes not specifically included, such as "gross

38 negligence," "strict liability," and "unseaworthiness."

39   That textual limitation in Paragraph 24.2 is further reinforced by the rule

40 under maritime law that an "extraordinary obligation" in an indemnity must

41 be "clearly express[ed] . . . in unequivocal terms." *Corbitt*, 654 F.2d at 333. An

42 agreement to indemnify another even for simple negligence is an "extraordinary

43 obligation" requiring a clear statement. *Id. A fortiori*, covering gross negligence

44 or violation of duties giving rise to strict liability requires unequivocal language.

45 Gross negligence, after all, "is substantially and appreciably higher in magnitude

46 than ordinary negligence." *Houston Exploration Co. v. Halliburton Energy Servs.,*

47 *Inc.*, 269 F.3d 528, 531-32 (5th Cir. 2001). Accordingly, this Court has held that

48 "silence dictates . . . exclusion" of gross negligence from an indemnity. . . . *In re*

49 *Torch, Inc.*, 1996 WL 185765, at *8-9 (E.D. La. Apr. 16, 1996). . . .

50   And the Fifth Circuit . . . has held that the logic demanding "clear and

51 unequivocal" language to cover negligence applies equally to strict liability. . . .

A Just as Example 7.1 argued that the plain meaning of "individual" was unambiguous, BP argues that the contract is crystal clear. Lawyers try to project confidence (without overdoing it); if you seem like you doubt your own position, judges will doubt it too.

B This section begins with a long sentence. The point is complicated, so the lawyers might have benefited from breaking the sentence into small pieces. The frenzied pace of high-stakes trial litigation affords less time for editing than when preparing appellate briefs. Thus, commit to muscle memory the writing principles discussed in Chapter 16.

C Passages that rely on textual arguments tend to emphasize more words than other passages because lawyers want to be especially sure that judges focus on the right words.

D Notice that all three cases cited here involved oil companies. Short explanatory parentheticals might have been helpful.

E We see here an interpretive technique that mirrors the way that litigants help courts to construe a statute, as Example 7.2 demonstrated.

F BP uses the district court judge's own words from an earlier stage of the lawsuit to advance its argument. This powerful trick can be effective when used gently — to remind the Court of its own conclusions. BP uses the you-already-decided-this-issue technique again later in the same paragraph.

G BP invokes a subject-specific canon that governs maritime disputes. Consult treatises and cases (and previous motions and briefs) that relate to the subject of your dispute to ensure that you do not overlook helpful interpretive tools. The lawyers' expertise is on display here.

H When a contract or statute is silent, lawyers fight to show that the default rule (about how to construe that provision) favors their client.

FREQUENTLY ASKED QUESTIONS ABOUT TEXTUAL ARGUMENTS

Q. Do I need to memorize all fifty-seven (or more) canons for resolving textual ambiguities?

A. No, although familiarizing yourself with them makes sense, especially if your practice regularly entails interpreting statutes or contracts. Many briefs and motions simply *use* the canons without naming them; thus, cultivate instincts for the sorts of interpretive clues that will help you. Many of the text-based canons are built on common sense. For instance, if a statute says that "dogs and cats are banned from all national parks" and then the legislature enacted another statute in the same section stating that "cats are banned from all national monuments," it's reasonable to think that a judge would infer that the omission of "dogs" from the second statute was deliberate, reflecting the legislature's intent to permit dogs into national monuments

But knowing the names of canons is helpful, both because some doctrinal canons are not intuitive and because knowing the names makes it easier to find cases that relied on the canon that you are invoking.

Q. This chapter lists a variety of techniques for making textual arguments. In what order do I present these arguments?

A. In federal courts, litigants most frequently begin with the text's plain meaning and then move to various canons for interpreting ambiguous statutes or clauses. Only then do they refer to legislative history, which is discussed in the next chapter. Some state courts (and some federal judges) reprioritize these elements and add others, and lawyers, of course, adapt accordingly. But starting with plain meaning, moving to textual clues and other interpretive canons, and then invoking legislative history (and policy) is a standard and fairly safe sequence.

Q. My argument is based on a long statute. Do I need to include the entire section (or the entire act) in my motion or brief?

A. No. Reprint short statutes or the relevant part of a longer statute in your motion or brief in the Applicable Statutes section. But consider including the full text of lengthy statutes in an appendix. Ensure that, in some manner, you give judges access to the relevant statute.

Q. I noticed that Example 7.1 cited statutes without adding a space between "§" and the section number; for instance, it referred to "§214" rather than "§ 214". Was that a Bluebooking error?

A. Textual arguments tend to cite many sources. The Supreme Court rules require merits briefs to contain no more than 15,000 words, and the brief reprinted in Example 7.1 uses the "§" exactly 281 times. By removing the space between the "§" and the following number, the lawyers gained almost two extra paragraphs of substantive argument. Just don't think that judges are unaware of the lawyers' motivations.

Chapter 8

Arguments Based on Legislative History

When lawyers try to persuade judges, they often find it advantageous to discuss the process by which a legislature enacted a law. Collectively, the materials from the legislative process — other than the final statute or ordinance — are referred to as "legislative history." There are many reasons to inform judges of the legislative history of a statute, and this chapter explores some of the principal ones. For instance, legislative history can help judges to construe an ambiguous statute, can strengthen a lawyer's policy-based argument by using the legislature's own words, or can show that the legislative either failed to consider an issue or acted for an improper reason.

CHAPTER OVERVIEW

1. Some judges treasure legislative history, some ignore it. Assess the preferences of your judge before you spend time building arguments around legislative history. Even its critics, however, concede that most judges rely on it and that lawyers should cite it in their motions and briefs.

2. In general, legislative history is most effective when lawyers use it to resolve an ambiguous statute or to discuss the legislature's goals, thereby legitimizing policy arguments. (Policy arguments are discussed more extensively in Chapter 9.)

3. Use legislative history to back up your primary argument.

4. When you want to use legislative history to show what a statute means, consider making your legislative history look like a textual or doctrinal argument, such as by juxtaposing the final language of a statute against earlier drafts of the same statute or by citing cases that relied on legislative history rather than by citing the legislative history itself.

5. Legislative history usually *proves* nothing, but it can provide important or persuasive hints about a statute. Chapter 7 referred to the canons of interpretation as clues; legislative history also provides clues about what the legislature intended.

6. Learn which types of legislative history courts favor (e.g., committee reports and juxtapositions of the final statute against earlier bills) and which types they tend to doubt (e.g., comments from individual legislators who did not even introduce the legislation). The legislative history that best advances a client's goal, however, will vary from case to case, so use legislative history creatively. And even an individual member's statement is better than nothing.

7. When you use legislative history for atmospheric effect — such as to show that Congress was worried about a specific problem — consider including it in your Statement of Facts rather than in your Argument. (*See* Chapter 3).

Example 8.1	**Takeaway point 8.1:** Use legislative history — especially committee reports and earlier drafts or versions of the legislation — to corroborate your client's reading of a statutory provision.

The following passage focuses on two important types of legislative history: committee reports and bills that preceded the final act. Those two types of materials are often powerful clues of what a statute means.

We revisit the case that assessed whether a foreign group that allegedly tortured and killed a U.S. citizen was liable under the federal Torture Victims Protection Act (TVPA), which makes any "individual" liable for violations of the law. The Palestinian Authority's lawyers argue here that, based on the word "individual," Congress intended for the TVPA to apply only to human beings — not to groups.

Source: Palestinian Authority's brief from *Mohamad v. Palestinian Authority,* 132 S. Ct. 1702 (2012).

---

1   **C. The Legislative History Confirms That Congress Deliberately Used the Term**
2   **"Individual" To Limit the TVPA to Natural Persons**
3   Consistent with the ordinary meaning of "individual," the legislative history
4   makes clear that Congress deliberately used that term to limit the TVPA's cover-
5   age to natural persons. Congress did not merely use the term "individual" rather
6   than "person" in the TVPA. It substituted the word "individual" for "person" for
7   the precise purpose of excluding organizational liability.
8   1. Earlier versions of the Act provided a cause of action against any "per-
9   son" who subjected another to torture or extrajudicial killing under color of
10   foreign law. 132 Cong. Rec. 12,950 (1986) (text of S. 2528); *see* H.R. 4756, 99th
11   Cong. (1986). But the House Committee on Foreign Affairs rejected that phrasing
12   because it would have extended liability beyond natural persons. During the
13   committee markup, Representative Leach proposed an amendment to "make it
14   clear we are applying [the Act] to individuals and not to corporations." *Hearing*
15   *and Markup on H.R. 1417 Before the H. Comm. on Foreign Affairs,* 100th Cong. 87
16   (1988) (*"1988 Hearings"*). The House counsel responded that this change would
17   require only "a fairly simple amendment," as it would entail only "changing the
18   word, 'person' to 'individuals' in several places in the bill." *Id.* at 88. "[T]he
19   intention [of the amendment]," he noted, was "to limit the application of this
20   civil action so that only individuals who engaged in torture could be the defen-
21   dants." *Id.* at 87. . . .
22   The Committee then adopted that amendment by unanimous consent. *1988*
23   *Hearings* 88. The TVPA as enacted retained the term "individual," affording a
24   cause of action against the responsible "individual" rather than "person." Pub.
25   L. No. 102-256, §2(a), 106 Stat, at 73.
26   There is thus no need to speculate about the reason for Congress's choice
27   of the term "individual." Congress replaced "person" with "individual" to limit
28   the category of those subject to suit under the statute to natural persons. While
29   petitioners belittle the significance of that change, Pet. Br. 44, this Court has not
30   hesitated to rely on such amendments when construing statutes: "Few principles
31   of statutory construction are more compelling than the proposition that Congress
32   does not intend *sub silentio* to enact statutory language that it has earlier dis-
33   carded in favor of other language." *INS v. Cardoza-Fonseca,* 480 U.S. 421, 442-443
34   (1987) (quotation marks omitted) . . . . That canon is all but conclusive here.

2. Petitioners attribute a different rationale to Congress's use of the term "individual" — a desire to exclude *state* entities. Pet. Br. 43-44. As they note, the 1991 Senate Report explains that "[t]he legislation uses the term 'individual' to make crystal clear that foreign states or their entities cannot be sued under this bill under any circumstances: only individuals may be sued." S. Rep. No. 102-249, at 7 (1991). And the House Report confirms that "[o]nly 'individuals,' not foreign states, can be sued under the bill." H.R. Rep. No. 102-367, at 4 (1991); *see also* Pet. Br. 44-45 & nn.10-12 (similar floor statements and hearing testimony). But the ordinary meaning of "individual" achieves that goal by limiting the Act to natural persons — thereby excluding *both* state entities *and* other organizations. Congress's deliberate decision to use "individual" to exclude state entities thus confirms that Congress was using the term in that ordinary sense.

If Congress had intended to exclude only foreign state entities, it would have been easy enough to write the liability provision broadly and then explicitly exempt those entities. *See, e.g.*, 18 U.S.C. §2337(2) (barring actions against "a foreign state" or "an agency of a foreign state"). Alternatively, Congress could have kept the term "person," which this Court has repeatedly construed not to include sovereigns (at least when referring to potential defendants). *See, e.g., Will v. Mich. Dep't of State Police*, 491 U.S. 58, 64-71 (1989); . . . . *United States v. Cooper Corp.*, 312 U.S. 600, 604 (1941) ("[T]he term 'person' does not include the sovereign, [and] statutes employing the [word] are ordinarily construed to exclude it."). Indeed, as this Court explained in *Ngiraingas v. Sanchez*, 495 U.S. 182 (1990), Congress amended the Dictionary Act's definition of "person" in 1874 precisely to make clear that it does not cover sovereigns. . . .

Congress thus had ample means to exclude states, and only states, from the TVPA. Instead, Congress limited the Act's coverage to "individuals." That word choice certainly made it "crystal clear that foreign states or their entities cannot be sued." S. Rep. No. 102-249, at 7.

Ⓐ This section *followed* the brief's textual arguments: legislative history is best used as a backup argument.

Ⓑ **When interpreting legislation (and clauses in the U.S. Constitution), courts often scour drafts of the law (bills and amendments) for evidence of what the final language means. Prior *enacted* versions of a law are referred to as "statutory history." Both resources can provide valuable clues about a statute's meaning.**

Ⓒ These citations refer to bills that were proposed in the House of Representatives (H.R. 4756) and the Senate (S. 2528). The bills appear in the *Congressional Record*, which logs the events that occur on the floor of each chamber of Congress.

Ⓓ Many judges deride citations to the statement of a single legislator, saying that cherry-picking helpful language is like looking for "a friend in a crowd." Here, however, the lawyers expertly contextualize the quotation, noting that the House counsel opined on how to achieve Leach's goal and that the committee then unanimously adopted this language.

Ⓔ Use precedent to validate legislative history.

Ⓕ The lawyers use textual and doctrinal arguments (as well as legislative history) to counter the other side's legislative history argument. You do not need to fight fire with fire; you help your cause when you remain flexible and invoke varied authorities to rebut the other side's arguments.

Ⓖ As we have seen throughout the book, lawyers try to end sections with strong points or punchy quotes. The "crystal clear" remark comes from a committee report, lending credibility to this great quotation.

Example 8.2	**Takeaway point 8.2:** Use legislative history to reveal a statute's invisible meaning and to let elected officials make your client's policy arguments.

Let's look at one more prototypical example of building a legislative history argument. It relies on a larger array of legislative history clues than the prior example. In April 1992, Hannah Bruesewitz — then an infant — received a vaccine for diphtheria, tetanus, and pertussis. Within twenty-four hours, she began experiencing recurring seizures. Her parents filed a claim in a special federal court that had been established to award quick, fixed payments when a vaccine caused harm (i.e., a strict liability system). That court, however, denied the Bruesewitzes' claims, finding insufficient evidence that the vaccine had caused Hannah's seizures. Hannah's parents then filed a lawsuit based on state tort law, alleging that the vaccine had caused their daughter's condition. The trial and appellate courts, however, barred these claims, holding that the National Childhood Vaccine Injury Act of 1986 conflicted with — and therefore blocked under the doctrine of federal preemption — the parents' state law claims. Here, the vaccine maker uses legislative history to argue that Congress intended to preempt state-law claims like those filed by Hannah's parents.

Source: Brief for the vaccine's manufacturer in *Bruesewitz v. Wyeth*, 131 S. Ct. 1068 (2011).

---

1 II. THE LEGISLATIVE HISTORY CONFIRMS THAT SECTION 22(b)(1)
2   PREEMPTS DESIGN-DEFECT CLAIMS
3   Because the text . . . and the structure of the Vaccine Act demonstrate
4   Congress's intent to preempt state-law design-defect claims arising from vaccine-
5   related injuries, the Vaccine Act's legislative history need not be consulted, but
6   if consulted, that history confirms Respondent's and the Third Circuit's interpre-   **A**
7   tation. . . .
8   H.R. Rep. No. 99-908, prepared in 1986 in support of the Vaccine Act by
9   the Committee on Energy and Commerce (the "1986 House Report"), provides
10   "the authoritative source for finding the Legislature's intent." *Garcia v. United*   **B**
11   *States*, 469 U.S. 70, 76 (1984) ("Committee Reports on the bill, . . . '[represent]   **C**
12   the considered and collective understanding of those Congressmen involved in
13   drafting and studying proposed legislation.'") (quoting *Zuber v. Allen*, 396 U.S.
14   168, 186 (1969)). *Accord, Eldred v. Ashcroft*, 537 U.S. 186, 210 n.16 (2003). The
15   1986 House Report sets out the rationale for the Vaccine Act and the compensa-
16   tion program, expresses concern that state tort liability will undermine vaccine
17   manufacturers and the nation's vaccine supply, and expresses Congress's intent
18   that the Act's preemption clause be read broadly to preempt state law actions
19   like the one here.
                                                                                              D
20   As the Committee explained, "in light of the availability of a comprehensive
21   and fair compensation system," the Vaccine Act established standards of respon-
22   sibility for manufacturers that were designed to lessen their potential liability
23   for vaccine-related injuries. 1986 House Report at 25. Directly addressing the
24   question presented in this case, the 1986 House Report explains:
                                                                                              E
25   Given the existence of the [no-fault] compensation system in this
26   bill, . . . [v]accine-injured persons will now have an appealing
27   alternative to the tort system. Accordingly, *if they cannot demon-*
28   *strate under applicable law either that a vaccine was improperly*
29   *prepared or that it was accompanied by improper directions or*

> 30   *inadequate warnings [they] should pursue recompense in the com-*
> 31   *pensation system, not the tort system.*

32   *Id.* at 26 (emphasis added). Thus, the 1986 House Report makes clear that the
33   Vaccine Act differentiates manufacturing-defect and failure-to-warn claims from
34   other claims, including design-defect claims, and allows persons alleging vaccine-
35   related injuries to pursue tort claims under only the former two theories.

36   In preempting other claims, the Committee recognized that, by the mid-
37   1980s, the "great difficulty in obtaining insurance . . . coupled with the possibility
38   that vaccine-injured persons may recover substantial awards in tort claims . . .
39   prompted manufacturers to question their continued participation in the vaccine
40   market." 1986 House Report at 6-7. The Committee further recognized that these
41   circumstances had the potential to create a public health crisis, as the "with-
42   drawal of even a single manufacturer would present the very real possibility of
43   vaccine shortages, and, in turn, increasing numbers of unimmunized children
44   and, perhaps, a resurgence of preventable disease." *Id.* at 7. Through the Vaccine
45   Act, the Committee sought to create "a more stable childhood vaccine market"
46   by giving vaccine manufacturers "a better sense of their potential litigation
47   obligations." *Ibid.*   F

A Once again, legislative history is used as an argument in the alternative. Litigants argue that the text is clear but that even if the court doesn't agree, the legislative history also supports the client's position.

B WARNING! Don't begin sentences with unseemly numbers and abbreviations: the term "H.R. Rep. No. 99-908" is a confusing way to begin a sentence because readers will think it is a citation, not the subject of the sentence.

C Precisely because some judges doubt the insightfulness of legislative history, you can and should try to find statements from courts themselves that validate either specific uses of legislative history or, as the lawyers do here, the very document on which their brief relies. As Example 8.1 explains, committee reports — in which the legislative committee that hammered out the details of a bill describes what the committee did and why it did so — tend to be one of the most valuable types of legislative history.

D Sometimes statutes are silent about an issue, but that silence can nevertheless influence a lawsuit. One common way that litigants spar over the meaning of silence is the doctrine of "implied preemption," which applies when a federal law nullifies state law or common law without specifying that it has done so. And as this passage shows, legislative history can reveal the sounds of silence. In other words, this sentence uses legislative history to make a thinly veiled policy argument.

E The lawyers' approach with this block quote is an ideal way to convince judges to read the passage: promise them a payoff, such as information that "[d]irectly address[es] the question presented in this case." Moreover, the block quote *emphasizes* the critical sentence, making it easier for judges to skim the lengthy quote. If you use a block quote, this one exemplifies the way to present it.

F In purporting to explain the statute, the brief actually does something else: it again uses Congress's words to advance a compelling policy argument, namely that the other side's position would endanger public health.

Example
8.3

Takeaway point 8.3: When courts disfavor legislative history, let cases — including those that relied on legislative history — explain what the legislative history intended.

When judges dislike legislative history, camouflage it. The next passage makes its legislative history nearly invisible. We look again at Exxon's attempt to escape liability for an oil spill in Alaska. One of its several arguments asserted that the Clean Water Act (CWA) implicitly prohibited any award of punitive damages against oil companies that pollute oceans and other waters. Exxon's main argument here is that Congress made numerous remedies available to plaintiffs and therefore intended to exclude any alternative remedy that the statute did not specify. The annotations point out how Exxon smuggles legislative history into its brief.

Source: From Exxon's brief in *Exxon Shipping Co. v. Baker*, 554 U.S. 471 (2008).

1	Apart from these provisions aimed at punishing and deterring spills, the CWA
2	provides for a limited private right of action. It includes a citizen's suit provision
3	allowing an injured private party to abate a continuing violation of the statute
4	and even to enforce the statute's prescribed civil penalties. *Id.* § 1365(a). But
5	the CWA did not and does not include in its enforcement scheme a private ac-
6	tion for punitive damages, even for willful misconduct. The public interest in
7	punishing and deterring negligent and intentional oil spills is left exclusively to
8	the calibrated *public* enforcement mechanisms established by the Act.
9	The CWA reflects Congress's "comprehensive long-range policy" for punish-
10	ing and deterring maritime oil spills, and includes "the most comprehensive and
11	far-reaching" provisions ever enacted on the subject. *Milwaukee*, 451 U.S. at 317-
12	18; *see Middlesex County Sewerage Auth. v. Nat'l Sea Clammers Ass'n*, 453 U.S.
13	1, 22 (1981) (noting "comprehensive scope of the [CWA]"). The CWA thus in-
14	volves an explicit *balance* of Congress's twin goals of protecting the environment
15	*and* limiting the liability of shipowners and other carriers so as not to impair
16	commerce, consistent with longstanding maritime policy generally favoring lim-
17	ited liability for seagoing accidents. *See* S. Rep. No. 91-351 at 5 (1969) (citing as
18	important factors "the effect of too rigid a liability test on maritime commerce"
19	and "the economic impact of any specific amount of liability on the owner of
20	the vessel, the shipper of the oil, and the consumer"); *see also Tull*, 481 U.S. at
21	422-23 & n.8 (describing balancing of factors Congress wished courts to use in
22	imposing CWA punishments).
23	The CWA thus speaks directly and comprehensively to the only issue pre-
24	sented by plaintiffs' claims for punitive damages: what punishment is necessary
25	and appropriate to satisfy the *public* regulatory goals of punishing and deterring
26	maritime oil spills? The CWA's answer is that these objectives are satisfied by
27	cleanup costs and natural-resource damages, as well as substantial but calibrated
28	monetary civil and criminal penalties — and even potential imprisonment — all
29	subject to the prosecutorial judgment of federal administrators and prosecutors.
30	Of course Congress knows how to provide punitive damages — when it thinks
31	they are necessary.[11] Its failure to provide them here speaks volumes.
32	11. *E.g.*, Commodities Exchange Act, 7 U.S.C. § 18(a)(1)(B). [Exxon cites eight
33	additional statutes in its brief.]

Markers in right margin: A, B, C, D, E, F, G

A This paragraph begins by building credibility. It introduces the plaintiff-friendly remedies that *are* enshrined in the CWA in order to set up the main point: that one, critical remedy (punitive damages) is precluded by the CWA. In general, begin with your strong points. But realize that, on occasion (such as when you are making a controversial point), this start-with-the-unfavorable-information strategy can be helpful.

B The word "calibrated" does a lot of work here. It implies that Congress and the CWA implemented a thoughtful, measured approach. It further hints that punitive damages in private actions are unpredictable and wild. As Mark Twain observed, the difference between the almost-perfect word and the perfect word is the difference between a lightning bug and lightning. "Calibrated" is perfect.

C Exxon engages in brilliant, sophisticated (but as we see below, dangerous) laundering of legislative history here. After building the lawyers' credibility, the brief cites cases — almost no legislative history is in sight. Many judges who disdain legislative history would read these citations without thinking twice, but digging into these cases reveals that Exxon's argument about what Congress intended — the main purpose of this part of Exxon's brief — relies on legislative history. And flimsy legislative history, at that. For instance, Exxon's quotation from *Milwaukee* comes from this sentence: "A House *sponsor* described the bill as 'the *most comprehensive and far-reaching* water pollution bill we have ever drafted,' 1 Leg.Hist. 369 (Rep. Mizell). . . ." (emphases added). Exxon thus claimed that a single member's statement was the definitive statement of the Supreme Court. (And that member did not even introduce the bill.) And the next case that Exxon quotes, *Middlesex*, cited *Milwaukee* for the proposition that the CWA was "comprehensive." In other words, Exxon's two Supreme Court citations that the CWA was "comprehensive" both sprouted from a single statement by a single legislator. But it *looks* like Exxon's position is supported by multiple Supreme Court opinions. Exxon achieved this effect by for-

getting to include the phrase "internal quotations omitted" or "quoting Representative Mizell" after the *Milwaukee* quote. Exxon was lucky that it did not get caught by opposing counsel for misidentifying the original source of the quotation, namely one elected official rather than the seven justices who joined the *Milwaukee* opinion. The passage is otherwise an ingenious use of invisible legislative history.

D Exxon smuggles in more information here. It suggests that the CWA vindicated "longstanding maritime policy," but it provides no support for this claim. The two citations that follow support *other* propositions in the sentence. Exxon is engaged in very aggressive advocacy, such as substantiating only part of a sentence that contains multiple claims. But the techniques, not the language, reveal its aggression.

E Yet again, Exxon smuggles in legislative history — in a perfectly acceptable way — by citing a case that relied on legislative history. The case that Exxon paraphrases says this: "The legislative history of the Act reveals that Congress wanted the district court to consider the need for retribution and deterrence, in addition to restitution, when it imposed civil penalties. 123 Cong. Rec. 39191 (1977) (remarks of Sen. Muskie)." Thus, this citation, like most of the paragraph, demonstrates how to use language from cases *that relied on legislative history* in order to make legislative history invisible in your own brief.

F Use only one or two rhetorical questions in an entire brief. But in the right spot, and Exxon picks a good one, a rhetorical question can crystallize and simplify an issue.

G Exxon springs the trap that it laid by building its stealthy legislative history argument: it returns to the language that now seems indisputable — that the CWA was "comprehensive" — to imply that *all* common law doctrines are subsumed by the CWA. Exxon has leveraged two comments from two legislators that were cited by the Court decades earlier into an entire theory of how the CWA interacts with *all* state laws. This is extraordinary advocacy.

Example
8.4

Takeaway point 8.4: Use legislative history to reveal that a legislature acted with an unlawful motive, for a reason other than the government's current position in litigation, or without the proper factual basis to invoke constitutionally prescribed powers.

Although legislative history is most frequently used to construe an ambiguous statute or to illuminate a legislature's goals, it serves three other valuable roles:

1. to spotlight the legislature's unconstitutional or unseemly motives;

2. to show that the legislature's motive for enacting a law differs from what its lawyers claim its goals were; and

3. to show that the legislative process failed to uncover facts that must exist for the legislature to invoke limited powers (e.g., if Congress failed to assess whether a problem that it sought to address through its Commerce Clause powers involved any interstate commerce).

The passage below illustrates the third technique. (Example 3.6 shows the other two moves.) Here, three Caucasian men attacked a developmentally disabled Navajo man, branding a swastika into his arm and drawing white supremacist symbols on his body. They were convicted of various felonies in New Mexico state court. They were also tried and convicted in federal court under a new federal law, the Hate Crimes Prevention Act (HCPA). The attackers were convicted under a provision of the HCPA (§ 249(a)(1)) that Congress enacted under the Thirteenth Amendment. But, as argued below, that amendment allows Congress to enact legislation only if states have failed to punish hate crimes. Here, the defendants use legislative history to assail the constitutionality of Section 249(a)(1).

Source: Brief of convicted hate-crime perpetrators in *Hatch v. United States*, 2012 WL 1966198 (10th Cir.).

---

1   3. *Because the states are already vigorously prosecuting hate crimes,*
2   *§249(a)(1) is unnecessary. . . .*
3   The legislative findings and legislative history of the HCPA offer almost no
4   evidence that states are failing to appropriately punish violent acts motivated
5   by racial hatred. Although the HCPA was "pending in the Senate for more than
6   a decade" before it was passed and numerous hearings were held on it (S.Hrg.
7   1), Attorney General Holder conceded that there was no data pertaining to state
8   prosecution of hate crimes and no known pattern of inadequate state enforce-
9   ment. (S.Hrg. 62). Senator Coburn noted that forty-five States have hate crimes
10   laws and asked whether the states that do not are worse in terms of the pros-
11   ecution of similar events. Holder replied, "I don't know." (S.Hrg. 14). Senator
12   Sessions pointed out that in the Matthew Shepard case, the criminal prosecution
13   by the State of Wyoming, which had no hate crimes law on the books, resulted
14   in imposition of two life sentences. (S.Hrg. 19).

                                                           A

15   Senators Hatch, Sessions, and Coburn pointedly asked Holder for numbers
16   or examples of cases that have not been vigorously prosecuted by states. . . .
17   Holder managed to supply only one example of such a case that would fall under
18   § 249(a)(1): a California assault case in which the State court dismissed hate
19   crime charges because it "refused to acknowledge that the crime was motivated
20   by the victims' ethnicity." (S.Hrg. 7, 171). He did not identify any region or local-
21   ity plagued by inadequate enforcement of laws penalizing hate crimes.

22   "[P]rophylactic legislation designed to enforce the Reconstruction Amend-
23   ments must identify conduct transgressing the . . . substantive provisions it seeks

24   to enforce and be tailored to remedying or preventing such conduct." *Northwest*
25   *Austin Municipal Utility District Number One v. Holder*, 557 U.S. 193 (2009) [in-
26   ternal quotation and citation omitted]. As the Court explained with respect to the
27   Act at issue in *Austin*, congressional legislation "imposes current burdens and
28   must be justified by current needs." *Id.* at 203. "There can be no remedy without
29   a wrong." *Katzenbach v. Morgan*, 384 U.S. 641, 667 (1966).

30   Given that the HCPA had been pending for a decade before passage, that
31   Congress held numerous hearings, and that hate crimes occur at a frequency of
32   "one for every hour of the day, 24 hours a day" (S.Hrg. 2), the citation of a single
33   case in which a state may not have adequately prosecuted a racially-motivated
34   crime does not suggest significant justification existed for Congress to intervene
35   in the prosecution of intrastate hate crimes. The legislative history of the HCPA
36   reflects that the states are exercising their responsibility to punish such violent
37   crimes. . . . The congressional record on § 249(a)(1) reflects a solution in search
38   of a problem. The federal government does not significantly advance the elimi-
39   nation of badges and incidents of slavery by duplicating states' efforts, as it did
40   in this case.

41   While Congress is not required to make formal findings supporting the need
42   for particular legislation, *Morrison*, 529 U.S. at 612, the Supreme Court's consti-
43   tutional analysis often involves painstaking examination of legislative history. In
44   *Jones*, for example, the Court carefully examined the legislative record and relied
45   on it in upholding Congress's 1866 enactment of 42 U.S.C. § 1982. *Jones*, 392
46   U.S. at 426-430. In *South Carolina v. Katzenbach*, 383 U.S. 301 (1966), where the
47   Court addressed whether the Voting Rights Act constituted "appropriate" legisla-
48   tion to "enforce" the Fifteenth Amendment prohibition against racial discrimi-
47   nation in voting, the Court thoroughly studied Congress's documentation of a
50   pattern of conduct that violated the Fifteenth Amendment. *Id.* at 308. In *Morrison*,
51   the Court parsed Congress's detailed findings with respect to the adverse impact
52   of gender-motivated violence and noted the uniform application of the statutory
53   remedy, despite indications that the discrimination targeted by the statute at
54   issue did not exist "in all States, or even most States." *Id.*, 529 U.S. at 626.

A The brief uses the *absence* of legislative evidence to suggest that Congress lacked power to fix the supposed problem of unpunished hate crimes. The lawyers do not try to excuse the crimes of their loathsome defendants; instead, they focus on the adequacy of *state* prosecutions to address the problem. Moreover, by emphasizing that states punish hate-crime defendants adequately, the brief unobtrusively advances a second goal: making judges somewhat more willing to strike down a law that they, most likely, favor (because the criminals wouldn't avoid prison if the HCPA were invalidated).

B The brief strengthens its legislative history argument by tying it to relevant case law. This brief shows how to make a credible argument out of a difficult,

unpopular position. Remember this attack-the-law approach if you find yourself with unpalatable clients.

C Hate crimes are common. That fact should *hurt* the defendants' position because it shows that hate crimes occur frequently enough to worry Congress. But the lawyers transform this bad fact into a useful one by suggesting that the vast number of hate crimes should have enabled Congress to identify more than one case in which a state failed to prosecute a hate-crime perpetrator.

D The brief lists multiple cases to try to convince the appellate court that it should scrutinize the grounds on which Congress acted. These cases provide anxious judges with confidence that they can probe Congress's fact finding.

FREQUENTLY ASKED QUESTIONS ABOUT LEGISLATIVE HISTORY

Q. **How do I find legislative history for federal statutes?**

A. The legislative histories for some statutes are collected in pre-assembled databases. For instance, Westlaw and Lexis offer the precollected legislative histories of several dozen major statutes. The Library of Congress's index of legislative history (http://thomas.loc.gov) is a great place to find materials about recent statutes (including drafts of bills). HeinOnline also has a good legislative history library.

Legislative history is often spread out, making it hard to find (and very hard to find inexpensively), so consult a law librarian or an attorney with experience researching these sources. Here are two quick tips:

- Look at the annotated versions of statutes (e.g., in West's U.S.C.A. series). The notes that accompany these annotations often cite committee reports and relevant pages in the *Congressional Record* or West's legislative materials collection (U.S.C.C.A.N.).
- Pick up the research trail by searching for terms like "legislative history" and "committee report" (along with the name or citation to your statute) in databases that compile opinions, briefs, motions, and articles.

Q. **Do I need to use legislative history in my brief or motion?**

A. No. Finding legislative history can be very time consuming and may not reflect a sensible investment of resources for your client when the stakes are low or when you have a formidable doctrinal or textual argument. For a routine trial motion, digging into legislative history may be overkill. When the stakes are high, however, lawyers tend to include legislative history.

Q. **When I am construing a state statute or a municipal ordinance, should I use legislative history?**

A. You should use state and municipal legislative history just as you would include clues from Congress's legislative process—if you can find those materials. Some states and cities preserve their legislative materials, but others do not. Example 3.6 showed that a state's legislative history can be useful. Once again, you may need to speak with a law librarian or an administrator in the state or city government to assess which records and archives exist and how to search them. In cases with great stakes, lawyers have often flown to statehouses to rummage through archives.

Q. **What is the range of materials that I can cite as legislative history?**

A. If it's useful, cite it. That said, courts are likely to assign significant value to committee reports from the committee with primary jurisdiction over the bill. Other useful legislative materials, as noted earlier in this chapter, include amendments that the legislature adopted or rejected, as well as past versions of a statute (so that you can point out differences between the two laws). If you're citing a less inherently reliable source, like the statement of a single legislator or hearing testimony, show why that evidence matters.

Q. **Is legislative history only useful to resolve an ambiguous statute?**

A. Legislative history can also show that the legislature acted rashly or carefully, hatefully or magnanimously, unconstitutionally or lawfully. It can show that the legislature was aware of a specific problem or that the legislature failed to consider an issue. Legislative history can also use the words of various legislators to make (or to help you think of) policy arguments.

Chapter 9

Policy Arguments

Many judges ascribe to Judge Richard Posner's observation that lawyers should empha-size the facts that "influence a legislative decision" and "the practical stakes in their cases."[1] In other words, lawyers should explain the policy implications of their legal positions.

   Some judges, however, don't want to acknowledge that they occasionally legislate from the bench. "Policy" is a dirty word in many courts, so lawyers who explicitly discuss policy tend to get rebuked — as we see in this line from a bankruptcy brief: "As a last resort, Appellees invoke 'policy.'"[2] The scare quotes around "policy" pander to judges' dis-dain for naked policy arguments; even so, the next paragraph of that very brief made, you guessed it, a policy argument. Policy matters. Just be discreet when you rely on it. This chapter explores several examples of policy arguments.

CHAPTER OVERVIEW

1. Familiarize yourself with the policy arguments that most frequently appear in briefs and motions. The examples in this chapter present several common techniques.
2. Camouflage your policy arguments. Add them to doctrinal or textual arguments, or use legislative history to discuss the policy goals that the legislature empha-sized. Discuss policy without using the actual word: none of the six examples in this chapter use "policy."
3. Use policy arguments to counteract the other side's strongest point or to address your client's greatest weakness.
4. The stronger the policy arguments advanced by your adversary, the greater the need either to undercut those arguments or provide an alternative policy rationale.
5. Keep policy arguments short. Ideally, you will finish your policy argument before the judge even realizes that you have been peddling prudential considerations rather than legal authorities.
6. Policy arguments offer room for creativity — and fun. A section or paragraph about policy is often one of the most absorbing passages in a motion or brief.

---

1. Richard Posner, *How Judges Think* 118-19 (2008) (footnotes omitted).
2. Reply Brief by Appellant Official Comm. of Unsecured Creditors, *In re* Tousa, Inc., 680 F.3d 1298 (11th Cir. 2012) (No. 11-11071).

Example
9.1

Takeaway point 9.1: Emphasize that the other side's position is harmful or that your client's position is beneficial or, at least, harmless.

Judges are often influenced by outcomes. Many judges will resist the cold, grey tug of the law if it would lead to drastic consequences. Therefore, you will sometimes want to show — without hysterics — that the other side's position would lead to grave results. Or, when your client's position is alleged to pose grave risks, you need to tamp down the rhetoric and show that the consequences are actually beneficial, or at worst, minimal.

To demonstrate this principle, let's take a look at a dispute that arose after California enacted a law that prohibited anyone from selling violent video games to minors. Video-game sellers and manufacturers challenged the law. In response, California relied on a doctrine that enables states to restrict the sale of sexual material to children, even when adults have a First Amendment right to acquire those materials. California argued that it had a comparable interest in protecting children from violent content. Here, the trade group uses policy arguments to counter California's position.

Source: Brief of video-game industry in *Brown v. Entertainment Merchants' Ass'n*, 131 S. Ct. 2729 (2011) (some citations omitted).

---

1   California's attempt to equate portrayals of violence with sexual materials
2   ignores an important reality: violence, unlike explicit descriptions of sex, is
3   a central feature of expression intended for minors. Eliminating depictions of
4   sexual obscenity from children's literature would hardly require any revision
5   because they are so rare; in contrast, eliminating depictions of violence, even
6   extreme violence, would require dramatic change. *AAMA*, 244 F.3d at 578
7   (depictions of sex, as opposed to depictions of violence, are "an adult invasion
8   of children's culture").

9   To take just a few examples, *Hansel and Gretel,* one of Grimms' Fairy Tales,
10   recounts how children murder a witch by locking her in a burning oven. Jakob
11   Grimm & Wilhelm Grimm, *Grimms' Tales for Young and Old* 56 (Ralph Manheim
12   trans. 1977). *Snow White*, another of the Tales, ends with the evil Queen be-
13   ing forced to wear red-hot iron shoes until she dies from pain. *Id.* at 184. The
14   Greek myths and Ovid's *Metamorphoses*, long fixtures of high school humanities
15   classes, contain violence of the harshest variety. [Details omitted.] And of course
16   the Bible includes some of the most famous depictions of violence in Western
17   culture. *E.g.*, Judges 16 (Samson's decimation of the Philistines); 1 Samuel 17
18   (David slays Goliath and cuts off his head).

19   Contemporary tales for children are no less violent. Generations of children
20   have watched violent movies like *Star Wars* and *Lord of the Rings* (and Westerns
21   and serials before that). Harry Potter witnesses the violent death of his teacher,
22   Dumbledore, at the hands of so-called "Death Eaters." J.K. Rowling, *Harry Potter*
23   *and the Half-Blood Prince* (2005). Likewise, William Golding's *Lord of the Flies*
24   (1954), which depicts torture and killing *by children*, is commonly assigned in
25   middle and high school because it deals with social impulses towards violence.

26   California's claim that depictions of violence should be treated like sexual
27   obscenity thus fails not only because it would impermissibly create a new cat-
28   egory of unprotected expression, but also because the expression at issue is a
29   recurring theme in works for minors. . . .

A
B
C
D
E

30 California has vacillated as to precisely what harm it claims is at issue.
31 Although the Act's preamble speaks of a need to prevent "violence" by minors,
32 California has largely disclaimed a violence-prevention rationale, presumably
33 because video games could not possibly be viewed as "incitement" as defined in
34 *Brandenburg v. Ohio*, 395 U.S. 444, 447 (1969). Instead, California focuses on a
35 more amorphous harm — causing increased "aggressive thoughts and behavior"
36 in minors. Pet. Br. 3, 42-45.

37 However the harm is defined, California has failed to demonstrate that it
38 exists. California relies primarily on the research of Dr. Craig Anderson and a few
39 other research psychologists closely affiliated with him. *See* J.A. 122-27, 133-43
40 (article bibliography from Legislature). Dr. Anderson testified before a district
41 court considering a challenge to a similar law in Illinois, and his testimony is
42 in the record here. J.A. 1206-1339. The Illinois district court, along with every
43 court to have considered Dr. Anderson's and similar research, concluded that the
44 research does not show that violent video games are harmful to minors in any
45 material way. *See Entm't Software Ass'n v. Blagojevich*, 404 F. Supp. 2d 1051, 1063   **F**
46 (N.D. Ill. 2005).[13] [The brief then cites five other cases.]

47 As the Ninth Circuit described in detail, there are numerous flaws with these
48 studies. First, ...

_____

47 13. Dr. Anderson . . . published an article saying the "research to date on video
50 game effects is sparse and weak," and four years later he published another article
51 pointing to a "glaring empirical gap" in video game research — the absence of the kind
52 of longitudinal studies that can provide information about causation.

A This brief draws a line between sexual content and violent content. The following paragraphs appear to reply to California's doctrinal argument, but they actually carry a policy argument — that California has drawn an arbitrary line by allowing children to access some violent content (books and movies), but not other violent content (video games). We look more closely at line-drawing policy arguments later in this chapter.

B WARNING! The term "children's literature" does not foreshadow that the brief will also describe examples from movies. This phrase should more accurately foretell the sorts of examples that will follow, just as a topic sentence should foretell exactly what will be discussed in a given paragraph.

C The lawyers use creative, well-known examples to advance their point. In general, avoid piling on examples; however, in some instances (such as if the other side heaped examples on the court or claimed that something never happened), you might want to cite numerous illustrations. Here, the number suffices to convey the point. Your key challenge is to make your examples look representative, not anecdotal.

D Instead of listing children's books and then children's movies, the examples could have shown that children often read or watch the *exact* content banned by the challenged law, such as in this example: "California barred children from acquiring games in which any character is decapitated; but children can freely acquire the Bible, in which David decapitated Goliath (1 Samuel 17)." The brief then could have provided a similar example for each type of violent act that California's law banned. Examples often are most effective when they track the exact law or provision that is being disputed. Even so, these examples reflect excellent advocacy.

E The brief interrupts its policy discussion by making a double-barreled doctrinal point: that the Court had recently opined that it would not create new categories of unprotected speech *and* that California's law impermissibly distinguishes between violent video games and other violent content that children read or watch.

F The brief rebuts California's attempt to show that it has a strong interest in protecting children from violence. Showing that a law is harmful or ineffective can persuade judges.

Example 9.2

Takeaway point 9.2: Courts are especially receptive to policy arguments based on the consequences that a decision would have on the legal system.

Lawyers often raise policy arguments based on procedural concerns such as forum shopping, abusive discovery practices, increased litigation costs, or — as in the following passage — frivolous and invasive litigation. These arguments are an important subset of the harm-based policy arguments discussed in Example 9.1.

This example comes from the West Virginia case in which a judge reversed a $50 million award against a coal company whose chair had contributed $3 million toward the judge's campaign. Here, the coal company discusses the risks of making it easier for parties to force judges to recuse themselves.

Source: Brief arguing that the West Virginia judge did not need to recuse himself, from *Caperton v. A.T. Massey Coal Co.*, 556 U.S. 868 (2009).

---

1   Petitioners contend that, under their due-process standard, campaign expen-
2 ditures will only rarely require recusal. But because their "vague and malleable
3 standard" cannot identify where the constitutional line should be drawn in any
4 particular case, it would almost certainly "open the gates for a flood of litigation." **A**
5 *Baze v. Rees*, 128 S. Ct. 1520, 1542 (2008) (Alito, J., concurring).
6   Resolving disqualification motions consumes scarce judicial time and
7 resources. As courts have recognized, an increase in the number of such
8 motions would interfere with "the conduct of judicial business" (*In re Petition*
9 *to Recall Dunleavy*, 769 P.2d 1271, 1275 (Nev. 1988)), and make it more difficult
10 to "carry[] out [courts'] essential responsibilities" (*Adair*, 709 N.W.2d at 581
11 (Taylor, C.J., and Markman, J.)). Apart from slowing the judicial process,
12 petitioners' opaque standard seems bound to lead many judges to recuse them-
13 selves, either on motion or *sua sponte*, even where it might ultimately have been
14 determined that recusal was not constitutionally necessary. Particularly in smaller **B**
15 districts, staffing problems would frequently result. *See Fieger*, 714 N.W.2d at 286
16 (Markman, J.). The potential for strategic contributions, made "for the purpose
17 of obtaining a recusal" (*Shepherdson*, 5 F. Supp. 2d at 311), would only exac- **C**
18 erbate these problems. And because the disqualification standard would rest
19 upon federal constitutional law, States would be unable to rectify the problems
20 by adopting bright-line rules legislatively. Constitutionalizing this area of the
21 law would also lead parties in recusal fights to beat a path to this Court's door,
22 thereby increasing the workload of this Court as well.

A The "flood gates" metaphor has been used for decades to describe the risk that litigation will increase greatly. The metaphor is now stale — nearly a cliché. Metaphors can be incredibly useful and persuasive (see page 35), but lawyers need to assess critically when a metaphor has been overused.

B The brief makes rapid-fire policy arguments. Each of the sentences in the paragraph raises a distinct argument, reflecting good, brisk pacing. This sentence's specific concern — rampant motions to recuse — persuaded four (dissenting) justices, who predicted that the Court would "regret this decision

... when courts are forced to deal with a wide variety of *Caperton* motions."

C The first two policy arguments are simplistic, but this concern (about using contributions to manufacture a conflict) reflects the sort of creative thinking in which you should engage. The more sophisticated your judge, the more sophisticated you can get with your policy analysis. The brief's next sentence, which notes that an adverse decision would prevent state legislatures from crafting bright-line rules, is even more brilliant. (Example 9.5 elaborates on how to present a line-drawing argument.)

Example 9.3

Takeaway point 9.3: Meld your fact-based arguments and your policy arguments.

The following example highlights the essential difference between a fact-based argument and a policy argument: the former emphasizes the harm to your client, and the latter explores the effects that would befall third parties. The two often work well side by side. Describing how your client would be injured makes your policy argument concrete and clear. Showing that other parties would be hurt makes your client's arguments plausible and compelling. Example 9.5 also shows this technique.

Designer Christian Louboutin sells high-heeled shoes. The most distinctive feature of his shoes is the red sole or "upper," which he trademarked in 2008. Louboutin sued another leading designer, Yves Saint Laurent (YSL), that began selling monochromatic red-soled shoes, alleging trademark infringement. Louboutin sought injunctive relief to prevent YSL from selling any red-soled shoes in any shade of red. Here, YSL raises a simple policy argument to oppose a preliminary injunction.

Source: YSL's brief in *Christian Louboutin S.A. v. Yves Saint Laurent America*, 778 F. Supp. 2d 445 (S.D.N.Y. 2011).

---

1   [I]f Louboutin is permitted to maintain a monopoly on the use of red out-
2   soles[,] . . . YSL would be prevented from executing one of its own venerable
3   design traditions — monochrome shoes — in a color that has long been an
4   integral part of the brand's palette. As Mr. Louboutin himself admitted, using   **A**
5   another color on a portion of a monochrome shoe would throw off the balance
6   and ruin the concept. Hamid Decl. Ex. A (Louboutin Tr. 81:16-83:24). Indeed, if
7   Louboutin were to have its way, no other designer would ever again be permitted
8   to make an all-red shoe.
                                                                                              B
9   If Louboutin were able to maintain a monopoly on red outsoles (and by ex-
10   tension on any shoes that are all red), there would also be a significant danger of
11   color depletion. In *Qualitex*, the Supreme Court held that the problem of "color
                                                                                              C
12   depletion" was not a sufficient rationale to justify an *absolute* bar on use of color
13   alone as a trademark, but also held that [trademark] doctrine could be used to
14   prevent trademarking of a color in those factual contexts where "color deple-
15   tion" is a problem. 514 U.S. at 169-70. Fashion is such a context. If Louboutin
16   can trademark red for the soles of shoes (and, by extension, claim a monopoly
17   on making all-red shoes), others could claim similar protection in blue, yellow,
18   green, orange and purple. A small oligarchy could claim ownership of the right
19   to make any colored soles . . . .

A This is a fact-based argument: YSL discusses how *it* would be affected by an injunction. By the end of the paragraph, YSL has pivoted into a policy argument, focusing on how an adverse decision would affect third parties, such as other designers.

B This policy argument won the battle but lost the war. The Second Circuit ultimately agreed with YSL on this point, permitting it to make *monochromatic* red shoes. But the court also held that Louboutin had intellectual property rights to shoes on which only the soles were red. Lawyers frequently must choose, in conjunction with their clients, whether to pursue a broad vic-

tory (e.g. *Louboutin has no rights to red soles*), a modest victory (e.g. *Louboutin controls only a specific shade of red*), or a narrow victory (*Louboutin can control red-soled shoes unless the shoe is monochromatic*). This sort of strategic choice is a critical but nearly invisible decision in every filing.

C You can strengthen your policy arguments by analogizing to other fields. Here, for instance, the brief could have referred to the risk that Ferrari could ban U.S. automakers from selling red cars or that Coke could keep other companies from selling red cans.

Example
9.4

Takeaway point 9.4: Learn to build credible "slippery slope" arguments, which show courts that permitting a fairly modest action in one case would open the door to drastic consequences in the future.

Another common policy argument is based on the "slippery slope" — the idea that reaching a decision in onecase will lead to more dangerous and extreme results in future cases. We see below a version of this argument from the case in which police, without a valid warrant, attached a GPS device to a suspect's jeep to track his movements for an entire month. The passage also shows how to rebut the other side's policy arguments.

Criminal defendant's brief in , 132 S. Ct. 945 (2012).

---

1 **3. The Court Should Not Disregard The Threat That Warrantless GPS Surveil-**
2 **lance Poses To Core Fourth Amendment Interests**
3   The government's final response is that the Court "should not depart from its
4 established reasonable-expectation-of-privacy framework to account for hypo-
5 thetical misuse of technology that does not occur in reality." Pet. Br. 37. But the
6 question is not whether some hypothetical future technology might make indis-
7 criminate, perpetual, and mass surveillance possible; GPS presents those dangers
8 now. And this Court has never afforded the government free reign to use privacy-
9 threatening methods merely because of government promises that the power
10 will not be abused. To the contrary, the Court has recognized that "prosecutors
11 and policemen simply cannot be asked to maintain the requisite neutrality with
12 regard to their own investigations — the 'competitive enterprise' that must right-
13 ly engage their single-minded attention." *Coolidge v. New Hampshire,* 403 U.S.
14 443, 450 (1971) (quoting *Mancusi v. DeForte,* 392 U.S. 364, 371 (1968)). Reason-
15 able expectations of privacy must be protected by more than executive grace.
16   The government counters that "[t]he court of appeals pointed to no evidence
17 that law enforcement officers engage in GPS monitoring of vehicles without any
18 suspicion of criminal activity." Pet. Br. 35. It does not *deny* that misuse of GPS
19 technology is occurring; it merely notes the absence of evidence in the court of
20 appeals's opinion. *Id.* And some evidence of abuse exists. *See supra* p.3. More
21 might be available if the government were more forthcoming in disclosing the
22 scope and nature of its use of GPS, which it acknowledges has been increasing.
23 *Id.* In any event, the Fourth Amendment should be enforced even if the approxi-
24 mately 765,000 sworn state and local law enforcement agents and 105,000 sworn
25 federal agents across the nation — and the innumerable non-law-enforcement
26 employees at all levels of government — have not yet begun to abuse GPS tech-
27 nology.[6] The Fourth Amendment must be applied to "prevent stealthy encroach-
28 ment upon or gradual depreciation of the rights secured by [it], by imperceptible
29 practice of courts or by well-intentioned, but mistakenly over-zealous, execu-
30 tive officers." *Johnson v. United States,* 333 U.S. 10, 16 n.8 (1948) (citation and
31 internal quotation marks omitted). That is why the Court in *Kyllo* did not ask

---

32   6. *See* Orin S. Kerr, *Fourth Amendment Remedies and Development of the Law:*
33 *A Comment on* Camreta v. Greene *and* Davis v. United States, Cato Supreme Court
34 Review 256 n.83 (10th ed. 2011) (citing sources).

A

B

C

D

35 for evidence that thermal imaging technology was being abused — or that future
36 versions of the technology would be. 533 U.S. 27, 36 (2001) . . . .
37   The government also notes that privacy-protective statutes could be enacted.
38 *See* Pet. Br. 35-37. But this Court has never held that because legislatures could
39 protect privacy, the Fourth Amendment ought not. And when it reaffirmed the
40 application of the [Fourth] Amendment to wiretaps implicating domestic national
41 security in *United States v. United States Dist. Court*, 407 U.S. 297, 320 (1972),
42 the Court rejected the government's argument that "internal security matters are
43 too subtle and complex for judicial evaluation," and observed that "[i]f the threat
44 is too subtle or complex for our senior law enforcement officers to convey its
45 significance to a court, one may question whether there is probable cause for
46 surveillance," *id.* at 320.

A This brief rebuts the other side's suggestions that there is no evidence of actual harm and that courts should not restrain the government based on hypothetical risks.

B The vintage of these opinions hints that this principle might be less compelling to modern courts because the scope of the Fourth Amendment has contracted since the late 1960s. But these cases are far better than nothing, and they enable the lawyers to quote the Supreme Court rather than asserting an unsubstantiated policy claim. Where possible, let courts or legislatures make your policy arguments.

C These lawyers lack concrete evidence that the government has abused GPS technology. But they use the government's silence to imply that GPS technology has already been abused. Then they point out that the government has admitted that its use of GPS technology has recently increased; the huge number of law enforcement officials in the country hints ominously at the risks of giving investigators unfettered power to use GPS to track citizens. The brief exemplifies how to do a lot with a little.

D This footnote citing Orin Kerr shows the importance of knowing your judge: the lawyers probably predicted that Justice Kennedy would break a 4-4 tie in this case, and Professor Kerr is a former Kennedy clerk, making it more likely that Justice Kennedy would value his conclusions. Also, the source — a libertarian journal

— is designed to signal tacitly to the Court's conservative Justices that excessive governmental monitoring is a greater long-term risk than allowing a few petty criminals to go free. Profile your judges: study their opinions, their articles, their speeches, and their backgrounds to figure out which policy arguments will persuade them.

E In *Kyllo v. United States*, the Court prevented the government from using thermal readings to detect unusually warm homes in order to locate and prosecute marijuana growers. The case presumably lacked a pithy, helpful quote, but the lawyers extracted something even more helpful: a concise and clear principle that helps their client. This approach is also recommended in Example 4.4.

F Following one of this book's most important principles, the lawyers already had built Jones's affirmative case by this point. Only *then* do they counter the other side's arguments. The first party to file a motion or brief usually gets a chance to file a reply, so that party's opening filing does not need to predict and rebut the other side's arguments, except for the key points. But the second party, (typically the appellee or the respondent) will ordinarily file only one brief, so it needs to counter all of the arguments raised by the other side. Rebuttals should generally be concise: a single sentence that fells the adversary's point is better than fifteen middling points.

Example
9.5

Takeaway point 9.5: Emphasize that your adversary's position makes it impossible to draw a line between lawful and unlawful conduct.

Legal rules need to be administrable, so many judges will wince when the line between legal and illegal conduct is blurry. Thus, call the court's attention to any opposing argument that leads to an unworkable rule or requires enormous amounts of fact-finding to administer the rule. The following example reflects this skill, and it also shows how to camouflage a policy argument by making it look like a fact-based argument.

The dispute involves a federal statute that made it a crime to create, sell, or possess depictions of cruelty to animals if the depicted conduct is "illegal under federal law" (such as a dog fight or a bull fight). Stevens, a writer and documentary producer, was indicted under this statute for selling violent movies that depicted dog-fighting and wounded dogs. Stevens was convicted by a jury, but the Third Circuit vacated the conviction, holding that the statute violated the free speech protections embedded in the First Amendment. The government challenged this decision at the Supreme Court. There, a number of animal rights groups, including the Humane Society, submitted amicus briefs in support of the government. Stevens's brief counters amici's arguments by presenting facts that hint at the difficulty of distinguishing between legal and illegal speech.

Source: Stevens's brief in *United States v. Stevens*, 559 U. S. 460 (2010).

---

1   [W]hile the Humane Society tells this Court that "gruesome depictions" of
2   dogfighting "do not merit the dignity of full First Amendment protection" and do
3   not "convey[] any ideas or information" (HSUS Br. 20), the Humane Society's own
4   website employs such images as part of its advocacy effort to convey ideas and
5   information, *see* http://video.hsus.org (Video Search for "dog fight" leads to hy-
6   perlinks to, *e.g.*, *Dog Fighting: Brutal Bloodsport and End Dogfighting in Chicago*).   **A**

7   Furthermore, outside of Court, the Society lauds as a "must see" Hollywood
8   producer David Roma's documentary about Pit Bulls that contains horrific images
9   from modern-day dogfights of dogs with portions of their eyes, ears, and noses
10   torn away and a dog disemboweled after a fight in the pit. *See* Bobby Brown &   **B**
11   David Roma, *Off the Chain* (24/7 Food Inc. and Illucid Productions 2005) (Hu-
12   mane Society review on cover: "This film is a must see — exposing the ultimate
13   betrayal of man's best friend.").

14   Stevens' dogfighting images, by contrast, lack any such images of blood or
15   serious injury to the dogs both because he opposes dogfighting and because
16   his purpose is to illustrate the genetic traits of Pit Bulls — endurance, cour-   **C**
17   age, stamina, strength, and disposition — that make the breed so well-suited
18   for non-dogfighting activities like hunting, field [trials], and weight pulling.[6]

---

19   6. Tellingly, the prosecutor had to instruct the jury to "[l]ook carefully" to see any
20   blood droplets in Stevens' images of dogfighting, C.A. App. 439, and had to bring in
21   an expert to opine that the dogs might have suffered injuries, J.A. 80-84. The govern-   **D**
22   ment's claim (Br. 20-21) that the dogs in Stevens' films are "ripped and torn" and
23   "screaming in pain" overstates the record and underscores the government's refusal
24   to consider the work as a whole. There are no "ripped and torn" dogs in these films,
25   there are no dog sounds at all in *Winna* and there are, at most, 25 seconds contain-
26   ing yelps in *Japan Fights'* 108-minute film. *See Japan Fights* at 47:43-48:17, 1:44:57-
27   1:45:07 (visible wounds); *id.* at 43:01, 43:58, 44:00-01, 44:49-51, 44:55-56, 45:00-04,
28   47:11, 47:17, 47:20-22, 1:18:54-55, 1:23:24-25 (yelps).

29 Nowhere in its brief does the Society explain why its own or Roma's "gruesome
30 depictions" of dogfighting are constitutionally protected and "must see," but
31 Stevens' far tamer depictions are not. Unless, that is, they just object to Stevens'
32 viewpoint. . . .

E

33   Because, as a form of animal fighting, bullfighting is illegal in the Unit-
34 ed States, 7 U.S.C. § 2156, Section 48's definition of "depiction[s] of animal
35 cruelty" reaches books like Ernest Hemingway's *Death in the Afternoon* (Scrib-

F

36 ner 1960), with its pictures of bulls being wounded and killed in actual Span-
37 ish bullfights; the innumerable photographs of bullfighting that accompany the
38 annual Running of the Bulls in Pamplona, Spain (*see, e.g.*, Leigh Ann Heni-
39 on, *Ernest Hemingway's Spain*, Wash. Post. Magazine, Mar. 29, 2009, at 1, 24;
40 *Thrill-Seekers Run with the Bulls in Spain*, Wash. Post., http://www.wash-
41 ingtonpost.com/wp-dyn/content/gallery/2009/07/08/GA2009070802841.
42 html; *Running of the Bulls*, Philly.com, http://www.philly.com/philly/news/
43 world/50261147.html); and the Colbert Report's recent use of a bullfighting clip
44 in discussing the American soccer team's victory over Spain (Soccer by Ives:
45 Stephen Colbert Talks American Soccer, http://www.soccerbyives.net/soccer_
46 by_ives/2009/07/stephen-colbert-talks-american-soccer.html).

A The brief emphasizes that the Humane Society itself depicts grusome images of dog fighting on its website. The comparison suggests that the Humane Society's depiction of animal cruelty is indistinguishable from what Stevens did.

B The brief elsewhere tries to make Stevens's videos sound mild — they merely "contain[] yelps" — whereas the movie that the Humane Society praised is described in deliberately graphic terms. This part of the brief highlights the difficulty of drawing a line between acceptable depictions of animal violence and unlawful depictions.

C The brief slips in some helpful details about Stevens's motives to make him sound less loathsome. Even your policy arguments need to reflect the "victims and villains" principles discussed in Chapter 1.

D This footnote achieves three goals. First, it uses the prosecutor's own words from the trial to show that Stevens's depictions were not as horrific as the government suggested. Second, this footnote tries to confront the bad fact that the dogs' wounds *were* visible, as shown by the first two citations

to the film *Japan Fights*. And third, the footnote advances a separate, almost subliminal argument about the difficulty of drawing lines between legal and illegal movies: exactly how much violence or gruesomeness is enough to throw a filmmaker in jail? This sort of argument should sometimes be explicit, but can sometimes be most effective when it is subtle. *See* Appendix A, Principle B.4.

E The brief's argument is that the statute discriminates based on viewpoint. But rather than simply stating this, the brief leads the reader to the same conclusion by showing that the Humane Society's argument inexorably leads there.

F As we saw, Example 9.1 made a similar argument, discussing various violent books. Example 9.1 was extracted from a brief that cited the *Stevens* case almost a dozen times and discussed it extensively. The similarity demonstrates that top lawyers litigate similar cases in similar ways, meaning that you should read briefs and motions in your field so that you know the custom. Learn from your rivals — and then outlitigate them.

Example 9.6

Takeaway point 9.6: Use policy arguments to address the concerns that readers will have about the biggest weaknesses in your case.

Policy arguments are sometimes most powerful when they confront your client's biggest obstacle to winning. We see that technique here, where a municipal official falsely claimed that he had won the Congressional Medal of Honor. Congress had banned anyone from knowingly lying about having won this military award, and a trial court convicted the official. Lying about military service will strike many judges as despicable — and valueless. The public defenders who wrote this brief confront the instinct that lying is worthless.

Source: The convicted liar's brief in *United States v. Alvarez*, 132 S. Ct. 457 (2011).

---

1   Before relegating false statements of fact to second-class status, and before
2   creating a balancing test with broad implications, it is important to step back
3   from the case at hand and examine the myriad reasons why false statements are
4   valuable.

    A

5   First, this Court has recognized that "[e]ven a false statement may be deemed
6   to make a valuable contribution to public debate, since it brings about 'the
7   clearer perception and livelier impression of truth, produced by its collision with
8   error.'" *Sullivan*, 376 U.S. at 279 n.19 . . . .

    B

9   [H]uman beings are constantly forced to choose the persona we present to
10 the world, and our choices nearly always involve intentional omissions and
11 misrepresentations, if not outright deception. College students portray different
12 personae to their parents, their professors, and their peers. Individuals lie about
13 everything, from things as trivial as their weight, to things as fundamental as
14 their sexual orientation. . . . Falsehoods are therefore indistinguishable in value
15 from other speech because they facilitate the development of critical thinking
16 and because their utterance represents an aspect of self-determination. . . .

    C

17 In addition to lies about ourselves, there is a class of lies told about others
18 and about the world that is generally viewed as socially useful. These range from
19 the important — Kant's hypothetical of lying to a person intent on murdering
20 about the whereabouts of his would-be victim — to the mundane — lying to
21 one's spouse about whether an outfit is flattering. Such lies are part of the fabric
22 of our socialization, so innate as to be a milestone in child development and a
23 feature of most everyone's daily lives. *See* . . . Jochen Meckel, *Cultures of Lying*
24 8 (2007) (estimating that Americans tell somewhere between two and fifty lies
25 each day). The pervasiveness of such lies should give this Court pause before
26 balancing away the value of such lies as merely "derivative" in the search for
27 truth.

    D

28 Knowingly false statements also have secondary meanings that are valuable,
29 apart from the content of the speech itself. Lies often betray to the listener that
30 we are trying to flatter them, that we are clumsily trying to avoid causing them
31 pain, that we are trying to show allegiance with a group, and other secondary
32 meanings. In this sense, many false statements reveal important truths about
33 the world, apart from their content. Indeed, a person listening to Alvarez could
34 infer that Alvarez was willing to lie about himself to get ahead, that his easily
35 disproved lie meant that he was unsophisticated, that some mental pathology

36 was afoot, or that his desire to impress caused truth to fall to the wayside. Such
37 lessons are not valueless. . . .
38   [I]t is not impossible to imagine a legislature that viewed the value of strong
39 marriages and the harm caused by adultery as sufficiently important to prohibit
40 lying about extramarital dalliances. Or one that viewed the potential danger of
41 strangers meeting over the Internet as significant enough to permit prosecution
42 for factual lies or exaggerations in dating profiles. *See Cybersecurity: Protecting*
43 *America's New Frontier: Hearing Before Subcomm. on Crime, Terrorism, and*
44 *National Security* 7 (2011) (statement of Richard W. Downing, Dep't of Justice)
45 (arguing that violation of website's terms of service should continue to be a
46 crime); *United States v. Drew*, 259 F.R.D. 449, 454 (C.D. Cal. 2009) (prosecution
47 under Computer Fraud and Abuse Act for a fictitious MySpace profile where
48 website's terms of service required that "all registration information [be] truthful
47 and accurate"). Or one that viewed the integrity of the state's hiring process as
50 so important that any factual lies on one's resume were punishable by criminal **E**
51 prosecution. Or one that viewed the integrity of elections to require truth-telling
52 at all moments by all candidates for election. *See Rickert v. State Pub. Disclosure*
53 *Comm'n*, 119 P.3d 379, 387 (Wash. 2005) (en banc) (striking down a statute that
54 prohibited knowingly false statements by candidates for office). And certainly,
55 Congress, concerned about a distracted President during a time of war, might
56 make it a crime to falsely represent that the President is not "a natural born
57 citizen" of the United States. **F**

A When the facts disfavor your client, emphasize the law — or the policy.

B The brief begins by showing that the Court entertained a similar argument in the landmark First Amendment case, *New York Times Co. v. Sullivan*, 376 U.S. 254 (1964). In that case, a group of African American civil rights leaders had been sued in Alabama after making minor factual errors in an advertisement, and the suit intended to impede the civil rights movement. The Supreme Court vacated the trial court's award; the current Justices would know this case's history, so the citation to *Sullivan* is a gentle reminder that punishing falsehoods can lead to grave problems.

C The brief aggressively defends lying by drawing on familiar circumstances in which lying is reasonable or beneficial, thus addressing the biggest weakness in the case: the instinct that lying is worthless. This brief's robust defense of lying was inspired by Chief Judge Kozinski's dissent before the case reached the Supreme Court. His opinion listed *32* situations in which lies have social value. Wise advocates draw on the insights that judges and lawyers have offered in similar cases or at earlier stages of the same case.

D The lawyers use social science research to show the scope of the policy problems that the brief discusses.

E The brief shows that the government is already prosecuting MySpace users under the same theory it is advancing in this case and that a Justice Department official called for broader prosecution of lying — a slippery slope argument. This approach exemplifies how to use cases and legislative testimony to validate your policy arguments.

F The brief alludes to the "birther" controversy surrounding President Obama. This illustration reflects the skill that Example 9.5 explored by showing the risks of letting the government draw the line between permissible and impermissible lies. And it worked. The majority in *Alvarez* wrote, "Permitting the Government to decree this speech to be a criminal offense would endorse government authority to compile a list of subjects about which false statements are punishable. That governmental power has no clear limiting principle."

FREQUENTLY ASKED QUESTIONS ABOUT POLICY ARGUMENTS

Q. When should I use policy arguments?

A. Many motions and most briefs contain some form of policy argument — but subtly in most instances. Judges rarely decide cases primarily on policy grounds, but policy concerns may tilt a judge toward your position, especially when you disguise your policy arguments and place them alongside doctrinal, textual, and fact-based arguments.

Q. Isn't policy something for legislatures to consider, not courts?

A. Judges often need to fill in gaps that unclear statutes and constitutional provisions fail to resolve. Moreover, no judge wants to produce an outcome that is unfair or that has undesirable effects. A well-crafted policy argument focuses on these effects, persuading the judge to look for a way to resolve the legal issue without grave consequences.

Q. How can I make my policy arguments more credible?

A. Let courts or legislatures make your arguments for you. That is, find cases, legislative history, or even statutory preambles that confirm your policy concerns, and then quote or cite these documents. This approach bolsters your credibility and disguises the fact that you're making a policy argument.

Q. This chapter presented several common policy arguments. What are some others?

A. You may also want to emphasize the need to (1) create good incentives for future conduct ("immunizing drug companies from lawsuits will reduce their incentives to conduct safety testing"), (2) preserve settled expectations ("police departments have invested billions of dollars in surveillance equipment based on this court's past dicta"), and (3) let another branch of government or agency resolve an issue (e.g., "the agency, unlike courts, has great expertise about how to transport uranium safely").

Q. How can I argue against policy arguments?

A. There are several ways. The simplest rebuttal is to encourage the court to leave policy considerations to the legislature. Or, better yet, you can show that the legislature expressly rejected the policy claims that your adversary advances. You can also fight policy with policy. For instance, if the other side emphasizes the dangers of letting TSA security guards search children at airports, you can counter that terrorists and smugglers would plant weapons and drugs on kids if TSA never searched them. One final technique involves dismantling the other side's policy argument, such as by discrediting its citations, providing better or newer sources that rebut its arguments, or by showing that its arguments are based on faulty premises.

Chapter 10

Historical Arguments

Judges love precedent. Nothing comforts them like knowing that their actions reflect a traditional, sensible, time-tested approach to a problem. This comfort is sometimes provided by cases. In other instances, however, this comfort is provided by history itself. This chapter explores how to build effective historical arguments. For instance, recall that Chapter 2 of this book presented a motion filed by President Bill Clinton that began, "For the first time, a sitting President has been subpoenaed to testify before a grand jury." Most judges would not want to be the first jurist *ever* to order a president to testify. Do judges ever have this power?

But imagine that any of the following (hypothetical) facts were true:

- Contrary to the president's claims, courts have ordered *six* presidents to testify before a grand jury.

- Alexander Hamilton, James Madison, George Washington, John Adams, Thomas Jefferson, and sixteen delegates to the Constitutional Convention agreed that it was "obvious" that federal courts had the power to order presidents to appear in front of a grand jury.

- English courts, on more than a dozen occasions before the Constitution was ratified, ordered prime ministers to testify in court.

These statements are mere fabrications, but they illustrate how history can be weaponized: they provide an alternative type of precedent. The past is a tool for persuasion — just like facts, cases, statutes, and policy arguments.

CHAPTER OVERVIEW

1. Use historical facts to show a long-standing custom. Because the legal system in the United States was built around the English model, English cases from the eighteenth century and earlier can be especially illustrative when assessing common law principles.
2. Use history to show the original understanding of a provision, such as what the Founders wrote or said when they debated the U.S. Constitution.
3. Invoke the historical record to advance a policy argument.
4. Use history to show that a policy worked (e.g., historical evidence of dismal race or gender relations in the country before Congress enacted antidiscrimination laws might persuade courts not to disturb these laws).
5. History (like empirical evidence) is hard to rebut without finding counterevidence. If your adversary builds a strong historical argument, either dismantle it or counter it with historical evidence of your own.
6. As with some of the other types of arguments explored in Part 2, you will not need history in every case. But it is especially useful when text is scarce and doctrine is amorphous.
7. Learn some of the shortcuts to finding historical evidence (e.g., look in briefs, opinions, articles and books, doctoral dissertations, and research databases). When you lean on materials discovered by other lawyers or by researchers, check their work and corroborate their conclusions: don't reinvent the wheel, but check the tires.

Example
10.1

Takeaway point 10.1: Show that history condones your clients' actions or supports their other arguments.

History is a battlefield. Lawyers need to learn to frame or reframe the past favorably and to counter an adversary's use of history. The next two examples come from opposite sides of the same prominent case. In it, a gay man was arrested for violating Texas's anti-sodomy law. He challenged the law, and the case eventually required the Supreme Court to assess whether the Constitution protects same-sex intimate relations. In the first excerpt from this case, which appears below, Texas emphasizes the history of anti-sodomy laws.

Source: Brief for Texas defending the state's anti-sodomy law, from *Lawrence v. Texas*, 539 U.S. 558 (2003).

---

1   **C. This nation has no deep-rooted tradition of protecting**
2   **a right to engage in sodomy.**   A

3   Turning to the question of whether a right to engage in sodomy is "so rooted
4   in the traditions and conscience of our people as to be ranked as fundamental,"
5   the Court's previous resolution of that issue in *Bowers v. Hardwick* is unassail-
6   able. As noted in *Bowers*, sodomy was a serious criminal offense at common   B
7   law; it was forbidden by the laws of the original thirteen states at the time of the
8   ratification of the Bill of Rights; and it was punishable as a crime in all but five of
9   the thirty-seven states in existence at the time of the ratification of the Fourteenth
10   Amendment. *Bowers*, 478 U.S. at 192-193.
11   As further noted in *Bowers*, sodomy remained punishable as a crime in every
12   state of the Union prior to the year 1961, *id.* at 193, when Illinois became the
13   first state to adopt the American Law Institute's Model Penal Code approach to
14   decriminalization of some sexual offenses. *Id.* at 193 n.7.
15   Our nation's history has not been rewritten in the seventeen years since
16   *Bowers* was decided, and that history contradicts any assertion that a right to
17   engage in homosexual anal intercourse has been a valued and protected right of
18   American citizens. The fact that the states have traditionally prohibited the act as
19   a crime is utterly inconsistent with any claim that our legal tradition has treated
20   the choice to engage in that act as a "fundamental" right.
21   It is true that some change has occurred since *Bowers* was decided: three
22   more states and the District of Columbia, in appropriate exercise of the demo-
23   cratic process, have repealed or limited the scope of their statutes prohibiting
24   sodomy in general or homosexual sodomy in particular; and a small number of
25   state appellate courts have found that such statutes violate a state constitutional
26   right to privacy. *See* Brief of Petitioners 23 n.17. The State of Texas is now one   C
27   of thirteen states in which consensual homosexual sodomy remains a criminal
28   offense. *Id.* at 27 n.21. The fact that several states have ceased treating sodomy as
29   a criminal offense, however, is no evidence of a national tradition . . . .
30   The petitioners concede that this Court requires "objective guideposts,"
31   such as "history and precedent," in the process of identification of liberty inter-
32   ests protected by the Fourteenth Amendment. They point to the gradual trend
33   towards decriminalization of consensual sexual behavior among adults as the
34   necessary objective evidence of a fundamental right firmly rooted in the tradi-
35   tions and conscience of American citizens. *See* Brief of Petitioners 19-25. Four

36   decades of gradual but incomplete decriminalization does not erase a history of
37   one hundred and fifty years of universal reprobation. A recent trend towards un-
38   easy toleration — even a trend involving a majority of the fifty states — cannot
39   establish a tradition "deeply rooted" in our national history and tradition. The
40   petitioners mistake new growth for deep roots.

A This subheading emphasizes the theme of "rooted[ness]" — a concept drawn from the Court's prior opinion in *Bowers*, which was the linchpin of Texas's argument. Pay attention to how the lawyers repeat and play off of this word throughout the subsection.

B Notice that this entire subsection, which is one extended historical argument, presents no original research. Rather, it repeatedly cites *Bowers* to suggest that history supports Texas's legal position. Referring to precedential history comforts lawyers and judges alike given how few of them have formal training as historians. As seen later in the chapter, original historical research can also influence judges.

C In Chapter 5, we saw lawyers distinguish and downplay the other side's authorities. Here, the lawyers use the same technique with history. They concede a handful of bad facts so that they can frame these facts in a way that serves their own argument. The phrase "in appropriate exercise of the democratic process" slips in a policy argument: that legislatures, not courts, should repeal anti-sodomy statutes.

D This sentence captures the common technique of concluding that history, either wholly or on balance, favors your client rather than the other party.

E Texas drives home its theme by repeating the words "history," "trend," "rooted," and "tradition." These words do a lot of heavy lifting for Texas, which is trying to depict the petitioners' evidence as a trend and its own position as the one rooted in history. The passage here ends with a powerful, elegant metaphor.

Example

10.2

Takeaway point 10.2: The best way to counter an argument based on history is with an argument based on history.

Lawyers fight history with history. Here, a number of groups that supported gay rights counter Texas's historical argument in a battle over Texas's anti-sodomy statute. This passage uses history to recast Texas's law and to build the case that gay men and lesbians have historically been victims of discrimination, thus strengthening Lawrence's equal protection argument.

Source: Amicus brief arguing that anti-sodomy laws are unconstitutional, from *Lawrence v. Texas*, 539 U.S. 558 (2003) (numerous footnotes and citations omitted).

I. TEXAS' HOMOSEXUAL CONDUCT LAW IS A PRODUCT OF ANTI-GAY
    ANIMUS

   Texas' Homosexual Conduct Law, limited to same-sex intimacy, was enacted in 1973. It is not a statute woven from the fabric of the common law, reflecting an "ancient" anti-sodomy morality. It grows from a different, more recent tradition: one of anti-gay animus and bigotry. . . .

   What offended traditional notions of morality, as reflected in English and early American common law, were a range of nonprocreative sexual practices. **A** Because nonprocreation was the central offense, those practices were criminalized by early sodomy laws regardless of whether they were engaged in by same-sex or different-sex couples. Most of today's sodomy laws continue to reflect this traditional disapproval of nonprocreative sexual activities regardless of the sexual identity of the couple involved. Of the thirteen states that continue to outlaw private consensual sodomy, nine apply their bans to all couples. Only four states, including Texas, punish solely same-sex conduct. **B**

   Sodomy proscriptions limited to same-sex relations are thus a distinctly modern phenomenon. The first Texas sodomy law enacted in 1860, for instance, prohibited anal sex whether committed by husband and wife, unmarried heterosexuals, or two male partners. Tex. Penal Code art. 342 (1860). In 1943, the state added a proscription of oral sex, but still without reference to the sexual identity of the partners. Tex. Penal Code art. 524 (1943). It was not until 1973 that Texas repealed its general prohibition on sodomy and enacted the Homosexual Conduct Law in its place, specifically criminalizing consensual relations only between people of the same sex. Tex. Penal Code § 21.06. **C**

   B. The Modern Criminalization Of Homosexual Sodomy Reflects
       Modern Patterns Of Discrimination Against Gay People As A Class **D**

   There is, then, no ancient tradition of same-sex sodomy proscriptions that explains Texas' Homosexual Conduct Law. The explanation lies elsewhere: simple animus, not against sodomy generally, but against individuals physically and emotionally attracted to members of the same sex.

   Although same-sex relationships have been documented throughout history, the concept of homosexuality (or heterosexuality) as a defining characteristic of one's identity is relatively recent. American "colonial society lacked even the category of homosexual or lesbian to describe a person," though colonial court records refer to incidents of sexual acts between two women or two men. **E**

36   D'Emilio, *Capitalism and Gay Identity, in* Cases and Materials on Sexual Orien-
37   tation and the Law 46, 47 (Rubenstein ed., 2d ed. 1993). It was only in the late
38   19th century that American scientific literature began describing homosexuality
39   as a pathological "condition, something that was inherent in a person, a part of
40   his or her 'nature.'" *Id.* at 29.

— F

41   The turn of the 20th century saw the rise of numerous forms of public
42   attacks on gay people. Police targeted for arrest people perceived to be gay and
43   raided institutions that served a predominately gay clientele. Gay-themed plays
44   and films were censored and books were banned. In Europe, discrimination
45   against gay people reached a horrific apogee in World War II, when thousands
46   were exterminated in Nazi concentration camps. After the war, discrimination
47   against gay men and lesbians took its most virulent American forms. Led by
48   Joseph McCarthy, who grouped homosexuality with communism as a "grave
47   evil to be rooted out of the federal government" the U.S. Senate conducted a
50   special investigation into government employment of gay people and "other sex
51   perverts." In 1953, President Eisenhower terminated all gay people from

— G

52   federal employment, and the FBI sought to enforce the order by gathering data
53   on local arrests for gay-related charges and membership in gay and lesbian civil
54   rights organizations. Gay aliens were excluded from admission into the United
55   States as psychopaths or sexual deviants. . . .

56   No credible authority disputes that gay people have been subjected to the
57   most dehumanizing forms of discrimination employed by American government
58   at any level in the 20th century. It is in this ugly tradition that Texas' Homosexual
59   Conduct Law follows: the modern practice of condemning gay people for who
60   they are, as opposed to the more ancient tradition condemning acts in which
61   anyone can engage.

A Historical arguments are usually written in a more scholarly tone than other types of arguments. Don't overdo this approach — you are an advocate, not a historian — but realize that historical arguments tend to sound slightly less aggressive than neighboring parts of a brief.

B The brief rebuts the "vote counting" presented by Texas. It makes Texas look like an outlier rather than, as Texas claimed, a guardian of a tradition.

C The brief emphasizes that anti-sodomy laws traditionally focused on banning an *activity* (sodomy), not on preventing a single group (gay men) from engaging in that activity. The brief shows that history can be read, framed, and interpreted just like a case. Here, the brief rejects Texas's "reading" of the historical record.

D This subsection's heading repeats the adjective "modern," preparing readers for the brief's argument that Texas's sodomy law is a new — a modern — innovation.

E The brief shifts from the history of anti-sodomy laws to the history of gay men and lesbians in America, focusing on the history of people rather than of laws.

F This argument is subtle and brilliant. The level of scrutiny that would apply to Texas's law depended in part on whether the law discriminated based on an immutable trait. The brief uses history to note that homosexuality has been perceived as an inherent trait since the word "homosexual" developed, increasing the likelihood that the Court would apply heightened scrutiny.

G This paragraph, too, taps into the legal test: the level of scrutiny that courts apply depends partly on whether there is a history of discrimination against the group challenging a law. The brief places Texas and its anti-sodomy law within an ugly "tradition" that includes Nazism and McCarthyism.

Example 10.3	**Takeaway point 10.3:** History can provide clues about the meaning of a constitutional provision or the scope of a legal tradition.

History can be especially helpful when courts need to assess the bounds of a constitutional provision (such as what "privileges and immunities" meant to the Founders) or a legal tradition (such as the scope of habeas corpus rights). Here, we see the former example — using history to assess the meaning of a constitutional amendment.

A school in California required schoolchildren to recite the Pledge of Allegiance, which has contained the words "under God" since Congress, by statute, added those words. One father, upset that his daughter was required to recite these words, filed a lawsuit. The suit alleged that forcing children to recite the Pledge of Allegiance violated the First Amendment's Establishment Clause, which prohibits state-sponsored religiosity. The federal government used history to argue that the words "under God" do not violate the Establishment Clause.

Source: Brief of the United States in *Elk Grove Unified School District v. Newdow,* 542 U.S. 1 (2004) (some citations and footnotes omitted).

---

1   **2. The Framers considered official acknowledgments of religion's role in**
2   **the formation of the Nation to be appropriate.**
3   [F]rom the Nation's earliest days, the Framers considered references to God
4   in official documents and official acknowledgments of the role of religion in
5   the history and public life of the Country to be consistent with the principles
6   of religious autonomy embodied in the First Amendment. Indeed, two docu-   **A**
7   ments that this Court has looked to in its Establishment Clause cases — James
8   Madison's Memorial and Remonstrance Against Religious Assessments (1785),
9   and Thomas Jefferson's Bill for Establishing Religious Freedom (1779) — repeat-
10 edly acknowledge the Creator.[20] . . .
11 The First Congress — the same Congress that drafted the Establishment
12 Clause — adopted a policy of selecting a paid chaplain to open each session of
13 Congress with prayer. *See Marsh v. Chambers,* 463 U.S. 783, 787 (1983). That
14 same Congress, the day after the Establishment Clause was proposed, also urged
15 President Washington "to proclaim 'a day of public thanksgiving and prayer, to
16 be observed by acknowledging with grateful hearts the many and signal favours
17 of Almighty God." *Lynch v. Donnelly,* 465 U.S. 668, 675 n.2 (1984) (citation omit-
18 ted). President Washington responded by proclaiming November 26, 1789, a day
19 of thanksgiving to "offer[] our prayers and supplications to the Great Lord and
20 Ruler of Nations, and beseech Him to pardon our national and other transgres-
21 sions." *Ibid.* (citation omitted). President Washington also included a reference
22 to God in his first inaugural address: "[I]t would be peculiarly improper to omit
23 in this first official act my fervent supplications to that Almighty Being who rules
24 over the universe, who presides in the council of nations, and whose providential
25 aids can supply every human defect, that His benediction may consecrate to the
26 liberties and happiness of the people of the United States a Government insti-
27 tuted by themselves for these essential purposes."

---

28   20. *See McGowan v. Maryland,* 366 U.S. 420, 437 (1961) (Jefferson's and Madi-
29 son's statements are "particularly relevant in the search for the First Amendment's
30 meaning").

31   Later generations have followed suit. Since the time of Chief Justice Marshall,
32   this Court has opened its sessions with "God save the United States and this
33   Honorable Court." *Engel v. Vitale*, 370 U.S. 421, 446 (1962) (Stewart, J.,
34   dissenting). President Abraham Lincoln referred to a "Nation[] under God" in
35   the historic Gettysburg Address (1863): "That we here highly resolve that these
36   dead shall not have died in vain; that this Nation, under God, shall have a new
37   birth of freedom, and that government of the people, by the people, for the people
38   shall not perish from the earth." Every President that has delivered an inaugural
39   address has referred to God or a Higher Power, and every President, except
40   Thomas Jefferson, has declared a Thanksgiving Day holiday. In 1865, Congress
41   authorized the inscription of "In God we trust" on United States coins. Act of
42   Mar. 3, 1865, ch. 102, § 5, 13 Stat. 518. In 1931, Congress adopted as the National
43   Anthem "The Star-Spangled Banner," the fourth verse of which reads: "Blest with
44   victory and peace, may the heav'n rescued land Praise the Pow'r that hath made
45   and preserved us a nation! Then conquer we must, when our cause it is just,
46   And this be our motto 'In God is our Trust.'" *Engel*, 370 U.S. at 449 (Stewart,
47   J., dissenting). In 1956, Congress passed legislation to make "In God we trust"
48   the National Motto, *see* 36 U.S.C. § 302, and provided that it be inscribed on all
47   United States currency, 31 U.S.C. § 5112(d)(1), above the main door of the Senate,
50   and behind the Chair of the Speaker of the House of Representatives. *See* Act of
51   Nov. 13, 2002, Pub. L. No. 107-293, §§ 1-2, 116 Stat. 2057-2060. The Constitutions
52   of all 50 States, moreover, include express references to God. *See* Appendix 13,
53   *infra.* There thus "is an unbroken history of official acknowledgment by all
54   three branches of government," as well as the States, "of the role of religion in
55   American life from at least 1789." *Lynch*, 465 U.S. at 674.

B

C

A Clear topic sentences like this one are especially useful in historical arguments. Without these sharp reminders of what a paragraph is discussing, historical facts can quickly seem random and dull.

B The brief uses cornerstones of American life — Thanksgiving, inaugural addresses, the national anthem, currency — to show that religion has been present in civic life in the United States throughout its history. Given that Jefferson's view is especially important (as the brief notes in footnote 20), the point about presidents declaring a day of thanksgiving is only moderately helpful given that Jefferson chose *not* to do so.

C The brief delves into what the Founders approved for public events. But the brief did not discuss religion in early American *schools*, including the following potentially useful examples:

- The first graduation ceremony (in 1804) of one of the nation's first public universities — the University of Georgia — included an invocation and a prayer delivered by reverends.

- Benjamin Rush, who led the ratification fight in Pennsylvania, called for "the universal education of our youth in the principles of Christianity by means of the Bible."

- The First Congress passed legislation in 1789, which presumed that religion would be taught in public schools.

- Representative Fisher Ames, who *drafted* the House's version of the Establishment Clause, wrote that "[m]ost young hearts are tender . . . why then . . . should not the Bible regain the place it once held as a school book?"

- Finally, Thomas Jefferson, who was in charge of the first public education program in the District of Columbia, used the Bible and a religious text called *Watt's Hymnal* as the primary texts for students, explaining, "The Bible is the cornerstone of liberty . . . a student's perusal of the Sacred volume will make them better citizens."

I found this evidence simply by reviewing earlier briefs and by conducting a bit of original research.

Example
10.4

Takeaway point 10.4: History can validate and help you develop policy arguments.

History can also help you to build powerful policy arguments by exploring the problems or benefits that occurred when our forebears experimented with a rule. And you don't need to travel back to the eighteenth century to find useful historical arguments, as we see below. Here is one of the most lauded briefs in recent years: in 2003, senior military officials filed it in defense of affirmative action, which many Court watchers expected that the Court would curtail in a case about a public law school's admission policy. The case was ultimately decided 5-4 in favor of affirmative action's supporters, and this filing is widely perceived to have flipped Justice O'Connor's vote. Justice Stevens later said that the outcome was "significantly influenced" by the "historical context" that this brief supplied.

Source: Amicus brief, from *Grutter v. Bollinger*, 539 U.S. 306 (2003) (some citations omitted).

1	Almost as soon as President Truman ordered the integration of the armed
2	forces, some in the military recognized the importance of integrating the officer
3	corps. After integration, however, the armed forces did not produce a substantial
4	number of minority officers for more than a generation. Both lingering discrim-
5	ination and the formal educational qualifications for officers precluded quick
6	racial integration of the officer corps. As a result, over time, the armed forces
7	became a racial mix of diverse enlisted ranks commanded by an overwhelmingly
8	white officer corps. In 1962, a mere 1.6% of all commissioned military officers
9	were African-American.
10	The chasm between the racial composition of the officer corps and the en-
11	listed personnel undermined military effectiveness in a variety of ways. For
12	example, military effectiveness depends heavily upon unit cohesion. In turn,
13	group cohesiveness depends on a shared sense of mission and the unimpeded
14	flow of information through the chain of command. African-Americans experi-
15	enced discriminatory treatment in the military, even during integration, but the
16	concerns and perceptions of African-American personnel were often unknown,
17	unaddressed or both, in part because the lines of authority, from the military
18	police to the officer corps, were almost exclusively white. Indeed, "communica-
19	tion between the largely white officer corps and black enlisted men could be so
20	tenuous that a commander might remain blissfully unaware of patterns of racial
21	discrimination that black servicemen found infuriating." Nalty, *supra*, at 282.
22	The military's pre-Vietnam racial problems generally were suppressed dur-
23	ing battle (*e.g.*, in Korea). During peacetime, violent incidents were met with
24	attempts to improve military life for African-Americans, but minority representa-
25	tion in the officer corps remained static. . . .
26	During the 1960s and 1970s, the military experienced a demoralizing and
27	destabilizing period of internal racial strife. Hundreds of race-related incidents
28	occurred. For example, in the 1960s, racial violence among the Marines at Camp
29	Lejeune was not uncommon. White officers were simply unaware of intense
30	African-American dissatisfaction with job assignments and the perceived lack of
31	respect from the Marine Corps. Nalty, *supra*, at 306-07. In the early 1970s, the
32	Navy endured similar racial violence on board the *Constellation*, the *Kitty Hawk*
33	and the *Hassayampa. See generally Special Subcommittee Report* at 17,674-79;
34	Adm. E. Zumwalt, Jr., *On Watch* 217-32 (1976). In each case, the officer corps

A

35 was caught off guard, unable to bring the situation under control, due to the
36 absence of trust and communication between the predominantly white officer
37 corps and frustrated African-American enlisted men.
38   Throughout the armed forces, the overwhelmingly white officer corps faced
39 racial tension and unrest. "Fights between black and white soldiers were en-
40 demic in the 1970s, an era now remembered as the 'time of troubles.'" Moskos
41 & Butler, *supra,* at 33. "In Vietnam, racial tensions reached a point where there
42 was an inability to fight." Maraniss, *supra,* at A01. African-American troops, who
43 rarely saw members of their own race in command positions, lost confidence
44 in the military as an institution. Mason, *supra,* at 2-3. And, African-American
45 servicemen concluded that the command structure had no regard for whether
46 African-Americans would succeed in military careers. 1 Dep't of Def., *Report of*
47 *the Task Force on the Administration of Military Justice in the Armed Forces* 38-48,
48 59-66 (Nov. 30, 1972), *reprinted in* 13 *Basic Documents*, item 66.
47   . . . Ultimately, "[t]he military of the 1970s recognized that its race problem
50 was so critical that it was on the verge of self-destruction." Moskos & Butler,
51 *supra,* at 142.
52   The painful lesson slowly learned was that our diverse enlisted ranks
53 rendered integration of the officer corps a military necessity. M. Neiberg, *Making*
54 *Citizen-Soldiers: ROTC and the Ideology of American Military Service* 166 (2000)
55 ("[t]he military came . . . to understand that having African American noncom-
56 missioned officers . . . and regular officers was critical to both the operational
57 efficiency of the military and to the creation of the more just and equal environ-
58 ment that military leaders . . . wanted to create"). "Racial conflict within the
59 military during the Vietnam era was a blaring wakeup call to the fact that equal
60 opportunity is absolutely indispensable to unit cohesion, and therefore critical
61 to military effectiveness and our national security." *President's Report* § 7.5.1.

A The brief uses historical data to show that the military's leadership reflected little diversity. Elsewhere, the brief notes that — because of a successful affirmative action program — "[m]inorities now comprise roughly 19% of all officers," with African Americans accounting for 8.8% of officers. These figures comport with the brief's argument that the ability to value diversity in selecting military officers is critical to national security.

B The historical record is used to show what happened when no affirmative action existed: national security was threatened, race-based conflict erupted, and morale plummeted.

C This is the theme of the brief. (Themes are discussed in Chapter 11.) The brief ends with this sentence: "Today, there is no race-neutral alternative that will fulfill the military's and the nation's compelling need for a diverse officer corps of the highest quality to serve the country." The brief uses history to show that diversity, and affirmative action, are necessary to a strong military.

FREQUENTLY ASKED QUESTIONS ABOUT HISTORICAL ARGUMENTS

Q. **Should I regularly include historical arguments in my motion or brief?**

A. Many legal issues won't require historical arguments. Of the arguments discussed in this book, this sort of argument will appear least frequently in your briefs or motions. But because your adversary is unlikely to raise these arguments, it gives you a great chance to outlitigate the other side in appropriate instances.

Q. **So what are the appropriate instances in which to present a historical argument?**

A. You *need* a historical argument only when your opponent advances one; you would then want to undermine the other side's research and present your own historical evidence. Also consider using historical evidence to

- show the meaning of a constitutional provision, as the debate surrounding the provision may be probative of a term's meaning or purpose;
- prove that courts, legislatures, or executive officials were aware of a problem or acted in a certain way in the past;
- convince a court that long-standing common law tradition requires, permits, disfavors, or prohibits a particular approach to a legal issue;
- build a policy argument by showing what happened in the past when a given approach was followed or avoided; and
- undermine the reasoning of a case (see Chapter 5's discussion about discrediting versus distinguishing authorities).

This list is just a starting point: use history whenever you think it will help your client—unless the costs of searching for it are too great.

Q. **How do I avoid relying on bad history?**

A. Reputable journals generally reveal the basic lines of historical consensus or dispute. Research whether subsequent articles criticized the accuracy of your sources. Moreover, those fault lines should allow you to decide whether you need to disclose adverse authorities. The duty of candor in most jurisdictions prevents lawyers from hiding bad historical evidence. Thus, you should generally deploy the evidence that best supports your case, while acknowledging (and strategically framing) enough of the opposing point of view so as to not be undermined later by a lack of disclosure.

Q. **Should I use historical evidence as an authority that compels a result or as a source of facts and policies that merely counsel for a result?**

A. The latter. History does not typically compel an outcome.

Q. **Some historical arguments seem really dry. Are they still effective?**

A. While you don't want your arguments to bore readers, a convention has emerged at the Supreme Court of citing history in scholarly terms — almost like a passage from a book about history, rather than as an argument that follows or adapts CRAC. *See* Introduction to Part II (discussing CRAC). This academic approach makes the history seem objective. In courts that less frequently see historical arguments, follow CRAC so that readers see the significance of each historical detail. Presenting history as an argument will improve your brief's flow and make the passage less dry and plodding (and will spare readers from feeling lost in detail). Just realize that your history will seem less objective when you are using it to argue a point.

Q. How long or hard should I look for historical evidence? And will supervising attorneys get angry if I bill a lot of hours for obscure historical research?

A. This issue applies to many legal research questions, not just historical issues. In general, discuss your research strategy with your supervisors and check in with them along the way to ensure that they feel like your incremental progress warrants further research. Historical research can be very time consuming, so the decision of whether your argument could benefit from historical evidence is tied to the larger strategic issues involved in crafting your motion or brief and to the stakes of the dispute.

Q. Is history really relevant outside of constitutional issues?

A. Not always, but often. For instance, shoe designer Christian Louboutin sued a competitor in New York to enjoin it from selling red-soled shoes. The competitor found a French judicial opinion which reported that "many models of women's shoes with red soles were marketed by other designers and distributors before and after the company Christian Louboutin decided to appropriate this feature." History weakened Louboutin's suggestion that he invented the red-soled shoe. Similarly, in a dispute about federal securities laws, showing the historical context of the Great Depression can help to validate your client's assessment of the statute's purpose — what problems led Congress to regulate stock markets?

Q. Are there shortcuts to conducting historical research?

A. This book is not a research guide, but here are some tricks to find useful historical arguments efficiently.

As a first step, use a library's database or an Internet search engine to conduct some preliminary research. Two options include Google Books (http://books.google.com) and Google Scholar (http://scholar.google.com). Search for useful titles and relevant terms.

Once you have gathered useful titles and some good search terms, supplement your search by combing research databases to find articles, books, briefs, and cases that have cited several or all of those books or articles. Why? Because anything that cites multiple relevant sources is likely to help you. You can conduct this follow-up research in numerous databases. HeinOnline is probably the best one-stop resource if you have access to it. You can also refer to the Making of Modern Law suite of legal archives, which compiles treatises, Supreme Court briefs, and various primary sources such as city charters and state constitutional conventions. For lawyers who have access to Westlaw/Lexis/Bloomberg, those electronic databases offer their subscribers access to journals and cases (which you can review and cite) and briefs (which compile useful resources that you can hunt down). You may also search databases that compile historical papers and other social science papers (such as JSTOR) or that compile old newspapers and dissertations (such as Proquest). Use free resources to help you gather the materials that will allow you to conduct efficient searches in subscription-based databases.

Conducting *original* historical research — as opposed to finding existing resources — is more involved. Start by reading the University of Michigan Law School Library's *American Legal History Resources Research Guide* (Feb. 21, 2006), *available at* http://www.law.umich.edu/library/students/research/Documents/am%20legal%20history%20resources.pdf. You will probably want to visit a library or a law library (depending on the topic). Consult a reference librarian who specializes in historical research. Or, if you cannot locate a specialist who will work with you, search the library's database for books and microfiche (or microfilm) about your topic; go to that section of the library and flip through the table of contents and index of each seemingly relevant source that you find. And, of course, consult judicial opinions about your topic.

OTHER ISSUES RELATING TO BRIEFS

Having explored the two bulkiest parts of a typical motion or brief — the Statement of Facts and the Argument — we turn to several other vital advocacy skills. Chapter 11 discusses how to select and organize arguments. Next, Chapter 12 dicusses Questions Presented, which introduce the legal issues implicated by the case. Chapter 13 then explores how to write a strong Introduction and Summary of Argument — two parts of a brief that are conceptually linked to one another, but distinct. Part III of the book ends by exploring trial motions (Chapter 14) and several common situations in appellate briefing that require additional advice (Chapter 15).

Chapter 11

Selecting and Organizing Arguments

Your Table of Contents is so pivotal to good advocacy that this chapter may be the most important in the book.

Yes, you read that correctly: the *Table of Contents*. To understand why this is true, you first need to broaden your ideas about what a Table of Contents does. In a motion or brief, it does much more than list the document's headings and corresponding page numbers. It implicates critical choices about how to select and sort your arguments and how to frame your client's story. That is, it becomes a tool to use in selecting and organizing the components of your client's case, not simply a rote list of headings that you compile immediately before you submit the brief to the court. You can use the Table of Contents, for instance, to decide issues like these:

- Which argument should I feature?

- Should I include a backup argument? A backup to my backup?

- Should I include an argument that I know will lose just to preserve the issue for appeal?

- Which argument should I place first: a long-shot argument requesting substantial remedies or a strong argument requesting limited relief?

- Should I place a weak procedural argument in front of strong substantive arguments, and risk weakening the brief by leading with a loser?

- If I am trying to reverse a decision below, how many issues can I raise before the appellate judges infer that none of my points deserve their attention?

These and countless other choices are reflected in the words (and omissions) of your Table of Contents.

There are no hard-and-fast rules about how to pick, ditch, and sort your arguments. You must rely on your judgment and experience, knowing, of course, that different cases will require different approaches. But by looking at a few strong Tables of Contents, you can infer how some great advocates make their choices, which will improve your instincts about how to select and sequence your own facts and arguments. This exploration is just the beginning, however; throughout your career, you will cultivate your ability to spot and build a winning strategy.

CHAPTER OVERVIEW

1. Because the Table of Contents appears early in your brief, a well-written table represents a valuable opportunity to persuade readers. Some judges read the Table of Contents first to preview the argument and to see whether the case presents any unfamiliar legal issues. Accuracy matters; incorrect page numbers or typos will hurt your credibility and leave a negative first impression.

2. The movant/appellant/petitioner should ordinarily raise *procedural* issues first, then *substantive* issues, then *remedies*.[1]

3. If you are the appellee/respondent (or the party opposing a motion), organize your response differently: present strong, affirmative points first. Do not feel compelled to copy the sequence of the other side's arguments. Sort the arguments to favor your client's position and phrase your position positively. (For example, your heading should state "Smith's complaint amply stated a cause of action for nuisance" rather than "Smith's nuisance claim should not be dismissed.")

4. Raising arguments in the alternative is generally fine, but avoid arguments that contradict one another. Readers loathe logically contradictory or inconsistent arguments. Also, many judges report that raising too many issues jeopardizes your case, so aim for four or fewer arguments.

5. When deciding which arguments to advance or discard, think through the remedy that your client will get if it prevails. Favor arguments that have better chances of securing a better victory, and deprioritize weak arguments. Likewise, pruning weak arguments from your filing is pivotal to good advocacy: cut dead branches so that judges can spot the fruit.

6. Do your best to prevent any heading or subheading from exceeding two lines (unless the court's rules demand more detail).

7. Avoid headings and subheadings that are too technical such as those relying on obscure cases or dense citations. Ideally, readers will understand your main headings and grasp the argument you are making even without reading your brief.

8. Avoid vague headings that fail to apprise readers of the argument. For instance, "DC's First Claim May Not Be Dismissed" does not tell the court what the section will discuss.

9. Use subheadings to explain why each heading is correct. Also, avoid placing your subheadings in all capital letters. All caps are harder to read, are not checked in most spell-check programs, and may seem aggressive to readers. All caps, however, are common in headings (as opposed to subheadings). Small caps are also acceptable in your main headings.

10. Your facts, too, can have subheadings. These are often sentence fragments. By contrast, headings and subheadings in the Argument are usually full sentences.

---

1. *Procedural issues* include arguments related to jurisdiction, forum *non conveniens*, improper service of process, sovereign immunity, standing, ripeness, mootness, the political question doctrine, statutes of limitations, and so on. *Substantive issues* include arguments that provide or foreclose a remedy on a nonprocedural area of law; these sections are likely to rely on statutes, ordinances, regulations, doctrines, and other authorities on which your suit (or defense) is based. *Remedies* include issues such as the appropriate size of a damages award, what the scope of an injunction should be, whether the court should order rescission of a contract, whether to assess interest on the other side, and whether to award costs.

Example **11.1**

Takeaway point 11.1: Use your Table of Contents to convey your key points.

We begin with a Table of Contents that is flawed — but brilliant. It shows that the key roles of a Table of Contents are to highlight the central theme of your case, to shape a judge's impression of the litigants, and to advance your client's strategic goals. And that's true even if your prose is a little bit rough.

The technology titan Apple sued Samsung in August 2011, alleging that Samsung had infringed ten patents that belonged to Apple. Four days after filing the lawsuit (and before Samsung had even answered the complaint), Apple filed a Motion to Expedite Discovery. Moreover, Apple managed to place its key argument in front of the judge. You'll see it below. In less than thirteen months, the case reached a jury, which awarded Apple more than $1 billion.

Source: Apple's Motion to Expedite Discovery, from *Apple, Inc. v. Samsung Electronics Co.,* No. 11-cv.-01846-LHK (N. D. Cal. May 3, 2011)

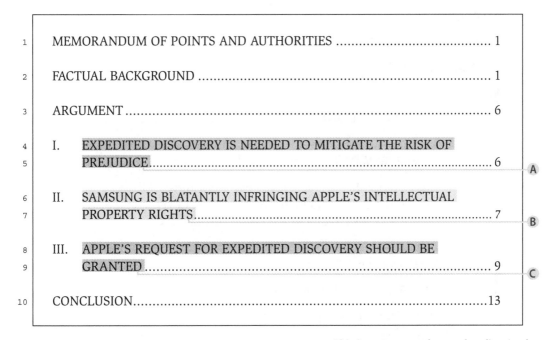

A Notice that the first heading does not specify who might be prejudiced or how. Nor does it specify who needs expedited discovery or why they need it. Stylistically, this heading is flawed.

B This heading advances Apple's core argument in the case and, in just eight words, brands Samsung as the villain in the case. Also, by moving to expedite discovery, the motion conveys to the court that Apple was eager to litigate the dispute, which signals strength and credibility. This motion also forced the judge to focus on the case promptly — and possibly before Samsung had a chance to perfect its defense strategy. This is a strong and savvy heading (and a clever motion) that helped Apple get its case to a jury quickly.

C As we see in this chapter's other examples, good headings in dispositive motions and appellate briefs usually "nest" their headings: they add subheadings to substantiate the claim contained in the major headings. But if your client has multiple, simple points or if the motion will not resolve a major issue in the case, unnested headings (which Apple uses here) may make sense.

Example	**Takeaway point 11.2:** Keep your Tables of Contents short, simple, and clean.

11.2

Tables of Contents should be short, simple, and clean, as we see below. In this case, Paul Konowaloff sued the Metropolitan Museum of Art to recover a painting created by the legendary impressionist Paul Cézanne. Konowaloff alleged that the painting was seized from his ancestor in 1918 by Russia's Bolshevik Party. He argued that because he was the heir of the painting's rightful owner, he should gain possession of the work. The museum moved to dismiss the complaint, arguing that Konowaloff's claim was barred by various legal doctrines, each of which provided an independent basis to preclude Konowaloff's lawsuit. The court agreed and dismissed Konowaloff's complaint.

Source: Museum's motion to dismiss in *Konowaloff v. Metropolitan Museum of Art*, 10 CIV. 9126 SAS, 2011 WL 4430856 (S.D.N.Y. Sept. 22, 2011).

Ⓐ Many briefs begin with an Introduction. When the applicable court rules are silent, skilled lawyers often add a thematic Introduction to the start of their brief to orient and persuade readers. Chapter 13 explores this technique.

Ⓑ When responding to the facts that appear in the complaint, you may want to remind the court that the facts are merely alleged. Frame the facts in a way that helps your client even when (as on a motion to dismiss) the other side's alleged facts are presumed to be correct.

Ⓒ Many courts require this section, which lets the court know the standard or standards that govern the issues in the case. For instance, which facts must the court presume to be true (if any)? What materials can the court consider at this stage? If the case is on appeal, how trustingly or suspiciously must it look at what the trial court did? In many cases, the standard of review can determine the outcome, thus dictating the prudence of raising an issue at all. For instance, if the trial judge denies sanctions and the "abuse of discretion" standard applies, it is wildly unlikely that an appellate court will second-guess the trial judge. Know the applicable standard and frame the standard helpfully — just as you would any other legal doctrine.

Ⓓ The motion to dismiss raises multiple, independent grounds to dismiss the complaint. This approach is effective because winning on of the arguments will doom Konowaloff's lawsuit. When an argument requires multiple steps or showings, the chance of winning plummets. Note, further, that a Table of Contents typically will not explain terms like the "act of state doctrine," but the subheadings may provide contextual clues to help readers figure out what the doctrine entails. Other than the act of state doctrine, the arguments in this motion are quite common, so they do not require the sort of explanatory hints that the subheadings to section I of the motion provide. This Table also offers another clue: by providing detailed subheadings about only the first argument, it signals that this issue (the act of state doctrine) is the most important point. And sure enough, the court resolved the issue based on this argument. As an aside, the presiding judge had submitted a brief involving the act of state doctrine when she was in private practice, demonstrating the value of profiling judges to learn their preferences, jurisprudential approach, and substantive experience. The lawyers were able to assume that she was familiar with this doctrine.

Ⓔ This Table of Contents does a stellar job of writing short, clear headings. In general, however, use your headings to explain why a given doctrine or rule applies, such as by adding "because X and Y." Alternatively, you can use subheadings to convey these points as the subheadings to Section I demonstrate. Try to keep your Table of Contents to one page—and rarely (if ever) more than two pages because less effort makes for happier judges. Tables of Contents should be short *and* helpful.

Ⓕ Notice that the "fourth" argument actually combines two distinct but related points. The lawyers apparently wanted to comply with Judge Ruggero Aldisert's "primo" rule, which appears on page 192, that a brief should not advance more than four issues. Combining related issues into one heading is a clever trick to make your brief seem like it addresses fewer issues than it actually does, provided that the issues actually fit together when placed alondside one another.

Example
11.3

Takeaway point 11.3: Use subheadings to explain and substantiate your primary headings.

The Table of Contents in Example 11.2 uses subheadings to explain why the court should follow its first argument, but it did not do so for the other arguments. Appellate briefs and major motions (like summary judgment motions) often use subheadings to provide the rationale for the proposition contained in all of the major headings of the brief. We see this technique below.

We looked earlier at an example from Exxon's brief opposing the award of punitive damages after the *Exxon Valdez* oil spill in 1989. Here, the plaintiffs' lawyers try to defend their clients' multibillion dollar award.

Source: Baker's brief in *Exxon Shipping Co. v. Baker*, 554 U.S. 471 (2008).

A

B

C

D

E

F

A   The brief begins with a theory of vicarious liability. That's fine; the lawyers concluded that the evidence that Exxon's agents had acted recklessly was more powerful than the evidence that Exxon itself had acted badly enough to warrant punitive damages. But see the next comment.

B   Subheadings should match the heading. Here, the first subheading mirrors what the heading promised. But subheading I.B refers to "Exxon's *Own* Recklessness" (emphasis added). Heading I, however, did not mention Exxon's recklessness — just that of its "top management." As a legal matter, Exxon is liable for the actions of its top managers, and the brief lucidly explains this point. Even so, the headings *seem* inconsistent, which could jar judges when they first read this brief.

C   This heading raises a procedural argument — that Exxon failed to raise (and thus waived) the argument that the Clean Water Act prohibits punitive damages. In general, place threshold arguments first. But here, the lawyers wisely begin by making their affirmative argument in Section I — that Exxon and its agents behaved badly enough that punitive damages were warranted. Then they deal in Section II with the "negative" argument raised by the other side; they make readers *want* to award punitive damages before countering Exxon's arguments.

D   **The subheadings in Section II each substantiate the main heading — a prototypical approach. But notice the tricky choice about how to sequence these two sub-points. Placing the procedural issue first (i.e., that Exxon waived the argument) could signal to the Court that Exxon's substantive argument is strong. But reversing the order would cause** the opposite problem, weakening the argument that Exxon waived this issue. Whichever argument comes second is hobbled. One possible solution: stick with the order that the lawyers use here, but shorten the waiver argument to signal that the issue is open-and-shut and to maintain the flow of the substantive argument. As Example 11.4 will show, you generally should discuss procedural issues before substantive ones. Baker and the other plaintiffs sensibly follow this principle within Section II of his argument.

E   The brief's sequence of arguments is reasonable, but Sections II and III *could* be reversed to emphasize that the punitive award was reasonable and to place at the end of the brief the defensive point that is currently in section II. Here is a possible revised order: (I) Exxon is liable for punitive damages, (II) the size of those damages was appropriate, and (III) the Court should not permit Exxon's meritless attempt — which it waived — to use the Clean Water Act to shield itself from liability. I don't present either approach as right or wrong, merely as evidence that the same case can be sensibly litigated in different ways or sequences.

Separately, notice that heading III is defensive; the damages are merely "permissible." Phrase your headings more positively, such as "The Size of the Punitive Award Comports Fully with This Court's Precedents and with Traditional Maritime Law."

F   Most court rules allow litigants to append materials to a brief or motion. Do so when statutes or other materials are bulky enough that they would clog the body of your brief. In trial courts, remember that record materials, such as documents and deposition transcripts, should be attached to a witness's declaration.

Example 11.4

Takeaway point 11.4: Raise procedural issues before you raise substantive issues.

The next Table of Contents reflects the principle that, in general, procedural issues should be raised before substantive issues. We have looked several times at the brief that sought to force a judge in West Virginia to recuse himself: the judge's chief benefactor had spent close to $3 million trying to elect him, and the judge voted to reverse a huge jury award against his benefactor's company. The plaintiffs argued that the unusually large contribution created a constitutionally unacceptable risk that the judge would feel indebted to his backer. Here is the Table of Contents from the other side's brief, which sought to fend off the effort to force recusal.

Source: Coal company's brief in *Caperton v. A.T. Massey Coal Co.*, 556 U.S. 868 (2009).

A Federal rules often require corporate parties to disclose their ownership structure so that judges can assess — ironically for this case — whether to recuse themselves.

B The Table of Authorities lists every authority cited in the brief, including articles and websites, but not including materials from the case you are litigating. It also lists the pages on which each authority appears.

C You may notice that the brief omits pages 1 and 2; the litigants added an Introduction, but they chose not to label it as an Introduction, presumably to comport with the letter of the Supreme Court's rules. As Chapter 13 will explain, Introductions are so important that lawyers often include them even when the rules are silent about whether lawyers may do so. At the Supreme Court, lawyers usually add their would-be Introduction to the beginning of their Statement.

D **Before getting into the substance of the argument, the lawyers try a procedural move: they ask the Court to dismiss the case. This is usually the correct place for this sort of move. The heading is not especially interesting, but this move itself is a bold ploy because the court already decided to review the case.**

E We see another successful example of an argument in the alternative. The context alerts readers that this argument needs to be considered only if the Court rejects the primary argument.

F The brief reminds readers that this party won in the lower court by using the word "affirmed." This brief uses all caps for its headings, which is typical of Supreme Court briefs; avoid all caps, however, in your subheadings (as this brief has done).

G Notice that each type of argument gets its own subsection, and the historical argument was so important (or so strong) that it preceded the doctrinal argument and the fact-based argument about the Court's own practice. Some readers may dislike the repetition of "probability of bias," but it coins a phrase, thus winning the battle to control the semantics of the case. The lawyers calculated that they would win if the issue was whether there was merely some unspecified "probability of bias," and they therefore wanted this phrase to stick.

H Yet another argument in the alternative appears in the brief. Headings do not need to reflect that an argument is "in the alternative," but they may do so.

I The policy arguments follow the historical, doctrinal, and fact-based arguments. This is standard positioning for a policy argument — near the end. Subsections II.B.2 and II.B.3 sound very similar, but they raise the distinct points that, respectively, (i) there is no sensible way to test whether a judge feels indebted to a contributor and (ii) many lawsuits would be filed to disqualify judges. Ideally, the subheadings would unambiguously foretell what each subsection was going to discuss.

J To round out the brief, we see one more argument, which asserts that the other side's proposed rule would not justify the remedy that it requested. Notice that the brief focused first on its best points — the *general* problem with forcing judges to recuse themselves — and addressed the specific dispute only at the end of the brief. Why? Because the facts were bad for this party, but the law and policy were strong.

Example

11.5

Takeaway point 11.5: Raise substantive issues before you discuss remedies.

Make your reader want your client to win before you ask for a remedy. The next case arose in 2007 when Missouri indicted Galin Frye for driving with a revoked license. Frye's three previous convictions for the same offense elevated his charge to a felony, and he faced up to four years in prison. The prosecution's plea agreement offered Frye a three-month sentence, but his counsel never conveyed this offer to Frye. Instead, Frye pled guilty and accepted a three-*year* sentence. When he later learned that his lawyer failed to mention the three-month plea offer, he appealed, raising an "ineffective assistance of counsel" claim. Under *Strickland v. Washington*, 466 U.S. 668 (1984), criminal defendants can attack their convictions if counsel performed deficiently *at trial* and if that deficiency was prejudicial. Later cases had extended *Strickland* to both guilty pleas and the plea negotiations that preceded a guilty plea. Frye sought to further extend *Strickland* to plea offers that a defendant did not accept — or hear about. And as you'll see in section II of Frye's Argument, he needed to overcome one other major hurdle. Thanks to this brief, he succeeded.

Source: Frye's brief in *Missouri v. Frye*, 132 S. Ct. 1399 (2012) (omitting Question Presented, Tables, Statement, and Summary of Argument from the Table of Contents).

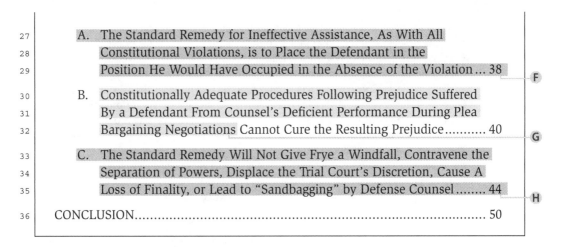

A Briefs need not raise multiple arguments. This Table of Contents raises just one argument and then places in subheadings the supporting points needed for the argument to succeed. The first heading discusses the substantive issue; the second heading addresses the appropriate remedy. These two issues are joined at the hip. If the brief had raised a second, unrelated argument, it probably would be sensible to discuss the first substantive issue, then the first substantive issue's remedy, and then the second substantive issue, followed by its remedy. This advice merely elaborates on the general rule that briefs should discuss procedural issues, then substantive issues, and then remedies.

B Under *Strickland*, a defendant can establish that he received ineffective assistance during a trial by showing (1) "that counsel's representation fell below an objective standard of reasonableness" and (2) that the bad lawyering harmed him significantly. Here, Frye relies on a case that extended *Strickland* to *pretrial* proceedings, thus referring to settled law in order to stretch it.

C As reflected in this heading, Frye's lawyers have a crystal-clear theory of the case, which allows them to be precise and direct about what they want the Court to rule, namely that Frye had a constitutional right to learn of the plea offer.

D WARNING! Notice that "would" is not capitalized and that other words (*of, is*) are capitalized inconsistently. There's no rule requiring initial caps, and you (like these lawyers) may capitalize certain words

inconsistently if you use initial caps for only certain words. I recommend using the same approach to capitalization as in any other sentence, but make headings bold and indented to signal that a new section is beginning. At a minimum, be consistent.

E This argument rebuts the other side's position in three ways: by stating that Frye's preferred test is "well established," by reminding the Court that Frye won below, and by using language from *Strickland* that spells out how the test would operate for this new procedural protection. Thus, this subheading is a perfect example of how to make a rebuttal look like an affirmative argument.

F Frye argues for a remarkable remedy: to let him rescind his guilty plea and retroactively accept the three-month plea offer that he never heard about. But the brief brilliantly tries to make this exceptional remedy look "standard" and reflective of what happens for "all constitutional violations."

G WARNING! Avoid adding too many modifiers to your nouns. The highlighted text is one long noun. Page 257 (Tip 9 in Chapter 16) discusses how to avoid this problem.

H Frye waits until the end to rebut — just as this book recommends. Missouri's various policy arguments are pooled to make the state's brief sound hysterical and implausible. In general, restrict headings to two lines of text. This three-line heading, however, signals that the section will rebut *five* points, making it much shorter than bogging down this section with a subheading for each of the state's arguments.

Example **11.6**	**Takeaway point 11.6:** Your Table of Contents can and should reflect arguments in the alternative.

Your Table of Contents can signal to judges that you are making an argument in the alternative. Several of the other tables contained arguments in the alternative (e.g., Examples 11.2 and 11.4), but the following one does so even more explicitly, telling the Court that the backup argument "independently" supports a victory.

This Table of Contents comes from a famous recent case: the dispute at the Supreme Court over the Affordable Care Act, or "Obamacare." The Affordable Care Act requires millions of Americans to buy health insurance or pay a penalty that increases their tax liability. The Act was challenged as exceeding Congress's powers. Below, we see the skeleton of the government's arguments from the key brief in the case, which raised two alternative theories as to why Congress acted within its constitutional powers.

Source: The federal government's "minimum coverage provision" brief in *HHS v. Florida*, 132 S. Ct. 2566 (2012).

A

B

C

D

E

F

A Court rules differ about which sections must appear in a brief. In addition to checking the rules, study other lawyers' recent or similar briefs (or motions) filed in the same court to spot problems with your own filing. This specific section is perfunctory; the *detailed* discussion of the case's procedural history appears at the end of the statement.

B As we saw in Chapters 1, 2, 3, and 6, facts can argue. Here, the facts begin by recounting the problems that necessitated the Affordable Care Act.

C Notice that the brief forgoes chronological order: it discusses the law that Congress enacted and *then* discusses prior efforts. The lawyers presumably felt that some compelling rationale made it advisable to discuss recent legislative measures before discussing past efforts. One obvious explanation: the current law matters more, so discussing it first arms readers with the facts that they most need. The statutory history is illuminating but less critical than the embattled law, so the brief gave the critical information to the Court first.

D Chapter 13 discusses how to prepare a strong Summary of Argument.

E The term "minimum coverage provision" might be unfamiliar to some readers; avoid using unfamiliar terms in your headings. In this case, however, the Justices were quite familiar with this legal issue.

F WARNING! Ideally, every heading should be easily comprehensible. The phrase "the financing of participation" is hard to absorb because it is a double "nominalization" — it uses the gerund "financing" and the noun "participation" rather than telling readers who acted. *See* Chapter 16, Tip 6 (discussing nominalizations). This subheading, however, does a lovely job of camouflaging a policy argument.

G Avoid using case names in a heading unless the cases are likely to be familiar to the court (as these two would be) or unless a particular case so governs your dispute that the court will need to consider it.

H This heading may be the most important line in any brief filed in this millennium. The government lost on its primary argument, but won on this one. Notice that the second argument is consistent with the first: the government argues that it wins on both grounds. This is the optimal way to argue "in the alternative." By contrast, inconsistent arguments in the alternative jeopardize your credibility.

I The language in these two subheadings is complicated. Try instead to mimic the light, simple writing in subheading II.A of this brief.

J This brief raises only two arguments, but numerous other arguments in the case were briefed separately. When a case becomes complicated, remember that courts have the discretion to schedule a case in stages. If your case is getting too complicated, consider filing a motion that asks the court to separate the proceedings or to stagger the briefing schedule. Resist passivity and press courts to administer cases in a way that favors your clients. (That process is easiest with trial courts.)

FREQUENTLY ASKED QUESTIONS ABOUT SELECTING AND ORGANIZING ARGUMENTS

Q. **To what extent should I select my arguments based on my judge's preferences, expertise, jurisprudential outlook, and so on?**

A. Adapt to the judge without being obvious about it. He or she resolves your case, so please your most important reader. That said, ensure that you preserve arguments that you will want to raise on appeal, even if they may not please the trial judge.

Q. **In my Argument, which numbers or letters should I use in my headings?**

A. Your headings should use uppercase Roman numerals (I, II, III). Your first level of sub-headings should use uppercase letters (A, B, C). Your next level of subheadings should use numbers (1, 2, 3). Try to avoid further nesting. If, however, you need sub-sub-sub-headings, use lowercase letters (a, b, c) followed by lowercase Roman numerals (i, ii, iii).

Q. **Can I repeat my heading in the first sentence of a section?**

A. Avoid doing so because your brief or motion will sound too repetitive.

Q. **How can I keep headings to two lines *and* adequately explain my premise?**

A. Lots and lots of editing. You may also move the explanation for your heading's premise to subheadings. Consider this approach when your argument is complex or has multiple parts. If necessary, use a longer heading. As you saw in this chapter, many headings and subheadings consume more than two lines. The two-line principle should guide you, not torment you.

Q. **This chapter presented lots of tips about how to sequence arguments. Can you restate your recommendations about how to organize arguments in one list?**

A. Sure. Here they are:
  - Place procedural and other threshold arguments first.
  - Sort procedural arguments chronologically (e.g., discuss the other side's failure to serve notice to your client before you discuss the trial judge's failure to instruct the jury properly because serving notice happens long before a trial occurs).
  - If procedural arguments occurred concurrently (e.g., as defects in a complaint), follow the rules about how to sort substantive arguments, which appear in the next bullet.
  - After you raise procedural or threshold arguments, assert your substantive argument with the highest expected payoff, then your next-best-yielding argument, and so on.
  - Place requests for relief after arguments that relate to substantive law.
  - If a given argument has multiple sub-arguments, then use the same sequence within any given section of your Argument: raise procedural issues first, then substantive arguments, and then issue relating to remedies.
  - Deviate freely from the above approach if sound reasons exist, such as to improve the flow of your argument.

Chapter 12

Questions Presented

In an appellate brief, the Question Presented is a statement of the legal issue or issues that each party wants the court to resolve.[1] Trial motions generally do not contain a stand-alone section dedicated to the Question Presented, but effective motions usually specify within a page or two which issue or issues the motion requires the trial judge to resolve.

This chapter is less prescriptive than other parts of the book. As you will see throughout the following pages, lawyers have widely divergent styles, and different customs prevail in different courts. Each approach has strengths and shortcomings. I promised you in the Introduction that you would get to cultivate your own style, and that is truer for this chapter than for any other. Review the examples and move toward an approach that suits you.

Only one rule is rigid: a Question Presented must frame the issue *precisely*. Lawyers spar, however, over how long Questions Presented should be and whether Questions Presented should frame issues neutrally or in a partisan way.

The most common Question Presented is short, precise, and neutral (or nearly neutral). According to one study of Questions Presented in the courts of six states, 95 percent of issue statements were phrased in a single sentence, and issue statements averaged thirty-seven words in length.[2]

Many top lawyers, however, have begun to make their Questions Presented longer and more partisan. This approach, which is common among private-sector, appellate specialists who litigate in federal courts, may jar some readers who expect the Question Presented to frame the issue neutrally. But many elite lawyers have realized that the prime real estate owned by the Question Presented — near the beginning of briefs — is too valuable to be squandered with a vague, tepid statement. Instead, these lawyers usually both add some trenchant details and signal how they want the case to be resolved. Thus, Questions Presented are becoming longer and more aggressive, though this choice remains a minority approach.

This chapter provides examples of a variety of styles. Do not believe anyone who tells you that there is only one way to draft a Question Presented; top lawyers follow widely divergent approaches. In general, my view favors aggressive Questions that provide some pivotal facts about the case, but no empirical work has proven that any specific approach yields superior results, no approach has built a consensus among top lawyers, and plenty of great lawyers prefer a different convention.

In the absence of any definitive guidelines, please your bosses and clients, and follow this tip from one of the nation's top appellate lawyers, Roy Englert: "Woe unto the lawyer who has," by the end of the Question Presented, "both irritated the judge by trying the judge's patience *and* lost credibility." Unlike earlier chapters in this book, this chapter provides no background about the cases in which the Questions Presented appeared. That approach puts you in the same position as judges who are introduced to a case by the Questions Presented.

---

1. This part of a brief is sometimes called "Statement of Issues" or "Issues Presented for Review." This chapter generally uses the name "Questions Presented," "Question," or "issue."

2. Judith Fischer, *Got Issues? An Empirical Study About Framing Them*, 6 J. A.L.W.D. 1, 3 (2009).

CHAPTER OVERVIEW

1. Check the court rules before writing your Question Presented. Not all courts require one. Court rules also dictate where in the brief the Question Presented appears.

2. Make your Questions Presented precise so that readers know exactly what issue or issues your case implicates. Avoid using the word "should," which connotes a moral or pragmatic choice rather than a legal one.

3. Frame the *legal* issue in a way that helps your client.

4. Consider following the trend of adding *facts* that frame the Question favorably. Just don't add too many facts or you will irritate judges.

5. Make your prose in a Question Presented resemble ordinary sentences. Many lawyers, for no evident reason, believe that a Question Presented must be crammed into a single sentence. A 100-word sentence in a Question Presented will be just as impenetrable as that same sentence elsewhere in a brief.

6. Harmonize these six competing goals: (i) write precisely, (ii) write succinctly, (iii) frame the legal issue favorably, (iv) frame the facts positively, (v) reason and write clearly, and (vi) project credibility. These goals often tug in different directions, so expect to compromise on one or more of these ideals.

7. The exact wording of a Question Presented matters, but it matters less than the insight and judgment reflected in the choices of (i) which issues to raise, (ii) how to frame those issues, and (iii) how to sequence them. (See generally Chapter 11.) Examples of how to select, frame, and sort issues appear throughout this chapter. Be absolutely sure that you are raising sensible issues before you agonize about how you phrase them.

Section	**Short, Neutral Questions**
12.1	

Takeaway point 12.1: Most lawyers use, and many judges expect, short and almost-neutral Questions Presented: this is the "safe" way to write a Question Presented.

The most typical Question Presented is short and neutral — or almost neutral. We begin by considering some examples of that approach. As you review them, recall from the chapter overview that the ideal question is precise, short, persuasive, informative, pellucid, and beneficial to the lawyer's credibility.

That Question has never been written. Questions Presented entail difficult trade-offs, so lawyers need to compromise on one or more of those goals. The examples in this section excel at brevity and at one or more other categories; some of them, however, make difficult compromises on the other criteria. We begin with the worst Question in this chapter, which is also the shortest.

Example 12.1.a   Is this dispute moot?

This Question tells the judge nothing about the case. What happened in the dispute? Who are the parties? What sort of legal argument is involved? Why might the dispute be moot? What is the standard for mootness? Notice, too, that this Question uses a question mark; ironically, many Questions Presented are not framed as questions.

With just a little more information, however, Questions Presented can frame the legal issue helpfully. Here is another short, neutral Question Presented, which is superior to the first example (but still flawed).

Example 12.1.b   Whether Congress has the power under Article I of the Constitution to enact the minimum coverage provision of the Patient Protection and Affordable Care Act, Pub. L. No. 111-148, 124 Stat. 119, as amended by the Health Care and Education Reconciliation Act of 2010, Pub. L. No. 111-152, 124 Stat. 1029.

Can you tell which side submitted this Question? It's certainly neutral — at least at a quick glance. And it does a number of things well. It introduces the basis of the legal challenge: whether Congress had power under Article I of the U.S. Constitution to enact this law. And, to remain concise, it conflates two distinct issues raised by the case: whether Congress had the power to enact this law under (i) the Commerce Clause or (ii) the tax power. Because this brief is, in fact, trying to invalidate the disputed law, it avoids airing both theories under which the government sought to defend the statute. And finally, by adding a precise citation and by framing the issue neutrally, the brief builds the lawyers' credibility.

But this Question Presented, like all others, entails tradeoffs. The citation to the Act is longer than the rest of the Question, and readers may lose their focus midway through. It is also dry, so much so that readers might not realize immediately that the Question comes from a hugely important case — the battle over President Obama's signature program, the Affordable Care Act.[3] Moreover, the Question tells us nothing

---

3. That choice, however, probably reflects the lawyers' attempt to make this case look like an ordinary dispute about a statute, rather than a historic battle. The bigger the stakes, the greater the risk that the Justices would get cold feet.

about what the law actually does, but using the word "minimum" makes the law sound modest, which conflicts with the brief's goals. And it certainly does nothing to make readers *want* to strike down the law. Finally, the issue is framed so that the lawyers win if the Question is answered negatively; by contrast, psychology research has led some writing experts to favor issue statements that let your client win if the Question is answered affirmatively because most people like to answer questions affirmatively. (But I doubt that this choice matters in law.) In sum, this Question is capable and professional, but it hardly primes readers to want to resolve the case in either side's favor — much less to yearn to read the brief.

Framing the issue in a punchy way matters even more in two specific situations. First, an issue should be catchy when a court is busy or is likely to be disinterested in your issue. For instance, harried trial judges do not want to spend their time on intricate discovery battles, so you may need to market the issues raised by uninspiring motions in a way that will intrigue the judge. See generally Chapter 14 (offering advice about how to increase a court's focus on a quotidian motion.) And second, when an appellate court has discretion about whether to hear a case, your Question Presented may be the only part of the brief that judges or clerks read; thus, the Question needs to state the issue in a way that compels readers to plod ahead. If the Question fails to allege some meaningful legal problem, for instance, judges may never look at the pages that follow. But a request that a court review another court's decision need not scream.

The next example illustrates that principle. It tries to obtain a writ of certiorari while also preserving the lawyers' credibility and an appearance of neutrality. This Question tries to seem even-handed, but it also tries to motivate readers; you may notice that it is, by design, less neutral than it seems if you read it quickly.

> Example 12.1.c   Whether the district court violated petitioner's Sixth Amendment rights by limiting his cross-examination of a government witness.

This question is short. And it is framed in a fairly neutral style, although it hints gently at an answer. (Read it again if you don't see immediately which way it leans.) It tells us who did what to whom: the district court cut off the defendant's cross-examination of a witness. The question orients readers, letting them know which facts to focus on in the ensuing Statement. And although the lawyers do not specify either what the Sixth Amendment provides or which of its four provisions they are invoking, they made the reasonable judgment call that Supreme Court Justices would be familiar with the Sixth Amendment and would recognize that the challenge arose under the Confrontation Clause, which lets defendants confront their accusers. This is a short, effective Question.

But it, too, makes tradeoffs. Was the cross-examination of an inconsequential or major government witness? How limited was the cross-examination? Presumably, after all, a defendant could not question a witness indefinitely to prevent the jury from ever beginning its deliberations. Is there any reason to think that the district court abused its discretion in managing the trial? Brevity trumps comprehensiveness in this Question.

There is more. This Question reflects the importance of knowing one's audience: the Supreme Court does not take run-of-the-mill cases in which a defendant thinks the trial judge mismanaged the case. Thus, the brief *tries* to elevate the case from a typical abuse-of-judicial-discretion case (i.e., *we think we should have had a little extra time for cross-examination*) into a major constitutional issue (i.e., whether the Constitution imposes meaningful limits on a trial court's ability to curtail cross-examination). The lawyers *needed* to heighten their claim to catch the Court's attention. The Court, however, saw through this attempt to frame a mundane dispute into a constitutional clash, and it denied certiorari. This Question is nevertheless a good example of how to play a losing hand capably: the lawyers had little to work with, but they made their argument seem important.

Later in this chapter, we see how to organize multiple Questions, but lawyers sometimes eschew that approach and cram multiple issues into a single Question Presented. For instance, the Question about the Affordable Care Act (Example12.1.b) refers to "Congress's power under Article I of the U.S. Constitution." But there are *ten* sections in Article I. The lawyers deliberately lumped together multiple congressional powers to avoid over-specifying the basis of Congress's power. If you are too vague, courts won't know your theory; if you are too specific, you might omit a winning argument. We see another version of this tension next.

Example 12.1.d	Whether the Federal Communications Commission's current indecency-enforcement regime violates the First or Fifth Amendment to the United States Constitution.

This Question bundled two separate theories: that the restrictions on indecency violated the Free Speech Clause and that the vague restrictions failed to provide fair warning under the Due Process Clause as to when the government would penalize misconduct. Most lawyers would divide these issues; the government's decision to merge them was probably designed to maximize the chances that the case would catch the Court's attention while keeping the Question trim.

Before we evaluate more aggressive Questions, here are several other short, mostly neutral Questions.

Example 12.1.e	Section 704(b) of Title 18, United States Code, makes it a crime when anyone "falsely represents himself or herself, verbally or in writing, to have been awarded any decoration or medal authorized by Congress for the Armed Forces of the United States."
	The question presented is whether 18 U.S.C. § 704(b) is facially invalid under the Free Speech Clause of the First Amendment.

Example 12.1.f	Whether threatening a robbery victim with a firearm constitutes "physical" restraint of the victim requiring enhancement of a defendant's sentence under United States Sentencing Guidelines § 2B3.1(b)(4)(B) and related Guidelines provisions.

Example 12.1.g	Whether the decision of a court of appeals to stay an alien's removal pending consideration of the alien's petition for review is governed by the standard set forth in 8 U.S.C. § 1252(f)(2), or instead by the traditional test for preliminary injunctive relief.

> Example 12.1.h   **Whether a municipal personal property tax that falls exclusively on large vessels using the municipality's harbor violates the Tonnage Clause of the Constitution, Art. I, § 10, Cl.3.**

In general, new lawyers favor the approach described above: short and almost-neutral. But as we see in the next section, some lawyers tweak this approach and make their Questions Presented short and *aggressive.*

Section

12.2

Short, Aggressive Questions

Takeaway point 12.2: Short, aggressive Questions Presented are ideal when your issue is fairly simple because they pack a punch and will not bore readers.

Short Questions need not be meek Questions. Many lawyers craft short Questions Presented that manage to pack a punch. As noted earlier, one survey found that the average Question Presented contains thirty-seven words, so this section uses examples of approximately that length. Here is an example of how aggressive a lawyer can get in thirty-seven words.

Example 12.2.a	Whether the Executive's use of military power inside the United States to detain, without charge or trial, a person who is lawfully in the United States violates the Constitution where Congress has not expressly authorized such detention.

Reread this Question to count how many little details in this Question hint at the answer. Done? Let's scrutinize the lawyers' choices.

TEXT OF THE QUESTION PRESENTED	ANALYSIS
Whether the Executive's use of military power inside the United States	The key detail is that *military* power was used *domestically*. The military rarely acts within U.S. borders, so the actor and the location raise a red flag.
to detain, without charge or trial,	Here's another fact designed to sway judges, who are likely to fret when citizens are detained (by the military) without even being charged.
a person	But wait — are we talking about *citizens* or *noncitizens*? If this case involved a *U.S. citizen*, you can be certain that the lawyers wouldn't have used the word *person*. That word is designed to paint over the fact that the detainee is not a U.S. citizen.
who is lawfully in the United States	But here's a favorable detail: this person is in the U.S. *lawfully*, hinting that he has various rights.
violates the Constitution	Notice that the lawyers fail to specify which provision of the Constitution is implicated. Is this vagueness problematic? Not at all — in this case, the lawyers were raising multiple, distinct constitutional arguments. Rather than list each of the issues (and thereby having multiple Questions), the lawyers pooled the various arguments together as the previous section demonstrated. If the brief had raised only one or two provisions, the Question Presented probably would (and should) have specified which ones the case implicated.
where Congress has not expressly authorized such detention.	Congress's inaction is yet another helpful detail because it hints at an argument: that letting executives *unilaterally* use soldiers to jail suspects without trial paves a road to despotism.

Let's look at another short, aggressive Question.

> Example 12.2.b   Whether a monument bearing the Ten Commandments, which has stood for over forty years and is surrounded by sixteen other monuments on the Texas Capitol Grounds, constitutes an impermissible establishment of religion in violation of the First Amendment.

Four of this Question's choices merit your attention. First, the challenged monument is merely "bearing" the Ten Commandments. Thus, the lawyers — deliberately — gloss over whether the monument is exclusively about or only *partially* about religion. The word "featuring," by contrast, would have suggested that the Ten Commandments dominated the monument. Second, the monument "has stood for over forty years," which establishes the monument's history and assuages the justices' potential concerns that Texas is actively (and freshly) injecting religion into a public space. This detail featured prominently in the 5-4 decision that allowed the monument to stand. Third, "sixteen other monuments" surround the Ten Commandments, suggesting that the religious text is incidental to a visitor's overall experience. The brief does not mention whether any of those other monuments mention religious content. Two others did. But the Question Presented need not, and should not, air bad facts, which can wait until the Statement. And finally, the monument is *outside* the statehouse (i.e., on the "Grounds"): thus, it is merely part of a predominantly secular walking tour that allows viewers to breeze past or skip the religious content. Had the lawyers written "at the Texas Statehouse" readers might have inferred that the commandments were inside the statehouse, which might be more objectionable to some judges. Pay similar care to the details and words that appear in your Questions Presented.

Here's one final example of how to frame a Question concisely and aggressively. The lawyers sought a writ of certiorari, so they highlighted both the "split" among courts that had considered this issue and the weight of authority favoring their client.

> Example 12.2.c   Whether the Supreme Court of South Carolina erred in holding — in conflict with twenty-two federal courts of appeals and state courts of last resort — that an indigent defendant has no constitutional right to appointed counsel at a civil contempt proceeding that results in his incarceration.

Section
12.3

The Trend Toward Longer Questions Presented

Takeaway point 12.3: If your legal issue is complicated or if you favor an aggressive style, consider using a longer Question Presented that mentions some helpful authorities, some helpful facts, or both.

With one exception, the short examples that this chapter has presented so far contain only one sentence. But, when permitted by court rules, many top lawyers favor longer Questions Presented. Here is an example from a brief that this book has discussed several times.

> Example 12.3.a   Justice Brent Benjamin of the Supreme Court of Appeals of West Virginia refused to recuse himself from the appeal of the $50 million jury verdict in this case, even though the CEO of the lead defendant spent $3 million supporting his campaign for a seat on the court — more than 60% of the total amount spent to support Justice Benjamin's campaign — while preparing to appeal the verdict against his company. After winning election to the court, Justice Benjamin cast the deciding vote in the court's 3–2 decision overturning that verdict. The question presented is whether Justice Benjamin's failure to recuse himself from participation in his principal financial supporter's case violated the Due Process Clause of the Fourteenth Amendment.

Even readers who know nothing about that case now grasp what it is about: they're oriented. And they would probably conclude that Justice Benjamin isn't the world's most ethical jurist, so they're also motivated. Orienting and motivating a judge (in three sentences) is a great start. This approach *can* be incredibly powerful, as we see above.

But that power comes with risk. Lengthier Questions increase the chances that lawyers will undermine their credibility or bore judges. The above example is three times the length of a typical Question Presented. Students and lawyers with whom I have discussed this example react in mixed ways. Some love it and believe it wins the case, landing a knockout punch on the first page. Others think it hobbles the lawyers' credibility by framing the issue so aggressively. Different lawyers will favor different approaches; just realize that the length and aggression may irk some readers.

Many legal writing commentators encourage advocates to adjust this approach and to build Questions Presented around modified syllogisms. A syllogism is a logical device in which the first two sentences lead inexorably to the conclusion in the third sentence:

> *A contract requires consideration.*
>
> *Jane provided no consideration to John.*
>
> *Therefore, Jane and John have not entered into a contract.*

A modified syllogism presents the last statement as a question:

> *A contract requires consideration.*
>
> *Jane provided no consideration to John.*
>
> *Have Jane and John entered into a contract?*

This approach makes the answer to a Question obvious.

In practice, however, few lawyers follow this form. And for good reason: these sorts of Questions Presented are usually ham-fisted because they become tautological. I would use this approach only for a case in which the right legal outcome really was crystal clear. Some of the nation's best advocates, however, have tweaked this approach by trying to obscure the fact that their Question is self-proving. Let's scrutinize an impressive example of this approach from a brief by John Roberts (from his time in private practice) that persuaded the Supreme Court to reverse a lower court's decision.

Example 12.3.b   A jury awarded respondents $55 million in compensatory damages, roughly $53 million of which was for "loss of consortium" and "pain and suffering." Petitioners appealed, arguing that the award — the largest by far in Indiana history — was grossly excessive. In doing so, they urged the Court of Appeals of Indiana to conduct a "comparability analysis," an approach endorsed by many federal and state courts whereby damage awards in similar cases are compared to determine whether a particular award is excessive. The Court of Appeals refused to adopt this method of review, ruling that it would improperly second-guess jury decisions "in a manner not permitted by the Seventh Amendment."

Whether the Court of Appeals correctly held — in clear conflict with this Court's established precedent that the Seventh Amendment applies only to the federal courts — that the Seventh Amendment constrains a state appellate court when reviewing a jury award for excessiveness?

The Question includes a slew of handy details, such as that the palintiffs received $53 million for, primarily, "loss of consortium," which will make many readers skeptical, especially given that these were *compensatory* damages. And the Question camouflages the following syllogistic reasoning: (i) the Seventh Amendment does not constrain state courts, (ii) a state court in Indiana said that it was constrained by the Seventh Amendment, (iii) did that court err? The entire first paragraph of the Question, in other words, is just a window dressing.

Do you think the case can really be this simple? If the Indiana court had directly violated a crystalline holding of the Supreme Court, it is unlikely that a full briefing process would need to occur; courts have the power to reverse summarily decisions that directly conflict with established precedent. So the lawyers are glossing over something, and the justices know it.

Notice that the Question doesn't tell you what the defendants *did* to trigger such a massive award. Rather, the lawyers present their clients as *victims* (of an unjust damages award) rather than wrongdoers. Whenever possible, make your client the proverbial good guy, as this Question does. The victims-and-villains strategy that Chapter 1 explored is relevant throughout your brief.

Does this Question slant the issue too far toward one side? Two elite appellate law-yers observed that "it is a mistake — and a common one — to slant the formulation of the issue too obviously in your own favor."[4] Likewise, new lawyers often bristle at the previous Question, finding it too pushy, too biased. But while it may rest at the outer edge of acceptable aggressiveness, don't overlook the strategic benefit of letting judges know exactly what your client is arguing and pressing them to see your case in your client's way from the first page. Advocacy is acceptable, so long as the Question Presented is also accurate. Aggressiveness is a hallmark of many of the nation's top lawyers, and it is reasonable to wonder whether they are successful *because* they are aggressive.

Here are several other examples of aggressive Questions Presented. I include Questions of different lengths and different levels of aggression; as you read, assess the point (if any) at which *you* think a Question goes too far or runs too long; as mentioned earlier, this chapter aims to have you decide for yourself how feisty and how long your Questions should be.

Example 12.3.c   In this case, the Illinois Supreme Court held that a state law transferring the revenues of four Illinois casinos to five Illinois horse-racing tracks is categorically not sus-ceptible to challenge under the Takings Clause of the Fifth Amendment because, in that court's view, "regu-latory actions requiring the payment of money are not takings." The question presented is:

Whether the State's taking of money from private parties is wholly outside the scope of the Takings Clause.

Example 12.3.d   18 U.S.C. § 924(c)(1)(A) criminalizes the "use" of a fire-arm during and in relation to a drug trafficking offense and imposes a mandatory consecutive sentence of at least five years' imprisonment. In *Bailey v. United States*, 516 U.S. 137, 144 (1995), this Court unanimously held that "use" of a firearm under § 924(c)(1)(A) means "ac-tive employment." The question presented in this case is:

Whether mere receipt of an unloaded firearm as payment for drugs constitutes "use" of the firearm during and in relation to a drug trafficking offense within the meaning of 18 U.S.C. § 924(c)(1)(A) and this Court's decision in *Bailey*.

---

4. Andrew L. Frey & Roy T. Englert, Jr., *How to Write a Good Appellate Brief* (1994), http://www.appellate.net/articles/gdaplbrf799.asp (last visited May 19, 2013).

Example 12.3.e   Petitioner admitted that she tried to injure her husband's paramour by spreading toxic chemicals on the woman's car and mailbox. Instead of allowing local officials to handle this domestic dispute, the federal prosecutor indicted petitioner under a federal law, 18 U.S.C. § 229(a), enacted by Congress to implement the United States' obligations under a 1993 treaty addressing the proliferation of chemical and biological weapons. Facing a sentence of six years in prison, petitioner challenged the statute and her resulting conviction as exceeding the federal government's enumerated powers and impermissible under the Tenth Amendment. Declining to reach petitioner's constitutional arguments, and in acknowledged conflict with decisions from other courts of appeals, the Third Circuit held that, when the state and its officers are not party to the proceedings, a private party has no standing to challenge the federal statute under which she is convicted as in excess of Congress's enumerated powers and in violation of the Tenth Amendment.

The question presented is:

Whether a criminal defendant convicted under a federal statute has standing to challenge her conviction on grounds that, as applied to her, the statute is beyond the federal government's enumerated powers and inconsistent with the Tenth Amendment.[5]

---

5. This Question was written by Paul Clement, a former U.S. Solicitor General and one of the nation's top lawyers. It starts slowly, but then makes the answer quite obvious. This Question arose in a petition for a writ of certiorari, which explains the reference to the circuit split. The version of the Question that arose during the *merits* stage of the case (i.e., after the Court agreed to hear it) dropped the following language: "and in acknowledged conflict with decisions from other courts of appeals." That information was merely a ticket into the Court, showing that the lower courts were fractured in their approach to a legal issue. But once the Court decided to hear the case, the importance of the discord in lower courts dwindled in the merits brief.

<table>
<tr><td>Section
12.4</td><td>

The Massive, Single-Sentence Question

Takeaway point 12.4: Avoid behemoth sentences in your Questions Presented.

</td></tr>
</table>

The first three subsections presented viable ways to write your Questions Presented. Short or long, tepid or aggressive: all are reasonable options. But this section urges you — begs you — not to follow a bewildering convention that lawyers often follow when they write Questions Presented. They squeeze a massive Question into a single sentence, like an elephant crammed into a Speedo. For example, the following is a real Question Presented.

Example 12.4.a   Did the Court of Appeals err in holding that the prosecution discharged its affirmative burden of establishing that the appellant's confession was not the product of his illegal arrest and detention and, therefore, was admissible against him, by concluding that the act of police interrogators in confronting the appellant with the inculpatory admissions of an alleged co-defendant prior to eliciting appellant's confession, constituted an adequate "intervening event" which supposedly broke the causal chain between his illegal arrest and detention rendering his confession "a product of a free will," notwithstanding the fact, [sic] that the record irrefutably demonstrates that the appellant was arrested illegally, without the benefit of a warrant issued by a neutral and detached magistrate, in violation of Chapter 14 of the Code of Criminal Procedure, was thereafter interrogated while illegally detained, was, at all times during his 22 hours at the homicide division, in the presence and under the control of the police, was never taken to a magistrate, never spoke with a lawyer and was misled by the interrogators about what he was actually being charged with?[6]

Don't ever write a Question like this one. It is incomprehensible to you, and it is just as incomprehensible to judges. Your writing style in a Question Presented should resemble your style in other parts of the brief.

The line, however, between incomprehensible Questions and powerful Questions is unclear. Some lawyers use long single-sentence Questions effectively, and two examples appear below. Just remember that things go haywire somewhere between the length of the above Question and the length of the following Questions.

Example 12.4.b   Whether the government violates a federal contract employee's constitutional right to informational privacy when it asks in the course of a background investigation whether the employee has received counseling or treatment for illegal drug use that has occurred within the past year, and the employee's response is used only for employment purposes and is protected under the Privacy Act, 5 U.S.C. 552a.

---

6. I learned of this Question Presented by reading Wayne Schiess & Elana Einhorn's article, *Issue Statements: Different Kinds for Different Documents,* 50 Washburn L.J. 341, 350 (2011).

Before joining the Supreme Court, Elena Kagan and her team of lawyers at the Office of the Solicitor General drafted the above question and won the case without any dissenters. Your Question Presented should hint, as the above Question does, at the type of decision that you want to obtain. For instance, if the contractors had access to classified information, the Question have sought to win on narrower grounds by limiting the government's right to conduct these background tests to contractors who have access to information. A victory on these narrower grounds might have been even more probable, but it would have been less desirable because it would secure comparatively limited rights for the government. Thus, the above Question reflects that, in addition to the tough tradeoffs mentioned throughout this chapter, you need to make tough choices about what relief you will seek. The Question is long, but it does not overwhelm readers.

But, sometimes you to overwhelm readers. For instance, if you are trying to show that the trial court had enough evidence to reach its conclusions, you might want to bombard readers with evidence even if the individual details blur together. For instance:

Example 12.4.c   Whether the district court committed clear error in finding that Barhoumi was part of an al-Qaida-associated force engaged in hostilities against the United States or its coalition partners in Afghanistan, where the Government presented evidence that Barhoumi traveled to Afghanistan to obtain terrorist training to wage jihad; received extensive training in weapons, explosives, and other military skills at different terrorist training camps, including a camp affiliated with Abu Zubaydah, and ultimately became a trainer himself; fought against U.S. forces in Afghanistan before retreating with the assistance of Abu Zubaydah and his affiliates; fled Afghanistan and regrouped with Abu Zubaydah in Pakistan; and was captured at a safehouse where Abu Zubaydah had gathered a cadre of men, including Barhoumi, to carry out future attacks against U.S. and coalition forces.

The length of the above question actually helps it. The evidence overwhelming because the lawyers present it in such rapid succession. The blast of information is designed to convince readers that the trial court had plenty of evidence to support its conclusion — whether or not readers absorb each detail.

In general, however, the sentences in your Questions Presented should not run longer than ordinary sentences.

Section	**Multiple Questions**
12.5	**Takeaway point 12.5:** You can raise multiple issues in a brief, but avoid raising more than four.

What if your case has multiple, distinct issues? List multiple Questions. Adding too many Questions, however, will frustrate judges and make them skeptical of your position, so avoid including more than four of them, even if adhering to this limit requires you to bundle and merge your issues. Beyond that number, judges report that they presume that your arguments probably lack merit. We see below a case implicating several distinct issues, so the lawyers, sensibly, posed three separate questions to the Court. Pay attention to the sequence: which issue would provide the biggest payoff? Which entailed the greatest chance of winning? If the order of these Questions were reversed, would the broader legal claims seem less credible?

> Example 12.5.a
>
> 1. Whether the First Circuit correctly held that the Massachusetts Burma Law, Mass. Gen. Laws ch. 7, §§ 22G-22M — which was undisputedly enacted to condemn the Nation of Myanmar and to influence the conduct of its government — unconstitutionally infringes upon the federal government's exclusive authority to regulate foreign affairs.
>
> 2. Whether the Massachusetts Burma Law, which discriminates against foreign commerce, violates the "speak-with-one-voice" principle, and seeks to regulate extraterritorial activity in a foreign nation, violates the Foreign Commerce Clause.
>
> 3. Whether the Massachusetts Burma Law, which upsets the delicate balance established by federal Myanmar sanctions, is preempted by federal law.

The above Questions about the Massachusetts law place the two broadest arguments before the narrower issue. First, they argue that there is a categorical constitutional prohibition against states' meddling in foreign affairs (whether or not Congress acts). The Supreme Court had largely evaded that issue for two centuries, so the Court probably did not want to declare a broad ban on state power. The second question is also broad: Massachusetts sought to avoid doing business with any company that dealt with Myanmar, so this issue sought to impose broad restrictions on how states spend their own money. But the third question is narrower and would apply only to this specific law and other instances in which Congress had imposed sanctions. (If you were frustrated by the unfamiliar information in these Questions — what's the Massachusetts Burma Law? What's the "speak-with-one-voice" principle? — consult Chapter 16, Tip 8, to learn how to avoid using terms that readers will not know.)

The lawyers won this case unanimously based on the argument in Question 3. Did the lawyers nearly bungle the case by putting their winning argument last? Hardly.

Admittedly, many lawyers offer advice like this: "In a case involving multiple issues, put the strongest issues first." That advice is alluring — and often correct — but you also need to attune yourself to the flow of your arguments, to the relative payoff of each argument, and to the iterative nature of making multiple arguments. Making a narrow (but strong) argument early all but admits that a subsequent, big argument is preposterous. And the potential rewards of fairly weak argument might be too great to place the strongest argument first: as Learned Hand observed with his famous

B > PL formulation, probability matters, but so does the potential payout. Thus, you might place a long-shot $100 million argument before a rock-solid $50,000 argument simply because you want the Court to focus on the claim that would allow your client to buy a yacht. Rather than raising your strongest arguments first, begin with the argument with the highest expected payoff for your client — whether that payoff is economic, doctrinal, injunctive or some other form of victory. Similarly, you might *need* to deal first with some threshold issue (such as jurisdiction, standing, mootness, ripeness, abstention doctrines, immunity from suit, or the political question doctrine). And some losing arguments set up winners; for instance, if you have an argument that is precluded by law but that makes a reader *want* you to win, you might put it before the more viable, but less compelling argument. The sequence of Questions, as discussed in Chapter 11, is a mix of art and science.

The three Questions about Massachusetts's Burma Law comply admirably with this advice. Placing the biggest arguments before the narrower Question made the broad arguments more credible. And placing the bigger arguments first probably made the Court eager to avoid allowing states to tamper with foreign affairs. Resolving the case on the third Question was the narrowest way to prevent states from embroiling the nation in showdowns and skirmishes with foreign nations. The first two Questions thereby motivated the justices to resolve the case based on preemption, the third Question.

When possible, each Question Presented should present an *independent basis for victory* — a series in which any of the issues, answered in your client's favor, will sink an opponent's case. The above Questions comport with this principle. Cases often buckle when each Question depends on a favorable resolution of the prior Question. Do your best to spare your client from needing to prevail on multiple issues. One is hard enough sometimes.

Finally, you will rarely ask a court to overrule itself. If you do that more than once or twice in your career, you're either too precocious or you have a wonderful and challenging legal practice. But here's an example of an outright request to abandon a prior opinion; this approach has the advantage of putting a court on notice that you're trying to overturn (and not merely escape the tug of) a precedent. And it, too, shows a sensible sequencing of the arguments.

Example 12.5.b   1. Whether Petitioners' criminal convictions under the Texas "Homosexual Conduct" law — which criminalizes adult, consensual same-sex intimate behavior, but not identical behavior by different-sex couples — violate the Fourteenth Amendment right to equal protection of the laws?

2. Whether Petitioners' criminal convictions for adult consensual sexual intimacy in the home violate their vital interests in liberty and privacy protected by the Due Process Clause of the Fourteenth Amendment?

3. Whether *Bowers v. Hardwick*, 478 U.S. 186 (1986), should be overruled?

Had the third Question appeared first, the brief would have basically admitted that the defendant could not win under existing case law. Instead, the brief first tries to win under existing law. Only then does it call on the Court to overrule its prior opinion.

FREQUENTLY ASKED QUESTIONS ABOUT QUESTIONS PRESENTED

Q. Does my Question Presented need to begin with the word "Whether," as nearly all of the examples in this chapter do?

A. No, unless your jurisdiction has unusual local rules. That said, one study found that 61.4 percent of Questions Presented began with "Whether."[7] In second place, 10.5 percent of Questions began with the word "Does," and "Is" finished in third place, appearing at the start of 7.0 percent of the briefs in the study. The Office of the Solicitor General is especially fond of beginning with "Whether," having done so in 94.1 percent of its briefs. This research suggests that beginning with "Whether" is safe, and that as with other elements of Questions Presented, the choice of an opening word is a matter of style that rests squarely within your discretion: almost 40 percent of briefs used a different convention, and briefs in other courts likely reflect an even greater variety of opening words. One pithy Question, for instance, asked "Are human genes patentable?"

Q. Do all motions and briefs contain a Question Presented?

A. Most opening appllellate briefs contain a Question. By contrast, motions do not typically include a Question Presented (but as noted earlier, lawyers often advise the judge immediately what issues the motion implicates). Reply briefs do not include a Question Presented; the opening brief already listed one. If you represent an amicus in a given court, consult the court rules to see whether you may reframe the Question Presented or whether you need to accept one of the party's formulations of the issue.

Q. What if my supervisor likes Questions that contain a single, long sentence?

A. Don't jeopardize your career over a Question Presented. As this chapter has suggested, crafting a Question Presented requires stylistic judgments and often reflects individual style. So follow your supervisors' instructions and attend to their preferences. If the Question is horrendous, consider revising it based on one of the models in this book or some other example—and then note that you were impressed by that Question, so you mimicked it. If your boss rejects your gentle hint, drop the issue.

Q. If a court uses its discretionary review to hear my client's case, can I revise the Question Presented that the court decided to address?

A. Yes, so long as the substance does not change. The petitioner and respondent often rephrase the Question Presented so that it frames the case favorably to their respective clients. Also, certiorari petitions to the Supreme Court routinely include information in the Question Presented that is designed to make the Court yearn to hear the case, such as noting that the court below deviated from the approach taken by every other circuit court. (See footnote 5 in this chapter.) Once the Court agrees to hear the case, those certiorari-supporting details become largely irrelevant, so parties omit that information when they file their merits briefs. Parties may not raise additional questions or substantively alter the issue that the Court has agreed to hear (unless the Court asks the parties to brief an additional issue).

---

7. Brady S. Coleman et al., *Grammatical and Structural Choices in Issue Framing: A Quantitative Analysis of "Questions Presented" from a Half Century of Supreme Court Briefs*, 29 Am. J. Trial Advoc. 329, 335 (2005).

Q. How many Questions Presented should I include?

A. The best advice I have seen comes from a Judge Ruggero Aldisert, who essentially warns lawyers not to raise more than four issues in a brief. He wrote:

No. of Issues	Judge's Reaction
3	Presumably arguable points. The lawyer is *primo*.
4	Probably arguable points. The lawyer is *primo* minus.
5	Perhaps arguable points. The lawyer is no longer *primo*. Probably no arguable points.
6	The lawyer has not made a favorable initial impression.
7	Presumptively, no arguable points. The lawyer is at an extreme disadvantage, with an uphill battle all the way.
8	Strong presumption that no point is worthwhile.[8]

This advice was offered for appellate briefs; trial motions often raise a large number of issues, but you can assume that trial judges, too, will bristle when they see that you ask them to resolve a heap of issues, so try to bundle issues together in trial motions to comply with Judge Aldisert's advice. In a complicated case, you might need to surpass the benchmark proposed above, but do so cautiously.

Q. Can I assume that local rules about Questions Presented largely track federal appellate rules?

A. No. Check whichever rules govern your dispute. Here is an example of a rule that varies significantly from the federal appellate rules, which this chapter has focused on: in one of New York's state appellate courts, briefs must contain "a concise statement, not exceeding *two pages*, of the questions involved in the matter, with each question numbered and *followed immediately by the answer*, if any, from the court from which the appeal is taken. . . ." N.Y. R. App. Fourth Div. 1000.4(f)(6) (emphasis added). The federal rules lack any analogous requirement. In addition to checking the rules, look at briefs filed in the court where you are litigating to see whether local lawyers do anything that reflects an unwritten local custom.

Q. Most of the Questions in this chapter are yes-no questions. But not Example 12.1.g. Do my Questions need to be framed as yes-no issues?

A. No, but nearly all Questions follow a yes-no format, so you will ordinarily adhere to that approach.

---

8. Ruggero J. Aldisert, Winning on Appeal: Better Briefs and Oral Argument 131 (2d ed. 2003).

Chapter 13

Introductions and Summaries of Argument

This chapter explores two related parts of a brief: the Introduction and the Summary of Argument. The chapter explains both how to write these sections effectively and how to prevent them from repeating one another.

Let's first discuss Introductions. Many appellate briefs (and most trial motions) contain some form of an introduction. Introductions should orient readers and frame the dispute, providing a barebones overview of the case that shapes the way that readers see either the overall dispute or the specific subject of a motion. For instance, here is an especially short Introduction:

> This is a case about a lawyer who, in the context of his own disciplinary proceeding, scolded a district court judge, labeled him a puppet, attacked his integrity, and then chose not to show up to defend himself when the judge set a hearing to decide if the lawyer should be found in criminal contempt. When the penalty was, not surprisingly, that he lost his ability to practice law in the district, the lawyer appealed.

Within thirty seconds of opening this brief, judges learn some of the lawsuit's key facts. They know that this brief will try to uphold the lawyer's punishment. And the Introduction primes readers to see the case in this party's favor: judges will view the suspended lawyer with skepticism, resent his disdain for the court system, and feel like *some* punishment was probably appropriate.

Not a bad start for two sentences. And that's the point. That's exactly what an Introduction should do.

Introductions are, in some ways, the closest that lawyers come to being spokespersons for politicians. When writing an Introduction, imagine that you are appearing on CNN or Fox News to explain a legislative proposal. If you begin by describing the nuances of the bill, viewers will yawn and change the channel. But you hook them when you begin with a short, compelling explanation about why the law was enacted, what problems it fixed, and why the law is important. So too with your Introductions. Unlike some political commentators, however, you need to preserve your credibility.

This Introduction, for instance, concisely conveys the brief's core points:

> Plaintiffs' suit is based on the remarkable contention that selected members of certain U.S. industries — alone among the billions of emitters of greenhouse gases throughout the world—are responsible, in tort, for all injuries allegedly caused by global warming, including enhancing the destructive force of Hurricane Katrina. Although Plaintiffs style this as a typical common-law nuisance case, it is not. . . . Plaintiffs' effort to squeeze the enormous "complexity of the initial global warming policy determinations" into the rubric of ordinary tort law stretches the judicial function well past the breaking point.

This Introduction, however, then went on for *five* more pages. That is far too long. Legal Introductions resemble social introductions: if you want to meet someone at a party, you'll be grateful if a mutual friend tells you the person's name and shares a few choice details to spark conversation. But if the same friend blabs for fifteen minutes, you'll crave silence long before he finishes talking. His bloviation is no longer an Introduction, but a lecture. Likewise, legal Introductions should be short and pithy. They should convey the theme or themes of the brief — for example, why it matters whether your client wins, what injustice the court should correct, and how the court should see the pivotal issue in the case.

Some great lawyers disagree with this advice and favor lengthy Introductions, but the judges with whom I have spoken share my view. As one example, Judge John Walker of the Second Circuit emailed me this observation, which perfectly mirrors my own view: "A brief introduction can help persuade a judge of the justice of your side. But don't overdo it with undue length or purple prose." Some lawyers nevertheless give judges more than what they want. Don't be one of them. (One partial exception, however, is explained in the paragraph about trial motions, just before the Chapter Overview.)

A Summary of Argument is different from an Introduction. As its name suggests, it summarizes. That does not mean that a Summary should repeat your headings. Rather, it should provide a boiled-down explanation of your key arguments and a short, sharp refutation of the other side's main points. The Summary does not need to include every subargument that appears in your brief, but it should outline your main points.

This chapter discusses the Introduction and the Summary side by side because so many lawyers are unsure how to apportion content between these two sections. To highlight the difference between a Summary and an Introduction, let's consider a short passage from each section. First, consider this clip from a hypothetical Summary of Argument:

> The district court erred for three reasons when it dismissed Adam King's lawsuit against the Detroit Police Department on the grounds that the Department was not liable for acts committed by off-duty officers. First, it elected not to follow two clear opinions from the Sixth Circuit that "plaintiffs may recover when off-duty officers cause injuries in furtherance of official police business." In cases nearly identical to this dispute, the Sixth Circuit has allowed a plaintiff to recover damages from off-duty officers and from their police departments. Second . . . .

By contrast, an Introduction might begin — and end — this way:

> Seven off-duty police officers received a report through their Department-issued radios that Adam King had exceeded a posted speed limit by seven miles per hour. Those officers then followed King — in their Department-issued cars — at 120 m.p.h. to catch him. They activated their patrol cars' sirens to pull him over and then used their Department-issued batons to dislocate King's jaw, break his hands and arms, and leave him in a coma for six weeks. After King sued the Police Department, one officer claimed that he was "just doing my job" and another testified that "the Department obviously needed our help, so we got called to action." The district court, however, barred King from collecting damages from the Department (even for his hospital bills) on the grounds that the officers were off duty. This brief argues that the trial court erred and that the police officers were acting on behalf of the Police Department, and that the officers and the Department are both liable.

In other words, the Introduction familiarizes readers with the dispute and *synthesizes* the brief down to a single issue, principle, or theme, almost as if to take the judge aside and say "here's what this case is really about." By contrast, the Summary of Argument provides an abbreviated glimpse of the brief's arguments — either all of them or the major ones, as if to say, "we win for the following three [or four, or more] reasons."

Trial motions, in particular, often do not include an Introduction; they instead use a Preliminary Statement, which combines your Introduction and your Summary of Argument. That approach gives judges enough information to resolve a case in your favor, even if they skim (or skip!) the rest of your motion. Nevertheless, be wary of letting the hybrid Introduction-Summary run for more than about three pages; you likely will lose your judge's attention if your Introduction runs longer than this.

CHAPTER OVERVIEW

1. Include an Introduction whenever court rules allow — unless your case is so straightforward factually and legally that you conclude that an Introduction is unnecessary. The more complicated the case, the more grateful readers are to receive an Introduction.
2. The Summary largely rephrases points that appear explicitly in the brief. But the Introduction conveys the *soul* of the brief — the core point that lingers in every word on every page, but that might never appear explicitly.
3. Think of an Introduction as a cookbook's description of a dish. By contrast, think of the Summary of Argument as the recipe for that dish. The description of the dish's subtle flavors, radiant color, and irresistible smell need to make the chef *want* to follow the recipe. The recipe simply tells the chef *how* to cook the dish and signals that doing so is easy and sensible.
4. Keep a Summary of Argument short. Keep an Introduction *very* short.
5. Take special care to ensure that you do not refer to unfamiliar terms, people, or concepts in your Introduction.
6. The Introduction can and usually should include some choice facts. The Summary of Argument ordinarily summarizes only your argument, not the facts. That said, it can certainly include facts that aid one of your arguments.
7. If the court in which you are litigating prohibits you from including an Introduction or a Summary of Argument, consider weaving them into some other section.
8. In writing trial motions, include a Preliminary Statement that combines your Introduction and your Summary of Argument concisely.

Example
13.1

Takeaway point 13.1: Introductions need to give judges a quick overview of what the case is about — the key facts and core principles.

Introductions should orient readers. The sample Introductions in this chapter omit case descriptions; after all, these are the first explanatory passages that judges will encounter about the case, so this approach lets you assess how well these Introductions orient and motivate you. Check the source of each passage so that you know which court is hearing each dispute.

Source: From an appellate brief for the plaintiff in *Adkins v. Wolever*, 692 F.3d 499 (6th Cir. 2012).

---

1   This case involves an important issue of due process: Whether a district
2   court abused its discretion when it failed to impose a spoliation sanction against
3   a prison guard who used a prison's internal policies as a shield to allow the
4   destruction of unfavorable evidence. This case involves abuse suffered by **A**
  B
5   Appellant Kenneth Adkins ("Adkins"), a prisoner of the Ionia Maximum Correc-
6   tional Facility ("IMAX"), at the hands of Appellee Basil Wolever, a prison guard.
7   Video surveillance of the incident, as well as color photographs of the injuries
8   Adkins suffered, existed at one time. However, at some point *after* Adkins filed
9   his lawsuit, the evidence was lost or destroyed in contravention of IMAX's **C**
10 internal retention policies. Previously, an *en banc* panel of this Court determined
11 that the standard [that controls] whether to punish a prison guard for spoliation **D**
12 of evidence is whether preservation of relevant evidence was *entirely beyond*
13 control of the guard. *Adkins v. Wolever*, 554 F.3d 650, 653 (6th Cir. 2009) (en
14 banc). On remand, the district court ignored this standard and, instead, applied a
15 standard that required the preservation of relevant evidence to be *entirely within*
16 the prison guard's control. **E**
17   This issue is of great importance, because, if the decision of the district court
18 is allowed to stand, evidence in prisoner rights cases can be destroyed with
19 impunity. Since state-run prisons are immune from suit, the prison or one of its **F**
20 employees/agents may "misplace" or destroy evidence without legal repercus-
21 sion. Whenever this substantive right is taken advantage of, the prisoner affected
22 will be even less likely to vindicate a violation of his Constitutional rights. The
23 prisoner will have a right without a real remedy, for he is unlikely to prevail in
24 a § 1983 action if he cannot corroborate his claims with reliable and accurate
25 physical evidence.

A   **This sentence orients readers and lets them know what the case is about. It provides key facts, the legal issue implicated by the case, and an overarching theory of why Adkins should win.**

B   A few vivid details here might have helped to convince readers that Adkins was victimized. The noble goals of brevity and persuasiveness sometimes conflict.

C   The lawyers do not know who destroyed the evidence, so they preserve their credibility rather than accusing a specific party. This caution reflects a sensible sacrifice. In other cases, such as when alleging

securities fraud in a complaint, lawyers must specify who engaged in improper conduct.

D   The term "spoliation," familiar to judges, refers to the destruction of documents or other evidence.

E   The Introduction lays out the trial court's legal error. The applicable standard was set forth by an appellate court in *this* litigation (i.e., Adkins's lawsuit), so the lawyers should have emphasized that the district court flaunted the Sixth Circuit's instructions.

F   And here we see the theme: in future cases, evidence that prisoners were abused would routinely vanish if prisons can destroy that evidence without penalty.

Example	**Takeaway point 13.2:** Introductions should frame how judges see your dispute.
13.2	The following Introduction presents key facts, key laws, and a valuable theme. Most important, it shapes the way that readers see the case. *Source:* From BAW's brief in *BMW v. Gore*, 517 U.S. 559 (1995).

1   In their journey from the assembly line to the dealer's showroom, automo-
2   biles occasionally experience minor damage requiring repair or refinishing. The
3   question then naturally arises whether, or in what circumstances, the fact of
4   repair or refinishing should be disclosed to the dealer or to the retail purchaser
5   of the automobile. By 1983, several states had answered this question by statute
6   or regulation. BMW canvassed these laws and adopted the strictest disclosure
7   threshold — 3% of the manufacturer's suggested retail price ("MSRP") — as
8   its nationwide policy. Since that time, numerous additional states have adopted
9   disclosure thresholds. The vast majority, including Alabama (which enacted its
10   statute after the trial in this case), require disclosure only if any repairs or refin-
11   ishing cost more than 3% (or some higher percentage) of MSRP. *See, e.g.,* Ala.
12   Code § 8-19-5(22) (the failure to give notice of repairs or refinishing costing less
13   than 3% of MSRP is not an unfair trade practice and "shall not . . . constitute a
14   material misrepresentation or omission of fact").
15   In this case, a jury found that BMW's 3% disclosure policy constituted fraud
16   under Alabama common law. It then proceeded to award $4 million in punitive
17   damages (later reduced by the Alabama Supreme Court to $2 million) to plaintiff
18   Dr. Ira Gore, not just for BMW's application of that policy to him but also for its
19   application of the policy to hundreds of cars sold outside of Alabama — despite
20   the absence of any showing that those sales were unlawful where they occurred.

A This phrase is critical, as it tries to get readers to imagine the difficulties of getting a car from Germany to a dealership in the United States — crossing the sea in huge boats that are pounded by giant waves, for instance. This phrase is designed to make readers think, "sure, it makes perfect sense that cars would suffer dings and dents on the way to dealerships."

B The other side alleged that BMW knowingly hid damage that compromised the durability of BMW's paint jobs. By contrast, this sentence refers to BMWs incurring "minor damage," on rare "occasion[s]." Moreover, the actor in the sentence is not BMW. Rather cars themselves "experience . . . damage." This clever phrasing avoids placing the blame on BMW or its delivery company.

C **Does every "minor" issue need to be disclosed? Or can minor dings and chips simply be fixed? The brief attempts to put readers in BMW's position and to lead them to the same conclusion that BMW reached about how to handle "minor damage." The brief seeks to frame the way that judges see the case.**

D BMW tries to become the good guy here: it adopted the "strictest disclosure threshold."

E This statement suggests that BMW's duty to disclose in Alabama was governed by *common law* (because Alabama had not yet adopted the 3 percent disclosure requirement). Thus, complying with the most rigorous *statutory* duties hardly immunized BMW from liability, but Alabama's eventual acceptance of BMW's policy makes punitive damages seem excessive. The next paragraph confirms that BMW's liability arose under common law.

F This sentence makes the jury award sound outlandish in two significant ways. First, the jury awarded $4 million to a man whose car was, at most, worth $1,000 less than he paid for it. Thus, the award was too large. And second, the sentence tells us that the plaintiffs failed to prove (or that the jury failed to find) that BMW's out-of-state practices were unlawful — making punitive damages seem less advisable. This Introduction conveys the theme that the plaintiffs are making a mountain out of few paint chips.

Example
13.3

Takeaway point 13.3: Introductions often work best when they frontload persuasive facts.

The following Introduction lacks the marvelous brevity of the previous two examples, but it reflects a stellar illustration of how to use facts and policy to motivate readers.

Source: Viacom's brief in *Viacom v. YouTube*, 676 F.3d 19 (2d Cir. 2012).

1   YouTube bills itself as "the world's most popular online video commun-
2   ity, allowing millions of people to discover, watch and share originally-created
3   videos." YouTube, About YouTube, http://www.youtube.com/t/about. But from
4   the time that YouTube launched in December 2005 until 2008 (well after this
5   litigation began), many of the videos that users "discovered[ed], watch[ed], and
6   share[d]," on YouTube were not their own home movies, but rather were "origi-
7   nally-created" by Viacom — and protected by the U.S. copyright laws.
8   Almost immediately after YouTube came online, YouTube became aware of
9   widespread infringement on its site. And it was the copyrighted videos — not
10 home movies — that people flocked to YouTube to see. Indeed, in an internal
11 email, YouTube acknowledged that if YouTube "just remove[d] the obviously
12 copyright infringing stuff," traffic would "go from 100,000 views a day down to
13 about 20,000 views or maybe even lower." JAII-159-60.
14   At this point, YouTube faced a stark choice: Like its competitor Google Video,
15 it could screen uploaded videos for unauthorized copyrighted content and build
16 its business on content that it had the legal right to reproduce, display, perform,
17 and distribute. Or it could attempt to grow its business more rapidly by display-
18 ing and performing the copyrighted creations of others without authorization. It
19 chose the latter course, stating "we need to attract traffic." JAII-171.
20   On these facts, there is no room to dispute the district court's view that You-
21 Tube "not only w[as] generally aware of, but welcomed, copyright-infringing
22 material being placed on [its] website" because "[s]uch material was attrac-
23 tive to users" and "enhanced [YouTube's] income from advertisements." SPA9.
24 Indeed, before Google bought YouTube for $1.65 billion, Google's own due dili-
25 gence team warned that *more than half* of YouTube's views infringed copyrights.
26 And the scope of the ongoing infringement was so broad — and the value to
27 Google of that infringement so great — that at one point, Google offered Viacom
28 a deal to license Viacom's copyrights that Google valued at a minimum of $590
29 million. JAI-302.
30   The district court nevertheless held that YouTube had *no* liability for the
31 rampant infringement of copyrights it "welcomed." To reach that implausible
32 conclusion, the district court held that the narrow safe harbor established by Sec-
33 tion 512(c) of the Digital Millennium Copyright Act, 17 U.S.C. § 512(c), shields
34 *any* infringing activity ("however flagrant and blatant") that "flow[s] from" a
35 user's upload of copyrighted material to a website, and is unavailable to a ser-
36 vice provider *only* when a copyright owner can demonstrate that the service
37 provider has actual knowledge of "specific and identifiable infringements of indi-
38 vidual items," including the "works' locations at the site," which is to say, actual
39 knowledge that the material appearing at a specific URL (web address) infringes
40 a copyright. SPA10, 20, 27, 32. Absent proof that a service provider possessed

A

B

C

D

E

F

41 this type of URL-specific knowledge, the service provider's responsibility under
42 the copyright laws was limited to timely responding to cease-and-desist demands
43 of copyright owners, *even if* the service provider already was "aware[] of perva-
44 sive copyright-infringing." SPA20.

45 If affirmed by this Court, that construction of Section 512(c) would radically
46 transform the functioning of the copyright system and severely impair, if not
47 completely destroy, the value of many copyrighted creations. It would immunize
48 from copyright infringement liability even avowedly piratical Internet businesses.
47 Even the very piratical businesses held to account in *Metro-Goldwyn-Mayer*
50 *Studios Inc. v. Grokster, Ltd.*, 545 U.S. 913 (2005), could be immune with just
51 minor tweaks to their business models.

52 Nothing in the text or history of the [Digital Millennium Copyright Act] even
53 remotely suggests that Congress intended such absurd, disquieting, and disrup-
54 tive results. In fact, the text of the DMCA compels the opposite conclusion:
55 Internet service providers that not only are aware of pervasive copyright infringe-
56 ment, but actively participate in and profit from it, enjoy no immunity from the
57 copyright laws and may be held to account for their theft of artists' creations.   **G**
58 Once YouTube is stripped of Section 512(c) immunity, well-established principles
59 of copyright law and the summary judgment record dictate that YouTube be held
60 liable for the rampant copyright infringement that, even on the district court's
61 telling, YouTube "welcomed."   **H**

A   The Introduction's theme is that YouTube exists to infringe copyrighted content.

B   This quote — a nightmare for YouTube — reflects a legal conclusion that content was infringing. We do not know (i) who said this; (ii) whether YouTube did, in fact, remove this content from its website; (iii) where within YouTube this content appeared; (iv) whether this "stuff" even belonged to Viacom; or (v) whether YouTube subsequently licensed this content. This quote, from YouTube's earliest days, nevertheless pummels YouTube; even if Viacom overreached, it is much easier to use a biting quote to attack an adversary than it is to dispel the impression that such a harmful quote creates. And Viacom's strategy of using damning quotes in its Introduction reflects savvy advocacy.

C   Yet again, the brief manages to show YouTube's (alleged) moral failings by focusing on a potentially benign comment from one of YouTube's documents. After all, almost *every* Internet business wants to attract traffic. This approach reflects the power of *post hoc ergo propter hoc* (as discussed in Appendix A): merely placing two facts next to each other suggests that the one caused the other. Use this same technique in your Statements of Fact to let readers draw their own inferences.

D   Viacom   below. But rather than acting defensively, it emphasizes some of the trial judge's conclusions .

E   This phrase is at the outer limit of how sharply lawyers may criticize judges.

F   This line — combined with the term "liability" in the first sentence — makes the district court's conclusions seem outlandish. The remainder of this sentence is the one clunker in this Introduction. It is long and hard to follow. But that's because Viacom wanted to keep readers from absorbing exactly what the district court decided.

G   The brief now makes one of its shrewdest moves, lumping YouTube in with the most-aggressive copyright pirates without even assessing whether YouTube satisfied the test laid out by the district court (i.e., whether YouTube removed videos when a copyright holder alleged infringement). This Introduction explains what the case is about, pummels YouTube, motivates readers to remedy the injury to copyright owners, and reflects a model of how to try to win a case in the opening pages.

H   Yet again, Viacom uses a snippet of a document brilliantly. The word "welcomed" singlehandedly answers the legal issue as Viacom see its, which is whether YouTube "actively participated in and profited from" infringement. And the Second Circuit agreed, remanding the case so that the trial court could assess whether YouTube remained willfully blind to the infringement on its site.

Example
13.4

Takeaway point 13.4: A Summary of Argument should generally present an abstract of your client's best arguments and should then rebut the other side's best arguments.

Let's turn to a Summary of Argument, a section that focuses on the *specific* reasons that a party should win. In the following case, a terrorist was caught smuggling bomb components across the border between the United States and Canada. A federal statute imposed a lengthy prison sentence on anyone who carried explosives "during" another felony. The defendant committed a felony when he lied on a customs form; thus, he was carrying explosives "during" his felony, but he alleged that common sense dictated that the explosives needed to be related to the felony. The Supreme Court rejected that argument based on the following brief.

Source: Government's brief in *United States v. Ressam*, 553 U.S. 272 (2008).

SUMMARY OF ARGUMENT

1
2 A. Section 844(h)(2) proscribes "carr[ying] an explosive during the commis-
3 sion of any felony which may be prosecuted in a court of the United States." 18
4 U.S.C. 844(h)(2). The statute does not say the explosive must have been carried
5 "in relation to" the underlying felony, nor does it contain any language that can
6 bear that construction. "[D]uring" suggests only a temporal connection; it means
7 "at the same time as," not "at the same time and in connection with." That
8 straightforward reading is reinforced by the fact that the adjacent prohibition
9 in Section 844(h)(1), which applies when a person "uses fire or an explosive to
10 commit" another felony, clearly requires a connection beyond a mere temporal
11 relationship between a defendant's possession of an explosive and the perpetra-
12 tion of the underlying felony.
13   B. Congress has expressly included the very words that the Ninth Circuit read
14 into Section 844(h)(2) in a closely related provision. Section 924(c)(1) of Title
15 18, United States Code, prohibits carrying a firearm "during and in relation to"
16 certain specified offenses. Because it is undisputed that Section 844(h) was pat-
17 terned on Section 924(c), the lack of similar language in Section 844(h)(2) is best
18 viewed as reflecting a deliberate congressional choice.
19   C. Because the text of Section 844(h)(2) is clear and unambiguous, there is no
20 need to resort to legislative history. Nonetheless, the statute's history confirms
21 the plain meaning of the text. As originally drafted, both Section 924(c) and Sec-
22 tion 844(h)(2) proscribed "carrying [an item] unlawfully during the commission
23 of" certain specified offenses. In 1984, Congress amended Section 924(c), the
24 firearms statute, by deleting the word "unlawfully" and adding the words "and
25 in relation to" after "during." In 1988, Congress amended Section 844(h)(2), the
26 explosives statute, by deleting the word "unlawfully," but Congress conspicu-
27 ously failed to add the words "and in relation to." A committee report prepared
28 in connection with the 1984 amendments to the firearms statute expressly rec-
29 ognized that, absent the words "unlawfully" or "and in relation to," the statute
30 would apply when a defendant's carrying of the firearm "played no part in" the
31 underlying offense. In addition, the Department of Justice advised Congress in
32 1985 that the elimination of the word "unlawfully" from Section 844(h)(2) would
33 result in the statute being expanded to cover "all cases in which explosives are
34 carried during the commission of a federal felony."

35   D. The Ninth Circuit's own previous decision in *United States v. Stewart*,
36   779 F.2d 538 (9th Cir. 1985) (Kennedy, J.), does not support reading into Sec-
37   tion 844(h)(2) a relational element that appears nowhere in the statutory text. **H**
38   *Stewart* construed a different statute that was amended at a different time and in
39   different ways, and did not purport to interpret Section 844(h).
40   E. The canon against reading general language in a statute to produce
41   absurd results has no application here. Given the inherent dangerousness of
42   explosives, as well the relative infrequency of situations in which a person will
43   have a legitimate reason for carrying one, there is nothing irrational or absurd
44   about mandating enhanced punishment for any person who carries an explo-
45   sive while committing a federal felony. Respondent relies on a few hypothetical
46   scenarios to which Section 844(h)(2) might potentially extend, but a party
47   who invokes the absurd results canon to create an exception to otherwise clear
48   statutory language must, at minimum, demonstrate that a straightforward read-
47   ing of the text produces an absurd result in his own case. Respondent has not
50   attempted to do so. In any event, it is unclear whether the examples respondent
51   posits would be truly absurd.
52   F.   The rule of lenity is inapplicable. The statutory text is clear and unambigu-
53   ous, and supplying an element that Congress itself omitted goes well beyond the
54   rule's limited role.

A The Summary of Argument usually appears after the Statement of Facts and before the Argument. This is one reason that Introductions are so vital; they appear *before* the facts, which can seem labyrinthine without an overview of the case.

B You may, but need not, demark where each argument begins. Use a new paragraph for each point.

C The Summary begins by telling readers what the disputed statute says.

D This sentence sought to lay out, with crystalline clarity, the positions taken by each side. This sort of juxtaposition offers much-appreciated help to judges.

E Notice that the first argument actually combines two separate points: that "during" means "during" and that an adjacent provision "reinforce[s]" this conclusion.

F As discussed in Chapter 11, arguing in the alternative is vital. The lawyers handle it here in a classic way. They affirm that they win on the prior grounds, but then add that they also win on additional grounds.

G **Pay special attention to the sequence in which the lawyers raise their arguments. They raise their** three main affirmative positions first, moving from strongest to weakest. Then the brief rebuts the other side's arguments in a carefully selected sequence that is discussed below. This is a paradigmatic example of moving from "affirmative to negative" arguments. The Summary of Argument should usually track the order in which the brief raises arguments.

H The Supreme Court is not bound to follow the Ninth Circuit's decision. So why does this counter-argument come first — or appear at all? Notice the author. This paragraph is a love letter to Justice Anthony Kennedy, telling him that the lower court opinion was based on a misreading of a case that he wrote when he served on the Ninth Circuit. Notice, too, that this is the only case cited in the Summary. You *can* cite cases in your Summary, but do so sparingly. The first "negative" argument thus discredits the opinion below to maximize the chances of winning 5–4, or better. The brief does not bother to refute every argument that the other side raised; that assault appears later, in the Argument. The Summary targets merely the pillars of the other side's position and a critical swing vote on the Court.

Example	**Takeaway point 13.5:** A Summary of Argument *may* present many arguments.
13.5	The next Summary of Argument reflects how to dart from argument to argument. The State Department refused to issue a passport to any American born in Jerusalem listing that citizen's birthplace as "Israel." Congress enacted a statute to override this policy. The State Department refused to comply. A federal court dodged the issue, invoking the "political question" doctrine. Here, the lawyers ask the Supreme Court to require the State Department to follow the statute.
	Source: Brief for the passport applicant from *Zivotofsky v. Clinton*, 132 S. Ct. 1421 (2012).

SUMMARY OF ARGUMENT

1. Senior Circuit Judge Edwards correctly dismissed as "specious" the contention that this case presents a "political question" that is nonjusticiable and that requires dismissal of the complaint. The "political question doctrine" is a prudential rule that removes the judiciary (a) from controversies that are "beyond judicial competence" because they turn on "policy choices and value determinations" that judges are not empowered to make and (b) from matters (such as impeachment) that are exclusively committed for decision to other branches of government. The central issue in this case is a constitutional separation-of-powers question that is well within the competence and expertise of federal courts: Does Congress have the constitutional authority to enact a law that entitles Jerusalem-born citizens to record "Israel" as their place of birth on passports . . . ?

2. The six criteria enumerated in the Court's opinion in *Baker v. Carr* as illustrative of a "political question" apply only when a court is asked to resolve a case in which Congress has failed to set legislative standards. The relevant precedent for this case — in which the lower courts were asked to enforce a clearly enunciated legislative mandate — is the *Japan Whaling Association* case. In that case, no member of this Court had any difficulty in deciding the controversy. . . .

3. On the merits of the constitutional issue, . . . [r]ecent historical research has established that the President's "power to recognize foreign sovereigns" was not intended, by the original understanding of the Founding Fathers, to be a "power" at all. It was a ceremonial duty . . . . A Congressional statute cannot be invalidated as interfering with this ceremonial function.

4. If a Presidential "power to recognize foreign sovereigns" does exist, it does not extend to determining whether a particular city or territory is within the foreign sovereign's boundaries. In two cases in which this Court had to determine jurisdiction over foreign territories, the Court assigned equal importance to legislative, as to executive, judgments. . . .

5. Although much-criticized dicta in the *Curtiss-Wright* opinion appears to give the President extra-constitutional exclusive control over America's foreign policy, this Court's decisions have adopted Justice Jackson's concurring opinion in the *Steel Seizure* case as the governing guideline. Under that standard, the President's power to make foreign-policy determinations is at "its lowest ebb" when those determinations are neither authorized by Congress nor reached following Congress' silence but actually conflict with Congress' enacted laws. Only Presidential actions that can survive cautious scrutiny may nullify Congress' expressed will in the foreign-policy arena.

6. The State Department's refusal to allow Jerusalem-born American citizens to record "Israel" as their place of birth cannot withstand such scrutiny. This prohibition has no rational basis other than a purported fear that Israel's enemies will criticize American policy because they will misperceive the significance of allowing "Israel" to be recorded on passports. The State Department's prohibition against recording "Israel" was, from its inception, erroneous and misguided. The government is now urging that it must be maintained permanently because changing it would be misconstrued. This reasoning justifies the maintenance of every poor . . . judgment that may be criticized by a foreign interest if corrected.

7. The folly of the State Department policy is also demonstrated by the fact that State Department personnel have occasionally failed to understand and apply the policy uniformly. Both before this lawsuit was brought and to this very day, individual citizens born in Jerusalem have reported that passports issued in Washington and New York to citizens born in Jerusalem record "Israel" as the place of birth. Moreover, other departments within the Executive Branch continue to issue official documents reading "Jerusalem, Israel." These documents have apparently not resulted in protests from Palestinians and the Arab world that the government has predicted in this case.

8. The Taiwan experience in 1994 demonstrates that the stated fear of harm to foreign policy is greatly exaggerated. In that case, the People's Republic of China had taken such great offense to passports recording "Taiwan" as a place of birth that it had refused to endorse visas on these passports. . . . Nonetheless, the State Department acquiesced in Congress' directive in 1994 and there was no harm to American foreign policy.

9. The State Department practice effectively repealed by Section 214(d) was discriminatory. . . .

10. Finally, the method chosen by the President to challenge Section 214(d) was an unconstitutional one. If the President believed that the law violated the Constitution, it was his obligation to follow the course described in Article I, Section 7, Clause 2, and issue a veto that would be subject to further consideration by the Congress. Not having vetoed the law and having chosen instead to sign it, the President is obliged to execute the directive of Section 214(d).

A The Summary tracks the sequence of the arguments that appear later in the brief. It begins with a threshold issue (the political question doctrine) and then moves to substantive issues. See Chapter 11 for advice about how to select and arrange arguments.

B As with Example 13.4, the lawyers rebut a counterargument quickly, noting that that argument is based on "much-criticized dicta" that clashes with the Court's precedent.

C Even in the Summary, the lawyers manage to follow CRAC. Paragraph 5 explained the Rule that governs this issue. Here in Paragraph 6, the brief explains why the other side cannot fulfill that standard.

D **The lawyers have concisely presented numerous reasons that their client should win.**

Example 13.6

Takeaway point 13.6: Trial motions often contain a Preliminary Statement that merges a thematic Introduction with a point-by-point Summary.

Next, we review a lean Introduction-Summary hybrid involving the estate of Mario Puzo (author of *The Godfather*). Trial motions often label these hybrids as a "Preliminary Statement." Pay attention to when you feel oriented about the case.

Source: Paramount's motion to dismiss counterclaims from *Paramount Pictures Corp. v. Estate of Mario Puzo* No. 12 Civ. 1268 (S.D.N.Y. Sept. 26, 2012).

I. *PRELIMINARY STATEMENT*

1   This motion is brought pursuant to Fed. R. Civ. P. 12(b)(6) to dismiss two of
2   the counterclaims alleged by Defendant and Counterclaimant Anthony Puzo, as
3
4   Executor of the Estate of Mario Puzo (the "Puzo Estate").

5   The action concerns a 1969 Agreement between Plaintiff and Counter-Defen-
6   dant Paramount Pictures Corporation ("Paramount") and the late author Mario
7   Puzo ("Puzo"), concerning the well-known novel *The Godfather*. In 1969, Para-
8   mount purchased from Puzo all rights and copyright interests in *The Godfather,*
9   including all "literary" rights and all rights to use any of the characters created in
10   *The Godfather* in "other works." The only right reserved to the Puzo Estate was
11   the right to publish the original novel *The Godfather* and to publish "versions and
12   adaptations thereof" and "to vend copies thereof." After entering into this 1969
13   Agreement, Paramount adapted the novel *The Godfather* into three famous films,
14   and the characters and story of Puzo's novel have become iconic throughout the
15   world for approximately 40 years.

16   Puzo died in 1999. In 2002, his Estate requested that Paramount permit the
17   publication of a sequel novel. Paramount consented to the publication of a single
18   sequel novel. The Puzo Estate then commissioned two additional sequel novels,
19   and licensed them for publication in 2006 and 2012. The Estate failed to obtain
20   Paramount's authorization for either the second or third sequels. Paramount al-
21   leges in this action that the unauthorized second and third sequel novels infringe
22   on the literary rights purchased by Paramount in 1969, and that the cover art on
23   the books also infringes on Paramount's trademarks. The Puzo Estate disagrees,
24   and has counterclaimed. Two of the counterclaims, however, are fatally flawed.

25   First, the Puzo Estate has asserted a counterclaim for "cancellation and ter-
26   mination" of the 1969 Agreement and seeks termination of Mario Puzo's grant
27   of rights in *The Godfather* in its entirety. As alleged by the Puzo Estate, the sole
28   basis for this radical remedy is Paramount's initiation of this lawsuit — no other
29   action by Paramount is alleged as a basis for the claim. Unsurprisingly, there
30   is no basis in law for terminating and canceling an agreement that has been in
31   place for over 40 years, during which Paramount has created a world-famous
32   literary and film franchise in reliance on the agreement, merely because Para-
33   mount alleges in this proceeding that the Puzo Estate has infringed Paramount's
34   rights. Under clear New York law, a cause of action for rescission (which is the
35   correct name for the Puzo Estate's alleged "cancellation" counterclaim) is only
36   available in the event of a "substantial and fundamental" breach that "may be
37   said to go the root of the agreement between the parties." *Septembertide Publ'g,*

A

B
C

D

E

F

B.V. v. Stein and Day, Inc., 884 F.2d 675, 678 (2d Cir.1989). The mere fact that Paramount has brought an action for copyright infringement based on unauthorized sequel novels, more than 40 years after the grant of rights, and without any alleged damage to the Puzo Estate aside from that stemming from Paramount's assertion of its rights, does not suffice to plead a fundamental breach of the parties' agreement. In addition, rescission is only available where monetary damages are an inadequate remedy, which is manifestly not the case here, since any injury to the Puzo Estate due to Paramount's assertion of its contractual rights could be compensated by monetary damages. Finally, rescission is available only when it is reasonably possible to restore the parties to the condition they were in before a contract was entered into. Given the more than 40 years since the contract was entered into, and the existence of the *Godfather* films and the state of the *Godfather* franchise, it is clear on the face of the Estate's pleadings that this element of the rescission claim is not met.

The Puzo Estate's third counterclaim, for tortious interference with contract, is equally flawed. It is well-established in this District that a cause of action for tortious interference with contract requires an allegation that some third-party contract was breached as a result of the alleged interference. *Kirch v. Liberty Media Corp.*, 449 F.3d 388, 401 (2d Cir. 2006). The Puzo Estate's counterclaims, however, do not allege that any third-party contract was breached due to Paramount's purported interference. Moreover, the Puzo Estate's tortious interference counterclaim fails because it is based exclusively upon Paramount's assertion of a claim in this litigation, which under Second Circuit law is protected activity that cannot support a tortious interference claim. These flaws are clear and are fatal to the third counterclaim.

Accordingly, the Court should dismiss the First and Third Counterclaims.

A The Preliminary Statement specifies that it seeks to dismiss two (but not all) of the counterclaims. The lawyers probably considered specifying which two claims they were targeting, but they waited two paragraphs to provide those details.

B The lawyers provide relevant details that nevertheless gum up the motion. They mention Paramount's procedural name in the case, which stalls the flow of the motion. This sort of extra detail is important, but be certain to write empathetically, making your case easy for the judge to follow.

C Avoid repeating the same uncommon word in a sentence, such as "concerns" and "concerning."

D Readers are most likely to be confused at the beginning of your motion or brief, so use short sentences to ensure that your points and facts are digestible.

E Here, readers would have benefited from a clue like, "After publishing the one sequel that Paramount authorized, the Estate commissioned two *additional*

sequel novels." That clue would clarify that the Estate published three sequel novels, not two.

F The "Introduction" side of this Preliminary Statement ends here. The remainder provides a summary of Paramount's argument.

G Even though the case is pending in federal court, a decision from the New York Court of Appeals was especially valuable because state law governed the contract.

H WARNING! Watch out for "circular" reasoning. This sentence basically says that monetary damages are not inadequate because they are adequate. Here, however, this circular reasoning is a reasonable move for these lawyers to make: if they try to predict what "irreparable harm" the other side will allege, the other side can simply assert other rationales. This approach basically adds a placeholder. Once the Puzo estate explains why money will not suffice to remedy its injuries, Paramount can counter those points in its reply.

FREQUENTLY ASKED QUESTIONS ABOUT INTRODUCTIONS AND SUMMARIES OF ARGUMENT

Q. You mention that Introductions generally convey the theme of a brief. Should *every* brief and motion have a theme?

A. Every brief and motion should have a theme and an Introduction; in practice, however, some briefs are less conducive to a unifying theme than others, such as filings that address multiple parties and multiple, distinct issues. Similarly, some motions (such as a battle over fifteen separate discovery issues) may be too sprawling or banal to have a unifying theme. But search for one. That's a key part of developing your persuasive powers.

For example, the theme of a broad discovery motion might be that the other side has systematically attempted to conceal documents that it was required to produce. The Introduction could provide an overview so that the individual points wouldn't seem rambling and chaotic. Indeed, Introductions are often *most* valuable when the brief or motion deals with numerous issues that do not relate to each other in obvious ways. The more convoluted and complicated the case, the more your Introduction can act as a beacon.

Q. If I include both an Introduction and a Summary of Argument, how do I keep the latter from being repetitive?

A. Place different type of points in the two parts of your brief. More specifically, think about how and where to use ethos, pathos, and logos, which are the three basic modes of persuasion. Ethos largely focuses on character, morality, and credibility — making readers believe you and your motives. Pathos appeals to a reader's emotions. Logos builds a logical argument. In an Introduction, ethos or pathos is usually the dominant element: your Introductions need to orient judges, build trust, and motivate them (without being melodramatic) to feel like some wrong has occurred that they must remedy. By contrast, the Summary's dominant mode of persuasion is logos: it provides a short recitation of the various arguments, mostly based on logic, that favor your client. Both of these sections may use all three modes of persuasion, but focusing on ethos or pathos (so long as you don't go overboard) will produce good Introductions just as focusing on logos will produce good Summaries.

Q. What advantages or disadvantages are there to combining an Introduction and a Summary of Argument?

A. When you combine an Introduction and a Summary, you provide a judge with one-stop shopping: the first few pages of the brief provide a sufficient overview to discern what happened, what the judge should do about it, and how to get there (i.e., the arguments that would support that outcome). On the flip side, a unified Introduction and Summary is often long — four to six pages is common for this approach — so it may bore readers before they even reach your Statement. Also, until readers have read your Statement, they may not understand all of the arguments in your Summary. California attorney Steve Hirsch is a master of this sort of merged Introduction-plus-Summary, and his work is recommended highly as a model of great advocacy, both in general and for lawyers who want to try the integrated approach. But this book recommends separate Introductions and Summaries because of the importance of brevity.

Q. Should I fear that the judge might read only my Summary of the Argument, and not the Argument itself? If so, how do I deal with that risk?

A. Few judges disclose which parts of briefs they read, skim, or skip, but one Supreme Court Justice has disclosed that he doesn't read the Summary of Argument, and multiple law clerks have told me that they skipped Introductions. So, because you do not know whether or when judges might cut corners, try to make your Introduction, your Summary of Argument, and your Argument independently capable of convincing a reader that your client's position is correct while limiting repetition.

Q. What should I do if court rules prohibit me from including an Introduction or a Summary of Argument in my brief or motion?

A. Consider weaving one or both of them into some other section. For instance, without labeling your opening page as an "Introduction" you can include a short paragraph or two — without a heading — before you describe the facts. Alternatively, your Statement of Facts can begin with a short overview — in other words, an Introduction — cloaked as facts. (And, yes, many judges have by now come to expect this approach.) You can then add some visual clue, such as a subheading or several asterisks in the middle of the page, to signal that the stealth introduction is ending. The same principle applies with the Summary of Argument; the rules governing trial motions often do not call for this section, so your *Argument* can begin with a short roadmap that summarizes the points that follow (if you choose not to summarize your arguments in your Preliminary Statement). Why are these tricks acceptable? Because hawk-eyed clerks watch for *headings* that the court rules prohibit, but they usually don't mind if the contents of a required section take a few minor liberties. Thus, even when court rules do not call for an Introduction or a Summary, you can usually introduce your case and summarize your arguments so long as you don't add a heading.

Chapter 14

Motions

Motions are how lawyers typically ask a trial court to resolve one or more issues within a case. This chapter describes three types: (1) motions to dismiss, (2) summary judgment motions, and (3) nondispositive motions. The first two categories are the best-known motions. The last category, which refers to motions that seek to resolve an isolated issue within the case, includes literally thousands of varietals — motions to amend complaints, to get a TRO, to quash a subpoena, to exclude evidence, to impose sanctions, to disqualify a lawyer, to delay a trial, to set aside a jury verdict, and on and on and on — even to "Require Plaintiff's Counsel to Count to Ten Before Making Categorical Statements that Are Incorrect." (A federal court actually granted that motion.)

Because motions are similar in many ways to briefs, this chapter predominantly fine-tunes the skills discussed in prior chapters. It explores the key differences between motions and briefs, all to meet its larger goal of helping you to grasp some of the nuances of writing motions. It also seeks to convey a broader point that is equally important to your success as a litigator: when you want a court to do something, the way to obtain that relief is probably to file a motion. Thus, if you want to exhume a body or get a blood sample from a defendant or force a client's former spouse to return intimate photos, do not buy a shovel, find a syringe, or break into the ex's apartment. File a motion. Learning how to use motions is critical to becoming an effective trial litigator.

CHAPTER OVERVIEW

1. For motions to dismiss, the party filing the motion (the "movant") is hamstrung. It must assume, with very limited exceptions, that the facts in the complaint are true. Thus, motions to dismiss succeed only when the complaint itself suffers from some defect. Filing a motion to dismiss can elicit information from the plaintiffs about their legal theory, lock plaintiffs into a position earlier than they would like, and color a judge's view of the merits of plaintiffs' claims. But if you lose, the judge's opinion will give the plaintiffs a clearer sense of exactly what they need to establish to win.

2. For summary judgment motions, the movant is again hamstrung. It generally needs to base its arguments on undisputed facts gathered during discovery.

3. When filing or opposing a nondispositive motion, introductions are especially important, as judges will be more inclined to grant (or deny) a motion if they can grasp quickly why the motion was filed and what it asks them to do. Keep these motions short.

4. Because motions are almost always considered by a single judge, you should gain information about the judge's experience and predilections. See Appendix A ("You are arguing to a particular tribunal. Everything else turns on that.").

Example 14.1	**Takeaway point 14.1:** When filing a motion to dismiss, scour the plaintiff's complaint (or amended complaint) to find relevant omissions, admissions, and revisions.

Motions to dismiss need to show a court that a complaint is, on its face, insufficient to provide the plaintiff with a remedy. These motions therefore need to base their arguments on facts alleged in the complaint (or in the amended complaint). Lawyers for the defendant therefore scour the complaint for statements and noteworthy omissions that might convince the court that the plaintiff's case may not proceed.

This case arose when a French citizen named Konowaloff sued a museum claiming to be the rightful owner of a painting by Paul Cézanne. Konowaloff alleged that the painting was seized from his ancestor (Morozov) in 1918. The complaint initially alleged that the Soviet government had taken the painting. The museum moved to dismiss the complaint based on the act of state doctrine, which prevents courts from unwinding valid actions taken by other sovereign governments. So what did Konowaloff do? He amended his complaint, alleging that the painting was seized by the Bolshevik *Party* rather than the official Soviet government. Here, the museum's lawyers confront this maneuver.

Source: Museum's motion to dismiss plaintiff's amended complaint from *Konowaloff v. Metropolitan Museum of Art*, 10 CIV. 9126 SAS, 2011 WL 4430856 (S.D.N.Y. Sept. 22, 2011).

C. Plaintiff's Attempts to Undercut the Act of State Doctrine Are Unavailing

In apparent recognition of the defects of the original Complaint, . . . the Amended Complaint adds a series of last-ditch attempts to plead around the act of state doctrine. These attempts are unavailing.   **A**

The "act of party" argument. Plaintiff tries to recast the 1918 Nationalization Decree and the 1933 sale as so-called "acts of party" rather than "acts of state." To set up this argument, plaintiff deleted the original Complaint's description of   **B** the 1918 Nationalization Decree as a "tak[ing] by the [Russian Government] by order of Lenin and Sovnarkom (the Council of People's Commissars)," Compl. ¶ 9, and substituted it with the allegation that the "Bolsheviks decreed" the Painting to be "state property." Am. Compl. ¶ 11. Plaintiff apparently hopes that the Court will overlook the allegation in the first Complaint that the Soviet government nationalized the Painting, and make the political judgment that the decrees and orders of Lenin and the Council of People's Commissars were merely "party" acts, and not "acts of state."

This argument is specious and futile. It contradicts well-established precedents in   **C** the Supreme Court, this Court, and the New York Court of Appeals, all of which have   **D** held that Soviet nationalization decrees issued in the same era by the same authorities are valid acts of state, not acts of party. *See supra* at 6-9. In any event, the Amended   **E** Complaint elsewhere effectively concedes the 1918 Nationalization Decree was an act of state. *See, e.g.,* Am. Compl. ¶ 57 ("[t]he Painting was confiscated by the RSFSR in 1918"); ¶ 11 (decree made the Painting "state property"); ¶ 14 (decree "was tantamount to a bill of attainder").

This attempt to characterize Politburo acts in 1933 as "acts of party" rather than "acts of state" similarly fails. Once again, the Amended Complaint is the source of its own undoing: It recognizes that the Soviet government controlled the sale, *id.* ¶ 20   **F** (money from Painting's sale was sent to "the Soviet government"); ¶ 27 (Clark cabled funds to "a Soviet-controlled bank account"); and that the Politburo exercised sovereign powers, *id.* ¶ 33 ("power was concentrated in the hands of Politburo members and . . . no one dared try to prosecute them"); ¶ 34 ("The Politburo made the decision on art sales."). . . .

31 | Although the original Complaint did not mention Morozov's religion, the
32 | Amended Complaint now adds the allegation that Morozov was an Old Believer,
33 | Am. Compl. ¶ 10, in an apparent attempt to imply that the 1918 Nationalization
34 | Decree was an act of religious persecution similar to Nazi looting. There are three
35 | fatal problems with this new argument. First, no allegation affirmatively links
36 | Morozov's religion to the 1918 Nationalization Decree. Second, even assuming
37 | that a taking based on religion violated international law in 1918 (it did not), it
38 | would not affect the outcome here because the act of state doctrine applies to
39 | state expropriations "even if international law has been violated." *Sabbatino*,
40 | 376 U.S. at 431. Finally, the Old Believer allegations are ultimately irrelevant
41 | because even if the Court declined to apply the act of state doctrine to the 1918
42 | Nationalization Decree, at least two other Soviet nationalization decrees would
43 | have nationalized the Painting that have no alleged link to religion and have
44 | already been upheld by this Court. See *infra* at 14.

A This clear preview of the argument is built around the legal test that governs this stage of the briefing: whether the complaint (or, in this case, the amended complaint) states a valid cause of action. This section of the motion argues that the seizure of the disputed painting was a valid act of government. Defendants often want to argue facts in a motion to dismiss; that approach may slake their thirst to reject what the plaintiff alleged, but courts generally cannot consider those facts at this stage of the lawsuit.

B Here, we can see the chess moves that each side makes when a lawsuit begins. The plaintiff initially asserted that the Soviet government took his ancestor's painting. The museum countered that this allegation was squarely barred by the act of state doctrine. The plaintiff then amended his complaint to get around this problem. Before filing a motion to dismiss, the defendent must assess whether doing so will end the plaintiff's case or lead to a favorable settlement or, alternatively, whether the motion will simply provide free research to your adversary, who will amend its complaint and be in a better position to know what it needs to show to win its case.

C Notice that the argument is built around the plaintiff's allegations, not around what *actually* happened in 1918. The lawyers highlight the original complaint's admissions to make the plaintiff look less reliable, truthful, and diligent.

D Sharp language is an unfortunate reality of modern litigation.

E Courts are supposed to consider only the materials within the four corners of the amended complaint. But notice that the museum's lawyers brilliantly evade the legal standard here: they encourage the court to ignore what the complaint says — that the Cézanne painting was seized by a mere political *party* — and to reach instead the factual finding that the seizure was an official act given that other courts reached that conclusion. They try to convert a factual issue that the court cannot consider into a legal one that it can.

F The motion plucks quotes from the amended complaint to advance its argument. Exercise great caution in crafting your complaints because omissions *and* statements can be fatal.

G This sentence illustrates the risks of filing a motion to dismiss. The initial motion to dismiss caused Konowaloff to dig deeper for grounds to reclaim the painting. As a result, he learned that proving that Morozov was a victim of religious persecution would help his position, alerting his lawyers to pursue this issue during discovery, such as by getting an expert witness to discuss how Old Believers were persecuted by the Russian Orthodox Church. An unsuccessful motion to dismiss can strengthen a plaintiff.

H The amended complaint alluded to Morozov's religion but failed to allege that his painting was seized *because* of his religion. The Museum's lawyers thereby exploit the amended complaint's *silence* as well as what it said and what it altered from the original complaint.

I The amended complaint alleged that international law was violated. Rather than delving into this legal morasse, the museum rejects that point's relevance and uses the pithy phrase "it did not" to suggest that the plaintiff mischaracterized the law. This is an expert move that lets your client adapt to the applicable legal standard without letting the judge form unhelpful impressions about the facts or the law.

Example 14.2	**Takeaway point 14.2:** Use procedural defenses to support your client's motion to dismiss.

Let's review one more example of this vital type of motion. This example is based on a procedural argument — that a court lacked jurisdiction because of an arbitration clause. The lawsuit was filed by the world's most famous cyclist, Lance Armstrong. Armstrong, who achieved global fame when he won the Tour de France seven consecutive times, was hounded for years by allegations that he had used steroids to boost his performance. Years after his last victory, the United States Anti-Doping Agency (USADA) charged him with using performance-enhancing substances, and it announced that it would ban Armstrong from cycling and strip him of his titles. Armstrong filed a lawsuit in federal court to challenge this penalty. Here, USADA moved to dismiss Armstrong's lawsuit and force Armstrong to abide by an arbitration clause that he previously signed.

Source: Defendant-USADA's Motion to Dismiss for Lack of Subject Matter Jurisdiction or, in the Alternative, Motion to Dismiss or Stay Under the Federal Arbitration Act from *Armstrong v. USADA*, No. 1:12-cv-00606-SS (W.D. Tex. July 19, 2012).

INTRODUCTION

Under the Ted Stevens Olympic and Amateur Sports Act ("Sports Act"), 36 U.S.C. § 220501, *et seq.*, Congress has established arbitration as the exclusive forum for disputes relating to athlete eligibility in sports that are part of the Olympic movement, including cycling and triathlon. As an elite athlete member of USA Cycling and USA Triathlon, Lance Armstrong is subject to this mandatory dispute resolution framework. His claims, which attempt to bypass and enjoin the mandatory arbitration process, are preempted by the Sports Act. By bringing suit before completing the available arbitral process, he has also failed to exhaust the administrative remedies afforded him by the Act. The court lacks subject matter jurisdiction for both reasons.

With respect to USADA's alternative motion to dismiss or stay under Section 3 of the Federal Arbitration Act ("FAA"), undisputed facts show Armstrong agreed on multiple occasions to be bound by anti-doping rules applicable to competitors in cycling and triathlon in the United States. He further agreed that any necessary hearing regarding a violation of these rules would be an arbitration under the USADA Protocol for Olympic and Paralympic Movement Testing ("USADA Protocol" or "Protocol") and pursuant to the American Arbitration Association ("AAA") Supplementary Procedures for the Arbitration of Olympic Sport Doping Disputes ("AAA Supplementary Procedures").

With no apparent regard for his prior commitments to be bound by the sport rules, and indeed silent as to many of the applicable rules,[1] Armstrong asks this Court to enjoin the USADA adjudication process and prevent the enforcement of the anti-doping rules to which he agreed. He would have this Court ignore bot

---

1. Armstrong repeatedly refers to the UCI Anti-Doping Rules in his Amended Complaint as if those are the only rules which USADA is claiming he violated and the only rules by which USADA asserts jurisdiction. The USADA's June 28, 2012, charging letter includes violations under rules of the United States Olympic Committee ("USOC"), USA Cycling, USADA and the World Anti-Doping Code. As explained in this Motion, those rules — ignored in the Amended Complaint — also support USADA's jurisdiction over Armstrong.

32 the applicability of the Sports Act and settled case law which confirm that
33 (i) courts lack jurisdiction over controversies such as this, concerning athletic
34 eligibility, and (ii) Armstrong's only recourse is binding arbitration.
35   The rules applicable to Armstrong are the same rules applicable to every
36 other U.S. cyclist in the USADA registered testing pool (the "USADA RTP") and
37 are identical in material respects to the rules applicable to the nearly 3,000 U.S.
38 athletes from more than 40 Olympic [sports] in the USADA RTP. He attacks the
39 legal process establishing USADA's jurisdiction over the members of U.S. sport
40 national governing bodies ("NGBs"), a process repeatedly upheld by courts and
41 supported by the USOC, NGBs and athletes for more than a decade. USADA re-   F
42 spectfully requests that the Court reject Armstrong's effort to create a new set of
43 rules applicable only to him.[2]
                                                                                                G
_____

44   2. The Amended Complaint contains many inaccuracies and incomplete state-
45 ments. Exhibit 1 is a chart highlighting those inaccuracies.
                                                                                                H

A Each of the points mentioned in this example is explored in greater detail later in the motion. This Introduction, however, provides a strong example of how a motion should burst from the starting line: the entire dispute is laid out in the first paragraph. Concision is even more important in trial courts than in appellate courts because trial judges are often so awash in filings.

B The lawyers argue here that the court lacks subject matter jurisdiction. *See* Fed. R. Civ. P. 12(b)(1). This example comes from federal court; the procedural rules in state courts generally mirror these rules, but check state and local rules, as they vary somewhat across jurisdictions.

C This procedural move is commonly asserted in administrative cases. It alleges that a court lacks jurisdiction because the plaintiff has alternative steps that it must take before filing a lawsuit.

D This motion is basically two motions wrapped into one. The USADA asks for one form of relief (dismissal) *or* for an alternative remedy (staying Armstrong's lawsuit until the arbitration is complete). Motions may ask for multiple or alternative types of relief.

E The phrase "undisputed facts" usually appears in summary judgment motions rather than in motions to dismiss. I include this example precisely because it reflects the sort of aggressive advocacy in which skilled lawyers engage. The USADA found previous lawsuits in which Armstrong asserted that he was bound by USADA rules. By relying on court records from those lawsuits, the USADA smuggled into the motion materials that the judge could not otherwise weigh until a summary judgment motion. Even though courts cannot consider facts outside the complaint without risking reversal, it's hard for them to ignore facts like these in a motion to dismiss. Armstrong's past quotation will probably force Armstrong to lock himself into a position in his opposition brief: he will need to confront these bad facts, and the court's opinion can rely on his admissions. This sentence baits Armstrong into adding facts to the pile of what the trial judge can consider.

F WARNING! Using a lot of abbreviations tends to confuse readers. If you use abbreviations, try to space them out and keep sentences that use them very short.

G Even though this chapter is about motions rather than Introductions, notice how the lawyers advance their theme, which is that Armstrong is trying to get around the rules that apply to everyone else. And that's an especially clever theme in this lawsuit given the underlying misconduct of which Armstrong is accused: ignoring the rules that prohibit steroids. Several months after this motion was granted, Armstrong publicly admitted that he had used steroids throughout his racing career.

H This savvy approach — compiling errors in an Appendix — allows lawyers to point out the other side's misdeeds without focusing on them in the body of the motion. It also lets them register their disagreement with those facts without creating a factual dispute that, under Fed. R. Civ. P. 12(d), would convert this filing into a motion for summary judgment, which would entail discovery and delay.

Example	**Takeaway point 14.3:** Summary judgment motions should frontload key *undisputed* facts.
14.3	

The next example illustrates how to move for summary judgment. This passage appeared in a pregnancy discrimination case in which a female IBM employee claimed that, because she had become a mother, her supervisor withheld a scheduled $179,000 bonus to push her out of the company. IBM argues that any reductions in bonus compensation reflected cuts that affected its whole sales division, not bias against the plaintiff, and it emphasizes that key facts are, as required by the summary judgment standard, undisputed.

Source: Reply to Plaintiff's Opposition to Motion for Summary Judgment, *Gilmour v. IBM*, No. 2:09cv04155 SJO, 2010 WL 1340599 (C.D. Cal. Feb. 11, 2010).

---

1   Plaintiff focuses . . . on the "childless" "villain" Mary Webb, instead **A**
2   of addressing IBM's legal arguments. Such invective is unprofessional and
3   regrettable, but does not obscure the fact that this motion should be granted in **B**
4   its entirety. Plaintiff's tactics demonstrate one good reason why the summary
5   judgment procedure exists: to prevent claims with no legal merit from going to
6   a jury on the sole hope that Plaintiff can strike an emotional chord and provoke
7   a prejudicial recovery.

8   Plaintiff's opposition grossly mischaracterizes evidence, even to the point of
9   using ellipses to hide crucial portions of IBM policies on which she relies. Plain- **C**
10 tiff's opposition does clarify that the following **material** facts are undisputed:

11 ● This Court has correctly ruled there was no contract for IBM to pay com- **D**
12   missions to Plaintiff. The decision to reduce her commissions did not alter
13   her terms and conditions of employment, and it would not have made a
14   reasonable employee feel forced to resign.
15 ● Plaintiff was fully paid over $94,000 in commissions for sales in March,
16   April, and May 2007, all *after* she returned from maternity leave. The
17   grossly disproportionate $179,000 in commissions was to be paid for June
18   2007 sales, months after Plaintiff had returned from her leave. **E**
19 ● Three similarly situated men who reported to Mary Webb also had their
20   commissions reduced.
21 ● David Geras was one of these men. Like Plaintiff, he reported to both Jim
22   Cadenhead and Mary Webb. Like Plaintiff, he did not receive any of his
23   projected June 2007 commissions of $156,000. Unlike Plaintiff, he was
24   never pregnant and never took a maternity leave.
25 ● Plaintiff was paid more when measured by percent attainment of quota,
26   which is the method by which Webb reduced the commissions, than any
27   of her three similarly situated male colleagues reporting to Webb.

28 Plaintiff cannot avoid these facts. They dictate that she was not construc-
29 tively terminated, and that she cannot demonstrate a *prima facie* case of
30 discrimination or retaliation.

A The plaintiff violated an implicit rule of Chapter 1: *show* that your adversary is a villain, but do not use that pejorative label or else it might be thrown back at you and make you look unreasonable.

B Once again, we see evidence that trial motions are snarkier than appellate briefs. The word "regrettable" would have sufficed, but IBM's lawyers return that fire with the plaintiff's lawyers by calling them "unprofessional." I discourage this approach, but I don't want new lawyers to be blindsided by the tone that sometimes prevails in modern lawsuits. And as shown in the next annotation, this approach may be strategic.

C WARNING! When lawyers allege unethical conduct by an adversary, they should substantiate that allegation. This language — "grossly mischaracterizes" — again reflects how feisty name calling gets in trial courts. Alas, even worse insults are sometimes lobbed against opposing counsel, and many judges report that this sort of vitriol maddens them. But pointing out an adversary's misconduct in sharp language serves several strategic goals:

- signaling competence and hyper-diligence;
- coloring the judge's view of the adversary, even if judges don't *think* that they're being influenced;
- signaling to your adversary that your client does not want to settle; and
- diverting an adversary from landing its punches by luring it into a name-calling contest.

When deciding how to reply to a nasty comment, assess whether a spat between litigators will help your client. If you're representing a plaintiff and have the burden of proof, the answer is usually "no" because your task becomes more difficult when the judge is distracted by irrelevant skirmishes. By contrast, defendants tend to benefit if they can lure plaintiffs into a squabble about minutiae and the lawyers' behavior. As noted in the first annotation following Example 5.6, some judges report that these spats frustrate them and cause them to stop paying attention to the underlying arguments. That's the point.

D **Using bullets is an especially effective strategy for the first pages of a summary judgment motion, opposition, or reply. Summary judgment motions often turn on a handful of critical facts, so highlighting them early and prominently maximizes the chance that a judge will focus on the all-important facts that justify (or preclude) summary judgment. Emphasize that those facts are undisputed because summary judgment is unavailable if material facts are contested.**

E Notice that the defendant has stripped any actor from this sentence. In general, sentences should identify the actor and avoid passive verbs. Here, however, the dismal verb "was to be paid" reflects lousy writing but good strategy: it avoids saying something harmful such as "the bonus that *IBM promised* . . . ." Write well, unless there is a reason not to.

Example 14.4

Takeaway point 14.4: Adapt your motion to whatever legal standard applies.

The next example comes from another gender discrimination case — the largest class action ever tried in the United States. Approximately 6,000 current and former female employees sued a huge Swiss drug manufacturer for employment discrimination, alleging that Novartis demonstrated bias against female employees by (1) paying women less than men, (2) promoting them less frequently than men, and (3) discriminating against pregnant women. Here, the plaintiffs rely on their experts to fend off the drug manufacturer's attempt to win most of the case on summary judgment.

Source: Plaintiffs' Memorandum of Law in Opposition to Defendant's Motion for Partial Summary Judgment in *Velez v. Novartis*, No. 04 Civ. 09194 (GEL) (S.D.N.Y. May 7, 2009) (some citations omitted; table altered for simplicity's sake).

---

1   [D]uring the two years of class certification discovery and one and a half
2   years of merits discovery, Plaintiffs have obtained overwhelming documentary,
3   testimonial, and statistical evidence that demonstrates Novartis' culture of
4   discriminating against women. In addition to the seven regressions and three
5   statistical analyses in Dr. Lanier's three reports and the expert report of Dr.
6   Martin, Plaintiffs have produced the statements and/or testimony of ninety-six
7   class members and representatives, each of whom has suffered discrimination
8   at the hands of Novartis and each of whom tells a story that is striking in its
9   similarity to the others.   **A**

10   Novartis rehashes arguments from its opposition to class certification briefing
11   to bring the present "Motion for Partial Summary Judgment." [But] this Court
12   has already considered and rejected the precise challenges to Plaintiffs' evidence
13   Defendant raises in the instant Motion. Defendant's challenge to Plaintiffs' pay
14   disparity claims implicates a battle of the experts that this Court, in its Opinion
15   and Order granting class certification ("Opinion"), ruled is precisely the sort of
16   "statistical dueling" that "should be resolved by a factfinder." Op. at 28; *see also*   **B**
17   Op. at 29 ("the accuracy of [Dr. Lanier's] conclusion identifying classwide dis-
18   crimination presents a factual issue for trial"). . . .

19   There are significant statistical disparities in how Novartis compensates
20   women when compared to similarly situated men. Specifically, Dr. Lanier's anal-
21   yses of the pay disparities at Novartis between female employees and similarly
22   situated men revealed:

	Excess Dollars Paid To Men Per Month	Standard Deviations
Pay Disparity	$74.82	5.4

26   [T]he cornerstone of Plaintiffs' evidence regarding pay discrimination is Dr.
27   Lanier's analysis . . . .[7] Dr. Lanier controlled for differences in company tenure,   **C**

---

28   7. 5.4 standard deviations, which represents the odds of *a less than one in 15 mil-*
29   *lion chance* that the results are attributable to random chance, is more than sufficient
30   for a finding of liability in any court. *See infra* at III(B)(1)(a). . . .   **D**

31 tenure in a particular Novartis job, prior workforce experience, unpaid leave
32 taken in a year and paid leave taken in a year. Moreover, because of the way Dr.
33 Lanier designed the controls to allow for variations in the interactions of different
34 variables, his . . . regression actually controls for hundreds of variables which
35 might provide a non-discriminatory reason for the otherwise observable gender
36 disparities. . . .

37   Rule 56's directive that the evidence be viewed in the light most favorable to
38 the non-moving party and that inferences be drawn in favor of the non-movant
39 applies equally to statistical evidence as it does to other forms of evidence.   E
40 When evaluating statistical evidence, district courts should be wary of becoming
41 enmeshed in a battle of the experts. Disputes regarding appropriate statistical
42 methodology, control, or interpretation of results are "the sort of 'statistical duel-
43 ing' that should be resolved by a factfinder." *Velez, et al. v. Novartis Pharmaceu-*
44 *ticals Corp.*, 244 F.R.D. 243 (S.D.N.Y. 2007); *see also In re Joint E. & S Dist. Asbes-*
45 *tos Lit.*, 52 F 3d 1124, 1135 (2d Cir 1995) ("**Trial courts should not abrogate the**
46 **jury's role in evaluating the evidence and the credibility of expert witnesses by**
47 **simply choosing sides in the battle of the experts.**") (emphasis added); *Larson*   F
48 *v. Simond Indus.*, 337 F. Supp. 2d 331, 336 (D. Mass. 2004); *Victory v. Hewlett-*
47 *Packard Co.*, 34 F.Supp.2d 809, 824 (E.D.N.Y. 1999); *Munn v. Marine Midland*
50 *Bank. N.A.*, 960 F.Supp. 632, 641 (W.D.N.Y. 1996).

A Here and throughout the passage, the women's attorneys contextualize this motion by weaponizing procedural history, discovery, and prior rulings in the case. This context helps demonstrate how the plaintiffs have satisfied their burden for summary judgment.

B Just one month before this motion was filed, President Obama nominated to the Second Circuit the trial judge who had presided over this case for five years. The motion helps the new judge see that the defendant was trying to relitigate issues that the original judge had already resolved. This sort of command of the dispute's history illustrates what senior lawyers mean when they say that a junior lawyer "knows the case."

C Without lining up a skilled expert, without getting Novartis's data, and without slicing the data in a helpful way, the women's case might have been lost on summary judgment. A pay difference of 1 percent or 2 percent might look coincidental. But showing that the probability of this occurring randomly was 1 in 15 million (see footnote 7) saves the case. Trial lawyers need to battle to get helpful facts into the case.

D This passage helps the judge understand how these seemingly small pay disparities reflect bias: the chances that this pay disparity occurred randomly were infinitesimal. Another section of the brief reiterated this data and cited a Supreme Court opinion and a Second Circuit opinion to show, respectively, that "statistical evidence that supports the inference [of] discrimination" will overcome summary judgment and "refined statistical regressions . . . demonstrate disparities at a rate of 2.0 standard deviations or higher."

E Trial lawyers use boldface more than appellate lawyers — to ensure that judges don't miss key details.

F **After providing compelling statistical evidence of pay discrimination, the women's attorneys remind the court that their burden at this juncture is an easy one. It's always effective in dispositive motions to remind the judge about the standard of review, particularly when you (i) can link the standard of review to the particular type of evidence or claim at issue and (ii) convince the judge that, damn the standard, your client actually deserves to win. Here, the tiny likelihood that the pay discrepancy was random convinced the judge that the case should go to a jury.**

Example
14.5

Takeaway point 14.5: Nondispositive motions urgently need to frontload critical facts so that trial judges can assess the relevant issues quickly.

Nondispositive motions should help judges see quickly what the motion is about and why relief is appropriate. Introductions (discussed in Chapter 13) are especially important in nondispositive motions to help judges efficiently assess why they should grant or deny the motions.

In the next example, Milwaukee County brought a lawsuit for malpractice against Mercer, a financial consultant, over its role in advising the county about its pension plan for municipal workers. The complaint alleged that Mercer failed to warn the county of potential hidden costs — called the "backDROP" — which could cost the city $900 million more than it budgeted. The county alleged that Mercer's work thereby violated the Actuarial Standards of Practice (ASOPs). Mercer submitted expert testimony from Lauren Bloom, who claimed that Mercer fulfilled its legal obligations. Here, Milwaukee County moves to exclude Bloom's expert report.

Source: Plaintiffs' Brief in Support of Their Motion to Exclude Mercer's Expert Lauren Bloom in *Milwaukee County v. Mercer Human Resource Consulting, Inc.*, No. 2:06-cv-00372-CNC (E.D. Wis. Oct. 13, 2008) (some citations omitted).

---

1   Plaintiffs respectfully submit this brief in support of their motion to exclude
2   the testimony of Mercer's expert Lauren Bloom, a lawyer with no actuarial
3   training, skill, or experience — none — who nevertheless seeks to opine about
4   actuarial standards of care and tell the jury that "Mercer satisfied its professional
5   obligations under the Code and the ASOPs in this case" and was not "grossly
6   negligent." Bloom Report at 17. This Court should exclude Bloom from testifying
7   at trial for three independent reasons.

8   1. Bloom is not qualified and cannot testify competently about actuarial
9   standards and whether Mercer's work for the County met those standards.
10   Bloom is not an actuary and has no specialized knowledge or experience
11   concerning actuarial practice. Her purported expertise is based only on
12   her work as counsel for the American Academy of Actuaries, but her legal
13   work cannot substitute for actuarial skill.
14 2. Bloom's opinions are not reliable. They are unsupported bottom-line con-
15   clusions. They are based on Bloom's purported "common sense," not any
16   specialized knowledge, skill, or experience. And they are based on imper-
17   missible and unreliable credibility determinations.
18 3. Finally, Bloom seeks to offer impermissible legal opinions. Her testimony
19   would invade both this Court's role to determine the applicable law and
20   the jury's role to apply that law to the facts.

21 Indeed, Bloom has made some rather remarkable admissions that require the
22 exclusion of her testimony.   Ⓐ

23 • Bloom is not and does not consider herself qualified to opine on actuarial
24   practice. She testified that *"I'm not a qualified actuary, and I would defer*
25   *to a qualified actuary, particularly on the close questions."* She says it is
26   only "if something got *way outside the bounds* I might well be able to rec-   Ⓑ
27   ognize it." Bloom Depo at 86/16-20 (all emphasis in this brief is added).   Ⓒ

28 • Bloom seeks to tell the jury that "Mercer satisfied its professional obliga-
29 tions," but Bloom is not — by her own admission — "capable of looking
30 at an actuary's work and determining whether the actuary studying the
31 backDROP has acted reasonably and in conformance with accepted prac-
32 tice and the ASOPs." *Id.* at 89/13-22.

33 • Instead, *when asked about the backDROP, Bloom testified that "I would*
34 *be inclined to defer to an actuary on that particular point." Id.* at 89/13-
35 22. Hence, Bloom admits she is not competent to opine on one of the
36 central actuarial issues in this case.   D

37 • While Bloom seeks to opine that Mercer "took reasonable care to select
38 assumptions that in their professional judgment were reasonable," she
39 admitted that *"I have not seen their underlying work product, I can't*
40 *describe the process." Id.* at 143/7-19. . . .

41 Most damning of all, Bloom unequivocally admits that she is not qualified to
42 opine about Mercer's work on the backDROP benefit[:]

43 **Q** But within — let's take a less extreme example than someone embezzling.
44 Let's take an example of work on a — a backDROP benefit, okay? *Are you*
45 *capable of looking at an actuary's work and determining whether the*
46 *actuary studying the backDROP has acted reasonably and in conformance*
47 *with accepted practice and the ASOPs?*

48 **A** *I would be inclined to defer to an actuary on that particular point.*

47 **Q** *That's a no, right?*

50 **A** *That's a no.*   E

51 *Id.* at 89/12-22 (Exhibit B). . . .

52 In short, Bloom is not qualified to testify about actuarial standards and
53 whether Mercer's work for the County met those standards. Bloom's testimony
54 is not validated by sufficient (or any, for that matter) specialized knowledge or
55 experience to be competent and reliable expert testimony.

A Notice how the county's lawyers use Bloom's own concessions (from her deposition) to make their point. The judge doesn't want to get mired in factual disputes about the adequacy of an expert's qualifications. Using the expert's own description of her qualifications helps a judge to determine these issues. While block quotes are *generally* unadvisable, they are useful to show exactly what a witness said, especially when the key parts are emphasized.

B The motion steers the court to the exact page and line of Bloom's statement. Be aware that you must attach the relevant deposition testimony as an exhibit to a declaration that accompanies the motion.

C This clever move lets the lawyers avoid cluttering the remainder of their citations with "emphasis added."

D **Here, the lawyers focus the court's attention on a critical legal issue in the case and show how Bloom's testimony cannot assist the trier of fact in understanding that issue. This phrase reminds the judge what the case is about. The bullet points frontload the key information that the judge needs to resolve this motion.**

E The county's lawyers have presented a compelling argument that Bloom offers no value to this part of the case. The motion contained more than twenty *additional* pages of similar statements to undermine Bloom's comments about the backDROP and other parts of the case: a bit long for a nondispositive motion, but devastating.

| Example 14.6 | **Takeaway point 14.6:** Motions can be very, very short. |

You should perfect every motion you write because you are advancing not only your clients' causes but also your own reputation, which sloppiness or corner cutting will jeopardize. As you become more experienced, however, you will learn which motions need to be detailed and which ones can be very short. Nondispositive motions are usually shorter than dispositive motions — often *vastly* shorter. Why? These motions are abundant, and judges want to devote minimal time to them. Also, litigants often want a lightning-fast resolution of the motion; the shorter the motion, the faster a judge can resolve it.

Some motions even confirm the quip that "90% of success is just showing up." This principle was in full operation when a jury awarded more than $1 billion to Apple, which had alleged that arch-rival Samsung infringed its patents. Samsung's counsel knew that the jury had decided the case quickly — suspiciously quickly, which was likely an awful sign for Samsung. The speed also created a risk that the jury had, in its haste, made mistakes that Samsung might be able to exploit on appeal, but only if the jury clarified certain factual findings in its verdict form. Rather than simply waiting to see what the jury did, Samsung's lawyers raced into action and instantaneously asked the judge to force the jury to stay in court while Samsung reviewed the jury form. Keep in mind that Samsung filed this motion *before* the jury announced its verdict. The entire motion appears below.

Source: Samsung's Request for Thirty Minutes to Review the Jury Verdict Form Before the Jury is Dismissed for the Purpose of Seeking Clarification of Potential Inconsistent Verdict if Necessary, *Apple, Inc. v. Samsung Electronics Co.*, No. 11-cv-01846-LHK, 2012 WL 3633666 (N.D. Cal. Aug. 24, 2012).

---

1   *Introduction*

The verdict form in this complex case necessarily spans 20 pages and requires unanimous answers to more than 500 discrete questions across 5 different legal disciplines. (Dtk. No. 1890.) The likelihood of an inconsistent verdict is a possibility despite the jury's best efforts. Samsung respectfully requests thirty minutes to review the verdict form before the jurors are dismissed and the opportunity to determine whether it would be appropriate to seek clarification if an inconsistent verdict is reached. This will allow the parties and the Court to determine whether to seek clarification of any potential inconsistent verdict from the factfinders themselves, avoid waiver of potential inconsistent verdict arguments, and conserve the resources of the Court and the parties.

Samsung requested that Apple join in this motion. Apple declined.   **A**

Argument

The parties risk the possibility that any inconsistent verdict arguments may be deemed waived on appeal if not given sufficient time to review the verdict form for inconsistencies before the jury is discharged. *See Home Indemnity Co. v. Lane Powell Moss & Miller*, 43 F.3d 1322 (9th Cir. 1995) (holding that the district court "properly refused to amend the judgment because [the plaintiff] waived its objection to the jury's verdict on its contribution claim by not objecting to the alleged inconsistency prior to the dismissal of the jury").   **B** **C**

The parties and the Court here have expended substantial time, money, and resources to bring this case to verdict. Allowing the parties thirty minutes to identify any inconsistencies in the jury's verdict and the opportunity to seek

24 clarification from the original fact-finders will (1) give clarity to the verdict and
25 may avoid potential post-trial briefing on topics the jury could have easily rem-
26 edied if given the opportunity, and (2) allow the parties the time necessary to
27 object to the verdict in order to preserve those objections for any appeal. *See,*
28 *e.g., Duk v. MGM Grand Hotel, Inc.* 320 F.3d 1052, 1057 (9th Cir. 2003) ("We now
29 hold that where the jury is still available, a district court's decision to resubmit
30 an inconsistent [special] verdict for clarification is within its discretion.").
31   Thus, for all the reasons stated above, Samsung respectfully requests thirty
32 minutes to review the verdict form before the jurors are dismissed and the op-
33 portunity to determine whether to seek clarification if an inconsistent verdict is
34 reached.

D

A Remember that parties must confer before the movant files its motion.

B Samsung's lawyers demonstrate stellar advocacy here. Even though they are in the throes of trial and know that they have likely lost a huge verdict, they are still fighting to protect their client. They carefully refer to a "possibility" that the argument "*may* be deemed waived." This phrasing protects the company; on appeal, it could still argue that the issue has been preserved even if the judge denied this motion. This phrasing prevents Apple from stating that Samsung conceded that "the issue *is* waived." This sentence reflects how experienced lawyers develop the intuition — muscle memory — of when a phrase concedes too much or could be deployed against their clients.

C Apple declined to consent to this motion, probably to prevent Samsung from gathering information that would help it dismantle the jury award on appeal. Even though the jury had not announced its verdict, Apple expected to win; a blogger at the courthouse described Apple's counsel as "smiling" and "in a polo shirt" — confident and relaxed. Public records tell us when Samsung's lawyers filed this motion, but not when they *wrote* it. All of the likely possibilities are impressive: they may have planned to file this motion all along just in case the jury

award was adverse (good planning), or may have raced into action and filed the motion within minutes of learning that the jury was back unusually soon (good adaptation to an ominous sign). Either way, this short motion helped to strengthen Samsung's billion-dollar appeal. Filing it *fast* mattered more than anything else.

D Samsung probably debated whether to ask for more or less time. An hour might have sounded like an imposition on a jury that had labored for weeks and was ready to go home. Fifteen minutes might have provided too little time to review the twenty-plus-page jury form. Samsung also knew that the presiding judge was a no-nonsense jurist. (During the trial, for instance, Judge Koh responded to a motion to call witnesses by saying "Unless you're smoking crack, you know these witnesses aren't going to be called.") So Samsung's request was almost certainly a carefully calibrated remedy that adapted to its need, to the dispute, and (above all) to the judge. Did it work? Samsung's motion to keep the jury from going home hit the court's electronic filing system at approximately 3:20 p.m. The judge granted the motion at 3:22 p.m., allowing Samsung to gather the information it needed to help its post-trial motions and its appeal. The brevity of Samsung's motion helped it get a quick resolution.

Example 14.7

Takeaway point 14.7: At the trial court, you know who your judge is, so profile him or her and let your writing reflect that knowledge.

Trial lawyers usually know which judge will read their filings. As soon as a case is assigned to a trial judge, he or she (or a specific magistrate judge) typically resolves all further motions in that case. Use this knowledge to your advantage. Your adversary will. Research issues like these:

- In which subjects is the judge an expert (so that you know how much background to provide about the topic and how sophisticated your arguments can get)?
- How has she resolved similar cases in the past?
- Has she previously credited or praised any experts in the same subject as your dispute (so that you can hire them)?
- Which authorities in the subject of your dispute — including treatises and academics — have her past opinions relied on?
- What do the judge's past opinions tell you about her general jurisprudential views (which might affect the arguments that you raise and your willingness to settle the case)?
- In public speeches, what subjects did she talk about? Hunting? Human rights? Harry Potter? You can use analogies and anecdotes more effectively when you know what your judge likes and what she's interested in.

In other words, adapt your approach to your judge — the above questions are just a starting point.

This profile-your-judge approach was used successfully on behalf of a woman who was hounded by a debt collection agency. The woman (Hicks) filed a lawsuit against the company under the Fair Debt Collection Practices Act (FDCPA). She sought damages and an injunction to prevent the debt collector from calling her phone. The relevant statute prohibited collectors from engaging in various abusive and harassing "communicat[ions]" with consumers. The debt collectors, however, argued that they had not made "communications" with Hicks because they did not place the calls personally (they used an automated system) and because they had not spoken with Hicks (because the auto-dialer left only voicemail messages). Hicks's lawyers here counter the argument that no "communications" occurred.

Source: Plaintiff's Reply Memorandum in Support of Plaintiff's Motion for Summary Judgment from *Hicks v. Client Services, Inc.*, No. 07-61822-CIV., 2009 WL 2365637 (S.D. Fla. June 9, 2009).

---

1   Defendant claims that the voice mails it left for Ms. Hicks and the class mem- **A**
2   bers, which solicited return telephone calls to discuss their alleged debts, are not
3   "communications" under the FDCPA. Opposition, pp. 4-5. Although Defendant
4   points to one Court that found that a voice mail was not a "communication,"
5   this rogue opinion is contrary to the nationwide consensus that voice mails are, **B**
6   indeed, "communications."
7   The plain language Congress put into the FDCPA states that "'communica-
8   tion' means the conveying of information *regarding* a debt *directly or indirectly*
9   *through any medium.*" 15 U.S.C. § 1692a(2) (emphasis added). "'Communica- **C**
10 tion' is defined broadly." *Hollis v. Stephen Bruce & Associates*, 2007 U.S.Dist.
11 LEXIS 89683, *9 (W.D.Okla. 2007); *Foti v. NCO Fin. Sys*, 424 F.Supp.2d 643, 655
12 (S.D.N.Y. 2006). Given the FDCPA's broad definition of "communication," courts

13 | that have considered voice mails that are nearly identical to the message left by
14 | Defendant have held them to be "communications."

15 | Indeed, Your Honor does not need to go any further than your own recent
16 | opinion in *Berg v. Merchants Association Collection Division, Inc.*, — F.Supp.2d
17 | —, 2008 WL 4936432, Case No. 08-60660-CIV-DIMITROULEAS, DE 22 (S.D.Fla.,
18 | Oct. 31, 2008). Therein, Your Honor stated, "Courts generally consider pre-re-
19 | corded messages and voice mail messages from debt collectors to be 'commu-
20 | nications,' even if the messages do not state what the calls are regarding." *Id.*
21 | at p. 5. Your Honor cited *Belin v. Litton Loan Servicing, LP*, 2006 WL 2061340,
22 | 2006 U.S.Dist.LEXIS 47953, *12 (M.D.Fla. 2006), *Foti v. NCO Fin. Sys.*, 424
23 | F.Supp.2d 643, 655-56 (S.D.N.Y. 2006), and *Hosseinzadeh v. M.R.S. Assocs., Inc.*,
24 | 387 F.Supp.2d 1104, 1115-16 (C.D. Cal. 2005) in support of your conclusion. In
25 | *Belin*, the Middle District of Florida stated that even though the voice mails did
26 | not directly convey information about a debt, they were still communications
27 | "because they conveyed information about a debt indirectly, since the purpose of
28 | the message is to get the debtor to return the call to discuss the debt." *Belin*, 2006
29 | U.S.Dist.LEXIS at *12. In this case, like *Belin*, Defendant's voice mails conveyed
30 | information about a debt indirectly because they requested Ms. Hicks return the
31 | call to Defendant.

D

E

F

A Some writing professors believe that adding a salutation or title to a client's name makes him or her more dignified. This approach works sometimes, but don't always follow it. Assess whether the value justifies the increased wordiness. For instance, the salutation is usually worth including in a divorce case to avoid ambiguity or for someone like Hicks, whom you want to present as a dignified victim rather than as a someone who is avoiding her financial obligations (as the other side will try to depict her).

B Hicks shows one of the techniques that Chapter 5 explored: diminishing an adverse authority (rather than merely distinguishing it).

C Emphasize only the words in a document or authority that matter most. Here, the word "indirectly"

suggests that the communication can occur through a voicemail.

D Few authorities will be more convincing to a judge than cases he or she decided, but few techniques create a greater risk of seeming manipulative. Proceed, but do so carefully and respectfully.

E The motion reminds the judge that he *relied* on these exact cases, which is more persuasive than merely citing them.

F While this sentence is a bit long, it also manages to explain exactly what the case held in a way that likely resolves the issue in Hicks's favor. It also reminds the judge what the case held.

FREQUENTLY ASKED QUESTIONS ABOUT MOTIONS

Q. How long should my dispositive motions be?

A. While no empirical work has reported on the optimal length of various motions, here are some rough guidelines. A simple motion to dismiss or motion for summary judgment usually runs ten to twenty-five pages. A more complicated dispositive motion typically runs twenty to forty pages. A very complicated dispositive motion might exceed forty pages, but check the local rules to ensure that you comply with the page or word limit. Dispositive motions in complex federal cases sometimes devour fifty pages or more, including some behemoths that run several *hundred* pages. But those motions are outliers. Judges may resent such lengthy filings, so be sure that you truly need a whopper of a motion before moving for permission to file one. Oppositions to a motion usually mirror the length of the motion.

Q. How long should nondispositive motions be?

A. Try to keep your motions under fifteen pages; in general, shorter is better. Motions, however, can run anywhere from one page to one hundred pages (but both extremes are rare). At the short end, a motion can be just a page or two (see Example 14.6). By contrast, complex motions on major issues (such as striking a critical expert report, disqualifying opposing counsel, or compelling production of a wide array of documents) can easily run twenty to forty pages. They sometimes run longer, but proceed cautiously: judges value their time. A two- or three-page motion that thoroughly covers the issue conveys confidence and certitude, and it will please judges. Just realize, however, that supervising attorneys may want to see a longer, more exhaustive document, so a short document may make your boss think that you cut corners.

When the other side files a long motion, you may be tempted to respond with a comparably massive opposition, but resist or temper this urge. And never submit a 3,000 page document to a judge. *Cf.* Jenna Green, *ITC Judge Calls 3,000-Page Patent Fight Submission from Apple "Unacceptable,"* (May 8, 2012, 2:29 P.M.), http://legaltimes.typepad.com/blt/2012/05/itc-judge-calls-3000-page-patent-fight-submission-from-Apple-unacceptable.html.

Q. When I file a motion to dismiss based on a failure to state a claim, can I mention any facts that are not in the complaint?

A. Proceed cautiously, as your motion to dismiss may be treated as a motion for summary judgment if you dispute the other side's facts or introduce facts into the case that the plaintiff's complaint did not mention. The conventional wisdom about motions to dismiss is that defendants may steer the court only to issues "within the four corners of the complaint." That said, there are several exceptions that (subject to the local rules and case law) defendants may use to stretch the record on a motion to dismiss. These include (1) any attachments or declarations that accompanied the complaint; (2) records of which the court may take judicial notice (such as public government documents); (3) documents that are mentioned in the complaint, even if they are not attached (a rule called the incorporation by reference doctrine); (4) documents that the plaintiff relied on in bringing suit and that the plaintiff either currently possesses or was aware of when the case was filed; and (5) documents that both parties acknowledge to be authentic. Lawyers sometimes add additional facts for atmospheric background — and to influence judges — while being clear that those facts are not necessary to the resolution of the motion to dismiss.

Q. **How extensively should a given filing remind the court what the case is about?**

A. Lawyers tend to provide useful summaries to judges when they file dispositive motions. In nondispositive motions, however, lawyers tend to provide too little information to judges about how the issue fits into the case. For instance, when moving to compel production of documents, motions should help the judge see how the contested documents relate to the case. Instead, lawyers usually presume (incorrectly) that judges can infer why the movant needs those documents. To avoid these problems, motions should more frequently remind the judge what the case is about on the first page or two (either in the body of the document or in a footnote) and explain how the requested relief relates to the case as a whole. A notable exception applies when the judge has exerted special effort on the case and therefore is presumably familiar with it. For instance, if you file a motion mid-trial, you can safely assume that the judge knows what the case is about.

Q. **I'm part of a team writing a motion. I'm just writing a short section; how should I ensure that my colleagues can plug my section into the draft that they are managing?**

A. Many complicated briefs and motions are written by teams of lawyers. To maximize the likelihood that your portion can be added seamlessly, try to acquire and review the following documents: (1) the most recent complaint from the case so that you know what issues have been alleged; (2) samples of the lead author's work from earlier in the case (or a portion of his or her draft) so that you can mimic that lawyer's writing style and tone; and (3) a table of contents of the motion so that you know where your passage will be inserted. If you and your colleagues are opposing a motion, you will obviously want that document. In general, dull your style when you are writing as part of a team, as the group-writing process tends to remove colorful phrases, elaborate metaphors, and stylistic choices.

Q. **I know that this book is about written advocacy rather than trial practice, but are there any other important tips about writing motions that I should know?**

A. Court rules usually require parties to "meet and confer" before filing a motion. This duty requires lawyers to assess whether the other party (or nonparty) is willing to agree to the relief that the motion would seek. Lawyers usually need to certify to the court that they complied with this obligation. Your "motion" — which this book defines as a "trial brief" — will need an *actual* motion, which is a one or two page statement of the relief that you seek. You may need to jump through additional hoops when filing a motion, such as serving a "notice of motion" or preparing a draft order. And some state courts require parties to obtain the court's permission before filing a motion. Attach relevant declarations to your motion, and attach relevant exhibits to those declarations. And more generally, check the rules carefully before filing your motion, especially when you are appearing in an unfamiliar court.

Chapter 15

Specific Types of Appellate Briefs

Certain types of briefs raise distinct strategic challenges, so this chapter highlights those differences (some of which will help you when you write at trial courts, too). This chapter provides some specific tips about how to

- respond to an appellant's brief,
- prepare effective reply briefs,
- convince a court to hear your case when the court does not need to, and
- add value to a case when you represent an amicus curiae.

Attuning yourself to the nuances of each challenge is a hallmark of effective advocacy.

CHAPTER OVERVIEW

1. When you are the appellee, ensure that your brief advances your client's affirmative argument. Do not merely repeat the reasoning contained in the lower court's decision and hope that the trial court's decision will be affirmed on appeal. Rather, advance a positive argument that is customized to the appellate court that is hearing your case.
2. Be mindful of the standard of review, which is the level of deference that the appellate court gives to the court below. Some issues are reviewed anew. Other issues afford deference to the trial court or administrative agency.
3. Appellees should ordinarily include a Counterstatement of Facts to tell the story to the appellate court in a favorable way. Trusting the other side to fairly present the case's facts to the appellate court is naïve.
4. Reply briefs should be written so that judges can, if they want, read the reply *before* they read each side's opening brief. By the time the reply is filed, the crux of the dispute has usually revealed itself, which lets a reply brief focus on the issues that are likely to dictate the resolution of the case.
5. Cert petitions should try to show that the opinion that is being challenged will cause broad, recurring problems if it is not corrected. To oppose certiorari, show that a challenged opinion reached a sensible outcome on an uncommon issue on which judicial opinions are uniform.
6. Amicus briefs should not merely echo what the actual litigants say. Instead, they should provide a unique perspective or argument that the party itself lacks the expertise (or space in its brief) to offer.
7. If a major development occurs after the briefs are submitted, you may file a supplemental brief to advise the court about the breaking news.

Example 15.1

Takeaway point 15.1: When the other side filed its brief first, submit a counterstatement and point out which claims conflict with the jury's findings.

We have previously looked at Exxon's brief from the case in which that company's supertanker spewed oil into Alaskan waters. Here, the plaintiffs-respondents counter Exxon's version of what happened. Exxon claimed that its captain (Hazelwood) was sober when the accident occurred, that his instructions about how to steer the boat would have prevented the accident, and that Exxon behaved ethically by encouraging Hazelwood to get alcohol treatment. Examples 1.5 and 3.3 show Exxon's position. Here, the plaintiffs-respondents counter this version of the "facts."

Source: Respondents' brief in *Exxon Shipping Co. v. Baker,* 554 U.S. 471 (2008) (some citations omitted).

---

1   Respondents set forth the facts of this case as found by the courts below and
2   other governmental entities. . . . Exxon claims that some of these matters were
3   "hotly disputed"; points elsewhere to "Exxon's evidence"; and recites as "facts"
4   various snippets of friendly testimony. But the jury "plainly did not" interpret the
5   evidence according to the tale Exxon tells. Nor did the district court or the Ninth
6   Circuit in performing *de novo* due process reviews. More fundamentally, this is
7   not the place to argue about evidence that a district court observed over a five-
8   month trial and that it and a court of appeals already have examined, sorted, and
9   distilled from an immense record. *See Exxon Co., U.S.A. v. Sofec, Inc.,* 517 U.S.
10 830, 841 (1996) . . . .
11 Exxon Shipping Company ran Exxon's tanker operations out of the Port of
12 Valdez. An alcoholic culture pervaded the company. Supertanker crews partied
13 with alcohol aboard ship; drank together in port; "destroyed" confiscated liquor
14 by drinking it; and violated rules that forbade returning to duty within four
15 hours of drinking. Although on paper Exxon had an alcohol policy that prohib-
16 ited drinking aboard ship, it did not enforce the policy, and Exxon's crews were
17 "pretty conscious of" the fact that reporting alcohol violations by officers "could
18 come back to haunt you."
19 Exxon put Captain Joseph Hazelwood in command of the Exxon Valdez, one
20 of the thousand-foot supertankers that transited Prince William Sound. Hazel-
21 wood was a drinking alcoholic, and Exxon knew it. In 1985, Exxon officials
22 learned through internal complaints that Hazelwood had been drinking aboard
23 ship and had been drunk on several occasions when he boarded ship. Because
24 Hazelwood had not self-reported his on-duty drinking, Exxon's written alcohol
25 policy called for him to be fired. Exxon, however, did not fire him.
26 Hazelwood instead attended a 28-day alcohol treatment program and started,
27 but dropped out of, a prescribed after-care rehabilitation program. Neverthe-
28 less, after "fail[ing] to evaluate" his fitness for duty or "consider[ing] whether
29 he should be given a shoreside assignment," Exxon reassigned him to command-
30 ing supertankers. Hazelwood's supervisor held his back-to-work meeting while
31 enjoying a beer in a bar.
32 Less than a year after returning to duty, Hazelwood relapsed. He did not hide
33 his drinking. He drank — often with other Exxon personnel — "in bars, parking
34 lots, apartments, airports, airplanes, restaurants, hotels, at various ports, and
35 aboard Exxon tankers." He also ignored rules requiring him to remain on the
36 bridge while transiting Prince William Sound.

A

B

C

D

Hazelwood's supervisors promptly began receiving reports that he "had fallen off the wagon." The first report was relayed to the President of Exxon Shipping, who was told that "Hazelwood was acting kind of crazy or kind of strange."

Shortly before the official 1988 stewardship review for the Exxon Valdez, Hazelwood's supervisors, one of whom reported directly to the President, witnessed Hazelwood's relapse. Following a loud encounter in which Hazelwood was "erratic" and "abusive" toward his boss, the supervisor told another officer that "Joe had perhaps gone back to drinking because of his behavior." During the review meeting itself, the drunken Hazelwood, whose "physical appearance was very bad" and whose "eyes were bloodshot," fell asleep. The supervisor and his boss signaled the officer conducting the review to "just keep rolling . . . as if nothing happened."

"[T]he highest executives in Exxon Shipping" continued to receive reports concerning Hazelwood's drinking. Less than two weeks before the grounding of the Exxon Valdez, Hazelwood's supervisor was told that Hazelwood had been drinking and insulting another captain over the ship's radio. JA693-707, 727-35, 745-46. It was apparent that "[s]omething was wrong with" Hazelwood. As the district court summarized:

> For approximately three years, Exxon's management knew that Captain Hazelwood had resumed drinking, knew that he was drinking on board their ships, and knew that he was drinking and driving. Over and over again, Exxon did nothing to prevent Captain Hazelwood from drinking and driving.

c. On the night of March 23, 1989, the Exxon Valdez departed Valdez loaded with 53 million gallons of crude oil. Hazelwood was the captain and the only officer aboard licensed to navigate through Prince William Sound. Predictably, he also was drunk — "so drunk that a non-alcoholic would have passed out." Before boarding the ship, Hazelwood had consumed between five and nine double vodkas (between fifteen and twenty-seven ounces of 80-proof alcohol) in waterfront bars. . . .

A Exxon, in its opening brief, sought to revisit factual disputes that the district court already resolved. Here, the respondents fire back and prevent Exxon from escaping the pro-plaintiff findings from the trial. In other words, the plaintiffs subtly ask the Supreme Court to defer to the lower court (based on the standard of review that applies to factual findings).

B In *Sofec*, another accident occurred that involved an Exxon-owned oil tanker and a captain's negligence. The brief hints that Exxon is a repeat offender — a technique that Example 3.3 explored — but this approach is probably too subtle without a parenthetical.

C Exxon sought to show that the oil spill resulted from the unforeseeable negligence of a single employee. The respondents need to show that Exxon itself is liable, so this paragraph and the next one provide that critical information, observing that Exxon had an "alcoholic culture" and knowingly put a lapsed alcoholic in charge of its supertanker, even though its own policy called for him to be fired.

D The issue on appeal was whether the $2.5 billion punitive damages award against Exxon was excessive. A beer at a bar may seem insignificant, but this fact supports the finding of gross negligence, and shows that Exxon officials knew that Hazelwood was drinking again.

E Notice that the citations that follow this sentence could support either point — that Hazelwood was drinking *or* that he was insulting another captain. This common trick lets lawyers add multiple citations for a critical proposition (i.e., that Hazelwood was drinking and boating), even though most of the citations might support the innocuous point (i.e., that he insulted someone).

Example 15.2

Takeaway point 15.2: A reply brief should begin with an Introduction explaining why your client wins and why the other side's position is fundamentally flawed.

Let's turn to reply briefs. A reply is the appellant's last shot to make its case in writing. Your primary challenges in writing a reply are to rebuild arguments that the other side has attacked, to highlight any arguments that your adversary failed to counter, and to rebut your adversaries' arguments. In general, the reply brief should stick to arguments raised earlier in the briefing rather than present new arguments. But reply briefs often reframe or provide alternative justifications for arguments that the other side obliterated. Try to make these new positions *look* like you raised them before, even if they're largely new. And finally and perhaps most importantly, think of the Introduction in a reply brief as a closing argument of sorts — a chance to explain why, even in light of the other side's brief, your client should still prevail. We see this technique below.

This reply brief comes from a landmark First Amendment case. Citizens United is a nonprofit organization that wanted to display a Video On Demand movie that criticized Senator Hillary Rodham Clinton. A federal statute called the Bipartisan Campaign Reform Act (BCRA), however, prohibited corporations from using their general treasury to fund election-related communications within thirty days of a primary or sixty days of a general election. Citizens United challenged the law, arguing that political spending is a form of protected speech under the First Amendment and that the statute therefore violated the group's speech rights. We see here the beginning of its reply brief in its case against the federal government.

Source: Citizens United's brief from *Citizens United v. FEC*, 558 U.S. 310 (2010).

---

1 The government defends its effort to criminalize Citizens United's political
2 documentary by repeatedly invoking its authority, purportedly exercised "[s]ince
3 1907," to suppress political expression that might influence federal elections by
4 individuals who have organized themselves into corporations or labor unions.
5 FEC Br. 2; *see also id.* at 15.   A

6   If the government had started instead with the First Amendment's impera-
7 tive that "Congress shall make *no* law . . . abridging the freedom of speech"
8 (U.S. Const. amend. I (emphasis added)), it would have been forced to articulate
9 some compelling constitutional justification for prohibiting dissemination of a
10 90-minute movie by a nonprofit, ideologically motivated group concerning the
11 qualifications, character, and fitness of a candidate for the Nation's highest of-
12 fice. Because Citizens United's documentary engages in precisely the political
13 debate the First Amendment was written to protect, only a narrow restriction
14 carefully crafted to prevent actual or threatened electoral corruption could be
15 used to suppress it.

16   Yet nowhere in its brief does the government make any effort to advance a
17 remotely plausible theory as to how Video On Demand dissemination of Citizens
18 United's movie could have been a corrupting influence in last year's Democratic
19 Party presidential primaries. The government certainly does not even hint that   B
20 Senator Clinton's opponents might have been so grateful for Citizens United's
21 documentary movie that they might have been tempted to endow Citizens United
22 or its members with *quid pro quo* benefits.   C

23   Instead, the government rests its case on the simple but disturbing proposi-
24 tion that election-related speech by a union or corporation (unless licensed by

25 the government as an "*MCFL*" corporation or defined by the government as
26 "news media") is so inherently evil that it must be prohibited and, if attempted,
27 punished as a felony with a five-year prison term. The government's position
28 is so far-reaching that it would logically extend to corporate or union use of a
29 microphone, printing press, or the Internet to express opinions — or articulate
30 facts — pertinent to a presidential candidate's fitness for office.

D

31 Citizens United's documentary movie is condemned by the government as
32 the functional equivalent of express advocacy because it focuses on, and criti-
33 cizes, Senator Clinton's character, fitness, and qualifications for office. FEC Br.
34 18. Indeed, it is the government's position that the movie is to be suppressed pre-
35 cisely because it expresses a point of view on issues that bear upon a presidential
36 candidate's suitability for the Nation's highest office. That is a perverse basis for
37 pronouncing election-related debate unworthy of First Amendment protection.

38 It is the government's deep suspicion of election-related debate — not
39 Citizens United's efforts to participate in that debate — that "reflects a jaundiced
40 view of American democracy." FEC Br. 25. That cynicism is flatly incompatible
41 with any reasoned or historically grounded understanding of the First Amend-
42 ment. As applied to Video On Demand dissemination of *Hillary: The Movie*,
43 BCRA's criminalization of election-related debate plainly exceeds Congress's
44 sharply limited authority to abridge the freedom of speech.

E

A   A common move in a reply brief is to synthesize and reject the other side's view of the case. Citizens United uses this technique here, suggesting that the government's position boils down to an attempt to "criminalize" a "political documentary" that might "influence federal elections." Moreover, the first two sentences frame the dispute as a conflict between the core purpose of the First Amendment and an antiquated line of cases: This is an excellent way of presenting each side's vision of what the case is about in a way that favors Citizens United. And this 1907-case-law-versus-the-First-Amendment's-core-meaning paradigm reflects why some judges read reply briefs first. Namely, the reply spells out the key battleground between the parties — the crux of the dispute.

B   This is another common move in an appellee's brief or a reply brief: pointing out that the other party has failed to meet its burden. Just as importantly,

notice that the reply provides several hints of what the case is about, just in case any Justices or clerks decided to read this brief first.

C   The brief emphasizes that the government's brief omitted any evidence of one of the key traditional rationales for allowing restrictions on corporate speech — the risk of politicians improperly rewarding groups that helped them during the election.

D   A reply is the appellant-petitioner's best chance to point out the ramifications of the other side's argument. Here, Citizens United shows that the government's regulation of speech reaches too far, resulting in a chilling effect on other forms of communication.

E   Unless a point is truly, indisputably obvious, avoid terms like "plainly" and "clearly," which are lazy words. If the issue were actually plain or clear, the case would not require the Court's attention.

Example
15.3

Takeaway point 15.3: After explaining in an Introduction why your client should win, your reply brief should rebuild your client's arguments and rebut the other side's position.

After both sides have submitted their briefs, each side's arguments may lie in shambles, bludgeoned by the intellectual force of fine lawyering. A reply offers a valuable chance to restore order to the case by explaining why your client's arguments can withstand the other side's onslaught and why the other side's arguments fail. We see this technique below in an aggressive reply brief from a case we considered in Chapter 5: the City of Valdez taxed certain boats that docked in the city's port, and the tax fell exclusively on large oil tankers. Polar Tankers, which owned large oil tankers, challenged the tax, alleging that it violated the Tonnage Clause, which blocks states from discriminating against specific ships or shipowners.

Source: Shipowners' reply brief from *Polar Tankers, Inc. v. City of Valdez*, 557 U.S. 1 (2009).

1   The City's brief confirms the aberrational nature of its tax. Valdez is unable
2   to identify any other jurisdiction that imposes vessel-only discriminatory taxes,
3   let alone a judicial decision upholding such a tax. . . . The Constitution precludes
4   the imposition of a tax with such features.   A

5   I. THE VALDEZ VESSEL TAX VIOLATES THE TONNAGE CLAUSE.

6   The City wisely does not assert that its vessel tax may be justified under the
7   Tonnage Clause as a charge for services uniquely rendered to vessels.[1] Instead, it
8   hangs its case almost exclusively on the contention that property taxes are per se
9   exempt from scrutiny under the Clause, asserting that "this Court has never held
10 an *ad valorem* property tax to be an unconstitutional duty of tonnage." Resp. Br.
11 10; see *id.* at 15-23. The latter observation is correct as far as it goes; the Court
12 has never had occasion to strike down a vessel tax precisely like the one imposed
13 by Valdez. But the City omits the more interesting part of the story. This Court
14 also has never *upheld* a property tax that discriminates against vessels. Neither,
15 so far as we can determine, has any other court, ever. Indeed, we can find no
16 instance in which any other jurisdiction ever even attempted to *impose* such a

---

17   1. Although Valdez notes generally (Br. 5-8) that it undertakes certain municipal
18 activities because it is a port, it does not contest the trial court's finding "that the tax is
19 not one for specific services to the vessels." Pet. App. 29a. It hardly could; the Valdez
20 City Council was commendably candid in announcing that the tax was imposed to
21 offset a decline in the City's tax base and would be used "for the funding of the build-
22 ing of a hospital, school, and the needed repairs of city infrastructure and facilities."
23 *Id.* at 54a. As we noted (Br. 24-25), early congressional action confirms the under-
24 standing that a levy on vessels imposed to finance municipal improvements (there, a
25 South Carolina tax to finance construction of a seaman's hospital) is a tonnage duty   B
26 requiring congressional consent. Valdez responds (Br. 22 n.4) that the South Carolina
27 tax was imposed on the basis of tonnage. But this misses the point; the relevance of
28 the congressional action is its recognition that such a tax for municipal improvements
29 is not a user fee that escapes the Tonnage Clause. The form of the tax is immaterial;
30 as Valdez itself acknowledges, fees denominated by tonnage that *are* for services ren-
31 dered to vessels are not proscribed by the Tonnage Clause. *Id.* at 16 n.2.   C

32 tax. There is a reason why Valdez can find no parallel for its tax in more than
33 two centuries of state and municipal practice: its levy is manifestly inconsistent
34 with the Tonnage Clause.

D

35 A. Discriminatory Property Taxes Violate The Tonnage Clause.

36 The City . . . insists that a levy wholly evades review under the Tonnage
37 Clause if it is denominated a property tax, even if that tax is identical in amount
38 and practical effect to a duty falling on a vessel's tonnage. For several reasons,
39 Valdez's wolf in sheep's clothing must be turned away.

40 1. To begin with, the City's distinction is wholly inconsistent with the
41 Framers' unquestioned intent in adding the Clause to the Constitution. Valdez
42 declares that the Tonnage Clause is "seldom-invoked" (Resp. Br. 1), which is
43 true today. But two centuries ago, the Clause and its companion provision, the
44 Import-Export Clause, were of central importance to the Framers as a principal
45 response to the destructive interstate commercial rivalry that led to the failure of
46 the Articles of Confederation; Madison's graphic image of North Carolina as "a
47 patient bleeding at both arms" from the commercial depredations of neighboring
48 States reflected the seriousness of the Framers' concern. See Pet. Br. 13.

E

A The reply uses a very short Introduction to reiterate its main point: that a state tax that discriminates against certain boats is unconstitutional.

B Notice that the brief inverts the order of "Rule" and "Application" from the CRAC organizational strategy (discussed at the beginning of Part II of this book). This approach (declaring several facts from the case and *then* mentioning the relevant legal standard) is a good way to occasionally tweak CRAC so that your arguments don't take on a rote or repetitive quality.

C The reply walks through the critical exchange, explaining what Polar Tankers argued, how Valdez countered, and why Valdez is wrong. The language is hard to follow; see Chapter 16 for tips about clarity and simplicity, including that briefs should minimize the verb "to be" (which appears five times in the last two sentences of the reply's footnote 1). Notwithstanding the density of these sentences, this passage demonstrates how a reply can become one-stop-shopping for readers, allowing them to get up to speed on a case just from reading a reply brief.

D This stellar passage judo throws the respondent's brief: the Court has never invalidated this type of tax because this type of tax is so plainly unlawful that everyone knows better. Here the lawyers argue from an absence of evidence. When you make bold historical claims such as these, diligent research is critical.

E The reply uses a historical argument (see Chapter 10) and a vivid metaphor (see page 35) to show that the dispute is about more than just vessel taxes: it's about correctly interpreting a clause of the Constitution that was central to nationhood. The previous paragraph characterizes Valdez as being formalistic, suggesting that a bogus tax can survive just by placing it "in sheep's clothing." And here, Polar Tankers shows that the need to prevent discriminatory taxes matters — a policy argument (see Chapter 9) as shown by the need to save "patient[s]" from "bleeding at both arms."

Example
15.4

Takeaway point 15.4: When trying to convince a court to exercise its discretion to hear your case, focus on broad problems that the lower court's opinion will create unless it is reversed.

Appellate courts are required to hear some challenges, but not all. When these courts determine their own dockets, you need to convince judges to exercise their discretion to hear your case.

We see below some of the elements that affect a judge's calculus as to whether a case is worth reviewing. Xerox refused to license parts or patents to companies that repaired its copiers. It wanted to control the lucrative business of repairing jammed and busted copiers. A company called CSU wanted to compete against Xerox, so it filed a lawsuit claiming that Xerox's practices violated antitrust laws. After Xerox won on summary judgment and on appeal, CSU asked the Supreme Court to hear the case. The initial petition reflected a typical request to hear a case, beginning with this sentence: "This petition calls upon the Court to resolve a direct conflict among the courts of appeals over a recurring question of national importance. . . ." But the following example reflects the more-interesting and challenging task of getting the Court to hear a case after it asked for the Solicitor General's view and the Solicitor General advised the Court not to hear the case.

Source: Supplemental Brief of CSU in Support of a Petition for a Writ of Certiorari from *CSU L.L.C. v. Xerox Corp.*, 531 U.S. 1143 (2001) (some citations removed).

---

1   We agree with much of what the Solicitor General has said about this case.
2   Most importantly, we agree that "[w]hether the unilateral refusal to sell or
3   license intellectual property protected by a patent or copyright may constitute a
4   violation of Section 2 of the Sherman Antitrust Act . . . is an important issue that
5   may well warrant this Court's resolution. . . ." U.S. Br. 8. We likewise agree that
6   "[t]he court of appeals in this case rejected the Ninth Circuit's decision in [*Image*   A
7   *Technical Services, Inc. v. Eastman Kodak Co.*, 125 F.3d 1195 (9th Cir. 1997).]"
8   We agree that neither the Patent Act nor the Sherman Act should be construed
9   "as making patent holders immune from liability under Section 2" even when
10 they have "not engag[ed] in an express tying arrangement." And we agree that
11 Section 271(d) of the Patent Act "does not address antitrust liability for monopo-
12 lization or attempted monopolization by refusal to deal."
13 Yet like an O. Henry story, the Solicitor General's brief ends with a bizarre
14 twist. Rather than advocating that the Court resolve the important issue, the   B
15 Solicitor General says that this case is not the appropriate vehicle for doing so
16 solely because, in his view, "the Federal Circuit's opinion is susceptible of vary-
17 ing interpretations." As shown below, the sole predicate for the Solicitor Gen-
18 eral's position — his anomalous interpretation of the Federal Circuit's opinion
19 — is incorrect. As the Court can conclude for itself, the Federal Circuit did in fact
20 grant absolute antitrust immunity for unilateral refusals to sell or license mate-
21 rial subject to valid intellectual property rights — a holding that directly conflicts
22 with those of other circuits.
23 The Solicitor General's misreading of the opinion below is the only basis
24 for his position that this case is not the appropriate vehicle to address the con-
25 cededly important question presented. Accordingly, the Court should reject the
26 Solicitor General's suggestion that the confusion in the lower courts be allowed
27 to persist even longer.   C

28 It is noteworthy that the Solicitor General's brief does not purport to repre-
29 sent the views of the Federal Trade Commission, one of the two federal agencies
30 charged with enforcing the Nation's antitrust laws. As we have noted, the FTC
31 has taken enforcement positions that are at odds with the holding of the Federal
32 Circuit, and its Chairman has specifically criticized that holding. In the past
33 when this Court has asked for the views of the United States on issues affecting   D
34 antitrust enforcement, the FTC has joined the briefs filed by the Solicitor General
35 when it has agreed with them. . . . Yet the FTC is conspicuously absent from the
36 brief filed by the Solicitor General in response to the Court's invitation in this
37 case.

38 While we do not know the precise nature of the disagreement between the
39 FTC and the Department of Justice, the conflict between the Nation's antitrust
40 enforcers is yet another factor supporting certiorari. Whatever confusion exists
41 within the Federal Government can only add to the confusion that exists among
42 the private entities that must determine how to comply with the Nation's anti-
43 trust laws. Contrary to the Solicitor General's view, the solution is not to prolong
44 the confusion indefinitely. The solution is for this Court to grant certiorari in
45 order to bring uniformity to the law.
                                                                                              E
46 The myriad business transactions affected by the question presented in this
47 case demand nationwide uniformity in the law. It would be intolerable to any
48 businessperson — particularly one considering investing in or expanding [a]
47 service business — for that uniformity to await what the Solicitor General would
50 consider sufficient percolation. The conflict exists now. It is clear and direct. The
51 issue is concededly one of national importance. It was directly addressed by both
52 the District Court and the Federal Circuit. And there are no impediments to this
53 Court's reaching the issue. The petition should therefore be granted.
                                                                                              F

A The certiorari petition follows the classic strategy of trying to win before rebutting. The brief observes that the Solicitor General confirmed that the legal issue is important and that the case created a circuit split. The next two sentences in the brief discuss additional issues on which the Solicitor General agreed with the petitioner.

B This playful transition draws a clear line: the previous paragraph outlines the issues on which CSU and the Solicitor General agree, but now shifts into how and why they disagree. In addition to marking this shift, the sentence is designed to defuse the tension of disagreeing with the government by adding a bit of lightheartedness. The sentence also exemplifies that, when using cultural references, lawyers should provide a large hint so that readers will grasp the point even if they don't know the reference. That the phrase "ends with a bizarre twist" helps readers to grasp the brief's point whether or not they have read O. Henry's stories.

C This paragraph presents a stark choice: deny the petition and allow confusion to reign in the lower courts, or grant the petition and provide clear instructions to the judiciary.

D The brief emphasizes that the FTC's Chair has decried the lower court's opinion. Several hints suggest that something else is motivating the Solicitor General's "bizarre" position. The Solicitor General's brief opposing certiorari was filed in the final weeks of President Clinton's administration; the Department of Justice may have preferred to preserve the Ninth Circuit's anti-monopolist decision in *Image Techincal Services* rather than risk letting the incoming laissez-faire Department of Justice officials litigate this case at the Supreme Court.

E This paragraph presents another persuasive reason for granting certiorari: the administrative agencies charged with enforcing antitrust laws disagree on critical issues affecting enforcement.

F This conclusion emphasizes a number of common, traditional grounds that lead the Court to hear a case.

235

Example 15.5

Takeaway point 15.5: When you want to convince a court to decline to hear an appellate challenge, emphasize that the decision is sound and that it does not create a conflict among lower court opinions, and show that the issue rarely arises.

When you are opposing certiorari (or some other kind of discretionary appellate review), you want to be able to submit an argument like this one, which appeared in opposition to a petition for a writ of certiorari:

> This Court is not likely to see a less meritorious petition for certiorari on the regular docket this Term. The petition here embodies literally every factor that counsels against certiorari: it implicates no circuit conflict, it is entirely factbound, it is interlocutory, it involves state law issues, the decision below is non-precedential, and the questions ostensibly presented were neither pressed by petitioners below nor passed on by the court of appeals. Any one of those grounds is normally a good and sufficient reason to deny certiorari. This petition runs the table on all of them .

SAFG's Brief in Opposition from *Altus Fin. S.A. v. SAFG Retirement Servs., Inc.,* No. 09-1578, 2010 WL 4022692 (U.S. Oct. 8, 2010).

In the more detailed example below, Sony accused Joel Tenenbaum of ille-gally downloading songs. Instead of seeking actual damages, Sony sought statutory dam-ages for copyright infringement, which is permitted under federal copyright law. The jury awarded $675,000 to Sony, but the district court lowered the jury's award to $67,500 based on due process grounds. The First Circuit reversed this part of the decision, holding that the district court judge breached constitutional avoidance principles by reducing the award on due process grounds rather than on common law principles. It remanded the case to the district court, but Tenenbaum neverthe-less petitioned for certiorari to try to reduce his damages to zero. Here Sony opposes Tenenbaum's petition for a writ of certiorari.

Source: Sony's Brief in Opposition from *Tenenbaum v. Sony BMG Music Entertainment,* No. 11-1019, 2012 WL 1384653 (U.S. Apr. 18, 2012).

---

1   Petitioner Joel Tenenbaum is a willful and repeated infringer of Respondents'
2 copyrighted sound recordings who is on a crusade to avoid any responsibility for
3 his unlawful actions. In this latest effort, Petitioner presents this Court with a
4 series of splitless and meritless questions, many of which are unpreserved
5 and all of which are rendered uncertworthy by the interlocutory posture of his
6 petition. As is clear from his arguments and the unfounded assumptions upon   A
7 which they rest (as well as from the ongoing proceedings in District Court on
8 remand), Petitioner's real gripe is with the jury's decision to award Respondents
9 substantial statutory damages for the very real injury that his willful infringe-
10 ment inflicted. But the question whether that damages award passes constitu-
11 tional muster is neither presented nor ripe for review, as the lower courts have
12 yet to resolve Petitioner's remarkable claim that the jury's statutorily authorized
13 award is unconstitutionally excessive. If and when the lower courts resolve that   B
14 question, Petitioner will have his chance to convince this Court to review that
15 and any interrelated questions. In the meantime, the Court should deny this
16 interlocutory petition in its entirety. . . .

REASONS FOR DENYING THE PETITION

The questions presented in this interlocutory petition are all varying combinations of premature, splitless, and unpreserved — not to mention meritless. Petitioner's broad-ranging attacks on the scope and validity of section 504(c) of the Copyright Act are foreclosed by decisions of this Court reaching back nearly a century. For the most part, Petitioner simply ignores those binding precedents, as well as the wealth of lower court decisions that are equally fatal to his arguments. Indeed, Petitioner does not even attempt to identify any case law adopting any of the arguments he advances. Nor could he, as no such case law exists. Petitioner similarly neglects to mention that the Court of Appeals explicitly concluded that at least three of the arguments he now presses were not preserved. Moreover, every question he presents is premised on a bald assertion that the jury's statutorily authorized damages award is impermissibly "excessive." But Petitioner cannot and does not present that predicate question because the lower courts have yet to resolve his excessiveness challenge to the jury's award. That issue remains pending, after full briefing and argument, in District Court. . . .

Nor is [Tenenbaum's] question the subject of a circuit split. Indeed, the First Circuit is the only Court of Appeals that has ever addressed whether section 504(c) applies to the kind of infringement at hand. It is also not a question of recurring importance, as there is only one other analogous case pending in all of the federal courts. *See Capital Records, Inc. v. Thomas-Rasset*, Nos. 11-2820, 11-2858 (8th Cir.).

A In this aggressive, short introduction, Sony paints Tenenbaum as the villain, recasting the lawsuit as one man's quest to evade the consequences of his illegal activity. Facts matter — even at the Supreme Court.

B The procedural posture of the case is critical to Sony's effort to avoid review by the Supreme Court.

C Sony gives the Court an easy out: procedural grounds for denying certiorari. In opposing a cert petition, lawyers should try to make denial simple and compelling. If the petition is unripe and the arguments are unpreserved, the Justices can avoid the case without grappling with the underlying legal questions. The brief goes on to add several additional grounds for denying the cert petition, including that Tenenbaum's arguments are "meritless."

D In addition to the various procedural grounds for denying Tenenbaum's petition, Sony emphasizes that the Court has previously addressed the relevant legal issue. There is, therefore, no need for the Court to resolve Tenenbaum's arguments (because it has already done so).

E We see yet another argument based on a procedural defect in Tenenbaum's case: his arguments were not preserved.

F Courts are more likely to review problems that are major and recurring. The Supreme Court, for instance, is most likely to grant certiorari when the disputed legal issue (i) creates or exacerbates a "split" about the same legal issue (i.e., conflicting decisions among circuit courts or state supreme courts), (ii) recurs frequently or is enormously important, (iii) is already producing problems (such as forum shopping and inconsistent results), and (iv) involves a final judgment about an issue that is not fact-bound. In the above example, Sony showed that this issue rarely arises and that nearly all of these other factors disfavor granting certiorari, making the Justices more likely to think that this issue is unworthy of their time.

Example
15.6

Takeaway point 15.6: When you represent an amicus, your strongest move is often to present insights and perspective that the actual litigants lack.

Too many amicus briefs merely reiterate the arguments raised by the parties, a practice that some judges deride as submitting a "me too" brief (i.e., the actual litigant says what it thinks and the amicus essentially writes "me too!"). Briefs add more value when they provide a distinctive argument, and that argument will often rely on amici's expertise or unique perspective. Think carefully about what your amicus client knows that the litigants and the judges do not. Example 10.4 presented this technique: senior military officials explained why the armed forces needed affirmative action to run the nation's volunteer army effectively.

The same technique appears below. A company challenged the *Dr. Miles* antitrust doctrine, which prohibited companies from agreeing with their retailers to set a "floor" on the price that vendors charge for the company's goods. Such agreed-upon price floors, called "vertical minimum resale pricing," were per se illegal under the federal antitrust law called the Sherman Act. The golf equipment manufacturer PING filed an amicus brief to argue against the per se rule and to advocate a more lenient "rule of reason" standard, which would enable courts to examine vertical price agreements on a case-by-case basis. PING had unilaterally imposed price floors on its retailers *without* their agreement (making the policy legal); this brief explains what happens to vendors who sold products below PING's price floor.

Source: Amicus brief of PING, Inc. in *Leegin Creative Leather Products v. PSKS*, 551 U.S. 877 (2007).

---

1   PING, Inc. submits this brief *amicus curiae* to provide a unique, real-world
2   view of the extraordinary lengths to which a company must go to implement and
3   administer a vertical minimum resale pricing policy that complies with *Dr. Miles*
4   *Medical Co. v. John D. Park & Sons Co.*, 220 U.S. 373 (1911), and *United States*
5   *v. Colgate & Co.*, 250 U.S. 300 (1919). In 2004, PING unilaterally adopted, and   A
6   since has unilaterally administered, a vertical minimum resale advertising and
7   pricing policy, referred to as the PING "*i*FIT Pricing Policy." PING developed the
8   *i*FIT Pricing Policy to ensure that its retailers have the resources and incentives
9   necessary to service and custom fit consumers who choose to purchase PING's
10 golf products.

11 Since PING adopted the *i*FIT Pricing Policy in 2004, it has:

12 • Spent several million dollars to administer the Policy;
13 • Employed as many as 12 full-time people to administer the Policy;
14 • Unilaterally terminated nearly 1,000 PING retailers that violated the Policy
15   — retailers that had generated millions of dollars of revenue for PING
16   prior to their closures; and
17 • Strained its relations with PING retailers and the golfing community in
18   general through its enforcement of the Policy.
                                                                                              B

19 . . . Under *Colgate*, PING cannot discuss, without risk [of a price-fixing law-
20 suit], potential corrective measures with retailers, and it therefore enforces its
21 *i*FIT Pricing Policy by terminating all retailers that violate PING's unilaterally
22 set pricing terms — to its own detriment and that of retailers and consumers.
23 PING does not warn its retailers when it becomes aware of a violation; it does
24 not contact the retailer to investigate whether the violation was intentional; it
25 does not consider how long that retailer has been a PING account or the size
26 of the retailer's sales numbers. PING simply closes the account. In fact, PING   C

has closed accounts with nearly *one thousand* PING retailers during the past 30 months. PING sold millions of dollars of golf equipment to these retailers the year before their closures.

As indicated, PING makes no exceptions in the administration of its *i*FIT Pricing Policy. . . . For example, PING closed the account of the country club in Phoenix once owned by PING, and which still serves as the home club of many PING employees, including its CEO and Chairman of the Board. PING also closed the accounts of several golf retailers located on military bases. These termina- **D** tions led to significant negative media attention in outlets as varied as Golfweek, USA Today and The San Jose Mercury News.[10]

. . . Companies like PING that adopt resale pricing policies for procompetitive purposes should not be forced to damage their relationships with retailers and consumers, and limit consumer choice, in order to avoid risking per se liability. A better alternative, one that is consumer-oriented and market-driven, is to change existing law to apply the rule of reason to vertical minimum resale price agreements to allow companies like PING to enter into pricing agreements with retailers that would involve negotiation and the free flow of communication between a manufacturer and its retailers.

We acknowledge and appreciate the Court's reluctance to overrule existing precedent, but the rule of stare decisis should not serve as a roadblock to common sense. *See, e.g., State Oil*, 522 U.S. at 20-21 ("[s]tare decisis is not an inexorable command. . . . Accordingly, this Court has reconsidered its decisions concerning the Sherman Act when the theoretical underpinnings of those decisions are called into serious question. . . .") (quotation and citation omitted). Where, as here, the very purpose of the antitrust laws is thwarted by precedent that is economically obsolete, the Court should not be reluctant to order a change. **E**

---

10. *See, e.g.*, "Pings pricing policy sparks PR fiasco," http://www.golfweek.com/pro/pro-other/287239709880948.php.

A   The first sentence sounds the theme of the brief: companies must go to "extraordinary lengths" to comply with the Court's doctrine. The brief immediately presents its distinctive value to readers to grab their attention: this sort of aggressive marketing of a brief's usefulness is necessary for amicus briefs, which are often skimmed or ignored.

B   The list signals that PING took the Court's doctrine seriously and invested money and human capital in compliance. That builds credibility and good will. Then the last two bullets show the negative consequences of compliance. This list sets up the transition to PING's critique of *Dr. Miles* and *Colgate*.

C   Notice how powerful a short sentence is after a long one. Pay attention to the rhythm of your writing, as discussed further on pages 250-51.

D   Once again, PING uses its unique knowledge (of which retailers it terminated) to inject facts into the dispute that the other side cannot cross-examine PING about. Amicus briefs add power when then add facts and specialized knowledge. The Supreme Court cited PING's brief favorably in overruling *Dr. Miles*.

E   Amici can more aggressively call for the overruling of a precedent than litigants. They should be sure that they do not undermine their ally's goals (such as by saying that a case *needs* to be overruled when the actual litigant says that the case can be distinguished). Try to confer with the party's counsel to learn its key arguments. Likewise, if you line up amici, think about which groups will help your cause and how to make sure that they do not inadvertently sabotage your case.

FREQUENTLY ASKED QUESTIONS ABOUT BRIEFS OTHER THAN THE "OPENING" BRIEF

Q. I see that most briefs require me to include a section that discusses the standard of review. Is that section perfunctory? And do all of the issues need to be governed by the same standard?

A. The standard of review is *very* important. It controls how the appellate court will assess what the trial court did. For instance, *de novo* review means that the trial court's decision gets no deference, whereas the "clearly erroneous" standard and the "abuse of discretion" standard cause appellate courts to give more latitude to trial courts. As you might suspect, empirical research confirms that appellate courts that apply *de novo* review are far more likely to reverse a lower court than appellate courts applying more deferential standards.

Each issue in your brief may be governed by a separate standard. And if a single issue raises multiple subissues, each of them might be governed by a different standard. You might decide which issues to appeal based partly on how they implicate the standard of review. Bear in mind, too, that parties sometimes argue in the alternative over the standard of review, suggesting (for example) that the appellate court should apply *de novo* review, but that the trial court's order should be vacated even if the appellate court applies the "clearly erroneous" standard.

Q. Should I always file a reply?

A. Basically, yes. Your adversaries are likely to raise at least one decent argument or to assert at least one incorrect fact, so you will usually want to counter what they submit (and, thereby, get the final word).

Q. Is a reply *really* the final word? Can I respond to a reply?

A. Some courts permit parties to file "surreplies," either by rule or with the court's permission. Exercise this prerogative only when necessary. Some courts, such as the Second Circuit, effectively ban surreplies, reflecting the judges' conviction that lawyers already submit too much paper.

Q. Should I always file an opposition to a petition for discretionary review, such as a cert petition?

A. No, you can refrain from filing an opposition if you conclude that no justice would find the case meritorious enough to hear. Also, at least at the Supreme Court of the United States, the Court won't grant certiorari without asking the respondent for its views. In state supreme courts, check the local rules to see whether you must — or may — oppose a petition for review. In federal *en banc* cases, the court of appeals will usually tell the appellee if it wants to receive an opposition to a petition for a rehearing *en banc*.

Q. If I'm writing an appellate brief, where do amici come from?

A. Some nonparties will hear of the case and will involve themselves in the case as amici. But you may also *recruit* amici. Thinking about which perspectives can help your client's cause and (as the saying goes) "lining them up" is an important part of good appellate advocacy. Remember that various ethical rules will govern what you can discuss with amici; in general, you can tell amici what your brief will argue, but you may not tell them what to write. Check amici's past positions because your client will be accountable for what its "friends" say. Amicus briefs often work best when they line up unlikely allies. As examples, an oil company will benefit if it has environmental groups as amici, just as an environmental group will benefit if it has oil companies as amici.

Q. What happens if I represent amici that have a view that differs from either party?

A. That's fairly common. You submit an "amicus brief in support of neither party." That caption signals to the court that you are advancing a position that differs from what either party is arguing. If, however, you support one side's conclusion (but you favor an alternative rationale), you may still support that party.

Q. Do all appellate courts follow the same rules?

A. Not at all — even within federal courts, there's great variation. For instance, an appellee must typically file its brief within thirty days. *See* Fed. R. App. P. 31(a)(1). But some courts alter the deadlines significantly. *See, e.g.,* 4th Cir. R. 31(a) ("the appellee shall serve and file appellee's brief within *twenty-one* days") (emphasis added). Many lawyers in the Fourth Circuit have suffered nausea (and awkward calls with clients) when their briefs were rejected for being untimely filed. Similarly, local rules differ on whether amici need permission to file, on the formatting of briefs (e.g., the Seventh Circuit dictates which *fonts* may be used), and so on. State appellate rules vary even more significantly.

PART IV

GENERAL WRITING ADVICE

Chapter 16

The *Writing* Side of Legal Writing

Most of this book focuses on the word *legal* in "legal writing" — challenges such as the art of building arguments and of weaving a client's facts into a story that compels a favorable legal conclusion. This chapter, however, focuses on the writing itself. It synthesizes many of the principles reflected in the examples that this book reprinted.

As you read those examples, you probably liked some and disliked others. Some examples probably seemed crystal clear to you. Others forced you to work harder. And if you're like most readers, you preferred the easier ones. As Daniel Kahneman (winner of the Nobel Prize in Economics) has observed, our brains have two "Systems" for processing information. "System 1" handles the easy tasks, and we're happy when we use it. We feel smart, life is easy, we can relax. In the language of psychology, "cognitive ease is associated with good feelings."[1] In other words, we like it when our brains aren't overworked.

But watch out when someone forces you to use System 2 — or when you force a judge to use it. System 2 deals with the tough stuff. When System 2 is triggered, your pulse quickens. Your breathing changes. Your muscles tense. Activating System 2 causes you to become "vigilant and suspicious,"[2] and it creates a risk that you'll "overload" your brain.[3] System 2 usually makes readers ornery.

But this Nobel Prize–winning theory is, as one might suspect given Kahneman's findings, oversimplified. The two Systems actually lie on a spectrum, as reflected in Table 1.

Table 1. Spectrum of Sentence Complexity

VERY EASY	EASY	DIFFICULT	VERY DIFFICULT
Two witnesses saw the crime.	Two witnesses, Allen and Cruz, each testified that Brody shot the victim.	Janice Allen, an accountant who works in St. Louis and was visiting Miami for a conference, and Juan Cruz, a dermatologist who has 20-20 vision, each testified that, on or around June 20, 2013, at 9:17 p.m., she or he, respectively, observed Brody's commission of the act.	Facts sufficient to acquire conviction pursuant to the statutory elements embedded within Section 782.04(1)(a) of the Florida Code were adduced upon the sworn testimony of witnesses who respectively were visiting from St. Louis for a conference and a dermatologist in possession of functionally perfect vision and who each from personal observation of the events provided confirmation that the commission of the statutorily relevant act was deliberately committed by Brody on or around Thursday, June 20, 2013, at approximately 9:17 p.m. at the northwest corner of Washington and 17th St.

---

1. Daniel Kahneman, *Thinking, Fast and Slow* 66 (2011).
2. *Id*. at 60.
3. *Id*. at 35.

Table 1 hints at the most important principle about how to convey your ideas: *your biggest writing challenge when drafting a brief or motion is to translate and synthesize your client's story and position into absorbable, engaging prose.* Or, to put this point in Kahneman's language, you need to help judges use System 1 (simple, happy) rather than System 2 (complicated, stressful). Your main job as a stylist is to ensure that readers grasp what you're saying. But you can't oversimplify the case or you'll omit critical information, as the "Very Easy" sentence in Table 1 demonstrates. So, while you'll know that you've become a competent lawyer when you can grasp complicated legal doctrines, you'll know that you've become a great legal stylist when you can explain complicated legal doctrines and complicated fact patterns precisely, simply, *and* persuasively.

CHAPTER OVERVIEW
1. Keep sentences short, averaging between seventeen and twenty words apiece. If you are struggling as a writer, keep *every* sentence to twenty-five or fewer words.
2. Vary the structure of your sentences to avoid making your prose monotonous.
3. Use topic sentences that clearly foretell what each paragraph will address.
4. Use strong verbs — especially monosyllabic verbs. And limit your use of passive verbs and nominalizations (former verbs that have mutated into nouns).
5. Avoid causing RAM problems for your readers. (RAM is a computing term.) A RAM problem occurs when you overload a reader's ability to process information.
6. Clear your writing of clutter and stylistic blunders. Thus, avoid clichés, wordy phrases, Latin and French phrases, abstract terms, throat-clearing phrases (e.g., "in my opinion"), and intensifiers (e.g., "very" and "highly").
7. Use "signposts" frequently to signal how a sentence relates to the sentence that preceded it (or to hint at what the next sentence will say). (Signposts are words that direct traffic in a sentence, such as "Therefore," "First," or "Although.")

There's more, of course. Some authors write entire books on legal style. But this chapter's tips will strengthen your writing quickly and reliably. And when you combine these pointers with your study of the examples in this book, you will soon be writing beautifully — *and* in a way that wins cases for your clients.[4]

---

4. The twelve tips that follow appear on the inside cover as Writing Tips 1 through 12.

TIP 1   **Write short sentences.**

Good writers control the length of their sentences. It would be silly, of course, to decree that *all* good writing averages *X* words per sentence; too many successful writers disregard this limit to defend a strict word count. But concise legal writing is rarely *bad* legal writing because brevity reduces the risk that your writing will irk or confuse readers. And judges report that they prefer documents that contain short sentences.[5] So give judges what they want.

Why is brevity so valuable? As the brilliant Karl Llewellyn explained (as shown in Appendix A), "[t]he Simple appeals, it is easy to follow, it persuades." By contrast, empirical studies show that writing verbosely makes writers sound *dumber*, not smarter.[6] The simple act of shortening sentences hones your prose, clarifies your points, keeps readers interested, and makes it easier for you to spot problems in your legal analysis. So, in general, keep sentences short. To minimize the risk of confusing readers (and to maximize the likelihood of pleasing them), average seventeen to twenty words per sentence.[7]

To reach my recommended words-per-sentence average, you can and should write some miniscule sentences. Others, of course, can be much longer. As we saw earlier in the book, you may *want* some sentences to be lengthy (to hide bad facts, to vary your prose, or to overwhelm readers deliberately with a long list of information).[8] More generally, however, avoid long sentences. You may sometimes catch yourself

---

5. *See , e.g.,* Sean Flammer, *Writing to Persuade Judges*, 90 Mich. B.J. 50 (Sept. 2011) (conducting a test to see whether judges preferred writing samples that averaged 17.8 words/sentence over similar samples that averaged 25.2 words/sentence and finding that 66 percent of judges preferred the revision with shorter sentences.

6. Daniel M. Oppenheimer, *Consequences of Erudite Vernacular Utilized Irrespective of Necessity: Problems with Using Long Words Needlessly*, 20 Applied Cognitive Psychol. 139, 156 (2006), *available at* http://web.princeton.edu/sites/opplab/papers/Opp%20Consequences%20of%20Erudite%20 Vernacular.pdf (finding, through five distinct tests, that "needless complexity in a text negatively impacts raters' assessments of the text's authors" — or, put another way, that trying to sound smart usually backfires).

7. This figure reflects a midpoint among writing experts who have advised lawyers how long their sentences should average. *See, e.g.,* Gerald Lebovits, *Sentences and Paragraphs: A Revisionist Philosophy*, 77 N.Y. St. B. Ass'n J. 64 (Jan. 2005) ("Strive for an average length of 15 to 17 words."); Mark Painter, *Appellate Practice — Including Legal Writing from a Judge's Perspective* 7, *available at* http://www.plainlanguagenetwork.org/Resources/appellate.pdf ("Keep sentence length to an average of no more than 15-18 words."); Joseph Kimble, *Lifting the Fog of Legalese: Essays on Plain English* 71 (2006) (encouraging lawyers to average 20 words per sentence); Bryan A. Garner, *Legal Writing in Plain English* 58 (2001) ("[Y]ou should have some thirty-five-word sentences and some three-word sentences, as well as many in between. But monitor your average, and *work hard to keep it to about twenty words.*") (emphasis added); *cf.* Richard C. Wydick, *Plain English for Lawyers* 36 (5th ed. 2005) ("[T]he average length of your sentences should be *below* twenty-five words.") (emphasis added).

8. Here's an example of the overwhelm-your-reader-intentionally approach, courtesy of Justice Antonin Scalia, who was rejecting the suggestion that a legislator's decision to vote for a statute reflected an intent to advance religion:

> In the present case, for example, a particular legislator need not have voted for the Act either because he wanted to foster religion or because he wanted to improve education. He may have thought the bill would provide jobs for his district, or may have wanted to make amends with a faction of his party he had alienated on another vote, or he may have been a

thinking, "this idea is complicated, so I need to use a long sentence." Wrong. You need to shorten that sentence precisely *because* it's complicated. If it's hard for you to write your idea in a digestible way, then readers will almost certainly struggle to grasp your point. Also, buff longer sentences until you're sure that readers will comprehend them.

For some lawyers, I'll go even further: if your boss doesn't like your writing, restrict every sentence to twenty-five or fewer words. That's right. *Every* sentence. That tip represents your best chance to quickly improve your boss's impression of your writing.

This twenty-five-word-limit — which will sound radical to some readers — produces remarkable results for struggling writers. Simply by keeping sentences under twenty-five words, writers ensure that they comply with many of the principles of good style. They hack wordy phrases, cut passive verbs, and limit the number of ideas in any single sentence, among other salutary changes. The results tend to thrill clients and supervisors, both because complying with the twenty-five-word-limit causes writing to sparkle and because short sentences are *vastly* easier for them to edit.

A friend who teaches undergraduates complained to me that her students' written work was incomprehensible. I suggested my rule to her, and she imposed it on her class. When she next saw me, she was beaming, and she explained that the trick had rendered a miracle, "especially for weaker students, the ones who don't have a built-in sense for what a good sentence looks like." I asked her to describe the improvements in her students' work. She explained that her undergraduates — like young lawyers — "stuff in thousands of dependent clauses and meaningless qualifiers in the mistaken hope that this will make us admire their prose." The twenty-five-word rule, she explained, "shows them that what they *want* to write is actually what I want."

Try it. You might like it. Your boss almost certainly will. (And yes, colons and semicolons reset the twenty-five-word limit.)

TIP 2   **Control the number of messages per sentence.**

Even a short sentence can be hard to absorb when it conveys too much information. For example, many readers will struggle to process this sentence, even though it contains only twenty-three words: "On Tuesday, experts inspected the car owned by Cohen that was in the accident west of Grove Street at 1:15 a.m. in Fresno."

Limit, then, both the number of words *and* the number of messages in your sentences. To achieve this goal, you may want to split a sentence. In particular, watch out for sentences with many prepositional phrases; the above example about Cohen's car

---

close friend of the bill's sponsor, or he may have been repaying a favor he owed the majority leader, or he may have hoped the Governor would appreciate his vote and make a fund-raising appearance for him, or he may have been pressured to vote for a bill he disliked by a wealthy contributor or by a flood of constituent mail, or he may have been seeking favorable publicity, or he may have been reluctant to hurt the feelings of a loyal staff member who worked on the bill, or he may have been settling an old score with a legislator who opposed the bill, or he may have been mad at his wife, who opposed the bill, or he may have been intoxicated and utterly unmotivated when the vote was called, or he may have accidentally voted "yes" instead of "no," or, of course, he may have had (and very likely did have) a combination of some of the above and many other motivations. To look for the sole purpose of even a single legislator is probably to look for something that does not exist.

Edwards v. Aguillard, 482 U.S. 578, 636-637 (1987) (Scalia, J., dissenting).

uses *on*, *by*, *in*, *west of*, *at*, and *in*. When you use multiple prepositions, place the critical detail at the end of the sentence to signal that fact's importance and to make it easier to flow into the next sentence.

TIP 3

Vary sentence structure.

Even as you follow my advice to write short sentences, beware of one grave risk. If every sentence resembles every other sentence, your prose will grow dull, sound robotic, or convey anger. Sometimes you'll want to sound cold, and a series of short sentences can convey your displeasure. For instance, the following example arose after a lawyer (named Bob) sent around a firm-wide email trumpeting his firm's victory for the National Football League's Washington Redskins in a lawsuit filed by a group of Native Americans; the Native Americans had objected to the Redskins' name. In response to the victory email, an associate hit "Reply All" and sent a critical, rambling message to the *entire* law firm. One of the firm's other partners sent this icy response to the associate:

> We have not met. I am in the NY office. I sit down the hall from Bob. Calling Bob out in front of the entire firm is a poor use of the "reply to all" function. Note the lack of any parentheses in this email. It makes it much easier to read.
>
> Bob and I represent clients, not causes. We like Native Americans. If Native Americans had hired Bob, the Redskins would have lost the case. But they didn't. They hired someone else. So it was incumbent on Bob to kick their ass in court. It is really that simple.[9]

Most of the time, however, you won't want to sound so contemptuous. You can easily defend your prose against that risk — and keep readers engrossed — by varying your sentence length and structure and by adding an occasional long sentence amidst the short ones. (And for those of you who want to try the strict twenty-five-word-limit, yes, even a twenty-five-word sentence can seem long and complex if many of your other sentences contain just six to fifteen words.)

Tip 1 emphasized that brevity will help almost any writer; Tip 3 reminds lawyers that variety is just as important as brevity. Table 2, which spans the next two pages, shows a dozen common ways to vary your sentences (accompanied by illustrations from a hypothetical post-trial motion to dismiss an indictment).

---

9. *See* Kashmir Hill & Elie Mystal, *Quinn Emanuel Associate Has Reservations About "Redskin" Victory*, Above the Law, May 19, 2009, http://abovethelaw.com/2009/05/quinn-emanuel-associate-has-reservations-about-redskin-victory/.

Table 2. Twelve Ways to Vary Sentence Structure

	TECHNIQUE	EXAMPLE
1.	Use a basic, simple sentence.	The government claims that Smith stole classified documents.
2.	Use an "independent marker word" (also called a "signpost") to tweak the basic structure of a simple sentence (e.g., *but, nor, yet, also, consequently, furthermore, thus, however, moreover, nevertheless, therefore*).	The evidence, however, overwhelmingly suggests otherwise. And that evidence requires dismissal of the indictment.
3.	Add a dependent clause to your sentence — at the beginning, in the middle, or at the end.	Although the government called nineteen witnesses during a two-week trial, none of these witnesses alleged that Smith took documents from the Department of Defense. The witnesses testified that the leak jeopardized troops in Afghanistan because the documents discussed future troop movements.
4.	Add a list to your sentence.	But the witnesses did *not* finger Smith as the culprit or suggest that he was a rogue employee. To the contrary, four of the government's witnesses testified that they knew Smith, trusted Smith, and believed that Smith would "never steal classified information." These witnesses included a four-star general, two ambassadors, and a U.S. senator.
5.	Use a relative pronoun (such as *who* or *which*).	The general, who supervised Smith for six years at the Pentagon, testified that Smith "was a loyal employee who probably couldn't have downloaded the highly encrypted documents if he'd wanted to." And the senator's committee, which investigated the leak, concluded that "foreign hackers, not Smith, breached Pentagon security and stole the classified documents."
6.	Use punctuation (e.g., colons, semicolons, em dashes).	Moreover, the government's three experts each offered testimony that exonerated Smith: that Smith's computer would bear some sort of "marker" if Smith had downloaded classified documents, but that — as each of them admitted during cross-examination — Smith's computer was "clean as a whistle."
7.	Link two sentences together by using one of the seven coordinating conjunctions, which form the mnemonic FANBOYS (*for, and, nor, but, or, yet, so*).	These experts found "convincing" and "well substantiated" Smith's evidence that the documents had been downloaded to a computer located in a section of the Pentagon to which Smith had no access, and they agreed that "someone else probably downloaded the documents."
8.	Use a rhetorical question (but use this technique sparingly).	So what evidence suggests that Smith stole classified documents?

	TECHNIQUE	EXAMPLE
9.	Use a sentence fragment (but use this technique even more sparingly). (Examples: *Wrong*, *Absolutely*, *Incorrect*, *False*, *Untrue*, *True*, *Nothing*, *None*; avoid snarkier examples like *Hogwash*, *Balderdash*, and *Nonsense*.)	One document.
10.	Use an occasional long sentence. (Often used to bury bad facts or law; to build up momentum, such as by listing a slew of helpful details; or to set up a very important sentence that follows.)	But this document, in which Smith merely joked that he "wanted" to leak sensitive information to the press, was inadmissible hearsay, was written more than three years before the classified documents were actually leaked to the media, and contained the following, critical sentence immediately after Smith's imprudent but innocent comment: "I would never actually leak documents, though."
11.	Use a present participle to extend a sentence.	The cumulative evidence bars any reasonable jury from convicting Smith, making a directed verdict wholly appropriate.
12.	Use bullet points.	Smith should not risk prison — for three decades — given the following uncontested facts: • no one testified that Smith downloaded or divulged classified information; • the government's witnesses doubted that Smith could have downloaded the documents; and • three government experts concluded that Smith's computer was not the source of the leak.

You can and should combine the approaches presented in Table 2, and you should also develop others. The above list is merely a starting point in the taxonomy of sentence structure. (I use fairly colloquial descriptions of sentence structure rather than the more formal language of grammarians, which deploys terms like "compound" and "complex" sentences.)

One other key tip about varying your sentences deserves some attention. Many legal writing professors encourage writers to begin each sentence in a paragraph with the same subject to improve comprehensability. But that approach can also make writing sound overly simplistic, as in this real example from a top law firm:

First, **Thompson** indisputably suffered an injury in fact, having been dismissed from a position as a metallurgical engineer which he had held for seven years. **Thompson** was unemployed for a year after that dismissal. **Thompson** and Regalado were married shortly after his termination, and had to live apart for nearly a year when **Thompson** was forced to move to another city to find comparable employment. **Thompson** testified that the resulting forced separation from his wife was a "huge hardship for our marriage." The injury to **Thompson** was not an incidental and indirect consequence of some economic harm done to Regalado. Precisely to the contrary, it was **Thompson** himself who suffered the immediate injury caused by the retaliatory dismissal; injuring **Thompson** was the means by which the employer sought to punish Regalado. "[T]he harm [to **Thompson**] was the intended consequence of the unlawful practice (albeit an intermediate harm in path to the ultimate goal of harming Regalado). . . ." Pet. App. 58a (White, J., dissenting); see Pet. App. 51a ("North American Stainless harmed **Thompson** in order to effectuate this retaliation [against Regalado]") (Moore, J. dissenting). **Thompson** clearly has a concrete interest in the monetary and injunctive relief sought in this action.

To prevent Thompsonitis, use pronouns (e.g., "he" instead of "Thompson"), combine sentences, and use a different subject from time to time — often enough to spruce up your prose, but infrequently enough that readers can easily follow the story.

Finally, let me offer one additional comment about my suggestion in Table 2 that you use bullet points to vary the shapes and sounds and structure of your sentences. Some readers get nervous about using bullets, which strike them as too reminiscent of corporate writing.

Get over it. Bullets are used often (and effectively) by a huge number of top advocates. Ross Guberman's stellar *Point Made* compiles numerous examples of the nation's most famous advocates using bullets in the nation's highest courts.[10] Bullets let you emphasize key information and make it possible to list multiple, similarly designed sentences consecutively without causing your prose to sound rote. Just to illustrate that top lawyers use this technique, an example follows. It comes from a brief filed by a team of Supreme Court specialists who asked the Court to invalidate Indiana's voter identification law:

> According to the State, the factual basis for the voter identification law is the risk Indiana faces from in-person voter identification fraud. Given that, the following uncontested facts bear repeating:
>
> - The State has not identified even a single instance of voter impersonation fraud occurring at the polls in the history of Indiana.
> - No Indiana voter has ever been charged with any crime relating to impersonation fraud in in-person voting.
> - No evidence of in-person impersonation fraud was presented to the Indiana legislature when it was considering the challenged legislation.
> - No such evidence was presented in this litigation.[11]

So use bullets, but even more importantly, remember the key point of the above Tip: ensure that your sentences don't all resemble one another.

TIP 4   Use strong topic sentences that match the contents of the paragraph.

A topic sentence expresses a paragraph's main idea. It usually comes at the beginning of a paragraph.

Well, that statement is inaccurate: topic sentences *often* get omitted from paragraphs, either by accident or to avoid sounding repetitive. Yet that omission, especially in legal writing, can weaken your prose. Sharp topic sentences help readers, persuade readers, and ensure that your points appear in the right place within your document.

---

10. Ross Guberman, *Point Made: How to Write Like the Nation's Top Advocates* 228 (2011); *see also* Bryan A. Garner, *The Winning Brief: 100 Tips for Persuasive Briefing in Trial and Appellate Courts* 289-290 (2d ed. 2004).

11. Petitioner's reply brief from Crawford v. Marion Cnty. Election Bd., 553 U.S. 181 (2008).

Think of each topic sentence as a jurisdictional statement for that paragraph. It tells you what the rest of the paragraph will discuss. If the rest of the paragraph strays, you need to revise either your topic sentence or the rest of the paragraph.

Perfect topics sentences make it possible to read *only* the first sentence of each paragraph and still follow the argument. The first sentence of each paragraph implicitly says, "I will prove the claim that I make in the topic sentence." The rest of the paragraph does so — except that the last sentence might remind the reader what the paragraph just proved. So is it really possible to follow an entire argument merely from the topic sentences? Sure. Appendix B contains a sample passage that contains spectacular topic sentences. As you will see, those sentences allow readers to follow the author's argument simply by reading the first sentence of each paragraph.

You don't need, however, to be *that* obsessive about topic sentences. As with any other writing tip, your prose will become rote if you follow this suggestion too vigilantly. In your Statement of Facts, you may omit topic sentences lest they sound like unsubstantiated rhetoric. Even so, each paragraph in a Statement of Facts should have some logical break from the paragraphs that precede or follow it. In your Argument, however, most paragraphs should have a topic sentence that foretells what you're about to prove.

TIP 5   Use strong verbs, especially monosyllabic verbs.

This tip shares one of the secrets of good writing that most writing books overlook: the value of short, strong verbs. Books about writing typically warn readers what to *avoid* — and I do that, too. But avoiding bad choices won't make you an elite writer, just as avoiding Doritos and doughnuts won't make you an elite runner. You need to do something affirmative. You can't just resist the bad stuff.

So here's a secret: use vivid verbs, especially one-syllable verbs. There's magic in monosyllabic verbs because they are easy to comprehend and tend to please readers' ears. I love some longer verbs — *auger, dragoon, dwindle, plummet, renege, tether,* and many others — but I want to encourage you to pay attention to the punch that short verbs add to your prose.

Look back at Example 1.7, which I praised for its brisk pacing, and you'll see that most of the verbs are monosyllabic. That's no coincidence. Here's an excerpt from that passage in which I mark each monosyllabic verb:

> As Detective Murray ***stopped***, he ***saw*** that the defendant ***had*** his sweatshirt or coat ***wrapped*** around his right hand near his right hip. Detective Murray ***yelled*** to the defendant, "***show*** me your hand." At that point, and for the first time, Detective Murray ***raised*** his gun and pointed it at the defendant. The defendant then ***pulled*** his right hand out from under his clothing. As he ***did***, Detective Murray ***saw*** that the defendant ***had*** a silver revolver in his hand, which the defendant ***raised*** and pointed at Detective Murray; the defendant's finger ***was*** on the trigger. Detective Murray ***yelled*** "gun" to alert his fellow officers that the defendant ***had*** a weapon.

This paragraph, which is among the most engaging I've ever read in a brief, uses fifteen monosyllabic verbs. Do you really think the short verbs deserve none of the credit for the passage's success? (It also averages just sixteen words per sentence.) Strong verbs plus short sentences usually equals good prose.

Table 3. Typical verbs vs. monosyllabic Verbs

TYPICAL VERBS	MONOSYLLABIC VERBS
In June 2012, King's company **maintained** inventory in an amount that **equaled** $13 million. The inventory, however, was **consumed** by a fire at the warehouse. King at all times **remitted** full and proper payments to her insurer, SafeHands, Inc. SafeHands, however, **provided** King in a letter **dated** August 17, 2012, written notification that SafeHands would not **disperse** reimbursement as a result of a preexisting hairline gas leak that it had **reported** to King previously but that King allegedly **declined** to **repair** as of the time of the fire.	In June 2012, a fire **ripped** through King's warehouse. Everything **burned**. At the time, King **stocked** $13 million of office equipment in her warehouse. She had **paid** her premiums fully, so she **lodged** a prompt claim with her insurer, SafeHands, Inc. But SafeHands **balked**, alleging that it had **warned** King about a gas leak that King **failed** to **fix**.

And to see how verbs improve one's prose, consider the two versions of hypothetical fact pattern shown in Table 3. The version on the left reflects typical legal style. The one on the right uses a number of monosyllabic verbs.

I want you to revel in the power of short verbs, so I've built a list more than 2,000 options for you in Appendix C. But don't worry, the purpose of my list isn't to nag you into cutting every long verb. I just want to arm you with a list of verbs to make you think about the sound of your words.

If you use strong verbs — without overdoing it — your prose will improve. You can use the basic verbs from Appendix C's list nearly as often as you want: *want, take, find, act, clear, lead*. Avoid weak verbs (such as *seem* and *be*) unless you need to lean on those words. I recommend, however, that only one or two rarer monosyllabic verbs grace each page. (Those are the friskier verbs, such as *bilk, blind, cramp, dwarf, drown*, and *doom*.) If you use these verbs too often, readers will grow cloy to their charms.[12]

Try not to leash your verbs to a preposition. As the great stylist William Zinsser observed, "We don't face problems anymore. We face *up* to them when we can free *up* a few minutes." He then added, "Writing improves in direct ratio to the number of things we can keep out of it that shouldn't be there. 'Up' in 'free up' shouldn't be there."[13] Some of the verbs on my list tend to be stalked by prepositions — *bog down* and *glom onto* and *home in*. They're still better than most alternatives, but strive to find even leaner verbs.

In general, avoid both slang and extremely colloquial verbs that appear on the list.

Finally, realize that some of these verbs swell into two syllables when you use their past-tense form. For instance, "I *boarded* a plane and *acted* calm, even when the flight attendant *swatted* my phone from my hand." So be it. This version is still better than "I

---

12. Novelist Ray Bradbury's work exemplifies the risk of using too many strong verbs. The following passage comes from *Something Wicked This Way Comes* (1962). I have italicized the monosyllabic verbs:

> We *salt* our lives with other people's sins. Our flesh to us *tastes* sweet. But the carnival doesn't *care* if it *stinks* by moonlight instead of sun, so long as it *gorges* on fear and pain. That's the fuel, the vapor that *spins* the carousel, the raw stuffs of terror, the excruciating agony of guilt, the scream from real or imagined wounds. The carnival *sucks* that gas, ignites it, and *chugs* along its way.

13. William Zinsser, *On Writing Well* 12 (7th ed. 2006).

participated in the boarding of the plane and *attempted* to *appear* unnerved, even when the flight attendant *deployed* the back of his hand to *remove* my phone forcibly." When possible, use monosyllabic verbs (and past-tense verbs).

| TIP 6 | **Use verbs instead of nominalizations.** |

Watch out for verbs that have mutated into nouns. These words are called nominalizations, which are former verbs that have devolved into nouns or gerunds.[14] These words consistently drain vitality from prose. And they hide the identity of the actor, as in this sentence: "A violation [*of what? by whom?*] occurred."

Look at the italicized nominalizations in this example:

> There was not a *signing* of a contract with ZYX to commence the *production* of widgets, but that fact does not prevent the *binding* of the parties based on the *actions* that occurred later.

Notice how much more easily you can absorb the sentence when you convert the nominalizations back into verbs and specify *who* is acting:

> CBA *agreed* to *make* widgets for ZYX, but those two parties did not *sign* a contract. Under state law, however, the oral agreement binds both parties because of how they subsequently *acted*.

Good writers train themselves to eradicate most nominalizations. These words often end in *-tion*, *-ence*, *-ing*, *-ent*, or *-ess*, so shun the *-tion*, dispense with *-ence*, ding the *-ing*, and so on. But other nominalizations are stealthier, so try to convert into a verb most nouns that obscure an actor's identity. The word "of" and the verb "to be" (and variations of that verb like "is" and "was") often mark the presence of nominalizations. For instance, "The *goal* of the legislature was to prevent *waste*" could be changed to "Congress *wanted* to ensure that the military *wastes* less money."

Nominations, however, have some valid uses. For instance, it's fine to use legal terms of art that contain nominalizations: "Defendant filed a *motion* to dismiss is an acceptable alternative to "Defendant *moved* to dismiss the case." And sometimes you'll *want* to hide the actor's identity, such as when your client committed an "unlawful interrogation" or "a violation." Thus, it's much better to say "no one was hurt during the *robbery*" than "no one was hurt when my client *robbed* the bank." Use nominalizations to obscure your client's misdeeds. Similarly, you might use a nominalization to summarize what you just discussed, as in this example: "Jane paid Juan. This *payment* . . . ."

These narrow exceptions, however, don't change the general principle: avoid nominalizations.

Remember that *present participles* look like gerunds, but they are perfectly good words, as in this example: "The client paid the bill, *acknowledging* that her lawyers had provided superb legal services." Present participles act like verbs. But the same word — "acknowledging" — acts as a nominalization in this sentence, which contains three nominalizations: "The *acknowledging* of the client that the *provision* of services was superb led it to make *payment* on the bill." Most top writers would remove the nominalizations from that sentence.

---

14. Gerunds end in *-ing* and function as nouns. For instance, "The *filing* [*of what? by whom?*] occurred in early 2013."

| TIP 7 | **Avoid passive verbs.** |

Passive verbs are wordy and often hide the identity of the actor in your sentence. "I was tickled" uses a passive verb that hides the identity of the tickler. It is not as interesting or as concrete a sentence as "Owen tickled me." Readers want to know who acted. So tell them (unless there's a good reason not to). Scour your writing for passive verbs and convert them into active verbs.

Passive verbs often use "is" or "was" followed by verbs that end in -*ed* or -*en*. Thus, "My client *was arrested* and *beaten*" contains two passive verbs. Instead, emphasize who wronged your client: "Officer Wilson *arrested* John and *beat* him with a police baton."

Passive verbs have some legitimate uses. For instance, you should introduce familiar information before you introduce unfamiliar information, even if doing so requires you to use a passive verb. For example: "In 2012, this Court followed *Myers*. But *Myers was subsequently overruled* by the Overturn Myers Act of 2013." The word "*Myers*" is familiar information; it should therefore appear earlier in the second sentence than the new information, which is the unfamiliar statute that overturned *Myers* — even though doing so requires you to use a passive verb (see generally Tip 8 below). You should also use a passive verb when you want to hide the agent's identity or when you don't know who acted. Unless you have compelling reasons to use passive verbs, however, avoid them. More often than not, their presence reflects undisciplined writing.

| TIP 8 | **Place familiar information before unfamiliar information.** |

This tip and the next three offer advice about how to avoid RAM problems, which refers to a sentence or idea that confuses readers or that overtaxes their brains.

The first of these tips is to tell readers what they already know before you tell them something new. This is the cognitive equivalent of what happens to most people when they walk into a crowded room. If they immediately see a few friends, they calm down. But if they see a slew of unfamiliar faces, most people will be anxious and uncomfortable. Likewise, your briefs and motions will make judges comfortable if your sentences greet them with old friends — familiar information.

But not all information is familiar, so how do you make unfamiliar information familiar? Explain it — *after* you mention information that is already familiar to readers. This "familiar to new" principle means that you should generally frontload familiar information (both within a given sentence and among the sentences that comprise a paragraph). This principle also requires that you explain new concepts *immediately* after using them or, better yet, that you introduce a new concept *before* you use the term for that concept.

For instance, compare the two passages that appear at the top of the next page. Unfamiliar information is italicized; familiar information, or information that is explained a split second after it is used, is boldfaced. Thus, passages should be easier to read if there's more bold, sooner. Notice that the confusing version of the Statement places familiar information near the end of the paragraph or the end of a given sentence; conversely, the clear version frontloads familiar information, both within sentences and within the paragraph.

Table 4. Frontload Familiar Information

NEW TO FAMILIAR (CONFUSING)	FAMILIAR TO NEW (CLEAR)
ChipCom's claims will be shown in this opposition to be incorrect because the *XB-427b* is not *prior art*. *CVX* invented the *XB-427b*. *ChipCom* argues that the *XB-427b* is *prior art*. The plaintiff in this case is **CVX**. Palo Alto, California, is where **CVX** is headquartered. The microchip that uses less energy than other chips and thereby lets computer batteries last up to 70 percent longer is the **XB-427b**. Looking at what information was public when a patented object was created and only upholding a patent that innovated on that information is the doctrine of **prior art**.	**CVX** is a technology company in Palo Alto, California. In 2011, **CVX** invented a revolutionary microchip that uses less energy than other chips and thereby lets computer batteries last up to 70 percent longer. **CVX** obtained a patent to protect **this microchip**, which is called the **XB-427b**. **CVX's patent on the XB-427b**, however, has been challenged by CVX's competitor, **ChipCom**. **ChipCom** alleges that the **XB-427b** did nothing new; **ChipCom** claims, in other words, that the **XB-427b** failed to improve upon the "**prior art**" — the information that was already public when a patented object was created. ChipCom thus alleges that CVX's patent is invalid. CVX will show that its patent is valid and that ChipCom's motion for summary judgment should be denied.

Few things confuse or frustrate readers more than when they do not recognize or understand words and concepts. Thus, be sure to adequately explain unfamiliar terms, parties, names, cases, doctrines — anything new.

Keep in mind, too, that some terms, even if you explain them, will *never* be familiar to a generalist judge; more specifically, using a barrage of abbreviations will confuse and annoy even the most talented jurists. For instance, one prominent judge blasted the litigants for using too many abbreviations: "Here," he wrote, "both parties abandoned any attempt to write in plain English, instead abbreviating every conceivable agency and statute involved, familiar or not, and littering their briefs with references to 'SNF,' 'HLW,' 'NWF,' 'NWPA,' and 'BRC.' . . ."[15] Avoid alphabet soup.

TIP 9 **Place the sentence's subject and principal verb near the beginning of the sentence.**

Readers can most easily absorb an author's point when sentences flow from short bundles of information (which are easy to absorb) to long bundles of information (which are harder to absorb). For instance, many readers will struggle to absorb this sentence: "The legislation that Congress enacted in response to the financial crisis that, in 2008 and 2009, nearly derailed the banking system will be signed by President King." Pretty tough, right? But if you place the short bundle of information — "President King" — at the sentence's beginning, the sentence becomes much easier to digest: "President King will sign legislation that Congress enacted in response to the financial crisis that, in 2008 and 2009, nearly derailed the banking system."

Lawyers often place long bundles of information too early in their sentences. This problem tends to occur in three distinct ways. First, "left-handed" sentences place too many words before — to the left of — the first principal verb. These sentences, then, use very long preambles, such as in the following hypothetical sentence:

---

15. Nat'l Ass'n of Regulatory Utility Com'rs v. U.S. Dept. of Energy, 680 F.3d 819, 820 n.1 (D.C. Cir. 2012) (Silberman, J.).

Although there are several factors that could support a contrary conclusion, including that GVK agreed to provide Illinico with twelve months of labor, that it agreed to install, test, and service the nuclear reactor, and that the parties agreed that Illinico would offer consulting services to address Illinico's questions about the reactor, this Circuit treats this sort of contract as . . .

The italicized preamble that precedes the subject ("this Circuit") and principal verb ("treats") contains fifty-two words! We all use long introductions when we speak, but we can do better in our prose. Long preambles make it hard for readers to follow your reasoning, and this sort of writing causes data absorption problems for readers because you hurl too much information at them. To avoid this problem, reach your principal verbs quickly so that readers know where your sentences are heading. A short preamble to a sentence is safe and often denotes good style. But the longer you force verbless readers to wander unguided in a sentence, the more likely you are to lose them.

Second, refrain from weighing down your nouns with modifiers. If you attach too many modifiers to a noun, readers will struggle to absorb your point. For instance, it is easy to absorb this sentence:

The investment adviser filed for bankruptcy.

But once you add more information about the adviser, the sentence becomes much trickier, as shown in this example (in which I italicized the sentence's 41-word subject):

The investment adviser who had embezzled money from his employer's parent company, made false representations to investors in more than thirty states, and refused to speak with SEC investigators when they approached him in July about his role in the embezzlement filed for bankruptcy.

At a minimum, place the lengthy bundle of information at the end of the sentence (even if you need to use a passive verb). Thus, this revision of the prior example is easier to absorb:

The investment adviser embezzled money from his employer's parent company. He then made false representations to investors in more than thirty states and refused to speak with SEC investigators when they approached him in July about his role in the embezzlement. Several weeks later, he filed for bankruptcy.

As we see above, breaking a lengthy subject into smaller bundles of information makes prose easier to absorb. This technique will sometimes require using two sentences to convey your point, and that's perfectly fine.

Third and finally, good writers avoid word gaps between either (i) subjects and principal verbs or (ii) verbs and objects. The following example contains a long word gap (which I have italicized) between the subject ("contract) and the principal verb ("is"):

The contract, *in spite of the fact that GVK agreed to provide services such as installing, testing, and servicing the nuclear reactor for twelve months*, is a sale of goods rather than a contract for services.

Periods, semicolons, and subordinate clauses are indispensable ways to frontload the subject and verb. For instance, this revision uses a subordinate clause to downplay the bad information:

The contract is a sale of goods — not a contract for services — *even though GVK agreed to install, test, and service the reactor for twelve months.*

All three of the points in this tip relate to the same goal, which is to ensure that readers can easily absorb the information that you present to them. To achieve this goal, keep your subject and principal verb close together at the beginning of each sentence, and place any long bundles of information near the end of sentences.

TIP 10   **Watch out for ambiguity.**

Write unambiguous sentences. Train yourself to spot words and concepts that a reader could misconstrue. Some ambiguities are fairly easy to notice, as in the following sentence: "John told Dan that he was about to be fired." Which of them is about to lose his job? The answer is ambiguous. But some ambiguities are subtler. For example, spot the ambiguity in this sentence: "Disclosing risks to investors occasionally helps to increase share value."

The word "occasionally" is ambiguous. Will shares *occasionally* rise in value when risks are disclosed? Or will shares typically rise as long as risks are disclosed only *occasionally*? We can't tell for sure. And while readers can sometimes figure out your meaning from the sentence's context, they are using RAM to do so — RAM that they could otherwise spend in productive ways, such as focusing on your main point.

There are many ways to remove ambiguity from your writing. You can use a synonym, move words within a sentence, revise the sentence, or use punctuation to save the reader from becoming confused. For instance, the above example could be revised to read in either of these two ways: "Disclosing risks to investors will occasionally increase share value" or "Shares usually rise when a company provides occasional disclosures to investors about the risks that the company faces." Even if you need to add a few words to prevent ambiguity, do so. Brevity is a great goal, but it should not be achieved at the expense of clarity.

Two words deserve special mention in any discussion about ambiguity: "this" and "such." A writer may intend for either of those words to refer to (i) one noun that she just mentioned or (ii) all of the nouns that she just mentioned. Further, "such" can refer to other, unspecified nouns that have some similarities to the noun(s) that the writer just mentioned. Consider this sentence: "Four lawyers angrily called me to discuss whether to settle their clients' cases. *This* meant that *such* cases would soon be resolved."

What does "this" mean? Will the case settle *because* the lawyers were angry? Because there were *four* of them? Because *they* opened the door to settlement talks? Or all of the above? And does "such" refer to the cases of the four angry lawyers? To all similar cases in which you're involved? To all cases, everywhere, that resemble the cases that the four lawyers are handling?

Using "this" as an adjective is fine. Thus, in the above example, no ambiguity is created by writing "*This tone* suggests that they plan to settle." But when "this" becomes a pronoun or when we use "such" as an adjective — or God forbid, "such" as a pronoun, like "and such" — those words almost always produce vague, ambiguous sentences.

TIP 11

Prune your prose.

Clutter sneaks into writing. The need to write precisely adds clutter. Citations add clutter. Trying to sound like a lawyer adds clutter. Quoting authorities adds clutter. Some clutter is almost unavoidable. Thus, lawyers need to find ways, in spite of these challenges, to simplify their prose. Here are six costless ways to achieve that goal.

First, avoid "throat clearing," which refers to terms like *it seems to me that*, *in my humble opinion, I honestly believe that, in my experience,* and so on. These phrases add nothing (unless you need to soften your tone). They often use the first person (*I* or *me* or *my*). But throat clearing doesn't involve only first-person pronouns: *one could argue, one might infer, if one imagines a world in which,* and *it should be noted* are also classic throat clearers. Cutting these empty phrases will sharpen your prose.

Second, use simple words. Lawyers often want to show off their vocabularies. Resist the urge. Use the simplest term that meets your needs. Complicated or obscure words can confuse readers; if they don't know the word, they'll either need to consult a dictionary or plod forward without fully understanding your point. And even if you use a word correctly, you may sound pompous. Worse, you are more likely to misuse a fancy word, jeopardizing your credibility. One caveat: some champions of the wonderful "plain language" movement think that *every* word needs to be simple. I reject that view, especially when you adjust the sophistication of your writing to your audience. But, in general, use simple words.

Third, avoid abstract writing in real-world documents. Academic writing has changed the world, but practicing lawyers should generally avoid words like "concept" and "notion" and "nexus" and "normative" and "heuristic" and "narrative" and "meme."

Fourth, avoid jargon. Lawyers once reveled in the monopoly that they held on both obscure Latin and French terms and other antiquated legal words. But over time, common sense triumphed, and top American lawyers began to write in plain English. And jargon and foreign phrases are unfamiliar to more and more judges. Consider the following example (from a real motion): "On April 17, 2006, Appellant filed a Petition for writ of habeas corpus ad subjiciendum and/or writ of coram nobis and/or modification of sentence nunc pro tunc." Some judges (and most law clerks) will beg for help. Common phrases — *res judicata, res ipsa* — are bearable, but if you need to use uncommon Latin or French phrases, be sure to explain those concepts, just as you would any other unfamiliar concept. Latin isn't the only culprit: jargon can be just as problematic in English, so writers should cut phrases like *the case at bar, the instant case, Now comes plaintiff, doth aver, forthwith, at present, heretofore,* and so on.[16] These terms make lawyers sound pompous. And judges loathe jargon and the verbosity that it tends to cause.[17] So stick with jargon-free English, even if you need to cull some *arguendo*s and *a fortiorari*s and *inter alias.*

Fifth, limit the number of negatives in your sentences — and certainly avoid double (or triple, or quadruple) negatives. Here's one of the most confusing sentences I've ever read, and it uses a quadruple negative: "This is *not* to say, however, that the prima facie case may *not* be met by evidence supporting a finding that a lesser degree of segregated schooling in the core city area would *not* have resulted even if the board had *not* acted as it did."[18] Feel free to read that sentence ten more times; it will still confound you. But even when "not" or "no" appears just once in a sentence, a reader's task grows trickier. For instance, this sentence is a bit tricky to absorb: "I did not fail to render payment." Readers will grasp your point more easily if you say "I paid."

---

16. For a useful list of jargon and wordy phrases, *see Legalese*, TransLegal, http://www.trans-legal.com/drafter/legalese (last visited Mar. 26, 2013).

17. See, e.g., http://cdn.abovethelaw.com/uploads/2012/11/Merryday-Order.pdf (last visited Mar. 26, 2013) (blasting lawyer for failing to eliminate "redundancy, verbosity, and legalism").

18. Keyes v. Sch. Dist. No. 1, 413 U.S. 189, 211 n.23 (1973) (emphasis did not not not appear in the original).

Finally, lawyers use too many compound prepositional phrases such as *a number of* (rather than "some"), *with respect to* (rather than "about"), or *as a result of the fact that* (rather than "because"). These phrases can usually be shortened or removed.

TIP 12   **Develop the confidence to break the general principles of style — completely, ruthlessly, and shockingly — if doing so will help your client win.**

Now that you've mastered the numerous tips and techniques in this chapter (and throughout this book), remember this: they are guidelines, not rigid laws. These principles will reliably sharpen your prose and your advocacy. But sometimes the rules won't meet your authorial needs. Develop your instincts and your confidence so that when a rule fails you in a particular situation, you can ignore it. As Strunk and White's classic writing book, *The Elements of Style*, reminds us, "The best writers sometimes disregard the rules of rhetoric" to achieve "some compensating merit, attained at the cost of the violation." So remember this chapter's tips, but don't follow them mindlessly. Your goal is to win your case, not to pass a writing test.

This book demonstrates that many top lawyers break the conventional rules of legal writing when necessary to help their clients win. At a recent conference in New Orleans, I presented the findings from my research for this book. I reported that top lawyers regularly violate these supposed rules:

- A Statement of Facts should include every fact that appears in your Argument.
- Don't use facts from outside the record in your brief.
- Don't include law in your Statement of Facts.
- Your procedural history should be neutral.
- A brief should disclose all bad facts.

After my presentation, a professor in the audience rose to ask whether top lawyers were able to take liberties that other lawyers cannot risk — that is, whether their reputations allow them to shake free of the restraints that bind everyone else.

I rejected this view then, and I do so again now. These lawyers, whose works this book has focused on, do not make daring choices because they are successful. They are successful, because, rather than adhering rigidly to principles of good style at any cost, they focus on winning. Writing is just a means to an end — victory.

FREQUENTLY ASKED QUESTIONS ABOUT WRITING TECHNIQUES

Note: The Frequently Asked Questions that follow address general writing issues, not merely the stylistic tips discussed in this chapter.

Q. How do I go from a blank page to a finished motion or brief?

A. Lawyers use various approaches, but here is one common technique to write briefs and motions:

- Review some materials from the case so that you have a rough sense of the dispute.
- Research the legal issue a bit, perhaps starting with treatises, cases that survey the main issue raised by your case, or the background section within academic articles.
- Begin a closer study of the facts of your client's case.
- Conduct more legal research, cutting and pasting helpful passages into a word-processing file (and marking the sources of those passages). Add notes, thoughts, and concerns alongside these passages. Jot down any felicitous phrases that occur to you.
- Repeat the prior two steps for other major issues in your case.
- Begin to outline your argument. From then on, insert the useful research materials that you find into your outline so that your cut-and-pasted authorities and your notes are in the "right" place in your document. That way, when you sit down to write, most of the materials you need are already in front of you.
- Write one section at a time, moving to whichever part of the document flows most easily for you at a given moment.
- Move sections around, if necessary. Edit your prose. Hone your argument. Polish your citations. Read critically and fill in any gaps, such as missing citations.
- Send the draft to your team or your client.
- Gather, harmonize, and enter your team's edits.
- Cite-check the brief to ensure that the citations are both accurate and supportive.
- Check the tables and the pagination (e.g., no headings at the end of a page).
- File.

Q. I am drafting a motion or brief, and the filing deadline is in two weeks. Can I give my draft to my boss on the morning that it is due?

A. No! Supervising attorneys will usually want significant amounts of time to review drafts. Additionally, clients — especially clients with in-house lawyers—will often want to review drafts. Paralegals will often cite-check the filing, which adds time. Finally, printing the document may take a significant amount of time in courts that lack e-filing, such as the Supreme Court, where briefs must be bound as a small booklet. Moreover, you may need to prepare various attachments, such as declarations, exhibits, proposed orders, and certificates. So work backward from your filing deadline. How much time will you need to enter your client's and colleagues' edits? How much time will those people need to review the draft? How much time will you need to prepare the documents that accompany your filing? How much time will a printer need, if you need to file a hard copy of your motion or brief? Given all these considerations, it is not uncommon for a first draft to be distributed more than a week before the filing deadline. So plan ahead.

Also, you might want to check in with your supervisor once you have outlined your arguments but before you write the entire document. Your boss can ensure that you're on the right track, which can spare you from wasted effort.

Q. What happens if my client disagrees with the approach that I propose in my draft of a motion or brief?

A. Be positive. Be diplomatic. Avoid committing to the client, but also avoid confrontation. Then take the issue to your supervising attorney. If you're in charge, validate the client's suggestions and then explain politely why you made your choice and what concerns you have about another approach. If the client still wants to raise a point (and if doing so is ethical), you will usually follow the client's wishes or follow a middle path. Ultimately, attorneys usually revise their drafts enough to placate clients but little enough that the brief still reflects the attorney's view about how to litigate the case.

Q. My supervising attorney edits my work heavily. How can I deal with the defensiveness and frustration I feel when this happens?

A. First realize that no writer finds it painless to have his or her writing shredded. Try to infer *why* your supervisor made the edits. You can usually learn from the changes if you study them — or, better yet, if your supervisor will explain them. Realize that the senior attorney may simply be writing in his or her own style or harmonizing your prose to sound like the rest of the document. Or the supervisor may worry that your argument, through excellent, might conflict with a position that the client took in another case. Or you might use a word that has a particular legal meaning. Pick one or two changes and ask the supervisor to help you learn by explaining those changes, as that approach is more focused than just asking your boss "what did you think of my draft?" or "how can I improve?"

Q. How do I defeat writer's block?

A. Jump to a section that feels easier to write: you don't need to write from the beginning — indeed, you usually *shouldn't,* because writing a good Introduction before you've written the rest of your motion or brief is inherently difficult. Alternatively, try setting a countdown timer and write as much as you can during a fixed time. *See, e.g.,* http://www.online-stopwatch.com/countdown-timer/ (last visited May 21, 2013). Or force yourself to write just one sentence. (Another one usually lurks behind that.) Also, try recording yourself and then have an assistant transcribe what you say. Or ask a friend to ask you questions about the case — "what's the main reason your client should win?" — and then jot down your answers. In general, remind yourself of Chief Judge Alex Kozinski's observation from a 2012 interview that I conducted: he knows that every word he writes will be rewritten multiple times, so he doesn't need to agonize about creating immaculate drafts. Drafts just need to get finished. It is editing that will draw you toward excellence.

Karl Llewellyn on Legal Advocacy

This book refers repeatedly to the advice about advocacy that one of law's juggernauts, Karl Llewellyn, offered in 1957. Llewellyn is one of law's titans, having drafted the Uniform Commercial Code, shaped legal realism, and written the legendary *Bramble Bush*. Toward the end of his career, he also offered some confidential advice about advocacy to his students. The advice has never been published until now.

I learned of this document from my dean, Robert Post, who forwarded it to me with a short message that captures my view:

I just came across these materials in my office. Best advice on legal writing I've ever seen.

I reprint this advice with the permission of Professor Llewellyn's nieces, Sandy Mentschikoff Levedahl and Jeanne Mentschikoff. They expressed interest in preserving their uncle's legacy and ensuring that his insights continue to inspire students and practitioners. May it be so.

MATERIALS ON LEGAL ARGUMENT

Revised, 1957

Selection, Annotations and Text

by

K. N. Llewellyn

Prepared for the private and
confidential use of students
in the course known as Technique of Legal Argument, given
in the Columbia Law School
and the University of Chicago
Law School

HYPOTHETICAL PRINCIPLES OF ARGUMENT.
(which may mean something by the end of the course.)

A. General strategy.

   1. You are arguing to a particular tribunal. Everything else
      turns on that.

   2. The facts are the next most important thing after the
      tribunal. Soak in them.

   3. The question must be divided your way. The fewer divisions
      the better. You are hunting for one single slicing of
      the material that settles the whole case your way. Then
      acceptance of your issue can win the case.

   4. Your statement of facts, made in the light of your division
      of the question, should conclude the case before you begin
      to "argue". Facts, properly arranged, phrased, and
      presented, are worth seven discussions.

   5. The Simple appeals, it is easy to follow, it persuades.
      This holds for facts, it holds for law. And slogan and
      labels, well-chosen, help both the seeing and the handling.

   6. Successive denials make concession. An "answering" case
      is a positive case.

   7. Atmosphere and policy are better done by indirection.

   8. Good hunches come because you have slaved over the stuff.
      If you haven't, don't trust a hunch.

   9. Points must never scatter, but always cumulate. Slogan
      and labels help build them together.

   10. The more you can safely concede, the better off you are.
       The essence of argument-strategy is to begin with the best
       your adversary has, and proceed from there. This is the
       first speaker's major defence: steal the adversary's stuff
       before he gets a chance to use it.

   11. A weak argument or point is best eliminated. If you can't
       eliminate it, sandwich it, coloring it by strong neighbors,
       and thereafter assuming its soundness.

   12. End with a punch.

B. Manner, style, words.

   1. Adjectives rarely pull their weight. Verbs rarely don't.

   2. One significant detail, made seen, beats forty epithets.

3. Statements are to point forward; arrangement argues; and a conclusion is to throw its shadow before.

4. <u>After</u> they have come to feel it, you can <u>say</u> it. Not before. But the less intelligent the tribunal, the more necessary it is to <u>say</u> it.

5. This holds doubly, as to unfairness by the adversary, except that that is better never stated. Shrug it.

6. Never tell 'em. Remind 'em. You are <u>serving</u> the tribunal.

7. Both law and facts bend and stretch, like an elastic. Stretched too far, they snap.

8. The tribunal must <u>want</u> to decide your way. But many of the reasons will probably be reasons the tribunal will prefer not to see too clearly. Again: atmosphere comes best by <u>indi</u>rection.

9. This is why <u>emotional</u> consistency in argument is so important.

10. If they are working with you, they convince themselves. Therefore: (a) you must get emotional contact.
            (b) you must guide the thought (or course of emotion).
            (c) the steps must be tailored to the tribunal.
            (d) the words must be such as not to disturb the emotional continuity, but to further it.

11. The appearance of fairness is the best road to denunciation Denunciation must seem forced by fact--though it can be prepared not only by fact-presentation, but by language-color in the paler tones. It is for the end, not the beginning--else no climax; and else risk of jumping too soon.

12. The more restraint you start with, the more room is left for climax.

13. Change of pace, style, tone, holds interest, widens range.

C. <u>Oral versus written</u>.

1. The eye can go back. Use page and folio references. The ear cannot go back. Repeat.

2. Short sentences for both oral and written, except when atmosphere is wanted. <u>Intellectual</u> points come best in very short sentences, <u>in cumulative order</u>. Attribution of causation comes best in short <u>post hoc propter hoc</u>

sentences. Atmosphere can be purveyed in rolling periods.

3. The rhetorical question is three times as effective orally as it is in print.

4. In division of the argument: the brief is for reference, for buttressing, for making its reader feel secure. It can go into law, at length. It can even risk complexity of points (though I hold this dangerous). The oral argument has only one job: to interest, to get them coming, and, thence to persuade. Facts and concentration are of its essence. It aims at an immediate, pressing, desire to decide your way. The brief provides the opinion.

5. No court ever objected to being instructed on the facts. No advocate ever had a better chance to win a case on the law than by presenting facts. Voice can do what print cannot.

6. Write your oral argument out in every detail. Write it for the ear. Read it aloud, and stay with it till you make it talk. Then you go in, and talk. With notes, if you must have them (a 3" x 5" card fits into a palm) but not reading or rehearsing a MS.

7. An oral argument has a brief to fall back on. But an oral argument has to get the brief read. This is point 4 over again; it might better be stated seven times.

8. If you have to argue law, one case neat and clear, shown neatly and clearly to do the work, is the goal of all oral argument. The brief can add bread, gravy, and the vegetable The oral argument calls for one something to hit the hearer where he lives: steak, rarish--maybe with an onion.

9. Oral or written, shun the subtle. It never persuades. Subtle argument may do for justification; but first, persuade!

10. Oral or written, shun scattering of points. If they scatter in necessary fact, then address your form to making them seem to cumulate. Most lawyers sin by cowardice, and jeopardize the good point by irresolution in staking on it.

11. You cannot play safe. There is no safety. If you have done an honest job with facts and law, your client has hired your best judgment as to what will work. And in argument as in business, as in life, faint heart means lousy poker. More: faint heart, in argument, commonly means not really thinking through what it is all about. The more you really think, the simpler becomes the advisable line of argument. Always.

12. Your bold-face statements of points can be shortened to half, and gain thereby, if you play for verbs, and verbs with a punch. (This is Point A, I. And also worth seven sayings.)

Topic Sentences

The fourth tip in Chapter 16 discussed the importance of topic sentences, emphasizing that they help readers follow your argument and help *you* organize your thoughts. Not every paragraph demands a topic sentence. But many will benefit from one. Topic sentences often act as the initial Conclusion or "C" in the CRAC organizational strategy discussed on pages 56-58.

As promised, this Appendix presents an example that contains unusually strong topic sentences. The passage is excerpted from *Atlantic Sounding Co., Inc. v. Townsend*, 557 U.S. 404, 408-18 (2009) (footnotes, section headings, and italics omitted). The topic sentences appear in bold; I encourage you to read only the topic sentences so that you see how well they guide readers. Only one topic sentence forces readers to wade into the paragraph, and it's still a strong sentence; all of the other topic sentences appear in bold, and they all foretell the contents of the paragraph spectacularly well.

This case evaluated whether a shipowner could be forced to pay punitive damages when it failed to provide "maintenance and cure" (basic support and medical treatment) to a sailor who fell onto the steel deck of the shipowner's tugboat. Note that this passage does not follow CRAC; each paragraph more closely resembles "CR": the body of the paragraph substantiates the topic sentence. You will usually follow CRAC more closely. Nevertheless, these topic sentences provide a strong illustration of what topic sentences should do: guide readers. And writers.

Respondent claims that he is entitled to seek punitive damages as a result of petitioners' alleged breach of their "maintenance and cure" duty under general maritime law. We find no legal obstacle to his doing so.

Punitive damages have long been an available remedy at common law for wanton, willful, or outrageous conduct. Under English law during the colonial era, juries were accorded broad discretion to award damages as they saw fit. See, e.g., Lord Townsend v. Hughes, 2 Mod. 150, 86 Eng. Rep. 994 (C.P. 1676) ("[I]n civil actions the plaintiff is to recover by way of compensation for the damages he hath sustained, and the jury are the proper judges thereof" (emphasis in original)); 1 T. Sedgwick, Measure of Damages § 349, p. 688 (9th ed.1912) (hereinafter Sedgwick) ("Until comparatively recent times juries were as arbitrary judges of the amount of damages as of the facts"). The common-law view "was that 'in cases where the amount of damages was uncertain[,] their assessment was a matter so peculiarly within the province of the jury that the Court should not alter it.'" Feltner v. Columbia Pictures Television, Inc., 523 U.S. 340, 353, 118 S.Ct. 1279, 140 L.Ed.2d 438 (1998) (quoting Dimick v. Schiedt, 293 U.S. 474, 480, 55 S.Ct. 296, 79 L.Ed. 603 (1935); alteration in original).

The jury's broad discretion to set damages included the authority to award punitive damages when the circumstances of the case warranted. Just before the ratification of the Constitution, Lord Chief Justice Pratt explained that "a jury ha[s] it in [its] power to give damages for more than the injury received. Damages are designed not only as a satisfaction to the injured person, but likewise as a punishment to the guilty, to deter from any such proceeding for the future, and as a proof of the detestation of the jury to the action itself." Wilkes v. Wood, Lofft 1, 18-19, 98 Eng. Rep. 489, 498-499 (C.P. 1763); see also Pacific Mut. Life Ins. Co. v. Haslip, 499 U.S. 1, 25, 111 S.Ct. 1032, 113 L.Ed.2d 1 (1991) (SCALIA, J., concurring in judgment) ("[P]unitive or 'exemplary' damages have long been a part of Anglo-American law"); Huckle v. Money, 2 Wils. 205, 207, 95 Eng. Rep. 768, 769 (C.P. 1763) (declining to grant a new trial because the jury "ha[s] done right in giving exemplary damages").

American courts have likewise permitted punitive damages awards in appropriate cases since at least 1784. See, e.g., Genay v. Norris, 1 S.C.L. 6, 7, 1784 WL 26 (C.P. and Gen. Sess. 1784) (approving award of "very exemplary damages" because spiking wine represented a "very wanton outrage"); Coryell v. Colbaugh, 1 N.J.L. 77, 1791 WL 380 (1791) (concluding that a breach of promise of marriage was "of the most atrocious and dishonourable nature" and supported "damages for example's sake, to prevent such offences in future" (emphasis in original)). Although some States elected not to allow juries to make such awards, the vast majority permitted them. See 1 Sedgwick §§ 352, 354, at 694, 700. By the middle of the 19th century, "punitive damages were undoubtedly an established part of the American common law of torts [and] no particular procedures were deemed necessary to circumscribe a jury's discretion regarding the award of such damages, or their amount." Haslip, supra, at 26-27, 111 S.Ct. 1032 (SCALIA, J., concurring in judgment).

This Court has also found the award of punitive damages to be authorized as a matter of common-law doctrine. In Day v. Woodworth, 13 How. 363, 14 L.Ed. 181 (1852), for example, the Court recognized the "well-established principle of the common law, that in actions of trespass and all actions on the case for torts, a jury may inflict what are called exemplary, punitive, or vindictive damages upon a defendant. . . ." Id., at 371; see also Philadelphia, W., & B.R. Co. v. Quigley, 21 How. 202, 214, 16 L.Ed. 73 (1859) ("Whenever the injury complained of has been inflicted maliciously or wantonly, and with circumstances of contumely or indignity, the jury are not limited to the ascertainment of a simple compensation for the wrong committed against the aggrieved person"); Barry v. Edmunds, 116 U.S. 550, 562, 6 S.Ct. 501, 29 L.Ed. 729 (1886) ("[A]ccording to the settled law of this court, [a plaintiff] might show himself, by proof of the circumstances, to be entitled to exemplary damages calculated to vindicate his right and protect it against future similar invasions").

The general rule that punitive damages were available at common law extended to claims arising under federal maritime law. See Lake Shore & Michigan Southern R. Co. v. Prentice, 147 U.S. 101, 108, 13 S.Ct. 261, 37 L.Ed. 97 (1893) ("[C]ourts of admiralty . . . proceed, in cases of tort, upon the same principles as courts of common law, in allowing exemplary damages. . . ."). One of this Court's first cases indicating that punitive damages were available involved an action for marine trespass. See The Amiable Nancy, 3 Wheat. 546, 4 L.Ed. 456 (1818). In the course of deciding whether to uphold the jury's award, Justice Story, writing for the Court, recognized that punitive damages are an available maritime remedy under the proper circumstances. Although the Court found that the particular facts of the case did not warrant such an award against the named defendants, it explained that "if this were a suit against the original wrong-doers, it might be proper to . . . visit upon them in the shape of exemplary damages, the proper punishment which belongs to such lawless misconduct." Id., at 558; see also Barry, supra, at 563, 6 S.Ct. 501 ("In The Amiable Nancy, which was the case of a marine tort, Mr. Justice Story spoke of exemplary damages as 'the proper punishment which belongs to . . . lawless misconduct' " (citation omitted)).

The lower federal courts followed suit, finding that punitive damages were available in maritime actions for tortious acts of a particularly egregious nature. See, e.g., McGuire v. The Golden Gate, 16 F. Cas. 141, 143 (No. 8,815) (CC ND Cal. 1856) ("In an action against the perpetrator of the wrong, the aggrieved party would be entitled to recover not only actual damages but exemplary, such as would vindicate his wrongs, and teach the tort feasor the necessity of reform"); Ralston v. The State Rights, 20 F. Cas. 201, 210 (No. 11,540) (DC ED Pa. 1836) ("[I]t is not legally correct . . . to say that a court cannot give exemplary damages, in a case like the present, against the owners of a vessel"); Boston Mfg. Co. v. Fiske, 3 F. Cas. 957 (No. 1,681) (CC Mass. 1820) (Story, J.) ("In cases of marine torts, or illegal captures, it is far from being uncommon in the admiralty to allow costs and expences, and to mulct the offending parties, even in exemplary damages, where the nature of the case requires it"). In short, prior to enactment of the Jones Act in 1920, "maritime jurisprudence was replete with judicial statements approving punitive damages, especially on behalf of passengers and seamen." Robertson, Punitive Damages in American Maritime Law, 28 J. Mar. L. & Comm. 73, 115 (1997) (hereinafter Robertson); see also 2 Sedgwick § 599b, at 1156 ("Exemplary damages are awarded in Admiralty, as in other jurisdictions"); 2 J. Sutherland, Law of Damages § 392, p. 1272 (4th ed. 1916) ("As a rule a court of equity will not award [punitive] damages, but courts of admiralty will. . . ." (footnote omitted)). . . .

Nothing in maritime law undermines the applicability of this general rule in the maintenance and cure context. See G. Gilmore & C. Black, Law of Admiralty § 6-13, p. 312 (2d ed.1975) (hereinafter Gilmore & Black) (explaining that a seaman denied maintenance and cure "has a free option to claim damages (including punitive damages) under a general maritime law count"); Robertson 163 (concluding that breach of maintenance and cure is one of the particular torts for which general maritime law would most likely permit the awarding of punitive damages "assuming . . . the requisite level of blameworthiness"). Indeed, the legal obligation to provide maintenance and cure dates back centuries as an aspect of general maritime law, and the failure of a seaman's employers to provide him with adequate medical care was the basis for awarding punitive damages in cases decided as early as the 1800's.

The right to receive maintenance and cure was first recognized in this country in two lower court decisions authored by Justice Story. See Harden v. Gordon, 11 F. Cas. 480 (No. 6,047) (CC Me. 1823); Reed v. Canfield, 20 F. Cas. 426 (No. 11,641) (CC Mass. 1832). According to Justice Story, this common-law obligation to seamen was justified on humanitarian and economic grounds: "If some provision be not made for [seamen] in sickness at the expense of the ship, they must often in foreign ports suffer the accumulated evils of disease, and poverty, and sometimes perish from the want of suitable nourishment. . . . [T]he merchant himself derives an ultimate benefit [because i]t encourages seamen to engage in perilous voyages with more promptitude, and at lower wages." Harden, supra, at 483; see also Reed, supra, at 429 ("The seaman is to be cured at the expense of the ship, of the sickness or injury sustained in the ship's service").

This Court has since registered its agreement with these decisions. "Upon a full review . . . of English and American authorities," the Court concluded that "the vessel and her owners are liable, in case a seaman falls sick, or is wounded, in the service of the ship, to the extent of his maintenance and cure, and to his wages, at least so long as the voyage is continued." The Osceola, 189 U.S. 158, 175, 23 S.Ct. 483, 47 L.Ed. 760 (1903). Decisions following The Osceola have explained that in addition to wages, "maintenance" includes food and lodging at the expense of their ship, and "cure" refers to medical treatment. Lewis, 531 U.S., at 441, 121 S.Ct. 993; see also Gilmore & Black § 6-12, at 267-268 (describing "maintenance and cure" as including medical expenses, a living allowance, and unearned wages).

In addition, the failure of a vessel owner to provide proper medical care for seamen has provided the impetus for damages awards that appear to contain at least some punitive element. For example, in The City of Carlisle, 39 F. 807 (DC Ore. 1889), the court added $1,000 to its damages award to compensate an apprentice seaman for "gross neglect and cruel maltreatment of the [seaman] since his injury." Id., at

809, 817. The court reviewed the indignities to which the apprentice had been subjected as he recovered without any serious medical attention, see id., at 810-812, and explained that "if owners do not wish to be mulct in damages for such misconduct, they should be careful to select men worthy to command their vessels and fit to be trusted with the safety and welfare of their crews, and particularly apprentice boys." Id., at 817; see also The Troop, 118 F. 769, 770-771, 773 (D.C.Wash.1902) (explaining that $4,000 was a reasonable award because the captain's "failure to observe the dictates of humanity" and obtain prompt medical care for an injured seaman constituted a "monstrous wrong"). . . .

The settled legal principles discussed above establish three points central to resolving this case. [This topic sentence was, deliberately, not placed in bold.] First, punitive damages have long been available at common law. Second, the common-law tradition of punitive damages extends to maritime claims. . . . And third, there is no evidence that claims for maintenance and cure were excluded from this general admiralty rule. Instead, the pre-Jones Act evidence indicates that punitive damages remain available for such claims under the appropriate factual circumstances. As a result, respondent is entitled to pursue punitive damages unless Congress has enacted legislation departing from this common-law understanding. As explained below, it has not.

The only statute that could serve as a basis for overturning the common-law rule in this case is the Jones Act. Congress enacted the Jones Act primarily to overrule The Osceola, supra, in which this Court prohibited a seaman or his family from recovering for injuries or death suffered due to his employers' negligence. To this end, the statute provides in relevant part:

> "A seaman injured in the course of employment or, if the seaman dies from the injury, the personal representative of the seaman may elect to bring a civil action at law, with the right of trial by jury, against the employer. Laws of the United States regulating recovery for personal injury to, or death of, a railway employee apply to an action under this section." 46 U.S.C. §30104(a) (incorporating the Federal Employers' Liability Act, 45 U.S.C. §§51-60).

The Jones Act thus created a statutory cause of action for negligence, but it did not eliminate pre-existing remedies available to seamen for the separate common-law cause of action based on a seaman's right to maintenance and cure. Section 30104 bestows upon the injured seaman the right to "elect" to bring a Jones Act claim, thereby indicating a choice of actions for seamen — not an exclusive remedy. See Funk & Wagnalls New Standard Dictionary of the English Language 798 (1913) (defining "elect" as "[t]o make choice of"); 1 Bouvier's Law Dictionary 979 (8th ed. 1914) (defining "election" as "[c]hoice; selection"). Because the then-accepted remedies for injured seamen arose from general maritime law, see The Osceola, supra, at 175, it necessarily follows that Congress was envisioning the continued availability of those common-law causes of action. See Chandris, Inc. v. Latsis, 515 U.S. 347, 354 (1995) ("Congress enacted the Jones Act in 1920 to remove the bar to suit for negligence articulated in The Osceola, thereby completing the trilogy of heightened legal protections [including maintenance and cure] that seamen receive because of their exposure to the perils of the sea" (internal quotation marks omitted)); Stewart v. Dutra Constr. Co., 543 U.S. 481, 487 (2005) (describing the Jones Act as "remov[ing] this bar to negligence suits by seamen"). If the Jones Act had been the only remaining remedy available to injured seamen, there would have been no election to make.

In addition, the only statutory restrictions expressly addressing general maritime claims for maintenance and cure were enacted long after the passage of the Jones Act. They limit its availability for two discrete classes of people: foreign workers on offshore oil and mineral production facilities, see §503(a)(2), 96 Stat. 1955, codified at 46 U.S.C. §30105(b), and sailing school students and instructors, §204, 96 Stat. 1589, codified at 46 U.S.C. §50504(b). These provisions indicate that "Congress knows how to" restrict the traditional remedy of maintenance and cure "when it wants to." Omni Capital Int'l, Ltd. v. Rudolf Wolff & Co., 484 U.S. 97, 106 (1987). Thus, nothing in the statutory scheme for maritime recovery restricts the availability of punitive damages for maintenance and cure for those, like respondent, who are not precluded from asserting the general maritime claim.

Further supporting this interpretation of the Jones Act, this Court has consistently recognized that the Act "was remedial, for the benefit and protection of seamen who are peculiarly the wards of admiralty. Its purpose was to enlarge that protection, not to narrow it." The Arizona v. Anelich, 298 U.S. 110, 123 (1936); see also American Export Lines, Inc. v. Alvez, 446 U.S. 274, 282 (1980) (plurality opinion) (declining to "read the Jones Act as sweeping aside general maritime law remedies"); O'Donnell v. Great Lakes Dredge & Dock Co., 318 U.S. 36, 43 (1943) ("It follows that the Jones Act, in extending a right of recovery to the seaman injured while in the service of his vessel by negligence, has done no more than supplement the remedy of maintenance and cure. . . ."); Pacific S.S. Co. v. Peterson, 278 U.S. 130, 134, 138-139 (1928) (holding that the Jones Act "was not intended to restrict in any way the long-established right of a seaman to maintenance, cure and wages").

Not only have our decisions repeatedly observed that the Jones Act preserves common-law causes of action such as maintenance and cure, but our case law also supports the view that punitive damages awards, in particular, remain available in maintenance and cure actions after the Act's passage. In Vaughan v. Atkinson, 369 U.S. 527

(1962), for example, the Court permitted the recovery of attorney's fees for the "callous" and "willful and persistent" refusal to pay maintenance and cure. Id., at 529-531. In fact, even the Vaughan dissenters, who believed that such fees were generally unavailable, agreed that a seaman "would be entitled to exemplary damages in accord with traditional concepts of the law of damages" where a "shipowner's refusal to pay maintenance stemmed from a wanton and intentional disregard of the legal rights of the seaman." Id., at 540 (opinion of Stewart, J.); see also Fiske, 3 F. Cas., at 957 (Story, J.) (arguing that counsel fees are awardable in "[c]ourts of admiralty . . . not technically as costs, but upon the same principles, as they are often allowed damages in cases of torts, by courts of common law, as a recompense for injuries sustained, as exemplary damages, or as a remuneration for expences incurred, or losses sustained, by the misconduct of the other party").

Nothing in the text of the Jones Act or this Court's decisions issued in the wake of its enactment undermines the continued existence of the common-law cause of action providing recovery for the delayed or improper provision of maintenance and cure. Petitioners do not deny the availability of punitive damages in general maritime law, or identify any cases establishing that such damages were historically unavailable for breach of the duty of maintenance and cure. The plain language of the Jones Act, then, does not provide the punitive damages bar that petitioners seek.

Appendix C

Monosyllabic Verbs

As I wrote in the fifth tip in Chapter 16, short verbs will enliven your prose. To prove that you can almost always find a trim verb to serve your needs, I present below a list of mono-syllabic verbs — roughly 2,000 of them.

Many of these words can invest your briefs and motions with energy and freshness. But don't litter your briefs with obscure verbs. Rather, just revel in the trove of short words that our language has bequeathed us. And then use the common ones. A plain, lean verb usually stands ready to serve your authorial needs. Save the rare ones for special occasions.

I ditched nearly all archaic verbs, a good deal of slang, and — to protect you from the contempt powers of the judiciary — all obscenities. With a single exception, I avoided words that are used in Great Britain: I included *prang*. Given the nation's ever-growing use of drone raids and airstrikes, I thought that our country needed to import this word from England. I couldn't resist.

I'm sure that I missed a few good verbs, so please let me know if you spot any gaps (or if you think I should cut any of these words). My email address is noah.messing@yale.edu.

aah	bar	bid	blot	bow
ace	bare	bide	blow	box
act	barf	bilk	bluff	brace
add	barge	bill	blunt	brag
age	bark	bin	blur	braise
aid	base	bind	blurt	branch
ail	bash	blame	board	brand
aim	bask	blanch	boast	brave
air	baste	blank	bob	breach
ape	bat	blare	bode	break
arc	bathe	blaze	bog	breathe
arch	bawl	bleach	bolt	breech
arm	bay	bleat	bomb	breed
ask	be	bleed	bond	breeze
awe	beach	bleep	bonk	brew
ax	bead	blend	boo	bribe
back	beam	bless	book	bridge
bag	bean	blight	boom	brief
bail	bear	blind	boost	brim
bait	beat	blip	boot	brine
bake	beep	bliss	booze	bring
ban	beg	blitz	bore	broach
band	belt	block	botch	bronze
bang	bend	blog	bounce	brood
bank	best	bloom	bound	brook

279

browse	change	cloak	crap	date	drench	fard
bruise	chap	clone	crash	daunt	drift	fare
buck	char	close	crate	dawn	drill	farm
bud	charge	clot	crave	daze	drink	fast
buff	charm	cloud	crawl	deal	drip	fault
bug	chart	clown	craze	deck	drive	fawn
build	chase	cloy	crease	deed	drone	faze
bulge	chat	club	creep	deem	drool	fear
bulk	cheat	clue	crest	deign	droop	feast
bum	check	clump	crib	delve	drop	feed
bunch	cheer	clutch	crimp	dent	drown	feign
burn	chew	coach	cringe	dice	drowse	feint
burp	chide	coast	crisp	die	drudge	fell
burst	chill	coat	croak	dim	drug	fence
bus	chime	coax	crook	dip	drum	fend
busk	chip	cock	croon	disc	dry	fess
bust	chirp	code	crop	dish	dub	fetch
butt	choke	coin	cross	dive	duck	fete
buy	choose	comb	crouch	do	duel	feud
buzz	chuck	come	crow	dock	duke	fib
cab	chug	comp	crowd	dodge	dull	field
cage	chum	con	crown	doff	dumb	fife
cake	churn	conk	cruise	dog	dump	fight
call	cinch	cook	crunch	dole	dunk	filch
calm	cite	cool	crush	don	dupe	file
camp	clack	coop	cry	doom	dust	fill
can	clad	cop	cube	dope	dwarf	film
cane	claim	cope	cue	dose	dwell	find
cap	clam	cost	cull	doss	earn	fine
card	clamp	cote	cup	dot	ease	fink
care	clank	couch	curb	dote	eat	firm
carp	clap	cough	cure	doubt	ebb	fish
cart	clash	count	curse	douse	edge	fit
carve	claw	course	curve	down	egg	fix
cast	clean	court	cuss	doze	eke	flag
catch	clear	cow	cut	draft	end	flail
caulk	cleave	cowl	dab	drag	err	flank
cause	clench	coze	dam	drain	etch	flap
cave	clerk	crack	damn	drank	eye	flare
cease	clew	craft	damp	drape	face	flash
cede	climb	cram	dance	draw	fade	flaunt
chafe	clinch	cramp	dare	dread	fail	flay
chaff	cling	cranch	darn	dream	faint	flee
chalk	clink	crane	dart	dredge	fall	fleece
chance	clip	crank	dash	dreg	fan	fleer

flesh	frown	grade	harm	hone	jeer	knead
flex	fry	graft	harp	honk	jell	knee
flick	fudge	grant	hash	hood	jerk	kneel
flip	fuel	grasp	hasp	hoof	jess	knell
flirt	fume	grate	hatch	hook	jest	knife
flit	fund	graze	hate	hoop	jet	knight
float	furl	greet	haul	hoot	jib	knit
flock	fuse	gride	haunt	hop	jibe	knob
flog	futz	grieve	have	hope	jig	knock
flood	gab	grift	hawk	horn	jilt	knoll
flop	gag	grind	hay	horse	jinx	knot
floss	gain	grip	haze	hose	jive	knout
flow	gall	gripe	head	host	job	know
flub	game	groan	heal	hound	jog	knurl
fluff	garb	groom	heap	house	join	kraal
flume	gas	groove	hear	howl	joke	lace
flump	gash	grope	heat	huff	jolt	lack
flunk	gasp	grouch	heave	hug	josh	lade
flush	gauge	ground	hedge	hulk	joss	lag
fly	gear	group	heed	hum	jot	lam
foam	geek	grouse	heel	hump	joust	lamb
fob	gel	grow	help	hunch	judge	lame
fog	get	growl	helve	hunt	juice	lamp
foist	gift	grub	hem	hurl	juke	lance
fold	gild	grunt	herd	hurt	jump	land
fool	gin	guard	hew	hush	junk	lap
foot	give	guess	hex	husk	jut	lapse
force	glean	guide	hide	hutch	keck	lard
ford	glint	gulf	hike	hype	keel	lark
forge	glitz	gull	hinge	ice	keen	lase
fork	glom	gulp	hint	imp	keep	lash
form	glow	gum	hire	inch	keeve	last
foul	gloze	gun	hiss	ink	kelp	latch
found	glut	gurge	hit	irk	kern	lath
fox	glutch	gush	hitch	itch	key	lathe
frag	gnarl	gust	hoard	jab	kick	laud
frame	gnash	gut	hoax	jack	kid	laugh
fray	gnaw	hack	hob	jag	kill	launch
free	go	hail	hock	jail	kiln	lave
freeze	goad	hale	hoe	jam	kilt	lawn
fret	golf	halt	hog	jape	kip	lay
fringe	goose	halve	hoist	jar	kiss	laze
frisk	gorge	ham	hold	jaunt	kit	lea
front	gouge	hand	hole	jaw	kite	leach
frost	grace	hang	home	jazz	knar	lead

281

leaf	loo	marl	molt	need	pal	phone
leak	look	mash	moo	neigh	pale	phrase
lean	loom	mask	mooch	nerve	pall	pi
leap	loop	mass	moon	nest	palm	pick
learn	loose	mast	moor	net	pan	piece
lease	loot	mat	moot	nib	pant	pierce
leash	lop	match	mop	nick	pap	pig
leave	lope	mate	mope	nil	par	pike
ledge	lord	matte	morn	nip	parch	pill
leech	lose	maul	morph	nit	pare	pimp
leer	lot	max	mosh	nix	park	pin
leg	lounge	may	moss	nock	parse	pinch
lend	louse	mean	moth	nod	part	pine
let	lout	meet	mound	noise	pass	ping
letch	love	meld	mount	noose	paste	pink
lick	low	melt	mourn	norm	pat	pip
lid	lube	mend	mouse	nose	patch	pipe
lie	luff	mense	mouth	nosh	pause	pique
life	lug	meow	move	notch	pave	piss
lift	luge	merge	mow	note	paw	pit
light	lull	mesh	muck	nudge	pawl	pitch
like	lump	mess	mud	null	pawn	pith
lilt	lunch	mete	muff	numb	pay	place
limb	lunge	mew	mug	nurse	peach	plait
lime	lunt	mewl	mulch	nut	peak	plan
limn	lurch	miff	mulct	oar	peal	plane
limp	lure	might	mull	off	pearl	plank
line	lurk	mike	mum	oink	peck	plant
link	lush	milk	mump	ooh	pee	plash
lip	lust	mill	munch	ooze	peek	plat
lisp	lute	milt	murk	opt	peel	plate
list	lye	mime	muse	orb	peen	play
live	lynch	mince	mush	ought	peep	pleach
load	lyse	mind	muss	oust	peer	plead
loaf	mace	mine	must	out	peeve	please
loam	mack	mint	mute	owe	peg	pleat
loan	mail	miss	mutt	own	pelt	pledge
loathe	maim	mist	nab	pace	pen	plink
lob	make	mix	nag	pack	pend	plod
lock	malt	moan	nail	pad	pep	plop
lodge	man	moat	name	page	perch	plot
loft	map	mob	nap	pail	perk	plotz
log	mar	mock	nape	pain	pest	plough
loll	march	mold	near	paint	pet	plow
long	mark	mold	neck	pair	phase	pluck

plum	pride	quilt	reeve	rough	scheme	shake
plumb	prim	quip	reign	round	scoff	shall
plume	prime	quirt	rein	rouse	scold	sham
plump	primp	quit	rend	roust	scoop	shame
plunge	prink	quiz	rent	rout	scoot	shank
plunk	print	quoin	rest	route	scope	shape
ply	prize	quoit	retch	rove	scorch	share
poach	probe	quote	rete	row	score	sharp
pod	prod	race	rhyme	rub	scout	shave
point	prompt	rack	rib	ruck	scowl	sheaf
poise	prong	raft	rick	rue	scram	shear
poke	proof	rag	rid	ruff	scrap	sheath
pole	prop	rage	ride	ruin	scrape	shed
poll	prose	raid	ridge	rule	scrawl	sheer
pond	prove	rail	rif	run	screen	sheet
pong	prowl	rain	riff	rush	screw	shelf
poof	prune	raise	rift	rust	scrimp	shell
pool	pry	rake	rig	rut	scrounge	shield
poop	psych	ralph	right	sack	scrub	shift
poor	pub	ram	rim	sag	scrum	shill
pop	puff	ramp	rime	sail	scuff	shim
pore	pug	ran	ring	salt	scull	shin
port	pule	ranch	rinse	salve	seal	shine
pose	pull	rand	rip	sand	seam	ship
post	pulp	range	rise	sap	sear	shirk
pot	pulse	rank	risk	sash	search	shirr
pouch	pump	rant	ritz	sate	seat	shiv
pounce	pun	rap	rive	sauce	see	shoal
pound	punch	rape	roach	save	seed	shock
pour	punt	rasp	roam	saw	seek	shoe
pout	pup	rat	roar	say	seem	shoo
praise	purge	rate	roast	scab	seep	shoot
prance	purl	rave	rob	scald	seethe	shop
prang	purr	ray	robe	scale	seize	shore
prank	purse	raze	rock	scalp	sell	short
prate	push	razz	rolf	scam	send	shot
prawn	put	reach	roll	scamp	sense	shout
pray	putt	read	romp	scan	serve	shove
preach	quack	ream	roof	scant	set	show
preen	quail	reap	rook	scar	sew	shred
prep	quake	rear	room	scare	sex	shriek
press	quash	reave	roost	scarf	shack	shrink
prey	quell	reef	root	scarp	shade	shrug
price	quench	reek	rope	scat	shaft	shuck
prick	queue	reel	rot	scent	shag	shun

shunt	slat	smelt	souse	spore	state	strike
shush	slate	smirk	south	sport	stave	string
shut	slave	smite	sow	spot	stay	strip
side	slay	smith	space	spout	steal	stripe
siege	sleave	smock	spade	sprain	steam	strive
sieve	sled	smoke	spall	sprawl	steel	strobe
sift	sledge	snack	spam	spray	steep	stroke
sigh	sleek	snag	span	spread	steer	stroll
sight	sleep	snake	spank	sprig	steeve	strop
sign	sleet	snap	spar	spring	stem	strum
silk	sleeve	snare	spare	sprint	step	strut
silt	sleigh	snarl	spark	spritz	stew	stub
sin	sleuth	sneak	spawn	sprout	stick	stud
sing	slice	sneer	spay	spruce	stiff	stuff
singe	slick	snick	spaz	spruik	still	stump
sink	slide	sniff	speak	spume	stilt	stun
sip	slight	snip	spear	spur	sting	stunt
sit	slim	snipe	speck	spurn	stink	sty
site	slime	snoop	speed	spurt	stint	sub
size	sling	snoot	spell	spy	stir	suck
skate	slink	snore	spend	squad	stitch	sue
skeet	slip	snort	spew	square	stock	suede
sketch	slit	snow	sphere	squash	stodge	suit
skew	slog	snub	spice	squat	stoke	sulk
ski	slop	snuff	spiff	squelch	stomp	sum
skid	slope	snug	spike	squib	stone	sun
skim	slosh	soak	spill	squid	stool	surf
skimp	slot	soap	spin	stab	stoop	surge
skin	slouch	soar	spit	stack	stop	swab
skip	slough	sob	spite	staff	store	swag
skirl	slow	sock	splash	stage	storm	swage
skirt	slue	sod	splay	stain	stot	swamp
skive	slug	sole	splice	stake	stow	swap
skulk	sluice	solve	spline	stale	strafe	sward
skunk	slum	soot	splint	stalk	strain	swarm
sky	slump	soothe	split	stall	strand	swash
slab	slur	sop	splore	stamp	strap	swat
slack	slurp	sorb	splosh	stanch	stray	swathe
slag	slush	sort	splurge	stand	streak	sway
slake	smack	sough	sponge	star	stream	swear
slam	smarm	sought	spoof	starch	streek	sweat
slang	smart	souk	spook	stare	stress	sweep
slant	smash	soul	spool	stark	stretch	swell
slap	smear	sound	spoon	start	strew	swerve
slash	smell	soup	spoor	stash	stride	swig

swill	tent	toss	tube	wad	whale	word
swim	term	tote	tuck	wade	wheel	work
swing	test	touch	tuft	waft	wheeze	worm
swinge	text	tough	tug	wag	whelm	worst
swipe	thank	tour	tulle	wage	whelp	would
swirl	thaw	tout	tune	wail	whet	wound
swish	thin	tow	turf	wait	whiff	wow
switch	think	toy	turn	waive	whine	wrack
swoon	thirst	trace	tusk	wake	whinge	wrap
swoop	thread	track	twang	wale	whip	wreak
swoosh	thrive	trade	tweak	walk	whir	wreck
synch	throb	trail	tweet	wall	whirl	wrench
tab	throw	train	twill	waltz	whish	wrest
tack	thrum	traipse	twin	wan	whisk	wring
tag	thrust	tramp	twine	wane	white	write
tail	thud	tranche	twirl	want	whiz	writhe
taint	thumb	trap	twist	war	whoop	wrong
take	thump	trash	twit	ward	whop	yak
talk	thwart	trawl	twitch	ware	whore	yank
tame	tick	tread	type	warm	whump	yap
tamp	tide	treat	up	warn	wick	yard
tan	tie	tree	urge	warp	wield	yarn
tank	tier	trek	use	wash	wig	yaw
tap	tiff	trench	vamp	waste	will	yawn
tape	till	trend	vat	watch	wilt	yawp
tar	tilt	tress	vault	wave	wimp	yean
tare	time	trice	vaunt	wax	win	yearn
tart	tin	trick	veer	wean	wince	yell
task	tinge	trill	veil	wear	winch	yelp
taste	tint	trim	vein	weave	wind	yield
tat	tip	trip	vend	web	wine	yip
taunt	tithe	trod	vent	wed	wing	yoke
taw	toast	troll	verge	wedge	wink	yowl
tax	toe	tromp	verse	weed	wipe	yuk
teach	tog	troop	vest	weep	wise	zag
team	toke	trot	vet	weigh	wish	zap
tear	toll	trounce	vex	weight	wisp	zest
tease	tone	troupe	vie	welch	witch	zing
tee	tool	truck	view	weld	withe	zip
teem	toot	trudge	vise	well	wolf	zone
tell	tooth	true	voice	welt	wont	zonk
temp	top	trump	void	wench	woo	zoom
tempt	tope	truss	vote	wend	wood	zoon
tend	torch	trust	vouch	wet	woof	
tense	tosh	try	vow	whack	wool	

Attribution of Examples

The motions and briefs reprinted in this book were written by talented lawyers all over the country. These attorneys deserve credit for their great work, so the following pages list the creators of each filing that I praised and used at length. In some instances, I needed to guess which lawyer was counsel of record. Please pardon any inaccuracies.

EXAMPLE NUMBER	CASE NAME	PARTY FILING THE BRIEF	TYPE OF BRIEF	WESTLAW LOCATOR	COUNSEL OF RECORD OR LEAD COUNSEL	ALL OTHER LAWYERS (listed as they appear in the brief)
1.1	Kelo v. City of New London, 545 U.S. 469 (2005)	Kelo	Petitioner's Brief	2004 WL 2811059	Scott G. Bullock	William H. Mellor, Dana Berliner, Scott W. Sawyer
1.2	Viacom Int'l v. YouTube, 676 F.3d 19 (2d Cir. 2012)	Viacom	Plaintiffs-Appellants' Opening Brief	2010 WL 4930315	Andrew H. Schapiro	Max W. Berger, John C. Browne, Charles S. Sims, William M. Hart, Noah Siskind Gitterman, Elizabeth A. Figueira, A. John P. Mancini, Brian M. Willen, David H. Kramer, Michael H. Rubin, Bart E. Volkmer
1.3	Caperton v. A.T. Massey Coal Co., 556 U.S. 868 (2009)	Hugh M. Caperton	Petitioners' Brief	2008 WL 5433361	Theodore B. Olson	David B. Fawcett, Matthew D. McGill, Amir C. Tayrani, Bruce E. Stanley, Robert V. Berthold, Jr.
1.4	Facebook v. Pac. N.W. Software, 640 F.3d 1034 (9th Cir. 2011)	Facebook	Appellees' Brief	2010 WL 5625003	E. Joshua Rosenkranz	Neel Chatterjee, Monte Cooper, Theresa A. Sutton, Theodore W. Ullyot, Colin S. Stretch
1.5	Exxon Shipping Co. v. Baker, 554 U.S. 471 (2008)	Exxon	Petitioners' Brief	2007 WL 4439454	Walter Dellinger	E. Edward Bruce, John F. Daum, Charles C. Lifland, Jonathan D. Hacker
1.6	U.S. v. Ressam, 553 U.S. 272 (2008)	U.S.	Brief for the U.S.	2008 WL 189554	Paul D. Clement	Kenneth L. Wainstein, Michael R. Dreeben, Toby J. Heytens, John F. De Pue
1.7	U.S. v. Bell, 584 F.3d 478 (2d Cir. 2009)	U.S.	Brief for the U.S.	n/a	Sandra Glover	Tracy Lee Dayton, Michael J. Gustafson, David Fein
1.8	Negusie v. Holder, 555 U.S. 511 (2009)	Negusie	Petitioners' Brief	2008 WL 2445504	Andrew J. Pincus	Dan Kahan, Terri-Lei O'Malley, Charles A. Rothfeld
2.1	Caperton v. A.T. Massey Coal Co., 556 U.S. 868 (2009)	Hugh M. Caperton	Petitioners' Brief	2008 WL 5433361	Theodore B. Olson	David B. Fawcett, Matthew D. McGill, Amir C. Tayrani, Bruce E. Stanley, Robert V. Berthold, Jr.
2.2	Florence v. Bd. of Chosen Freeholders, 132 S. Ct. 1510 (2012)	Essex County Correctional Facility	Respondents' Brief	2011 WL 3739474	Carter G. Phillips	Alan Ruddy, Eamon P. Joyce, Ryan C. Morris, Joshua J. Fougere, Robyn H. Frumkin

EXAMPLE NUMBER	CASE NAME	PARTY FILING THE BRIEF	TYPE OF BRIEF	WESTLAW LOCATOR	COUNSEL OF RECORD OR LEAD COUNSEL	ALL OTHER LAWYERS (listed as they appear in the brief)
2.3	Exxon Shipping Co. v. Baker, 554 U.S. 471 (2008)	Exxon	Petitioners' Brief	2007 WL 4439454	Walter Dellinger	E. Edward Bruce, John F. Daum, Charles C. Lifland, Jonathan D. Hacker
2.4	In re Motion to Continue, Misc. No. 98-267 (D.D.C. July 28, 1998)	President William J. Clinton	Memorandum in Support of Motion of William J. Clinton for Continuance	n/a	David E. Kendall	Nicole K. Seligman, Max Stier, Alicia L. Marti
2.5	Fox TV Stations v. FCC, 280 F.3d 1027 (D.C. Cir. 2002)	Fox TV Stations	Petitioners' Opening Brief	2001 WL 36037975	John G. Roberts, Jr.	Bruce D. Sokler, Christopher J. Harvie, Michael Pryor, Maureen A. O'Connell, Edward W. Warren, Richard A. Cordray, Ashley C. Parrish, Ellen S. Agress, Susan E. Weiner, Diane Zipursky, Michael D. Fricklas, Mark C. Morril, Stuart W. Gold
3.1	Selby v. AT&T Mobility, 2012 WL 2081644 (Cal. App. 4th Dist. May 9, 2012)	AT&T Mobility	Respondents' Brief	2012 WL 2081644	Donald M. Falk	John Nadolenco
3.2	Football Ass'n Premier League v. YouTube, 633 F. Supp. 2d 159 (S.D.N.Y. 2009), aff'd in part and vacated in part, 676 F.3d 19 (2d Cir. 2012)	YouTube	Defendant's Opposition to Plaintiffs' Motions for Partial Summary Judgment	2010 WL 3054854	Andrew H. Schapiro	A. John P. Mancini, Matthew D. Ingber, Brian M. Willen, David H. Kramer, Maura L. Rees, Michael H. Rubin, Bart E. Volkmer
3.3	Exxon Shipping Co. v. Baker, 554 U.S. 471 (2008)	Exxon	Petitioners' Brief	2007 WL 4439454	Walter Dellinger	E. Edward Bruce, John F. Daum, Charles C. Lifland, Jonathan D. Hacker
3.4	Watters v. Wachovia Bank, 550 U.S. 1 (2007)	Wachovia	Respondents' Brief	2006 WL 3243131	Robert A. Long	Lori McAllister, William J. Perrone, Stuart C. Stock, Keith A. Noreika, Emily Johnson Henn

EXAMPLE NUMBER	CASE NAME	PARTY FILING THE BRIEF	TYPE OF BRIEF	WESTLAW LOCATOR	COUNSEL OF RECORD OR LEAD COUNSEL	ALL OTHER LAWYERS (listed as they appear in the brief)
3.5	Fox TV Stations v. FCC, 280 F.3d 1027 (D.C. Cir. 2002)	Fox TV Stations	Petitioners' Opening Brief	2001 WL 36037975	John G. Roberts, Jr.,	Bruce D. Sokler, Christopher J. Harvie, Michael Pryor, Maureen A. O'Connell, Edward W. Warren, Richard A. Cordray, Ashley C. Parrish, Ellen S. Agress, Susan E. Weiner, Diane Zipursky, Michael D. Fricklas, Mark C. Morril, Stuart W. Gold
3.6	Crosby v. NFTC, 530 U.S. 363 (2000)	National Foreign Trade Council	Respondent's Brief	2000 WL 193325	Timothy B. Dyk	Michael A. Collora, David M. Osborne, Gregory A. Castanias, Jack W. Campbell IV, John B. Kennedy
3.7	Tenenbaum v. Sony BMG Music Entm't, 660 F.3d 487 (1st Cir. 2011), cert. denied, 132 S. Ct. 2431 (2012)	Sony	Brief in Opposition to Writ of Certiorari	2012 WL 1384653	Paul D. Clement	Jennifer L. Pariser, Matthew J. Oppenheim, Timothy M. Reynolds
3.8	Negusie v. Holder, 555 U.S. 511 (2009)	Negusie	Petitioners' Brief	2008 WL 2445504	Andrew J. Pincus	Dan Kahan, Terri-Lei O'Malley, Charles A. Rothfeld
3.9	U.S. v. Jones, 132 S. Ct. 945 (2012)	Antoine Jones	Respondent's Brief	2011 WL 4479076	Stephen C. Leckar	Walter Dellinger, Jonathan D. Hacker, Micah W.J. Smith
3.10	Perry v. Van Orden, 545 U.S. 677 (2005)	Texas	Respondent's Brief	2005 WL 263793	R. Ted Cruz	Greg Abbot, Barry R. McBee, Edward D. Burrach, Don R. Willett, Joel L. Thollander, Amy Warr, Paul Michael Winget-Hernandez
4.1	Liston v. Chertoff, No. CV-06-265-LRS, 2007 WL 681178 (E.D. Wash. Jan. 11, 2007)	U.S.	U.S.' Memorandum of Authorities in Support of Motion To Dismiss	n/a	James A. McDevitt	Andrew S. Biviano
4.2	Mayer v. Belichick, 605 F.3d 223 (3d Cir. 2010)	National Football League	Brief for Defendant-Appellee	2010 WL 2156904	Robert Del Tufo	Shepard Goldfein, Paul M. Eckles, Matthew M. Martino

EXAMPLE NUMBER	CASE NAME	PARTY FILING THE BRIEF	TYPE OF BRIEF	WESTLAW LOCATOR	COUNSEL OF RECORD OR LEAD COUNSEL	ALL OTHER LAWYERS (listed as they appear in the brief)
4.3	Kelo v. City of New London, 545 U.S. 469 (2005)	City of New London	Respondents' Brief	2005 WL 429976	Wesley W. Horton	Daniel J. Krisch, Thomas J. Londregan, Jeffrey T. Lodregan, Edward B. O'Connell, David P. Condon
4.4	Verizon Commc'ns v. Law Offices of Curtis V. Trinko, 540 U.S. 398 (2004)	Verizon	Petitioner's Brief	2003 WL 21244083	John Thorne	Michael K. Kellogg, Peter W. Huber, Mark C. Hansen, Aaron M. Panner, Henry B. Gutman, Richard G. Taranto
4.5	Football Premier Ass'n League v. YouTube, 718 F. Supp. 2d 514 (S.D.N.Y. 2010), vacated in part, 676 F.3d 19 (2d Cir. 2012)	YouTube	Defendant's Opposition to Plaintiffs' Motions for Partial Summary Judgment	2010 WL 3054854	Andrew H. Schapiro	A. John P. Mancini, Matthew D. Ingber, Brian M. Willen, David H. Kramer, Maura L. Rees, Michael H. Rubin, Bart E. Volkmer
4.6	Honda Motor Co. v. Oberg, 512 U.S. 415 (1994)	Honda	Petitioners' Brief	1994 WL 190913	Andrew L. Frey	Kenneth S. Geller, Charles A. Rothfeld, Evan M. Tager, Adam C. Sloane, James H. Gidley, Thomas W. Brown, Jeffrey R. Brooke, Paul G. Cereghini
4.7	Tenenbaum v. Sony BMG Music Entm't, 660 F.3d 487 (1st Cir. 2011)	Sony	Brief for Respondents in Opposition	2012 WL 1384653	Paul D. Clement	Jennifer L. Pariser, Matthew J. Oppenheim, Timothy M. Reynolds, Erin E. Murphy
4.8	U.S. v. Jones, 132 S. Ct. 945 (2012)	Antoine Jones	Respondent's Brief	2011 WL 4479076	Stephen C. Leckar	Walter Dellinger, Jonathan D. Hacker, Micah W.J. Smith
5.1	Facebook v. Pac. N.W. Software, 640 F.3d 1034 (9th Cir. 2011)	Facebook	Appellees' Brief	2010 WL 5625003	E. Joshua Rosenkranz	Neel Chatterjee, Monte Cooper, Theresa A. Sutton, Theodore W. Ullyot, Colin S. Stretch
5.2	Gonzales v. Raich, 545 U.S. 1 (2005)	Alabama, Louisiana, & Mississippi as Amici Curiae	Amicus Brief in Support of Respondents	2004 WL 2336486	Kevin C. Newsom	Troy King, Charles C. Foti, Jr., Jim Hood
5.3	U.S. v. Adams, 176 F.3d 493 (11th Cir. 1999) (table)	U.S.	Brief for the U.S.	1998 WL 34168493	Thomas E. Scott	Adalberto Jordan, Kathleen M. Salyer, Robin S. Rosenbaum

EXAMPLE NUMBER	CASE NAME	PARTY FILING THE BRIEF	TYPE OF BRIEF	WESTLAW LOCATOR	COUNSEL OF RECORD OR LEAD COUNSEL	ALL OTHER LAWYERS (listed as they appear in the brief)
5.4	Polar Tankers v. City of Valdez, 557 U.S. 1 (2009)	Polar Tankers	Petitioner's Reply Brief	2009 WL 788634	Andrew L. Frey	Richard A. Leavy, Kwaku A. Akowuah, Charles A. Rothfeld, Brian D. Netter
5.5	Smith v. Cain, 132 S. Ct. 627 (2012)	Smith	Petitioner's Brief	2011 WL 3608728	Kristin A. Feeley	Kathleen Kelly, Matilde J. Carbia, David E. Kendall, Kannon K. Shanmugam, Thomas H.L. Selby, George W. Hicks, Jr., April R. Rieger
5.6	In re Cipro Cases I & II, 200 Cal. App. 4th 442 (4th Dist. 2011)	Bayer Corp.	Brief of Respondent Bayer Corp. in Response to Law Professors' Amicus Brief	2011 WL 1054358	Charles A. Bird	Christopher J. Healey, Todd R. Kinnear, Peter B. Bensinger, Jr., Kevin D. McDonald
5.7	U.S. v. Jones, 132 S. Ct. 945 (2012)	Antoine Jones	Respondent's Brief	2011 WL 4479076	Stephen C. Leckar	Walter Dellinger, Jonathan D. Hacker, Micah W.J. Smith
6.1	Caperton v. A.T. Masseay Coal Co., 556 U.S. 868 (2009)	Hugh M. Caperton	Petitioners' Brief	2008 WL 5433361	Theodore B. Olson	Matthew D. McGill, Amir C. Tayrani, Bruce E. Stanley, Robert V. Berthold, Jr.
6.2	Office of Indep. Counsel v. Favish, 541 U.S. 157 (2004)	Office of Independent Counsel	Petitioner's Brief	2003 WL 21738777	Theodore B. Olson	Peter D. Keisler, Edwin S. Kneedler, Patricia A. Millett, Leonard Schaitman, Robert M. Loeb
6.3	U.S. v. Brown, 459 F.3d 509 (5th Cir. 2006)	Daniel Bayly	Appellant's Reply Brief	n/a	Lawrence S. Robbins	Thomas A. Hagemann, Marla Thompson Poirot, Gregory L. Poe, Alan E. Untereiner, Alice W. Yao
6.4	Christian Legal Soc'y v. Martinez, 130 S. Ct. 2971 (2010)	Hastings College of Law	Respondents' Brief	2010 WL 1513023	Gregory G. Garre	Ethan P. Schulman, Elise K. Traynum, Maureen E. Mahoney, J. Scott Ballenger, Lori Alvino McGill, Gabriel K. Bell
6.5	Van Orden v. Perry, 545 U.S. 677 (2005)	Public Policy Center	Brief for the Ethics and Public Policy Center as Amicus Curiae in Support of Respondents	2005 WL 240665	Mark A. Perry	Daniel J. Davis, Ryan P. Meyers, Dustin K. Palmer

EXAMPLE NUMBER	CASE NAME	PARTY FILING THE BRIEF	TYPE OF BRIEF	WESTLAW LOCATOR	COUNSEL OF RECORD OR LEAD COUNSEL	ALL OTHER LAWYERS (listed as they appear in the brief)
6.6	Viacom Int'l v. YouTube, 676 F.3d 19 (2d Cir. 2012)	YouTube	Defendants-Appellees' Brief	2011 WL 1357313	Andrew H. Schapiro	David H. Kramer, Michael H. Rubin, Bart E. Volkmer, A. John P. Mancini, Brian M. Willen
7.1	Mohamad v. Palestinian Auth., 132 S. Ct. 1702 (2011)	Palestinian Authority	Respondents' Brief	2012 WL 293720	Laura G. Ferguson	Jeffrey A. Lamken, Robert K. Kry, Martin V. Totaro, Richard A. Hibey, Mark J. Rochon, Dawn E. Murphy-Johnson
7.2	Kasten v. Saint-Gobain Performance Plastics Corp., 131 S. Ct. 1325 (2011)	Kevin Kasten	Petitioner's Brief	2010 WL 2481867	James H. Kaster	Adrianna S. Haugen, Eric Schnapper
7.3	CSX Corp. v. Children's Inv. Fund Mgmt. (UK), 292 Fed. App'x 133 (2d Cir. 2008)	Children's Investment Fund Management (UK)	Defendants-Appellees-Cross-Appellants' Opening Brief	2008 WL 7071554	Howard O. Godnick	Michael E. Swartz, Peter D. Doyle, Andrew M. Genser, Christopher Landau, P.C., Patrick F. Philbin, Theodore W. Ullyot
7.4	In re Deepwater Horizon, 2:10-md-02179-CJB-SS Dock. 4827-1 (E.D. La. Dec. 7, 2011)	BP	BP's Memorandum in Opposition to Transocean's Motion for Partial Summary Judgment and in Support of BP's Cross-Motion for Partial Summary Judgment Relating to Alleged Contractual Indemnities	n/a	Don K. Haycraft	R. Keith Jarrett, Robert C. "Mike" Brock, Joel M. Gross, Richard C. Godfrey, J. Andrew Langan, R. Chris Heck, Patrick F. Philbin
8.1	Mohamad v. Palestinian Auth., 132 S. Ct. 1702 (2011)	Palestinian Authority	Respondents' Brief	2012 WL 293720	Laura G. Ferguson	Jeffrey A. Lamken, Robert K. Kry, Martin V. Totaro, Richard A. Hibey, Mark J. Rochon, Dawn E. Murphy-Johnson
8.2	Bruesewitz v. Wyeth, Inc., 131 S. Ct. 1068 (2011)	Wyeth	Respondent's Brief	2010 WL 2962899	Kathleen M. Sullivan	Daniel J. Thomasch, Richard W. Mark, E. Joshua Rosenkranz, Lauren J. Elliot, John L. Ewald, Faith E. Gay, Sanford I. Weisburst, William B. Adams

EXAMPLE NUMBER	CASE NAME	PARTY FILING THE BRIEF	TYPE OF BRIEF	WESTLAW LOCATOR	COUNSEL OF RECORD OR LEAD COUNSEL	ALL OTHER LAWYERS (listed as they appear in the brief)
8.3	Exxon Shipping Co. v. Baker, 554 U.S. 471 (2008)	Exxon Shipping Co.	Petitioners' Brief	2007 WL 4439454	Walter Dellinger	E. Edward Bruce, John F. Daum, Charles C. Lifland, Jonathan D. Hacker
8.4	Hatch v. U.S., No. 12-2040 (10th Cir. filed May 23, 2012)	William Hatch	Appellant's Opening Brief	2012 WL 1966198	Richard A. Winterbottom	
9.1	Brown v. Entm't Merchants Ass'n, 131 S. Ct. 2729 (2011)	Entertainment Merchants Ass'n	Respondents' Brief	2010 WL 3535053	Paul M. Smith	Kenneth L. Doroshow, Katherine A. Fallow, Matthew S. Hellman, Duane C. Pozza, William M. Hohengarten, Jonathan F. Olin, David Z. Moskowitz, Krishanti Vignarajah
9.2	Caperton v. A.T. Massey Coal Co., 556 U.S. 868 (2009)	A.T. Massey Coal Co.	Respondents' Brief	2009 WL 216165	Andrew L. Frey	Evan M. Tager, Dan Himmelfarb, Jeffrey A. Berger, Eugene Volokh, Lewis F. Powell III, Ryan A. Shores, Robert W. Loftin, D.C. Offutt, Jr.
9.3	Christian Louboutin S.A. v. Yves Saint Laurent Am., 778 F. Supp. 2d 445 (S.D.N.Y. 2011)	Yves Saint Laurent America, Inc.	Defendants/ Counterclaim-Plaintiffs' Memorandum of Law in Opposition to Motion for Preliminary Injunction	2011 WL 2972933	David H. Bernstein	Jyotin Hamid, Jill van Berg, Rayna S. Feldman
9.4	U.S. v. Jones, 132 S. Ct. 945 (2012)	Antoine Jones	Respondent's Brief	2011 WL 4479076	Stephen C. Leckar	Walter Dellinger, Jonathan D. Hacker, Micah W.J. Smith
9.5	U.S. v. Stevens, 130 S. Ct. 1577 (2010)	Robert J. Stevens	Respondent's Brief	2009 WL 2191081	Patricia A. Millett	Lisa B. Freeland, Michael J. Novara, Karen Sirianni Gerlach, Robert Corn-Revere, Thomas C. Goldstein, Kevin R. Amer, Monica P. Sekhon, Faith E. Barter, Jeffrey L. Fisher
9.6	U.S. v. Alvarez, 132 S. Ct. 457 (2011)	Xavier Alvarez	Respondent's Brief	2012 WL 160227	Jonathan D. Libby	Sean K. Kennedy, Brianna J. Fuller

EXAMPLE NUMBER	CASE NAME	PARTY FILING THE BRIEF	TYPE OF BRIEF	WESTLAW LOCATOR	COUNSEL OF RECORD OR LEAD COUNSEL	ALL OTHER LAWYERS (listed as they appear in the brief)
10.1	Lawrence v. Tex., 539 U.S. 558 (2003)	Texas	Respondent's Brief	2003 WL 470184	William J. Delmore III	Scott A. Durfee
10.2	Lawrence v. Tex., 539 U.S. 558 (2003)	Human Rights Campaign	Amicus Brief for Petitioner	2003 WL 152347	Walter Dellinger	Pamela Harris, Jonathan D. Hacker, Brian V. Ellner, Matthew J. Merrick, Gayle E. Pollack
10.3	Elk Grove Unified Sch. Dist. v. Newdow, 542 U.S. 1 (2004)	U.S.	Brief for the U.S. as Respondent Supporting Petitioners	2003 WL 23051994	Theodore B. Olson	Peter D. Kisler, Paul D. Clement, Gregory G. Katsas, Patricia A. Millett, Robert M. Loeb, Lowell V. Sturgill, Sushma Soni
10.4	Grutter v. Bollinger, 539 U.S. 306 (2003)	Retired military officials	Amicus Brief	2003 WL 1787554	Virginia A. Seitz	Joseph R. Reeder, Robert P. Charrow, Kevin E. Stern, Robert N. Hochman, Carter G. Phillips
11.1	Apple, Inc. v. Samsung Electronics Co., No. 11-cv-01846-LHK 2013 WL 11570 (N.D. Cal. Jan. 1, 2013)	Apple, Inc.	Motion to Expedite Discovery	2011 WL 1938574	Harold J. McElhinny	Michael A. Jacobs, Jennifer Lee Taylor, Jason R. Bartlett
11.2	Konowaloff v. Metro. Museum of Art, 10 CIV. 9126 SAS, 2011 WL 4430856 (S.D.N.Y. Sept. 22, 2011)	Metropolitan Museum of Art	Memorandum of Law in Support of Metropolitan Museum of Art's Motion to Dismiss Plaintiff's Amended Complaint	n/a	David W. Bowker	Paul A. Engelmayer, Pamela K. Bookman
11.3	Exxon Shipping Co. v. Baker, 554 U.S. 471 (2008)	Baker	Respondents' Brief	2008 WL 194284	David W. Oesting	James van R. Springer, Brian B. O'Neill, Stephen M. Rummage, David C. Tarshes, Jeffrey L. Fisher
11.4	Caperton v. A.T. Massey Coal Co., 556 U.S. 868 (2009)	A.T. Massey Coal Co.	Respondents' Brief	2009 WL 216165	Andrew L. Frey	Evan M. Tager, Dan Himmelfarb, Jeffrey A. Berger, Eugene Volokh, Lewis F. Powell III, Ryan A. Shores, Robert W. Loftin

EXAMPLE NUMBER	CASE NAME	PARTY FILING THE BRIEF	TYPE OF BRIEF	WESTLAW LOCATOR	COUNSEL OF RECORD OR LEAD COUNSEL	ALL OTHER LAWYERS (listed as they appear in the brief)
11.5	Mo. v. Frye, 132 S. Ct. 1399 (2012)	Frye	Respondent's Brief	2011 WL 2837937	Emmett D. Queener	Craig A. Johnston
11.6	HHS v. Fla., 2012 WL 2427810 (June 28, 2012)	HHS	Brief for Petitioners (Minimum Coverage Provision)	2012 WL 37168	Donald B. Verrilli, Jr.	Tony West, Edwin S. Kneedler, Beth S. Brinkmann, Joseph R. Palmore, Mark B. Stern, Alisa B. Klein, Samantha L. Chaifetz, Dana Kaersvang
12.1.b	Nat'l Fed'n of Indep. Business v. Sebelius, 132 S. Ct. 2566 (2012)	State Respondents	Brief for State Respondents on the Minimum Coverage Provision	2012 WL 392550	Paul D. Clement	Pamela Jo Bondi; Scott D. Makar, Louis F. Hubener, Timothy D. Osterhaus, Blaim H. Winship, Erin E. Murphy, Greg Abbott, Bill Cobb, Alan Wilson, Luther Strange, Bill Schuette, Jon Bruning, Katherine J. Spohn, Mark L. Shurtleff, John W. Suthers, Robert M. McKenna, Thomas W. Corbett, Jr., Linda L. Kelly, Marty J. Jackley, Gregory F. Zoeller, Samuel S. Olens, Lawrence G. Wasden, Joseph Sciarrotta, Jr., Tom Horne, Wayne Stenejhem, Brian Sandoval, Michael C. Geraghty, Michael DeWine, David B. Rivkin, Lee A. Casey, Matthew Mead, William J. Schneider, Terry Branstad, Michael B. Wallace, Derek Schmidt, J.B. Van Hollen
12.1.c	Hogsett v. U.S., 129 S. Ct. 1308 (2009)	U.S.	Brief for the U.S.	2009 WL 52072	Gregory S. Garre	Matthew W. Friedrich, Daniel S. Goodman
12.1.d	FCC v. Fox TV Stations, 132 S. Ct. 2307 (2012)	Cato Institute	Brief of the Cato Institute, and other Amici in Support of Respondents	2011 WL 5562515	John P. Elwood	Eric A. White, Emma J. Llanso, John Bergmayer, Harold Feld, Thomas S. Leathurbury, Lee Tien, Berin Szoka

EXAMPLE NUMBER	CASE NAME	PARTY FILING THE BRIEF	TYPE OF BRIEF	WESTLAW LOCATOR	COUNSEL OF RECORD OR LEAD COUNSEL	ALL OTHER LAWYERS (listed as they appear in the brief)
12.1.e	U.S. v. Alvarez, 132 S. Ct. 2537 (2012)	Jonathon D. Varat	Brief of Professor Jonathan D. Varat as Amicus Curiae in Support of Respondent	2012 WL 195302	Cary B. Lerman	Leo Goldbard, Claire Yan, Richard C. Chen
12.1.f	Baylor v. U.S., 129 S. Ct. 1386 (2009)	Baylor	Petition for a Writ of Certiorari	2009 WL 157097	Meir Feder	Samuel Estreicher, Randolph M. Lee, Donald B. Ayer
12.1.g	Tesfagaber v. Filip, 129 S. Ct. 2074 (2009)	Filip	Respondent's Brief	2009 WL 208130	Edwin S. Kneedler	Michael F. Hertz, Donald E. Keener, Erica B. Miles
12.1.h	Polar Tankers v. City of Valdez, 129 S. Ct. 2277 (2009)	Polar Tankers	Petitioners' Brief	2009 WL 191838	Andrew L. Frey	Charles A. Rothfeld, Brian D. Netter
12.2.a	Al-Marri v. Spagone, 129 S. Ct. 1545 (2009)	Cato Institute	Brief of the Cato Institute and other Amici in Support of Reversal	2009 WL 230960	Ketanji Brown Jackson	Drew S. Days III, Beth S. Brinkmann, Brian R. Matsui, Boris Yankilovich
12.2.b	Van Orden v. Perry, 545 U.S. 677 (2005)	Perry	Respondent's Brief	2005 WL 263793	Ted Cruz	Joel L. Thollander, Amy Warr, Paul Michael Winget-Hernandez
12.2.c	Turner v. Rogers, 131 S. Ct. 2507 (2011)	Turner	Petitioner's Brief	2011 WL 49898	Seth P. Waxman	Paul R.Q. Wolfson, Catherine M.A. Carroll, Sonya L. Lebsack, Shivaprasad Nagaraj
12.3.a	Caperton v. A.T. Massey Coal Co., 556 U.S. 868 (2009)	Hugh M. Caperton	Petitioners' Brief	2008 WL 5433361	Theodore B. Olson	Matthew D. McGill, Amir C. Tayrani, Bruce E. Stanley, Robert V. Berthold, Jr.
12.3.b	Ritter v. Stanton, 536 U.S. 904 (2002)	Ritter	Petition for a Writ of Certiorari	2002 WL 32135997	John G. Roberts, Jr.	Karl L. Mulvaney, David C. Campbell, Nana Quay-Smith, Christopher T. Handman

EXAMPLE NUMBER	CASE NAME	PARTY FILING THE BRIEF	TYPE OF BRIEF	WESTLAW LOCATOR	COUNSEL OF RECORD OR LEAD COUNSEL	ALL OTHER LAWYERS (listed as they appear in the brief)
12.3.c	Empress Casino Joliet Corp. v. Giannoulias, 129 S. Ct. 2764 (2009)	Empress Casino Joliet Corp.	Petition for Writ of Certiorari	2009 WL 208133	Charles Rothfeld	Evan Tager, Jeffrey Berger
12.3.d	Watson v. U.S., 552 U.S. 74 (2007)	Watson	Petitioner's Brief	2007 WL 1319437	Mark T. Stancil	Karl J. Koch, David T. Goldberg, Daniel R. Ortiz
12.3.e	Bond v. U.S., 131 S. Ct. 1061 (2011)	Bond	Petition for Writ of Certiorari	2010 WL 1506717	Paul D. Clement	Ashley C. Parrish, Candice Chiu
12.4.b	NASA v. Nelson, 131 S. Ct. 746 (2011)	NASA	Petitioners' Brief	2010 WL 2031410	Neal Kumar Katyal	Tony West, Edwin S. Kneedler, Nicole A. Saharsky, Mark B. Stern, Melissa N. Patterson, Benjamin M. Shultz
12.4.c	Barhoumi v. Obama, 609 F.3d 416 (D.C. Cir. 2010)	President Barack Obama	Brief for Respondents-Appellees	2010 WL 2129069	Ian Heath Gershengorn	Robert M. Loeb, Sharon Swingle
12.5.a	Natsios v. Nat'l Foreign Trade Council, 530 U.S. 363 (2000)	National Foreign Trade Council	Respondents' Brief	2000 WL 193325	Timothy B. Dyk	Gregory A. Castanlas, Jack W. Campbell IV, John B. Kennedy
12.5.b	Lawrence v. Tex., 539 U.S. 558 (2003)	Lawrence	Petitioners' Brief	2003 WL 152352	Ruth E. Harlow	Paul M. Smith, William M. Hohengarten, Daniel Mach, Sharon M. McGowan, Patricia M. Logue, Susan L. Sommer, Mitchell Katine
13.1	Adkins v. Wolever, 692 F.3d 499 (6th Cir. 2012)	Wolever	Appellant's Corrected Brief on Appeal Oral Argument Requested	2011 WL 3006962	Joseph M. Infante	
13.2	BMW v. Gore, 517 U.S. 559 (1995)	BMW	Petitioner's Brief	1995 WL 126508	Andrew L. Frey	Kenneth S. Geler, Evan M. Tager

EXAMPLE NUMBER	CASE NAME	PARTY FILING THE BRIEF	TYPE OF BRIEF	WESTLAW LOCATOR	COUNSEL OF RECORD OR LEAD COUNSEL	ALL OTHER LAWYERS (listed as they appear in the brief)
13.3	Viacom v. YouTube, 676 F.3d 19 (2d Cir. 2012)	Viacom	Plaintiffs-Appellants' Opening Brief	2010 WL 4930315	Theodore B. Olson	Paul M. Smith, William M. Hohengarten, Scott B. Wilkens, Matthew S. Hellman, Susan J. Kohlmann, Matthew D. McGill, Stuart J. Baskin
13.4	U.S. v. Ressam, 553 U.S. 272 (2008)	U.S.	Brief for the U.S.	2008 WL 189554	Paul D. Clement	Kenneth L. Wainstein, Michael R. Dreeben, Toby J. Heytens, John F. De Pue
13.5	Zivotofsky v. Clinton, 132 S. Ct. 1421 (2012)	Menachem Binyamin Zivotofsky, by his parents and guardians, Ari Z. and Naomi Siegman Zivotofsky	Petitioner's Brief	2011 WL 3288337	Nathan Lewin	Alyza D. Lewin
13.6	Paramount Pictures Corp. v. Puzo, No. 12 Civ. 1268(AJN), 2012 WL 4465574, (S.D.N.Y. Sept. 26, 2012)	Paramount Pictures Corp.	Plaintiff's Motion to Dismiss Counterclaims	2012 WL 3019730	Richard B. Kendall	Nicholas F. Daum
14.1	Konowaloff v. Metro. Museum of Art, 10 CIV. 9126 SAS, 2011 WL 4430856 (S.D.N.Y. Sept. 22, 2011)	Metropolitan Museum of Art	Memorandum of Law in Support of Metro-politan Museum of Art's Motion to Dismiss Plaintiff's Amended Complaint	n/a	David W. Bowker	Paul A. Engelmayer, Pamela K. Bookman
14.2	Armstrong v. USADA, No. 1:12-cv-00606-SS, 2012 WL 3569682 (W.D. Tex. July 19, 2012)	USADA	Defendants' Motion to Dismiss for Lack of Subject Matter Jurisdiction or, in the Alternative, Motion to Dismiss or Stay Under the Federal Arbitration Act	2012 WL 3204626	John J. McKetta, III	Matthew C. Powers, William Bock, III, Richard R. Young

EXAMPLE NUMBER	CASE NAME	PARTY FILING THE BRIEF	TYPE OF BRIEF	WESTLAW LOCATOR	COUNSEL OF RECORD OR LEAD COUNSEL	ALL OTHER LAWYERS (listed as they appear in the brief)
14.3	Gilmour v. IBM, 2:09cv04155 SJO, (C.D. Cal. filed Feb. 11, 2010)	IBM	Reply to Plaintiff's Opposition to Motion for Summary Judgment or, in the Alternative, Partial Summary Judgment	2010 WL 1340599	Thomas G. Mackey	Jamie C. Chanin
14.4	Velez v. Novartis, No. 04 Civ. 09194 (GEL), 2010 WL 4877852 (S.D.N.Y. Nov. 30, 2010)	Velez	Plaintiffs' Memorandum of Law in Opposition to Defendant's Motion for Partial Summary Judgment	2009 WL 2442886	David Sanford	Jeremy Heisler, Steven Wittels, Grant Morris
14.5	Milwaukee Cnty. v. Mercer Hum. Res. Consulting, No. 2:06-cv-00372-CNC (E.D. Wis. Oct. 13, 2008)	Milwaukee County	Plaintiffs' Brief in Support of Their Motion to Exclude Mercer's Expert Lauren Bloom	2008 WL 4612693	Kenneth E. McNeil	James T. Southwick, John A. Busch, Chris J. Trebatoski
14.6	Apple, Inc. v. Samsung Electronics Co., No. 11-cv-01846-LHK (N.D. Cal. Aug. 24, 2012)	Samsung	Defendant's Request For Thirty Minutes to Review the Jury Verdict Form Before the Jury is Dismissed for the Purpose of Seeking Clarification of Potential Inconsistent Verdict if Necessary	2012 WL 3633666	Charles K. Verhoeven	Kevin P.B. Johnson, Victoria F. Maroulis, Michael T. Zeller
14.7	Hicks v. Client Servs., No. 07-61822-CIV., 2009 WL 2365637 (S.D. Fla. June 9, 2009)	Hicks	Reply Memorandum in Support of Plaintiff's Motion for Summary Judgment	2008 WL 7147473	Donald A. Yarbrough	Craig M. Shapiro
15.1	Exxon Shipping Co. v. Baker, 554 U.S. 471 (2008)	Baker	Respondents' Brief	2008 WL 194284	David W. Oesting	James van R. Springer, Brian B. O'Neill, Stephen M. Rummage, David C. Tarshes, Jeffrey L. Fisher

EXAMPLE NUMBER	CASE NAME	PARTY FILING THE BRIEF	TYPE OF BRIEF	WESTLAW LOCATOR	COUNSEL OF RECORD OR LEAD COUNSEL	ALL OTHER LAWYERS (listed as they appear in the brief)
15.2	Citizens United v. FEC, 558 U.S. 310 (2009)	Citizens United	Reply Brief for Appellant	2009 WL 693638	Theodore B. Olson	Matthew D. McGill, Amir C. Tayrani, Justin S. Herring
15.3	Polar Tankers v. City of Valdez, 557 U.S. 1 (2009)	Polar Tankers	Petitioner's Reply Brief	2009 WL 788634	Andrew L. Frey	Richard A. Leavy, Kwaku A. Akowuah, Charles A. Rothfeld, Brian D. Netter
15.4	CSU L.L.C. v. Xerox Corp., 531 U.S. 1143 (2001)	CSU	Supplemental Brief of Petitioner in Support of a Petition for a Writ of Certiorari	2001 WL 34116124	John G. Roberts, Jr.	David G. Leitch, Jonathan S. Franklin
15.5	Tenenbaum v. Sony BMG Music Entm't, 132 S. Ct. 2431 (2012)	Sony	Respondent's Brief in Opposition	2012 WL 1384653	Paul D. Clement	Erin E. Murphy, Timothy M. Reynolds, Matthew J. Oppenheim
15.6	Leegin Creative Leather Prods. v. PSKS, 551 U.S. 877 (2007)	PING	Amicus Brief of PING, Inc.	2007 WL 173680	Thomas C. Walsh	Aaron S. Bayer, Robert M. Langer, Suzanne E. Wachsstock, David A. Van Engelhoven, Lawrence G. Scarborough, J. Alex Grimsley

Index